Passover, Pentecost and Parousia
Studies in Celebration of the Life and Ministry of R. Hollis Gause

Journal of Pentecostal Theology
Supplement Series

35

Editors

John Christopher Thomas
Rickie Moore
Steven J. Land

ISSN 0966 7393

Deo Publishing

PASSOVER, PENTECOST *and* PAROUSIA

Studies in Celebration of the Life and Ministry of

R. Hollis Gause

Edited by

**Steven Jack Land
Rickie D. Moore
John Christopher Thomas**

deo
PUBLISHING

BLANDFORD FORUM

Journal of Pentecostal Theology Supplement Series, 35

Published by Deo Publishing
P.O. Box 6284, Blandford Forum, Dorset DT11 1AQ, UK

The Odyssea Greek font used in the publication of this work is available from Linguist's Software, Inc., www.linguistsoftware.com, P.O. Box 580, Edmonds, WA 98020-0580 USA, tel. (425) 775-1130.

Printed in the United Kingdom by Henry Ling Ltd, at the Dorset Press, Dorchester, DT1 1HD.

British Library Cataloguing-in-Publication data
A catalogue record for this book is available from the British Library

ISBN 978-1-905679-12-6

R. Hollis Gause

Contents

Preface and Commendation

Every one of the contributors to this volume, as well as the Church of God denomination as a whole, has been significantly affected by Dr. R. Hollis Gause. To be taught by, to teach with, to be mentored by or to serve on a committee with him is to be influenced by someone with a deep biblical integrity and personal commitment to the things of God. He brings a sense of devotion, competence and humor (often self-deprecating) to all his assignments. This preface will note only a few of the milestones in his life and lift up some of his distinctive emphases. A more detailed and outstanding account of his intellectual achievement is found in Dr. Alexander's essay in this volume.

Rev. and Mrs. Gause, Sr. had to have known they had a bright, devoted son as they watched him seek and receive new birth, sanctification and Spirit baptism. They loved him. They were proud of him. Born July 1, 1925, the second of two children, he was greatly influenced by their kind regard and godly lives. The family prayers, corporate worship and especially his father's preaching had a profound and lasting effect upon his life.

During his teen years, he joined his parents in transferring from the Pentecostal Holiness Church to the Church of God. His father had a theological concern related to polity. This must have impressed the younger Gause and partially accounts for his lifelong personal and scholarly interest in polity, resulting later, among other things, in the publication of the first comprehensive book of polity in the Church of God. Not all of the Gause extended family was pleased with the change of church membership. This was back when people took their denominational affiliation seriously – socially as well theologically. At any rate, one of his loyal Pentecostal Holiness aunts expressed her disappointment with the church change by remarking, 'I'd rather they brought you in a corpse!' This was a momentous change for the Gauses with significant, long-lasting implications for the future of the Church of God.

Dr. Gause has been a devoted, loving husband and father. On April 30, 1948 he married Beulah Hunt and they later had a son, Valdane

(Val). The Gause household was one of prayer, laughter and shared tasks. Everyone pitched in with housework, homework and scholarship. Dr. and Mrs. Gause delighted in one another and were devoted to their son. In the later years, through a strange and wonderful providence, after the passing of Sister Gause, Dr. Gause's only grandchild, April Dawn, came to live in his house, to be cared for and to care for her grandfather and father. Val had returned during the last months of his life having contracted cancer. April and her grandfather cared for Val. Dr. Gause and Val wrote a book together entitled *The Emmaus Road* (Xulon Press, 2005).

Dr. Gause was present at his son's home-going. The last thing Val heard on this side was the voice of his father praying in his ear as Christ came to receive him. Dr. Gause faithfully and sacrificially cared for his wife and his son who are now both together in heaven. These personal family matters are essential if one is to begin to grasp the depth of care and perseverance of this man.

Second only to his love of God and family is his commitment to God's word written, the Holy Bible. In that sense, like John Wesley, he is *homo unius libris* – a man of one book. His commitment to Scripture as truth has fed a lifelong effort to relate all other learning to the Word in his teaching and preaching and daily living. This deep devotion to Scripture is foundational to all his ministerial and educational pursuits.

Dr. Gause's educational background is an interesting theological mix of Reformed, Wesleyan and mainline Protestant influences. He graduated in 1942 from high school in Clinton, South Carolina and in 1944 from Emmanuel College in Franklin Springs, Georgia. Emmanuel was and is a Wesleyan institution. He completed his undergraduate studies at Presbyterian College (1945) in Clinton, South Carolina. The Reformed influence was prominent at Presbyterian College and later in Columbia Theological Seminary in Decatur, Georgia. He was recognized for his keen theological mind and powerful preaching at Columbia, from which he graduated with a Bachelor of Divinity (later changed to Master of Divinity) in 1971. From the Reformed he took a great appreciation for Scripture, the sovereignty of God, divine decrees, the Protestant scholastic *ordo salutis* (order of salvation) and the value of the Law of God in Christian ethics. Throughout his educational endeavors, his focus always seemed to return to the Cross as foundational for everything else.

While in the PhD program in New Testament studies at Emory University, Dr. Gause continued to teach and write for the denomination. His work week was enough to occupy two or three persons. He excelled in his doctoral studies and wrote his dissertation on *The Lukan*

Transfiguration Account (University Microfilms, 1975). Among the many anecdotes surrounding his studies at Emory, probably one of the best known occurred during his dissertation defense before a panel of Emory professors (all more liberal than he!). During his defense he was asked by one of his examiners whether he realized that if they accepted his thesis, it would upset a whole body of previously received liberal, critical scholarship. His classic reply: "That's okay with me!" They laughed with him and, of course, approved his excellent dissertation.

I first met Dr. Gause in the mid-1970's in Atlanta. He was engaged in doctoral studies, and we became friends. During this time he and his wife Beulah began visiting and later joined the Midtown Mission Church of God, which was founded by Jack Land (my father) and myself. Dr. Gause was a very popular Valentine banquet speaker and Sunday morning preacher. The saints loved the Gauses and the sinners and visitors were as disarmed by his humor as they were deeply moved by his preaching.

During the 1970's Dr. Gause, Dr. M.G. McLuhan and I initiated a series of studies in holiness. We met in the Mt. Paran Church of God facilities and discussed several papers, most of which were authored by Dr. Gause. We shared and sought to develop a revived and vigorous Wesleyan-Holiness Pentecostal hermeneutic. We were both convinced of initial sanctification (in union with Christ at justification – regeneration- new birth), of entire sanctification (perfect love reigning in the pure in heart) and ongoing growth in sanctification (from new birth through entire sanctification and into eternity). We were committed to the efficacy of the blood of Christ, the Word and the Holy Spirit to bring about the putting off of the 'old man', the 'crucifixion of the old nature' and the 'circumcision of the heart'. This purity of heart (holiness), without which no one would see the Lord (Heb. 12.14), we held to be the center of Christian spirituality (1 Cor. 13), and the desired pre-requisite motive for the baptism in the Spirit. This comprehensive doctrine of sanctification (initial, entire, ongoing) was never a philosophical perfection of performance; it was a perfection in love doing away with double-mindedness and resistance to the known will of God. Positively, it was a filling with divine love which reigned in the heart of the believer.

We were both against legalism, but afraid that a new libertinism (going from 'everything is wrong' to 'nothing is wrong') was on the horizon for the Church of God. Dr. Gause, in a church committee document entitled 'The Order of Church Discipline', had pointed out the distinction between the test of fellowship (actions disqualifying one for heaven, e.g. works of the flesh) and matters of cultivation in righteousness (on the way to a greater consecration and maturity). This gave a theological basis for rejecting the old practical commitments which required disfellowshiping persons for wearing unnecessary jewelry (vanity), public swimming (immodesty) or movie attendance (promoting immorality). But it also pointed the way, not subsequently followed very carefully by the denomination in North America, of heeding the biblical warning concerning the works of the flesh (Gal. 5.19-21). Along with this warning came the church's long-time teaching against the 'finished work' theory of atonement as a license to sin or a way to avoid moral striving with its attendant crucifixion of the deeds of the flesh and cultivation of the fruit of the Spirit. We feared that a pendulum swing from the old strictness to the 'finished work' and 'eternal security' influences circulating in evangelical circles, would lead to a new antinomianism which would de-emphasize obedience and moral striving in favor of a cheap grace without discipleship. These concerns Dr. Gause brought with him from his Wesleyan Pentecostal roots.

From his Reformed background, he brought a concern for the sovereignty of God whose divine decrees ordered all things according to His will. Although he did not embrace double-predestination, he did bring a strong emphasis on God as the King and moral ruler of the universe. In addition, he found useful the Protestant scholarship formulation of the order of salvation (*ordo salutis*), placing Wesleyan sanctification and Pentecostal Spirit baptism in the order of a *full* salvation purchased through Calvary, realized in the early Church and promised to all generations who will seek God for it.

From the mainline Protestant traditions, Dr. Gause came to understand more fully and to use to the advantage of a deeply conservative scholar, the historical critical method. Although rejecting its liberal philosophical and theological presuppositions, he used the results of this and other tools, to explicate more fully and apply the text of what he believed to be the inerrant, infallible, written word of God. His preaching and teaching never indicated any other norm or ultimate standard than that of the Holy Spirit inspired Scriptures. As a teacher of hermeneutics, he saw the importance of the didactic and transformative effects of the Holy Spirit among the faithful who gather around God's word to hear His voice.

At the center of all his teaching has been the Cross, which draws together the concerns of Sinai and Pentecost. It is in the Cross that the demands of the law and the possibility of full sanctification are secured. It is the same God with the same intention to save 'whosoever will', who came down at Sinai, Calvary and Pentecost. This is a salvation trajectory of righteousness, love and power. The power of Pentecost is given to us in order that the crucified One may be proclaimed and witnessed to in character, word and deed.

Dr. Gause showed his Wesleyan, Pentecostal roots in his long-time work on a polity of participation and formation for the whole people of God (see *Church of God Polity*, Pathway Press, 1958; revised, 1973). When he was asked to contribute a chapter to the book *Perspectives on the New Pentecostalism* (ed. Russell P. Spittler; Baker, 1976), he focused on the need for the purity of heart and life. From his emphasis on the ministry of women (*The Place of Women in the Body of Christ*, co-authored with his wife, Beulah, Pathway Press, 1983) to a decidedly Wesleyan-Pentecostal (non-dispensational) reading of the books of Revelation (*Revelation: God's Stamp of Sovereignty on History*, Pathway Press, 1982) and Romans (*The Preaching of Paul, A Commentary on Romans*, Pathway Press, 1986), he has powerfully demonstrated the hermeneutical and ministerial effects of the confluence of the Holiness and Pentecostal streams of Christianity. He has given this gift to generations of students in hundreds of popular and scholarly articles, a collection of doctrinal meditations (*The Heritage Papers*, edited with Steven J. Land; Pathway Press, 1989), an outstanding Pentecostal work on soteriology (*Living in the Spirit: The Way of Salvation*, Pathway Press, 1980), and scores of Sunday School lessons over twenty years (1952-72) in the *Adult Quarterly* and *Adult Teacher's Quarterly*, which he and his wife produced.

His ministerial journey in the Church of God began in 1943. After three series of written or oral exams, Dr. Gause received his full ordination in 1954. In addition to serving as the Chief Parliamentarian and advisor to decades of General Overseers at the denomination's biannual assemblies, he is broadly recognized as the most respected authority in doctrinal and polity matters in the Church of God. For the bulk of his sixty-plus years of ministry Dr. Gause has been a teacher. The first thirty years of his educational ministry were invested in Lee College (today, Lee University). His tenure there lasted from 1947-1975 and 1982-1984. During these years he served as instructor, Dean of the Bible College, Registrar, Dean of the Division of Religion, Dean of the College, Department Chair and Professor. Generations of Church of God laity, pastors, missionaries, teachers and leaders have come under his influence, which is considerable and memorable.

He has been known as a deeply spiritual intellectual in a revivalist church, which hasn't always understood or trusted intellectuals, especially those so steeped in the Scriptures. He has a deep abiding love for the Church of God as well as a deep desire to see its ministers and leaders have the best biblical and theological training possible. He has never seen the teaching gift as more valuable than others. He has only asked that the teaching gift not be denigrated, neglected or ignored. For example, he has wondered why there is no listing for 'teachers' in the monthly denominational ministerial report forms; or why, when bible teachers are selected for camp meetings, those who have given their lives to advanced biblical studies receive so few invitations.

His passion and prayers for greater ministerial training were rewarded in 1975 when he was appointed the first Dean and Director of the Church of God Graduate and School of Christian Ministries (today, Pentecostal Theological Seminary). Dr. Wade Horton, then General Overseer, was designated as President. This move as well as the decision to have the Seminary stand free of all other schools on its own underscored the Church's desire that the school be plugged directly into the ministry leadership of the Church with an exclusive holiness-Pentecostal focus. Dr. Gause was prepared for this opportunity all of his life. His concerns for biblically based, theological, practical curriculum and more emphasis on internships and field experience affect the school to this day.

Dr. Gause served as Dean until 1980. He then spent two years, from 1980-1982, as pastor, district overseer and state council member in Warren, Michigan. To this day his members recall his preaching, pastoral care and evangelistic passion. They continue to call and visit someone who clearly got deeply into their hearts.

In 1982, Dr. Gause returned to Cleveland and taught for two years at Lee University and the Seminary. After this, all his time was given to teaching and influencing the students and faculty at the Seminary where he is Professor of Theological and New Testament Studies. He is greatly beloved by students, faculty, staff and administrators alike. He has probably served in a formal teaching capacity longer than anyone else in the Church of God (six of his eight-plus decades of life!).

This book is written by 'sons and daughters' of Dr. Gause. We hope that you will be blessed by it. But by all means, read his books and articles. His life will live in those books and the lives of those who have been touched by his preaching and teaching.

I have prayed beside him as he interceded for family, friends, the lost and enemies (those who had hurt or disappointed him). I have been privileged to teach with this generous man who has worked so hard, for so long in a loving labor in word and doctrine. For this I will always be grateful.

Earlier I stated that the Cross was a theme running through his entire ministry of teaching, preaching and writing. This concluding story from Sister Gause's last days will underscore this and invite all of us to continue with Dr. Gause on the way home.

On the occasion of their fiftieth anniversary, Dr. and Mrs. Gause arrived in a large banquet room of a local Cleveland hotel where family and friends had gathered. Most, but not all, were Christians. We assisted Dr. Gause in bringing Sister Gause into the room in her wheelchair. Alzheimer's had afflicted her. She sat for most of the afternoon, head bowed to the side, eyes fixed, seemingly unaware of the proceedings. Near the end of the event, Dr. Gause asked me to read a love poem he had written to his bride. It was so overwhelmingly personal and intimate that he could not read it, and I could scarcely say the words without weeping. As I came to the concluding sentence, my voice broke, and as I paused, the Holy Spirit swept over everyone there as Sister Gause lifted her head and sang out, 'The Way of the Cross leads home!' Thus weeping and rejoicing, we were all called to join her following Jesus toward the Marriage Supper.

May this book be an encouragement and a guide as we journey together with him.

Steven Jack Land, Ph.D.
President, Professor of Pentecostal Theology
Pentecostal Theological Seminary
February 29, 2008

Abbreviations

AJPS	*Asian Journal of Pentecostal Studies*
BR	*Bible Review*
CBQ	*Catholic Biblical Quarterly*
CC	*Christian Century*
CTJ	*Calvin Theological Journal*
DCH	Clines, *Dictionary of Classical Hebrew*
DNTT	*Dictionary of New Testament Theology*
DPCM	Burgess and McGee, *Dictionary of Pentecostal and Charismatic Movements*
HALOT	Köhler, *Hebrew-Aramaic Lexicon of the Old Testament*
IDPCM	*International Dictionary of Pentecostal and Charismatic Movements*
IJST	*International Journal of Systematic Theology*
Int	*Interpretation*
JBL	*Journal of Biblical Literature*
JPsyT	*Journal of Psychology and Theology*
JPT	*Journal of Pentecostal Theology*
JPTS	*Journal of Pentecostal Theology Supplement Series*
JQR	*Jewish Quarterly Review*
JSNT	*Journal for the Study of the New Testament*
JSOT	*Journal for the Study of the Old Testament*
JTS	*Journal of Theological Studies*
NTS	*New Testament Studies*
PNEUMA	*PNEUMA: The Journal of the Society for Pentecostal Studies*
RevRR	*Review of Religious Research*
SJT	*Scottish Journal of Theology*
TDNT	Kittel, *Theological Dictionary of the New Testament*
ThT	*Theology Today*
TS	*Theological Studies*
VT	*Vetus Testamentum*
WTJ	*Westminster Theological Journal*

1

Under the Authority of the Word and in Response to the Spirit: The Written Work and Worship of R. Hollis Gause

Kimberly Ervin Alexander[*]

> The writing of theology or the teaching and preaching of theology must be one fabric with worship. The lecturer's classroom, theologian's study and the proclaiming-praying-singing congregation are identical. They are the body of Christ, the church of the living God. It is our intention to write under the authority of the word of God. All that is said is answerable to Scripture. It is also our intention to be responsive to the guidance of the Holy Spirit – in loving union with Him so that His leading and power are evident. Our writing is under the warning and promise of God that it is 'not by might, nor by power, but by my Spirit, saith the Lord of hosts' (Zechariah 4:6). We write with the understanding that we are immediately in the presence of God – the One who knows our thoughts afar off. We also write around the centrality of the Incarnation – Christ's birth, life, crucifixion, resurrection, ascension and return. These are all terms of worship, and such terms of worship are both promise and judgment. (R. Hollis Gause, 'The Distinctives of a Pentecostal Theology', unpublished paper)

For years students have been challenged by the rapid-fire delivery of Dr. Hollis Gause's logically ordered but tightly packed lectures in theology and biblical studies. The challenge to 'keep up' and 'get it all down' is complicated by the awe and wonder we experience as we hear what we've never heard before though it resonates within us. What amazes those of us who've studied under him and now have had the privilege of teaching with him is that though he is obviously drawing on an accumulation of scholarly work spanning five decades, he

* Kimberly Ervin Alexander (Ph.D., Open University [St. John's College, Nottingham]) is Associate Professor of Historical Theology at the Pentecostal Theological Seminary, Cleveland, TN.

continues to write new lectures, to think in new ways and to re-vision Pentecostal theology. As one student who 'sat at his feet' at both the undergraduate and graduate levels put it, 'I was always thrilled to see those fresh legal sheets.'

The yellow legal pad, for the most part has been replaced by the word processor (*sans* the grammar check, which he has disabled, for obvious reasons!) and he continues to articulate Pentecostal theology, re-thinking categories, looking anew at familiar texts not just through the lens of his keen intellect but also through the companion lens of years of experience in the classroom, the study and the church.

Dr. Gause, as your student, first and foremost, and now as your colleague, I want to thank you for what you have imparted to me and to generations of Pentecostal scholars and ministers. And I want to thank you for the model you have provided of what it means to worship in our discipline. I am forever grateful.

Academic and Ecclesiastical Writing as Worship

Perhaps the most important of Gause's contributions is one with which his students are quite familiar but as of this writing, remains unpublished. Undergirding everything written or said in the classroom is Gause's unique 'Theology of Worship'. In his doctoral work on Luke, Gause hammers out this understanding of worship in the Christian community. In his dissertation he discusses early Christian worship and its 'eschatological outlook'. He explains, 'This outlook combines present eschatological realization and future eschatological expectation.' Not only is there a 'backward look' and a 'forward look' in worship, there is also an 'existential perception of the kingdom of God.'[1] The kingdom is experienced presently as 'the worshiper is translated by the Holy Spirit into an experience of the kingdom that is depicted or described in Sacrament or Word.'[2] Gause here has built on the work of Oscar Cullmann, seeing this eschatological outlook in the proclamation and hearing of the Word as well as celebration of the Eucharist.[3] He distinguishes this being 'in the Spirit' from 'a forensic placement in the kingdom or in heaven.'[4]

In a later work, Gause delineates the elements of this Theology of Worship: rapture, rapport and proleptic. Rapture is 'the ecstatic quality of worship' ... in which 'the emotions are transported to the level of

---

[1] R. Hollis Gause, 'The Lukan Transfiguration Account: Luke's Pre-Crucifixion Presentation of the Exalted Lord in the Glory of the Kingdom of God', Ph.D. dissertation, Emory University, 1975, p. 213.

[2] Gause, 'The Lukan Transfiguration Account', p. 214.

[3] Gause, 'The Lukan Transfiguration Account', p. 215.

[4] Gause, 'The Lukan Transfiguration Account', p. 214.

worshipping in the Holy Spirit, both in song and prayer.'[5] Rapport is defined as 'a union of love between the worshipper and God, and between the worshipper and fellow worshippers.'[6] The third element, Proleptic, is 'anticipation of the worship to be enjoyed when believers will fall before the thrones of the Father and of the Lamb in the consummation of the kingdom of God ... it is foretaste and "guarantee in kind" of the kingdom state of worship. This is an experience in which heaven is transported to the believer and the believer is transported to heaven.'[7]

This Theology of Worship is presented as a proper way of understanding Pentecostal theology, a dialectical approach holding in tension the two poles of a Theology of the Word and a Theology of Experience. He writes, 'It is a theology of the Word in that the call to worship is by the Word of God, and the terms of worship and its direction are given in the Word. The most important aspect of the Word in this worship is that the Object of our worship is revealed in Scripture.'[8] But it is also a theology that 'possesses essential experiential qualities that involve the whole of human personality.' He continues, 'Scriptural worship envelopes the mind, the emotions and the will.'[9] For Gause, there is a salvific dimension to worship: 'In this experience of worship the congregation and all congregations are melded into a unit – the body of Jesus Christ.'[10]

With this understanding of worship, as involving mind, will and emotions, it is possible to see how Gause can view the act of writing as an act of devotion and worship. Theological writing must have integrity, and must therefore be 'under the authority of the word of God.' At the same time, it must be led by the Spirit, responsive to the Spirit. He writes 'with the understanding that we are immediately in the presence of God – the One who knows our thoughts afar off.'[11] This awareness of the presence of God is far removed from the more mechanical approaches often described by scholars. For instance, Gause's contemporary, Gordon D. Fee, in discussing the writing of his commentary on 1 Corinthians describes 'the several times when I had very personal encounters with the living God through the power of the text itself.'[12] He goes on, 'Much of the writing was simply hard work, keeping at it some twelve hours a day, six days a week, for fourteen months of ac-

---

[5] R. Hollis Gause, 'Distinctives of a Pentecostal Theology', unpublished paper, p. 36.
[6] Gause, 'Distinctives of a Pentecostal Theology', p. 21.
[7] Gause, 'Distinctives of a Pentecostal Theology', p. 21.
[8] Gause, 'Distinctives of a Pentecostal Theology', pp. 21-22.
[9] Gause, 'Distinctives of a Pentecostal Theology', p. 22.
[10] Gause, 'Distinctives of a Pentecostal Theology', p. 22.
[11] Gause, 'Distinctives of a Pentecostal Theology', p. 22.
[12] Gordon D. Fee, 'Reflections on Commentary Writing', *ThT* 46/4 (Jan. 1990), p. 391.

tual writing ... these moments of encounter with God through the text of the word were "seasons of refreshing."'[13] Notice the marked difference between Gause's more immanent view ('immediately in the presence of God') and the more transcendent one of Fee ('moments of encounter'). While in reality, their experiences were probably very similar, their perceptions and semantics are quite different.

For Gause, theological integrity does not simply mean one doctrine flowing logically from another. It means that the way one does theology must have integrity with the message. Rowan Williams seems to hold a similar view, 'The integrity of a community's language about God, the degree to which it escapes its own pressures to power and closure, is tied to the integrity of the language it directs to God.' He goes on to speak of language 'surrendered to God.'[14] It is with this integrated view that Gause has offered his talents and abilities in the service of God and His church.

Pentecostal scholars today, for the most part, have the luxury of being able to 'specialize', devoting their time, talents and energies to one discipline with an occasional foray into interdisciplinary experiments. But scholars of earlier eras within Pentecostal academia were called upon to be the primary resource person for the denomination or school that employed them.[15] Thus, though their degrees may have been in biblical studies, they were often called upon to teach theology, history or even practical theology. While obviously taxing for that first generation of scholars, they produced an invaluable pool of resources for future generations. R. Hollis Gause became that kind of resource for the Church of God. One may conclude that Gause is/was what Anglicans would refer to as a 'divine', a member of the clergy skilled in the study of divinity or theology; though now much more common in Pentecostal circles, for years this was something of a rarity.

As a result, a survey of his writing reveals that his contributions are found in a variety of genre. One finds in his portfolio works categorized as exegetical commentary, Bible lessons, theology, church polity, historical theology, practical theology, reflective essays and even free verse.

Gause, like his contemporaries in classical Pentecostalism, became an occasional writer, being called upon by the denomination to produce works that answered questions, explained positions or instructed and trained ministers and laypersons in the faith. The Gause catalog reminds one of that of Athanasius, of whom Gonzalez says,

---

[13] Fee, 'Reflections on Commentary Writing', p. 392.

[14] Rowan Williams, *On Christian Theology* (Oxford: Blackwell, 2000), pp. 7-8.

[15] See Rickie D. Moore, John Christopher Thomas, Steven J. Land, 'Editorial', *JPT* 1 (Oct. 1992), pp. 3-4.

Athanasius was a pastor rather than a systematic or speculative thinker. This does not mean that his thought is not orderly, or that it lacks system, but that his work and his theology developed in response to the needs of each moment rather than on the basis of the requirements of a system. Therefore, one would seek in vain among his works for one that attempts to present the totality of his theology. His works are pastoral, polemical, exegetical and there is even a biography among them; but in none of them does he attempt to theologize for the mere pleasure or curiosity of it.[16]

And like Athanasius, Gause's work was often pivotal, determining the direction the denomination or educational institution would take.

Engagement with Scripture

Whatever the occasion and whatever genre demanded by that occasion, Gause's work is always grounded in exegesis of Scripture. His view seems to be 'new occasions demand new exegesis.' This careful approach reflects his view that he writes 'under the authority of the Word of God'.

Gause's work might be classified as Exegetical Theology or Biblical Theology. This branch of theology, according to Orton Wiley 'is a study of the contents of Scripture, exegetically ascertained and classified according to doctrines.'[17] This category, if it may be applied to Gause's work, should not be confused with contemporary understandings of Exegetical Theology, such as that proposed by Walter Kaiser which calls for 'principlization' as a final step wherein one states '"the author's propositions, arguments, narrations and illustrations in timeless abiding truths with special focus on the application of these truths to the current needs of the Church."'[18] Instead, Gause employs the method more inductively, allowing the text to speak, but integrating its voice into the other voices of Scripture and Wesleyan-Pentecostal doctrine.

In an interview, Gause explains how he arrived at his own method. In 1948 he wrote lessons for the youth Sunday School quarterly for the Church of God. This was followed by an extended assignment of writing both the teacher and student quarterlies for adult Sunday School from 1952-1972. It was with this assignment that he derived a method which has been his basic approach ever since. He began with the pericope (which in this case was assigned) and did a verse-by-verse exegesis

---

[16] Justo L. Gonzalez, *A History of Christian Thought: From the Beginnings to the Council of Chalcedon*, vol. I (Nashville: Abingdon, 1970), pp. 291-92.

[17] H. Orton Wiley, *Christian Theology*, vol. I (http://wesley.nnu.edu/holiness_tradition/wiley/index.htm).

[18] Walter Kaiser, *Toward an Exegetical Theology: Biblical Exegesis for Preaching and Teaching* (Grand Rapids: Baker Book House, 1981), p. 151, quoted in Carl G. Kormminga, Book Review, *CTJ* 18/1 (1983), p. 89.

of the text. From here he wrote a didactic and inspirational discourse followed by a prescribed section called 'Pentecostal Viewpoint'.[19] What this method provided was, in his words, 'an intense engagement with Scripture.' In this way, Gause is, like Wesley, 'a man of one book.' This designation, which may be used for both men, is not a renunciation of other sources; indeed, both men may also be described as 'men of letters'. But it is an epithet, which describes the primacy that is ascribed to Scripture.[20]

Integrating Motifs

Readers and hearers of Gause's theology are struck by the integrity of his work. This integrated approach was arrived at in a deliberate way. Gause reveals that in his frustration with dispensational theology that was becoming prevalent at Lee College in the fifties he was inspired by the work of William Hendriksen, through a survey text being utilized in freshman Bible classes. In this work, _Survey of the Bible: A Treasury of Bible Information_, Hendriksen emphasizes the thematic unity of the Old and New Testaments. This idea, that one could see unifying themes in Scripture, set Gause on a course of unifying the whole biblical narrative in the cross.[21]

This salvation history motif complemented another motif inherent in Gause's Wesleyan-Pentecostal worldview. Joseph Hillery King, Bishop of the Pentecostal Holiness Church for decades, and a major influence in the Gause home, first set out his _Passover to Pentecost_ trajectory in the book's first publication in 1913. King's work, an apologetic (and often polemical) exposition of the Wesleyan-Pentecostal doctrines of salvation, sanctification and spirit baptism, utilized the Old Testament events of the Exodus and Pentecost to defend not only the concept of subsequence, but more importantly to explain the significance and meaning of the crisis experiences. Specifically, Pentecost of the New Testament was to Calvary what Sinai was to the Exodus event of the Old Testament. Building on this, and on the earlier three ages or dispensations interpretations of salvation history by Joachim of Fiore and John Fletcher, Gause constructed his understanding of the _via salutis_. So, the initial salvation experience (Passover) of the believer anticipates the writing of the law on the heart (Pentecost).

The title of this festschrift delineates three key themes or motifs found in Gause's writing: Passover (i.e. the cross), Pentecost and Pa-

---

[19] Gause says that section was sometimes forced and 'I guess I thought that's what I was doing [all along]!' Interview with R. Hollis Gause, 1 Nov. 2006, Cleveland, Tennessee.

[20] For a succinct discussion of Wesley's engagement with Scripture see 'Chapter 2 - Scriptural Christianity: John Wesley's Theology of Grace' in Thomas A. Langford, _Practical Divinity: Theology in the Wesleyan Tradition_ (Nashville: Abingdon, 1983), pp. 24-27.

[21] Interview, 1 Nov. 2006.

rousia. As discussed above, underlying all of these is the theme of worship. Originating in his Pentecostal origins, and informed by his early theological education in Presbyterian institutions (Presbyterian College, 1945; Columbia Theological Seminary, 1949) and the accompanying immersion in the Westminster Shorter Catechism, the creature's responsibility to worship the Creator is foremost in his thought: 'The chief end of humankind is to worship God and enjoy Him forever'. The cross, the upper room and heaven are places of divine worship.

Gause's doctoral dissertation (Emory University, 1975) is illustrative of this hermeneutic. The title, 'The Lukan Transfiguration Account: Luke's Pre-Crucifixion Presentation of the Exalted Lord in the Glory of the Kingdom of God', is telling. Gause explains, 'One of the theses of this paper is that the Transfiguration account in Luke is a proleptic presentation of the kingdom of God in the experience of Jesus and His three intimate disciples, and that this account is used in a similar manner in worship in the Christian community.'[22] Gause lifts up four themes of Lukan theology, each of which may be found in the Transfiguration account: Kingdom, Prayer, Glory and Exodus. This account is paradigmatic of the worship of the community, the idea of recapitulation being central to Gause's thought.[23]

Kingdom, as presented in this account, is a 'proleptical presentation ... of the kingdom as it will be gathered around the exalted Messiah.'[24] Prayer serves as the 'threshold of the Transfiguration.' It is also 'instrumental in their revelation represented' and as such is 'instrumental in proleptical translation into the glory of the kingdom of God.'[25] So, in the paradigm, prayer serves the proleptic dimension of worship in the church.

Gause's discussions of the theme of glory illuminate another of his undergirding motifs: salvation. He writes, 'In summary, the transfigured appearance of Jesus brings into a single scene most of the symbolism in Luke's use of δοξα the instrument of divine saving self-revelation, the apocalyptic appearance of the Son of man which is also His intermediate heavenly appearance, and the visible instrument of revelation and salvation.'[26] In seeing the whole of Scripture as revealing salvation history, this event in Christ's life is not episodic but a part of the redemptive fabric. The fourth theme, exodus, 'takes on the mean-

---

[22] R. Hollis Gause, 'The Lukan Transfiguration Account', p. 133.

[23] See an early exegetical piece by Gause, 'A Study of the Doxology of Ephesians 3:20, 21', unpublished paper. He writes, 'The epistle has set out to show that the church is a divine institution in which the glory of God is to be manifested because of the divine work upon and the divine presence in the church' (p. 7).

[24] Gause, 'The Lukan Transfiguration Account', p. 151.

[25] Gause, 'The Lukan Transfiguration Account', p. 165.

[26] Gause, 'The Lukan Transfiguration Account', p. 169.

ing of deliverance in Luke.'[27] Jesus' death is 'His own deliverance'[28] and 'the opening of the way into redemption',[29] 'the route by which the kingdom of God is brought to its fulfillment.'[30]

When one remembers that the majority of Gause's published work is occasional, that is 'assigned' by the Church of God in some way, it is striking that these themes and integrating motifs continue to emerge. Though it will be impossible to examine in depth each of Gause's published works, some attention will be given to the most noteworthy of these.

Collection 1: Biblical Studies

As already discussed, all of Gause's work begins with careful exegesis. However, much of what has been written and published falls into the category of commentary.

The earliest of these exegetical and expository works is the Sunday School literature written for the Church of God from 1952 to 1972. A survey of this literature reveals that over the two decades in which he wrote this literature, 60 of the 66 books of the Bible were examined.[31]

In 1983, Gause was commissioned by the Department of General Education of the Church of God to develop a commentary on the book of Revelation.[32] This commentary was to be utilized in Bible Institutes throughout the denomination, for the training of ministers and laypeople alike. The commentary, *Revelation: God's Stamp of Sovereignty on History*, was written from the perspective of historic premillennialism and a progressive and unified view of salvation history over and against a dispensational view. What must be noted and emphasized here is that given this alignment with a non-dispensational interpretation, this assignment placed Gause in the position of writing a commentary that would differ with the majority of interpreters within Pentecostal circles.[33] Gause opts for a combination of a preterist and

---

[27] Gause, 'The Lukan Transfiguration Account', p. 172.

[28] Gause, 'The Lukan Transfiguration Account', p. 174.

[29] Gause, 'The Lukan Transfiguration Account', p. 173.

[30] Gause, 'The Lukan Transfiguration Account', p. 178.

[31] Those for which there were no lessons written are 1 Chronicles, Song of Solomon, Lamentations, Nahum, Zephaniah and Titus.

[32] R. Hollis Gause, *Revelation: God's Stamp of Sovereignty on History* (Cleveland, TN: Pathway, 1983).

[33] See for example works on eschatology and Revelation by Gause's contemporary Stanley M. Horton, *The Ultimate Victory: An Exposition of the Book of Revelation* (Springfield, MO: Gospel Publishing House, 1991), pp. 18-21 and *Our Destiny: Biblical Teachings on the Last Things* (Springfield, MO: Logion, 1996), pp. 24-28 and 174-77. See also the discussion of 'The Great Tribulation' in *Bible Doctrines: A Pentecostal Perspective* (ed. William W. Menzies & Stanley M. Horton; Springfield, MO: Logion, 1993) in which the Church Age is described: 'The interlude is the age of grace, or the Church Age. When

futurist viewpoint in interpreting the book.[34] An example of this 'combination' interpretation may be seen in his discussion of the seven
churches in ch. 2. He explains that the seven churches are 'churches of
the day. As such they give us a composite picture of the Church as it
lived in a pluralistic and antagonistic society.' He continues, 'By studying these epistles we actually see the Church in every age and in all
ages. These are not seven ages of the Church predicatively described.
In every age of the Church there have been congregations that have
displayed the entire range of spirituality represented by these churches.
In every age the Church has lived with the same temptations and in
the midst of the same enemies.'[35]

Gause's work may be further contrasted with scholars who attempt a
literal interpretation of the events in the book. For instance, in describing the plagues described in ch. 8 he writes, 'With these plagues God
destroyed a third part of the trees and grass by burning. We need not
attempt mathematic calculations on this proportion – a highly symbolic
book such as this does not attempt to deal in such exactitude.'[36]

Perhaps the most explicit statement against dispensationalism is
found in his discussion of the history of salvation. He writes, 'The
Word of God embraces both law and promise. As the law is one over
both testaments, so is the gospel.'[37] God's dealings with humankind
have fallen under two covenants: one of works (or life) established
prior to Adam's fall in Gen. 2.15-17 and one of grace, also a covenant
of life, established in Gen. 3.15. All other covenants delineated in
Scripture are 'subordinate covenants', 'explications of the one covenant
of grace.' There is one aim of this covenant, established after the Fall,
and that is the restoration of humankind to relationship with God.[38]
Given the theological climate, this commitment, stated up front, was a
bold one.[39]

---

the restraining influence, the Holy Spirit's working in and through the Church, is removed at the time of the Rapture, apparently this is the signal for the unleashing of the
events which fall into that fateful, terrible 70th week. The "week" seems to have the
significance of 7 years' (p. 221).

[34] Gause, *Revelation*, p. 23. Horton (*Ultimate Victory*, p. 20) is obviously committed to a
futurist approach to the interpretation of the book.

[35] Gause, *Revelation*, p. 45.

[36] Gause, *Revelation*, p. 131. This approach is quite different from that of Horton who
says (*Ultimate Victory*, p. 21) that he is committed to 'as literal an interpretation as the
context allows'.

[37] Gause, *Revelation*, p. 20.

[38] Gause, *Revelation*, p. 21.

[39] Contrast this view with that of Horton in *Our Destiny* (p. 26): 'With the coming of
Jesus and His death on the cross, the Law's work was done, and it was no longer
needed.... The covenant of the law having been abolished, Christ's death and the shedding of His blood put a brand new covenant into effect (Heb. 8:13; 9:15–10:18).'

It is not surprising that Gause titles the first chapter 'The Glory of the Son of Man in the Church'. What may be seen in this chapter, and indeed in the entire commentary, is Gause's foundational understanding of worship. In addition, he emphasizes the centrality of Christ in this chapter, and throughout the book. Christ is the Mediator of the Revelation and its message or content is the will of God, the destiny of the world order.[40] The reader of this commentary easily finds the motifs of Kingdom, worship and salvation within this first chapter: the blessing of the Triune God is described by John and he offers a doxology in which Christ is praised for his work of redemption. Gause lifts up three aspects of this redemption: the love of Christ for us, deliverance from the bondage of sin and being made a kingdom of priests to God.[41]

Further, ch. 1 announces the return of Christ. John's response to this announcement is worship: he prays 'even so', a prayer that Gause calls a prayer of 'welcome and submission'.[42] As on the Mount of Transfiguration, prayer is the 'threshold' of this revelation of God. Later, what was described in the work on Luke as an eschatological outlook is seen by Gause in the description of the presence of Christ in the church: 'It is also important for the Church to know that this figure of the Son of man stands in the midst of the churches. It is His presence that makes them the Church.'[43]

In the earlier discussion of salvation history Gause expresses his view that 'Revelation is the culmination of what God has been doing in all ages. The concepts of the kingdom of God, Israel and the Church are unified. In definition these concepts may be distinguished, but spiritually and redemptively they are one.'[44] This viewpoint is clearly seen in his discussions of the visions of heaven and of the twenty-four elders. Whether elders of the Old Testament or the New, they are one in their testimony of redemption.[45] What follows is a discussion of the nature of the elders' worship as a paradigm for worship in the church. In the acts of bowing and of casting their crowns at the feet of the One who is on the throne, the elders show reverence but also intimacy. Their praise is a 'confession of personal relationship' as He is "'our Lord and our God"'.[46]

---

[40] Gause, *Revelation*, pp. 27-28.
[41] Gause, *Revelation*, p. 33. Gause points out John's recollection of the Exodus and Passover.
[42] Gause, *Revelation*, pp. 34-35.
[43] Gause, *Revelation*, pp. 39-40.
[44] Gause, *Revelation*, p. 25.
[45] Gause, *Revelation*, p. 90.
[46] Gause, *Revelation*, p. 93.

The Wesleyan-Arminian orientation of Gause may be seen in his understanding of the prayers of the saints (ch. 8). Prayer is a participatory act and is effective. Contrary to Reformed views which see prayer as only changing the one praying, Gause writes, 'Though they are always heard immediately by God, they are also reserved until this moment in the fulfillment of God's plan. The reservation of these prayers for this time and for this sacrifice and for this purpose makes the saints in their praying participants in God's eternal plan (Eph 1:9-12). The believer not only serves men for their good when he prays; he serves God and affects eternity.' [47]

As the judgment of God climaxes, as described in the book of Revelation, the songs in heaven become what Gause calls 'Hymns of Defeat'. These hymns are a 'reflection through song upon the events of Revelation 17.' [48] Those singing these dirges (specifically those found in vv. 9-19) are the kings of the earth, the merchants and the merchant marines. Of the mourning of the fallen kings Gause writes,

> In application, we may note the following. The believers in John's day could say to Rome. 'Your judgment was set as soon as you became the Babylon of your day.' In recent history the people of God could say to Germany of the Third Reich, 'When you vowed to make *Mein Kampf* the Bible of a thousand years from now, you set your own judgment.' To any oppressive society, whether it is Red China, Soviet Russia, or any other we may now say to the Babylon of our day, 'Helpless laborers may now fear you and all nations may try to negotiate with you, but in one hour your destruction will come because your deeds require it.' To any modern power, whether it is Red China, Central American dictators, communist rebels, the PLO, Israel, or the United States, the same warning must be given. To all of them, when they boast of their sins, when they try to escort God to the edge of the universe and dismiss Him, when they assume the right of oppression, murder and enslavement, in that day they will set their own judgment. Their name, their past history, their so-called democraticness, or any other assumed virtue of modern sophisticated politics will not save them. The character of Babylon guarantees the judgment of God. [49]

Once again, Gause's salvation history orientation may be seen. Similarly, he applies the buying and selling of the 'bodies and souls of men' to the evils of the slave trade throughout history:

> The United States ought to have learned the lessons of the Civil War. That war was not simply a test of the survival of a democratic society. it [*sic*] was God's judgment upon North and South alike – judgment

---

[47] Gause, *Revelation*, p. 129.
[48] Gause, *Revelation*, p. 227.
[49] Gause, *Revelation*, p. 233.

upon a nation that would profess the equality of all men, and yet would sell and trade men, treating them as if they were chattel.[50]

Gause goes on to apply this slavery to any political or economic practice that 'uses people as pawns in a massive chess game.'[51]

The salvation history orientation and the Covenant of Grace once again come in view as Gause describes 'Life in the Holy City' (Rev 22.1–5). The scene is depicted utilizing classic literary images of life and well being: a river and a tree. Gause sees in these images allusions to the provisions of the atonement:

> Both of these symbols – river of the water of life and tree of life – provide the benefits of the atonement. These benefits provide both life and healing. The tree bears its fruit every month and its fruit is life giving. The leaves to the tree are provided for the healing of the nations (Ezekiel 47:8). It can be said then, 'And there is no longer any curse' (22:3a). None of the blight of sin exists any longer. It is healed by the flow of water – atonement provision and application – out of the throne of God and of the Lamb.[52]

In this picture is the restoration of all that was lost in the Fall.

> The tree of life is a symbol picked up out of the first paradise of God on earth, the Garden of Eden (Genesis 2:9; 3:22, 24). There the tree of life provided for the maintenance of the life that God had given the first man Adam. God had established a covenant of life with Adam, and He provided a tree of life in that covenant. When man sinned against God, it was necessary to separate man from that tree. Under the curse of sin, man would have desecrated the tree of life to partake of it, and he would have been placed under a perpetual curse. Thus, God protected man from the tree and the tree from sinful man (Genesis 3:22, 24). In the last Adam, the paradise has been restored, and with it the tree of life. Man is no longer cursed to partake of it. He is made alive and healed in Christ by the flow of the water of life and by the fruit and leaves of the tree of life.[53]

With this image, salvation history has come full-circle. Like Irenaeus, Gause sees the Last Adam, Christ, as reversing the curse of the First Adam. Like Wesley, Gause sees salvation as restoration of the *imago dei*.

> To see God's face is the height of worship. The consistent testimony of Scripture is that men in this mortal life cannot see and have not seen the face of God (John 6:46; 1 Timothy 6:16). But in the holy city the face of God is always present. The face of God is the revelation of Himself. To

---

[50] Gause, *Revelation*, pp. 233-34.
[51] Gause, *Revelation*, p. 234.
[52] Gause, *Revelation*, p. 276.
[53] Gause, *Revelation*, pp. 276-77.

see His face is to see His nature and His glory. David anticipated this experience: 'As for me, I will behold thy face in righteousness; I shall be satisfied, when I awake, with thy likeness' (Psalm 17:15). To see the face of God is to be made like Him; therefore, worship is the response of those in whom the image of God has been fully renewed.[54]

Gause's commentary on the book of Revelation integrates his two prevalent themes of worship and soteriology. In Heaven is 'full realized redemption'.[55]

The second major biblical studies work is a commentary on the book of Romans, again produced for the Department of General Education of the Church of God. The work is titled *The Preaching of Paul: A Study of Romans*. It is not possible here to do a full review of this commentary but, as with the study of Revelation above, Gause's interpretive viewpoint and distinctive theological approach will be highlighted.

Gause contends that the Apostle Paul wrote to the Romans in order to give them a 'comprehensive statement of his message.' Gause reminds the reader that Paul called the material 'my gospel' and concludes, 'What is written here is what Paul preached.'[56] But Gause clarifies that Paul understood the gospel to be of or from God (1.1). It is its origin in God that gives it authority.[57] Again, in congruity with his non-dispensational reading, Gause states that Paul understands the Old Testament scripture as 'gospel promise and preaching'.[58]

Agreeing with other scholarship, Gause sees 1.16, 17 as central to the message of Romans. But Gause warns that this is more than a proposition; it is his 'entire message and mission'. Gause's emphasis on the authority of the Word surfaces in this discussion. Paul writes that the gospel is the 'power of God unto salvation' (1.16).

> It is the quality of a divine word that it accomplishes what it says. Divine word is not dependent upon another medium for the fulfillment of its decree; the fulfillment lies in the character of the word itself. The gospel is no less divine word than the decree of creation which fulfills its own command. So the gospel's announcement of salvation is the giving of salvation.[59]

Also in keeping with his non-dispensational interpretation is Gause's understanding of Paul's delimitations of the recipients of the gospel

---

[54] Gause, *Revelation*, p. 277.

[55] Gause, *Revelation*, p. 278.

[56] R. Hollis Gause *The Preaching of Paul: A Study of Romans* (Cleveland, TN: Pathway, 1986), p. 17.

[57] Gause, *Preaching of Paul*, p. 20.

[58] Gause, *Preaching of Paul*, p. 20.

[59] Gause, *Preaching of Paul*, pp. 26-27.

message, 'to the Jew first and also to the Greek'. Gause contends that
this describes the order of salvation history, not a prioritizing of the
recipients. He sees this same order being applied to 'the order of responsibility and judgment' in Rom. 2.9.[60] Later, in commenting on
9.1-5, Gause continues this thought. Paul delineates two truths with
regard to salvation: 'First, there is no respect of persons (or nations)
with God. Second, these blessings are not intended to terminate on
Israel.'[61] Paul goes on in ch. 9 to list seven advantages given to ethnic
Israel historically. But Paul then shows that 'the real issue of being
"Israel" is spiritual and not physical'. Gause explains: 'The Israel of
grace cannot be identified according to the fleshly descendants of Abraham (9:5, 6)'.[62] In keeping with his salvation history views, Gause
again emphasizes that it is not possible 'to imagine that God provides
New Testament salvation in a way different from Old Testament salvation. Salvation is one in all ages, and for all races. God deals with Israel
as He does with gentiles. This is not something new; this has always
been God's role in relation to Israel and redemption.'[63]

One significant contribution of this work is Gause's extensive discussion of living in the Spirit. This discussion is prominent in the
commentary on ch. 8. Moving beyond the juridical language often
prevalent in discussions of the soteriology of Romans, Gause utilizes
language that is more therapeutic. He begins this discussion by reiterat-
ing Paul's Christology that foreshadows Chalcedon: 'Christ's manhood
was complete; his body was the body of a man. His immaterial nature
(soul and spirit) was fully human. The incarnation was real, not simply
apparent.'[64] Gause states emphatically, 'The flesh of the incarnation was
not sinful; sin is not natural to the human body or to any aspect of
human nature. Sin is a foreign element that robs man of the fullness of

[60] Gause, *Preaching of Paul*, p. 27.

[61] Gause, *Preaching of Paul*, p. 124.

[62] Gause, *Preaching of Paul*, p. 126. On this point it may be that Horton can be classified
as a 'Progressive Dispensationalist' in that he acknowledges that Israel 'must come by
grace through faith in the risen Lord Jesus' (Horton, *Our Destiny*, p. 176). However, in
his work with Menzies (*Bible Doctrines*, pp. 236-37) there is a discussion of 'God's Promises to National Israel' in which they declare that according to Ezekiel 36 and 37, 'God is
going to restore Israel both materially and spiritually even though they have profaned His
holy Name. He will do it to honor His holy Name, that is, to demonstrate His holy
nature and character.... Consequently, there is no way that Ezekiel's prophecy can be
spiritualized and applied to the Church.' In *Our Destiny* (p. 177), Horton attempts to
clarify this tension: 'Clearly, God will be faithful to His promises to national Israel without splitting Israel and the Church into two peoples and two plans.'

[63] Gause, *Preaching of Paul*, p. 123.

[64] Gause, *Preaching of Paul*, p. 98.

his humanness.'[65] This very important presupposition anticipates a Wesleyan, and therefore transformational, soteriology.

If this 'foreign element' is to be dealt with, it must be done so through the Spirit. Contrasted with living according to the flesh is life in the Spirit. The work of the Spirit is described in therapeutic terms: cleansing, indwelling, and regeneration. Each of these terms denotes a change or alteration.

This indwelling of the Spirit is transformative in that death is no longer at work in the believer, but rather resurrection life is at work. In harmony with Eastern interpretations, particularly of Rom. 5.12, Gause concludes,

> This passage [8.12-14] is not dealing with the spiritual principle of the crucifixion of the old nature, but with the fact that the indwelling of the Holy Spirit reverses the results of sin. The death resulting from sin is not only the mortality of the physical body; it is the entire judgment of God which includes the mortality of the body. This passage refers to the death of the body.[66]

The Spirit of Life in us assures the believer of bodily resurrection. By emphasizing this aspect of physical death Gause moves the discussion from one of mere status or position in Christ to one of real change.

Like Wesley, Gause emphasizes the role of the Spirit in assurance. Wesley defined assurance as 'perception of the inward work of the Spirit'.[67] Gause concurs, 'If there is any point at which we are aware of the Spirit's leadership, we know that we are the children of God. If there is in our heart a hunger for holiness for life, this it [sic] the Spirit's witness that we are God's child.'[68]

One of Gause's emphases in Pauline studies through the years has been Paul's understanding of the place of suffering in the Christian life. Chapter 8 of Romans is, in many ways, central to this emphasis. As children of God, our redemptive heritage includes both suffering and glory. Gause writes, 'It is unfortunate that believers sometimes treat the suffering as a negative experience only to be endured (and barely tolerated) because it is necessary for the receiving of glory.'[69] He goes on to explain that for Christ the 'cross was His exaltation' and that Paul is told 'that he must suffer for Christ's sake'.[70] Because the Kingdom is at hand both experiences, suffering and glory, are participation in it.

---

[65] Gause, *Preaching of Paul*, p. 98.

[66] Gause, *Preaching of Paul*, p. 101.

[67] Randy L. Maddox, *Responsible Grace: John Wesley's Practical Theology* (Nashville: Kingswood, 1994), p. 125.

[68] Gause, *Preaching of Paul*, p. 104.

[69] Gause, *Preaching of Paul*, p. 104.

[70] Gause, *Preaching of Paul*, p. 104.

Gause explains, 'The Holy Spirit enables the believer to stand in both relationships of the kingdom [the 'already' and 'not yet'] so that the foretaste becomes participation in the kingdom and guarantee of its fulfillment.'[71] Because the Kingdom is already and not yet, the glory is already experienced in part by the presence of the Spirit. We as a part of God's creation wait with anticipation of the full realization of that glory. Gause discusses the 'cosmic nature of redemption' in his discussions of Rom. 8.17-22. Like a woman suffering the pains of giving birth, all of creation groans, but that groaning anticipates deliverance.[72] Gause writes,

> All of creation is together in this agony and in the anticipation of the age to come. The untamedness and viciousness of the beasts, and the fact that one lives off the life of another are witnesses to the coming mountain of God in which the lion, the bear, and the calf will lie down together, eat straw together like the ox and be led by a little child (Isaiah 11). The present turmoil witnesses to a new heaven and a new earth. The clap of thunder testifies to a clear sky. The earthquake testifies to a stable earth. The raging storm testifies to a world at peace. The raging and destroying flood testifies to the river of life.[73]

Because we have the 'firstfruit of the Spirit', we join the 'chorus of agony and witness'. With this firstfuit implanted, though we still live in this present age, we have within us 'the very character of the kingdom that is to come.'[74] It is in light of this already-not yet dialectic in which believers find ourselves, that Gause discusses praying in the Spirit. In fact, Gause points out that Paul's choice of words, 'unutterable groanings' is meant to reflect the groanings of all of creation described above. The origin of the groanings is the Spirit and these groanings are prayers to the Father, the 'One who searches the heart'. 'When we do not know our own mind, or the circumstances in which we pray, when we do not know the mind of God (and many times we do not), when we do not know the future (and always, [sic] we do not), there is for us an Intercessor who knows all these things because the Spirit knows the mind of God.'[75]

Collection 2: Theological Works
Though Gause's doctoral work was in the area of biblical studies, as one of the few formally trained scholars in the denomination's academy, he was often called upon to teach in the areas of theology or his-

---

[71] Gause, *Preaching of Paul*, p. 105.
[72] Gause, *Preaching of Paul*, p. 110.
[73] Gause, *Preaching of Paul*, p. 110.
[74] Gause, *Preaching of Paul*, pp. 110-11.
[75] Gause, *Preaching of Paul*, p. 115.

torical studies. For that reason, much of his written work would be categorized as theological discourse. There are several published works falling under this rubric.[76] Much of that writing has focused on soteriology. Perhaps the major contribution to Pentecostal theology made by Gause is his work *Living in the Spirit*.[77]

In this treatment of Wesleyan-Pentecostal soteriology, Gause asserts that 'the believer is living in the Spirit from the first moment of faith in Christ. To be saved and to live a godly life is to live in and by the power of the Holy Spirit.'[78] He goes on to identify the two major emphases of the book: (1) Reception of the Holy Spirit is a distinctive experience; (2) 'being filled with the Spirit is a quality of being and a manner of life.'[79] Gause's presupposition is the unique contribution of this book as it sets the experience of Spirit Baptism in the *via salutis*. He writes, 'All of the prior experiences in redemption anticipate and are culminated in baptism with the Holy Spirit.'[80] This view of the place of Spirit Baptism in the life of the believer is a particularly Wesleyan one in that it sees salvation as involving both crisis and process, and life in the Spirit as participatory with the grace of God. Gause has developed a metaphor that illustrates this understanding:

> As the pinnacle of the mountain is distinct from the path leading to it, baptism with the Holy Spirit is distinct from those experiences which anticipate it. On the other hand, as the pinnacle and the mountain are integral to each other, all the prior experiences are bound up in the life in the Holy Spirit. Though the base of the mountain is distinct from

---

[76] The following published works would be categorized as theology proper: 'Our Heritage of Faith in the Verbal Inspiration of the Bible', *Heritage Papers: Centennial Celebration: Declaration of Faith* (ed. R. Hollis Gause & Steven J. Land; Cleveland, TN: Pathway, 1989). 'The Holy Spirit: Your Personal Guide', *Endued with Power: The Holy Spirit in the Church* (Robert W. White, ed.; Nashville: Oliver Nelson, 1995), pp. 17-31; 'The Doctrine of Holiness', *Transforming Power: Dimensions of the Gospel* (ed. Yung Chul Han; Cleveland, TN: Pathway, 2001), pp. 87-147; 'Resurrection', *The Pentecostal Minister* 1.1 (Spring 1981), pp. 51-53; 'The Ministry of the Holy Spirit in the Life of the Individual', *Church of God Evangel* 57.9 (April 1967), pp. 405.

[77] R. Hollis Gause, *Living in the Spirit: The Way of Salvation* (Cleveland, TN: Pathway, 1980); *Living in the Spirit: The Way of Salvation* (Cleveland, TN: R. Hollis Gause, 2005); and now *Living in the Spirit: The Way of Salvation* (Cleveland, TN: CPT Press, 2009). All quotations, unless otherwise noted, are from the 2005 revision.

[78] Gause, *Living in the Spirit*, p. 6.

[79] Gause, *Living in the Spirit*, p. 7. Gause's emphasis in this work and elsewhere on life in the Spirit, and his view of salvation as participatory (see discussion of Romans 8 above) as well as his emphasis on the personal-relational nature of the Spirit seems clearly to contradict Steven Studebaker's interpretation of Gause's view of the work of the Spirit as following the 'well-worn path of Protestant soteriology by assigning the Spirit an instrumental role in soteriology' or as reductionist where the Spirit's only role is 'applying the redemptive provisions of Christ' (Steven M. Studebaker, 'Pentecostal Soteriology and Pneumatology', *JPT* 11/2 [2003], pp. 258-59).

[80] Gause, *Living in the Spirit*, p. 7.

the peak, it is one mountain. Progression along the slope of the mountain provides different experiences and vantage points. It is still one mountain. [Author's italics][81]

Gause goes on to identify these various points along the mountain or way, placing them in a 'logical and experiential' order. The experiences he identifies in the *via salutis* are repentance, justification, adoption, regeneration, sanctification and Spirit Baptism. He designates some, by virtue of definition, as a part of initial salvation (repentance, justification, adoption, regeneration). These initial experiences are 'changes of position' and changes in 'nature' and they 'occur in union with each other when one first trusts in Christ as Savior.'[82] Like Melvin Dieter, he recognizes that chronologically and in the view of the believer they may be indistinguishable.[83] Two of these experiences are designated as subsequent to initial salvation (sanctification and Spirit baptism). In keeping with Wesleyan theology Gause sees sanctification as subsequent to initial conversion; in discontinuity with Wesleyan theology, he sees Spirit baptism as an experience distinct from sanctification.[84] But Gause goes on to warn against a 'fragmentation in definition' that may in turn lead to a 'fragmentation in our experience of life in the Holy Spirit'.[85]

Sanctification is defined by Gause as grounded in the atonement provision of Christ 'whereby the body of sin is crucified and all unrighteousness is purged from the heart of the regenerate, making her/him free from the law of sin and death.'[86] By definition, then, this experience must be understood as subsequent to initial conversion; it is an act transforming the already regenerate person. In the prior experience of regeneration, a creative act of God, the 'seed of the life of Christ is implanted'. In the subsequent experience of sanctification, these implanted graces are 'released to a more fruitful growth in and by the Holy Spirit'.[87] Gause continues his defining of sanctification by including an emphasis on the pursuit of holiness, 'the normal manner of life for the believer'. This 'normal manner of life' is 'characterized by freedom from sinning, by the denial of lust of the flesh, lust of the eye and pride of life and by cultivation of the fruit of the Spirit.'[88]

---

[81] Gause, *Living in the Spirit*, p. 7.

[82] Gause, *Living in the Spirit*, pp. 8-11.

[83] Melvin Dieter, 'The Wesleyan Perspective' in *Five Views on Sanctification* (ed. Melvin Dieter; Grand Rapids, MI: Zondervan, 1987), p. 1987.

[84] Gause, *Living in the Spirit*, p. 12.

[85] Gause, *Living in the Spirit*, p. 15.

[86] Gause, *Living in the Spirit*, p. 10.

[87] Gause, *Living in the Spirit*, pp. 10-11.

[88] Gause, *Living in the Spirit*, p. 11.

As an experience in the way of salvation, baptism in the Spirit is 'transformational in the cultivation of the righteousness and its anointing for the pursuit of holiness'. In variance with other Pentecostal discussions of the purpose of the experience, both historic and contemporary, Gause suggests, 'There is a strong emphasis on vocational /missional purposes of this baptism, but its purpose is not vocational alone.'[89]

Though it is not possible in the scope of this essay to delineate and discuss all of the revisions and additions in the 2005 edition of this work, several should be noted. First, though *repentance* was delineated as an experience and aspect of salvation in the Introduction in the earlier edition, Gause has added a chapter titled 'Repentance' and a follow-up chapter titled 'Living the Penitential Life'. In so doing, Gause emphasizes that repentance is a part of the crisis of initial salvation but is also 'a grace which is to be practiced throughout one's life in Christ.'[90]

Initial repentance involves a recognition that the sinner has 'fallen short of the glory of God' (Rom 3.23). It is not surprising to find a discussion in this chapter on the glory of God that involves both His majesty and His ethical holiness. It follows then that a discussion of sin will describe human sin as sin against this glory. Though the law defines sin, and as a 'tutor' makes us aware of sin, thereby making us culpable, sin is primarily a 'violation of trust, and it is a disruption of relationship with God.' Sin is not inherent to human nature; it is foreign and alien. However, it occurs first in the heart, before being acted upon and in fact may remain a sin of the heart. Therefore, all who have come to knowledge of sin must repent.[91]

Repentance is a gift of God, not originating in the human heart. Once being awakened by the law to his/her guilt, the sinner is also awakened to the promise of the gospel. In keeping with the Pietist tradition, Gause sees repentance as 'a radical emotional experience' involving godly sorrow and remorse. It is a willful act on the part of the sinner, just as sin was a willful act. By the Spirit of God, the sinner is made repentant.[92] Like Wesley's synergistic soteriology, Gause's is a modified synergism, always initiated by God.

Radical repentance calls for forsaking of sin, audible confession of sin within the body of Christ. This initial repentance then calls for the living of a penitential life. This initial encounter sets the pattern for how we are to live. This penitential life is characterized by a hatred of

---

[89] Gause, *Living in the Spirit*, p. 12.

[90] Gause, *Living in the Spirit*, p. 17.

[91] Gause, *Living in the Spirit*, pp. 32-33.

[92] Gause, *Living in the Spirit*, p. 39.

sin and a continued rejection of evil and continued pursuit of holiness. This involves prayers of repentance which recognize union with Christ, a sense of shame, confession and restitution.

The second noteworthy addition is a chapter on justification in which justification is viewed as an act provided by and applied by both Word and Spirit. Here, Gause identifies Word as 'both law and promise, but more particularly the Word is the Person of Jesus Christ.'[93] Most significantly, Gause identifies the Spirit of God as the 'Power of God'.[94] Also in this chapter, Gause is careful to point out that justification is a declaration that concerns past sins not those which may be committed in the future. Adamantly he writes of the 'corruption of Pentecostal theology' which leads inevitably to a doctrine of perseverance of the saints and 'robs faith of its component of obedience.' He concludes that this naturally issues in antinomianism in which believers continue to practice sin.[95]

Perhaps more thoroughly than any writer before him, Gause has discussed the significance of baptism with the Holy Spirit. He begins, 'The significance of baptism with the Holy Spirit rests in the person of the Holy Spirit. To be baptized and filled with the Holy Spirit is to be indwelt of a divine person – a member of the Trinity.'[96] This, he writes, is 'an extreme elevation of man. It is elevation by the grace of God in which the unworthy hovel of the spirit of this world has become the glorious temple of the Holy Spirit (Eph 2:2; 1 Cor 6:19, 20).'[97] From Peter's sermon in Acts 2, Gause points out that the pouring out of the Holy Spirit is the 'primary proof, then, of Christ's presence with the Father'. Therefore, he continues, 'A personal Pentecost is our highest evidence of Christ's resurrection.'[98]

As stated earlier, Gause is influenced in his theology by early Pentecostal leader J.H. King. It is in this discussion that King's influence is so apparent. Pentecost, both historically and personally, is 'the interpretation of Calvary.' He explains, it 'instructs in the way of life to be followed subsequent to Calvary.'[99]

---

[93] Gause, *Living in the Spirit*, p. 73.

[94] Gause, *Living in the Spirit*, p. 73.

[95] Gause, *Living in the Spirit*, p. 79. See especially n. 17.

[96] Gause, *Living in the Spirit*, p. 196.

[97] Gause, *Living in the Spirit*, pp. 196-97.

[98] Against contemporary attempts at apologetics for the resurrection Gause writes, 'It is well and good to be able to point to the empty tomb to show the physical evidences of resurrection, and to list all of the polemic arguments for resurrection. But the only saving evidence of the resurrection of Christ is the testimony of the Holy Spirit (cf. Romans 1:4)' (Gause, *Living in the Spirit*, p. 198).

[99] Gause, *Living in the Spirit*, p. 199.

A third distinctive contribution of this volume, and this is found in both editions, is Gause's discussion of the 'pattern of experience' as established in the Acts narrative. Moving beyond, but in keeping with, the classical Pentecostal 'three out of the five' argument,[100] Gause views the Acts narrative as establishing not only Spirit baptism's distinction from and subsequence to regeneration, and glossolalia as initial evidence, but he also sees the pattern in Acts as establishing the normative way that the Spirit is poured out, corporately and individually, in 'situations of divine worship.'[101]

Fourthly, Gause contributes to the ongoing discussions among Pentecostal scholars about the significance of speaking in tongues.[102] Because Gause has established the initiatory event (as well all as subsequent fillings) as one of divine worship, he defines the manifestation (tongues speech) contextually. Out of his understanding of Pentecostal theology as a 'Theology of Worship', Gause describes glossolalia as representing 'a profound rapport between two persons: the divine Person, the Holy Spirit, and the human person, the believer. These two persons meet together through kinship and affection in such intimacy that the believer becomes fully responsive to the Holy Spirit. As He acts, wills, and communicates, the responding believer speaks and acts. This act of submission and responsiveness [speaking in tongues] is essential to other acts of submission and responsiveness to the Holy Spirit.' In this way, Gause is defining the manifestation of *glossolalia* as a *sign* of the transformation of the believer into one who is ultimately responsive and submitted to the Spirit of God. These inward effects and moral and ethical and spiritual evidences are discussed in subsequent chapters.[103]

---

[100] See Ray H. Hughes, *What is Pentecost?* (Cleveland, TN: Pathway, 1963), pp. 30-32; Ray H. Hughes, *Church of God Distinctives* (Cleveland, TN: Pathway, 1968), pp. 24-27; Noel Brooks, *Charismatic Ministries in the New Testament* (Greenville, SC: Holmes Memorial Church, 1988), pp. 3-4; David Petts, *The Holy Spirit: An Introduction* (Mattersey, UK: David Petts, 1998), pp. 72-75.

[101] Gause, *Living in the Spirit*, p. 217. It is this observation made by Gause with which noted scholar Harvey Cox was so taken when Gause responded to him at a conference in Cleveland, TN in 1998. Cox responded with great respect to Gause's observation noting that this insight made his entire trip to Tennessee worthwhile!

[102] See Land, 'Be Filled With the Spirit: The Nature and Evidence of Spiritual Fullness', *Ex Auditu* 12 (1996), pp. 108-20; Frank D. Macchia, 'Sighs too Deep for Words: Toward a Theology of Glossolalia', *JPT* 1 (1992), pp. 47-73 and 'Groans too Deep for Words: Towards a Theology of Tongues as Initial Evidence', *AJPS* 1 (1998), pp. 149-73; Blaine Charette, 'Reflective Speech: Glossolalia and the Image of God', *Pneuma* 28/2 (Sep 2006), pp. 189-201.

[103] Note especially Gause's discussion of the gift and use of tongues as discussed by Paul in 1 Corinthians 12 and 14. There is a significant revision with reference to Paul's words in 12.29-31. See n. 65. Gause interprets the rhetorical question in v. 31a as 'But are you seeking the best spiritual gifts' with the expectation of a negative answer, 'No, you are

Three other smaller theological works should be noted in this study. The first of these is a brief work on the role of the Spirit in personal guidance. This work, 'The Holy Spirit: Your Personal Guide'[104] focuses on the biblical understanding of the Spirit as *another Paraclete*. Gause contends that to understand the role of the Spirit, one must first see how Jesus, the *first Paraclete* functioned in the lives of his disciples while on earth. He concludes, 'What Christ did by His physical and local presence the Holy Spirit does in His invisible and universal presence.'[105] However, Gause goes on to delineate the dissimilarities in the transition from the physical presence of Christ to the Spirit's outpouring.

A second work of note is a doctrinal study titled 'The Doctrine of Holiness'.[106] This work takes seriously the scriptural exhortation to be holy and develops an understanding of the doctrine and exhortation identifying first the 'character of God's holiness' as foundational. From this basis, there is a consideration of the nature of holiness in the human experience as well as the provision for the experience in redemption. The study moves then to an examination of both the experience and pursuit of holiness.[107] Thoroughly Wesleyan-Pentecostal, Gause describes that process in terms of crisis ('cleansing') and process ('way of life').

A third (unpublished) work discusses sanctification in light of the Trinity.[108] This paper was prepared for the 'Oneness-Trinitarian Dialogue' sponsored by the Society for Pentecostal Studies and was read at the 2006 meeting. This work is significant for two reasons. First, it offers a thorough treatment of Gause's understanding of the doctrine of the Trinity. Secondly, it examines sanctification and holiness, in an intentional way, from a Trinitarian perspective. Gause describes the doctrine of Trinity as

---

not'. He writes, 'The original Greek uses a verb form that can be an imperative verb (as in the KJV) or an indicative interrogative verb.' He explains, 'This translation makes this sentence consistent with the language of vv. 29, 30. The questions in those verses are all rhetorical questions expecting a negative answer. I see this verse as the climax of a series of rhetorical questions. It shows that the Corinthian believers had misplaced their values and they were not seeking the best gifts, but were elevating the spectacular above the quiet and unostentatious manifestations of the Holy Spirit' (*Living in the Spirit*, pp. 252-53).

[104] R. Hollis Gause, 'The Holy Spirit: Your Personal Guide' in *Endued with Power: The Holy Spirit in the Church* (ed. Robert White; Nashville, TN: Thomas Nelson, 1995), pp. 17-31.

[105] Gause, 'Holy Spirit', p. 23.

[106] R. Hollis Gause, 'The Doctrine of Holiness' in *Transforming Power: Dimensions of the Gospel* (ed. Yung Chul Han; Cleveland, TN: Pathway, 2001), pp. 89-147.

[107] R. Hollis Gause, 'Holiness', p. 90.

[108] R. Hollis Gause, 'Pentecostal Understanding of Sanctification from a Trinitarian Perspective', unpublished paper.

a doctrine of worship. The patterns of worship are revealed progressively in the covenant of promise, the Old Testament period, through theophanies, oracles and the spiritual experiences of the faithful. In the covenant of fulfillment, the New Testament, the wonder of this understanding of God bursts forth in the Incarnation and is demonstrated repeatedly by such events as the baptism of Jesus, the Transfiguration, the resurrection of Christ, His ascension and the outpouring of the Holy Spirit.[109]

Gause issues a warning to Evangelicals and Pentecostals who have become or are becoming 'binatarian' by laying too much stress on the Word at the expense of Spirit. He defends the union of Word and Spirit in role and function in the Christian life:

> Word of God comes and fulfills its own commandments and promises only because of the union of Word with the Holy Spirit. This statement does not allow for a static deposit of truth. We have in mind Word that is divine in its Origin, dissemination and propagation; this Word goes forth by the continued activity of the Holy Spirit to fulfill His nature of holiness in those who hear. As the Word imparts His nature in believers, the Holy Spirit is no less the Agent of fulfillment of His nature in believers. Holiness of nature is paramount for both Word and Spirit because holiness of nature is ontological to both Word and Spirit. There can be no endowment of the power of the Holy Spirit that is not also an experience in righteousness and purity.[110]

Gause sees a danger in this neglect of Spirit in that (1) the result is a rationalistic-analytic use of the Word in which spirituality is confused with profession of faith and (2) there is a 'mantra-like use of Scripture' resulting in faith claims where there is no actual evidence of transformation, resulting in a positional righteousness or healing.[111]

The second significant contribution made by this paper is the development of the doctrine of sanctification out of a theology of sociality in God. Basing his argument, primarily, on 1 John, Gause describes a continuum of holiness–unity–love,

---

[109] Gause, 'Pentecostal Understanding of Sanctification', p. 2.

[110] Gause, 'Pentecostal Understanding of Sanctification, p. 4.

[111] Gause, 'Pentecostal Understanding of Sanctification', p 5. See also Kimberly Ervin Alexander, 'The Almost Pentecostal: The Future of the Church of God in the United States' in *The Future of the Pentecostal Movement* (ed. Rybarczyk & Patterson, publ. Roman and Littlefield, forthcoming) where the negative repercussions of the shift in Pentecostal circles from a view of a real transformational conversion experience to the emphasis on a 'decision for Christ' or 'profession of faith'. The effect of this shift to a more positional view and its effect on healing theology and practice are explored more fully in Kimberly Ervin Alexander, *Pentecostal Healing: Models in Theology and Practice* (JPTS 29; Blandford Forum, UK: Deo, 2006).

> That sociality is represented in the communion of Persons of the Holy
> Trinity by their love one for another and by their unity with one
> another. Their love one for another is eternally fulfilled in the exten-
> sion of love to each other and in the perfect/infinite reciprocation of
> that love. In its interrelatedness, this is social and in its essence it is
> eternal. As to the interrelatedness some sense of pluralism is necessary.
> As to its eternal quality, it is ontological to deity, necessary and un-
> changeable. Its ontological character and necessity are clearly an-
> nounced by the declaration, 'God is love' (1 John 4:8). Its necessity lies
> in God's eternal nature and in His personal nature.[112]

Finally, one other unpublished work should be considered. Gause
has recently developed a Pentecostal view of atonement which is not
bound to any one of the theories addressed in orthodox theological
studies but accepts truths found within the classic (Christus Victor), the
Latin (penal substitution) and the moral persuasion or influence theory
(Abelard), while rejecting universalism. The paper points out the
shortcomings of each theory and arrives at a conclusion that emphasizes
that no one event (cross or cross-resurrection) is responsible for atonement but that Christ Himself is our atonement. He writes, 'The advantage of this emphasis is that it makes the entire first advent of our Lord
the sacrifice that He became for us.'[113]

Collection 3: Practical Theology

As already noted, Gause is a theologian in the Athanasian tradition in
that he has written primarily for the church. While this essay has thus
far discussed several of Gause's works in the area of biblical studies and
theology, there are significant works that would be categorized as practical theology. Wesley preferred the term *practical divinity* for the entire
theological task as he saw that all theology had a practical goal. Thomas
A. Langford summarizes Wesley's thought on this subject: 'Christian
truth must be applied to both personal and social life. Doctrine is for
the purpose of Christian nurture and service.'[114] There are noteworthy
contributions to this field among the published works of Gause.

The most obvious contribution is his 1973 publication *Church of
God Polity*.[115] Though obviously a work written for use by the Church
of God, it is a work that was initiated by Gause, and not commissioned
by the denominational leadership. Gause explains that in addition to
serving as Parliamentarian for the denomination for a number of years,

---

[112] Gause, 'Pentecostal Understanding of Sanctification', p. 7.

[113] R. Hollis Gause, 'Atonement', unpublished paper, Cleveland, TN: R. Hollis
Gause, 2006.

[114] Thomas A. Langford, *Practical Divinity: Theology in the Wesleyan Tradition* (Nashville:
Abingdon, 1983), p. 27.

[115] R. Hollis Gause, *Church of God Polity* (Cleveland, TN: Pathway, 1973).

he had been teaching a course in the curriculum of Lee College which focused on Church of God history as well as polity. In both instances, one was dependent on the *Supplement to Minutes* (of the General Assembly) in order to determine matters of polity. He writes, 'I found that the church had made and recorded many of its decisions on the occasions of specific problems and issues; consequently, a decision was often made that touched on one or more different areas of government and order, but was recorded under only one heading. This, of course, caused some duties of various offices to be listed under other areas rather than under the office itself.'[116] It was his idea to develop a concise and well-ordered manual of the church's polity on all levels (local, district, state and general—in that order). The changing nature of church polity necessitated revisions on a rather frequent basis and eventually, these revisions were not seen as necessary. Several items of note may be found in the work. First, the Dedication is noteworthy. This work is dedicated to Gause's parents who '...won me to Christ and nourished me with grace and wise counsel and exemplified the order of the Church of the Lord Jesus Christ with its love, discipline and unity in our home.'[117] This brief statement of honor is profoundly theological, expressing an ecclesiology which sees the Church as Family of God, wherein is found 'love, discipline and unity'. Secondly, Gause includes an appendix which provides a 'brief study of scriptural words used to describe the ministry.'[118] It is noteworthy that this work of exegetical theology is an appendix. Gause comments that this study was not adopted by the Church of God but was 'an attempt to describe the ministry in its varied functions.'[119]

Three other publications in the field of practical theology are of note. First, Gause was a part of a committee formulated to study the reworking of the Practical Commitments of the Church of God. He recalls that the committee was divided and his offering was the 'minority report', not adopted by the General Assembly, but published and circulated among pastors. This document was titled 'The Order of Church Discipline' and attempted to develop a pattern in which the 'integrity of the Practical Commitments could be maintained without austerity'.[120] In the preface, then General Overseer Wade H. Horton instructs that 'THE ORDER OF CHURCH DISCIPLINE should be used in preliminary orientation of prospective members prior to their

---

[116] Gause, *Church of God Polity*, Preface (n.p.).
[117] Gause, *Church of God Polity*, Dedication (n.p.).
[118] Gause, *Church of God Polity*, p. 261.
[119] Gause, *Church of God Polity*, p. 261.
[120] Interview, 1 Nov. 2006.

reception into the Church.'[121] Horton encourages pastors, 'This book-let is provided by your Church and I urge each pastor to use it prayer-fully in counseling with prospective members.'[122] Gause approaches the issue by first examining how discipline is undertaken in Scripture. He notes that many things are rebuked but very few persons are excluded. He concludes that the purpose of church discipline is the perfection of the saints and their spiritual cultivation. If one is excluded or 'turned over to the flesh' it is so that they might be saved.

Related to this, is a paper published by the church that examined the issue of moral failure, the accompanying discipline and restoration of ministers. In the paper titled 'After Moral Failure (Forgiveness vs. Ministerial Fitness)' Gause does not see forgiveness and ministerial fitness as necessarily adverse to each other but as integral and 'two points in the spectrum of grace.'[123] Moral failure must be defined scrip-turally, not by one tradition or by the conditioning of society. Gause also reiterates that sin is not inherent to humanity and must always be treated as such. He goes on to emphasize 'that the violation of trust and privilege adds dimensions of egregiousness to sin.'[124] This is com-pounded when the offender is a minister due to his/her ordination by God and affirmation by the church. Restoration, therefore, involves the rebuilding of trust.[125] Gause emphasizes that 'the aim of forgiveness is restoration – unencumbered restoration.'[126]

Another publication to be considered in this category is the *Covenant of Dedication: A Ceremony of Infant Dedication.*[127] It is appropriate that Gause would write and publish for the Pentecostal worship context in light of his understanding of Pentecostal theology as a theology of wor-ship. This litany sets infant dedication in the context of biblical ste-wardship. Gause says of parenting,

> Parenthood is a stewardship. This child which we will dedicate today is not your own. He/she belongs to God. God gave him/her life and that life will be returned to God. You are the keepers of this treasure. You are the developers of this treasure. You are answerable to God for the

[121] 'The Order of Church Discipline' (no publication information), p. 3. The preface begins: 'At the fifty-fifth General Assembly, the following motion prevailed. "That the amplification on THE ORDER OF CHURCH DISCIPLINE be printed in booklet form and used in preliminary orientation of prospective members by each person prior to receiving members into the Church' (p. 3).

[122] 'Order of Church Discipline', p. 3.

[123] R. Hollis Gause, 'After Moral Failure (Forgiveness vs. Ministerial Fitness' (Cleve-land, TN: no publ.), p. 1.

[124] Gause, 'Moral Failure', p. 5.

[125] Gause, 'Moral Failure', p. 6.

[126] Gause, 'Moral Failure', p. 6.

[127] R. Hollis Gause, *Covenant of Dedication: A Ceremony of Infant Dedication* (R. Hollis Gause, 1988).

manner in which you keep and develop this treasure. God has given you a privilege. You have the opportunity to return to God a treasure developed to its full potential spiritually and socially.[128]

The litany continues by establishing that the act of dedication is a part of the parents' stewardship. The parents respond with commitments, as does the congregation, placing the responsibility in the hands of the community. Gause exhorts,

> These parents standing alone are not sufficient to the vows which they have just taken. This child on his/her own will not come to know Jesus Christ as Saviour and Lord. These vows and the goal of personal salvation can be realized only in a community of faith. You as the congregation of God are charged by God to provide a nurturing and supporting community of spiritual oversight and nurture for this child and his/her parents.[129]

As would be expected the prayer of dedication is thoroughly Trinitarian, addressing the Father ('the Author of Life'), the Son ('the Light who Lights everyone coming into the World') and the Holy Spirit ('the Breath of Life').[130]

Over the course of the last two decades, Gause has written two works on the role of women in the church, each co-authored with a woman. The first, *Women in the Body of Christ* was co-authored with his wife, Beulah Gause.[131] This book was commissioned and distributed by the women's department of the Church of God, then called 'Ladies' Ministries'. The second of these works, *Women in Leadership: A Pentecostal Perspective*, commissioned by the Center for Pentecostal Leadership and Care, provided me the privilege of co-authoring a work with Dr. Gause.[132]

In both works, Gause's discussions of the role of women begin with the Creation accounts in Genesis 1 and 2. In 1984, the Gauses began their study with a chapter titled 'God Created Woman in His Image'. They concede that this is a 'shocking statement'. 'Perhaps we have become so accustomed to saying "man" for mankind that we have come to think of humanness as being primarily male. Once we make such an assumption, it is easy to assume that male dominance and superiority are biblical teachings.'[133] They go on to consider the role of

---

[128] Gause, *Covenant of Dedication*, n.p.

[129] Gause, *Covenant of Dedication*, n.p.

[130] Gause, *Covenant of Dedication*, n.p.

[131] R. Hollis & Beulah Gause, *Women in the Body of Christ* (Cleveland, TN: Pathway, 1984).

[132] Kimberly Ervin Alexander and R. Hollis Gause, *Women in Leadership: A Pentecostal Perspective* (Cleveland, TN: Center for Pentecostal Leadership and Care, 2006).

[133] Gause and Gause, *Women in the Body of Christ*, p. 13.

women in both the Old and New Testaments. With the characteristic humor and insight for which both authors have been noted, they write, 'There are not a great many regulations that are singularly applied to women in Scripture, but there are enough to create reams of copy by male authors in particular'.[134] The regulations considered by the Gauses are those related to women speaking, women's appearance and the relationships of women in the home. The position taken is primarily what may be now called a complementarian view. There is a temporal order in creation but there is mutuality in redemption.

Twenty-two years later Gause would undertake a thorough reading of Scripture with reference to women, particularly their leadership roles. Gause writes, 'In this work we will not argue that the woman is equal to the man because that equation implies that man sets the standard and that woman must be "pulled up" to the level of the man.'[135] Gause centers this discussion in soteriology when he writes,

> Rather than argue that woman is equal to man, we argue that in their humanity (i.e., their being in the divine image), they are the same. We will also argue that while the fall obscured and defaced the divine, it did not destroy it because of God's grace. The aim of grace is the restoration of this image for humankind through Jesus Christ. The image of God is restored in His life, death and resurrection. Since this image *is* restored in Christ, no human hierarchical systems apply to the place and privilege of the redeemed in Christ.[136]

Gause holds that one should begin this examination with the Creation accounts. He contends that one cannot begin with the social sciences or historical studies, though those studies may inform. He goes further by stating that neither can one begin with the Gospel narratives or teachings of the epistles because 'Most apply to the secondary stage in the existence of the role of women – that is, the period of human history after the fall.'[137]

Connected to this examination of Creation in anthropological study is an examination of Redemption. He argues, 'If we would see woman as God sees her, we must see her as God created her prior to the fall, and as God sees her as redeemed after the Fall.'[138] In keeping with an egalitarian view, and in keeping with his earlier conclusions, Gause sees both woman and man as created in the *imago dei* and each are necessary

---

[134] Gause and Gause, *Women in the Body of Christ*, p. 70.
[135] Alexander and Gause, *Women in Leadership*, p. 25.
[136] Alexander and Gause, *Women in Leadership*, p. 25.
[137] Alexander and Gause, *Women in Leadership*, p. 26.
[138] Alexander and Gause, *Women in Leadership*, p. 28.

for the completion of humanity. Each draw the image directly from God and each share in the dignity of humanity.[139]

Again, Gause reiterates that sinfulness is not inherently human. Therefore, fallenness and the conditions determined by the curse of sin are not to be considered normative. In addition, he warns that the judgments of Genesis 3 are pronouncements of God and their fulfillment is not the responsibility of any creature.[140] Gause points out that even in Genesis 3 there is *promise* of restoration of the *imago dei* and elevation of woman.[141] This is fulfilled in the Incarnation, where the human woman Mary passes to her child all the qualities of being fully human.[142]

Gause explores the role of women in leadership in the Old Testament noting obvious examples such as Miriam and Deborah as well as often overlooked stories of female leadership, such as Huldah. Perhaps most notable is Gause's attribution of Hagar as tribal head.[143]

In examining the material in the New Testament, Gause suggests that the early Christian community was more influenced by OT Scripture than by the Jewish community or by the Hellenistic world and more importantly by the example of Jesus in His relationships with women.

Gause begins his survey by discussing the treatment of Mary in the birth narratives and, again, the transformational nature of the Incarnation with regard to the status of women. He writes,

> That He was born of a virgin lays emphasis on the fact that the promise of redemption would come through the seed of the woman (Genesis 3:15). This is important for New Testament writers because it is in the childbearing that salvation comes (1 Timothy 2:15).[144]

He continues,

> In His Incarnation Jesus went back through all the ages of human history. His Incarnation retraces the steps of Israel, the call of Abraham, the families of Noah, the entire antediluvian world. The aim of this spiritual journey was for Him to reenter the womb of the mother of all the living (Genesis 3:20) in order that He might come out of the womb of His mother, Mary, as the Seed of the woman – the Savior to humankind and the One to bruise the head of the serpent. Mary and Eve became one for the salvation of the descendents of Adam.[145]

---

[139] Alexander and Gause, *Women in Leadership*, p. 35.
[140] Alexander and Gause, *Women in Leadership*, p. 43.
[141] Alexander and Gause, *Women in Leadership*, p. 43.
[142] Alexander and Gause, *Women in Leadership*, pp. 34, 43.
[143] Alexander and Gause, *Women in Leadership*, pp. 48-49.
[144] Alexander and Gause, *Women in Leadership*, p. 60.
[145] Alexander and Gause, *Women in Leadership*, p. 61.

Further, Gause sees in the birth narratives significance in the employment of three women as primary witnesses: Mary, Elizabeth and Anna. Luke's elevation of women in seeing them as credible witnesses (in this and other events, especially the Resurrection) is evidence of the influence of Jesus on the Christian community as this was not characteristic of the Palestinian community at the time.

Jesus' interaction with women throughout His ministry and their place in His ministry is 'an anomaly for His time and place.'[146] He points out that the use of the language 'sat at Jesus' feet' in reference to Mary (the sister of Martha and Lazarus) in Luke 10 is telling, as this is nearly identical with the description of the relationship between Paul and Gamaliel (Acts 22.3).

Gause's treatment of the role of women in the Early Church as evidenced in the Acts narrative and the epistles breaks with or, at least, pushes further than the views expressed in his earlier work. He first discusses the nature of the church as Body of Christ (organic unity having its paradigm for sociality in the Trinity) and the understanding of submission as defined by Scripture (a submission among equals as evidenced in Trinity or mutual submission). He examines with careful exegesis the so-called 'texts of terror' pointing out that submission is not subjugation and that metaphors, analogies and language itself should not be forced beyond its intended meaning.[147] He concludes 'To be heirs together of the gift of life gives us equal access to the throne of grace and equal opportunity to minister the gospel of grace.'[148]

Collection 4: Other Genre

One last group of Gause's writing must be considered. In this category, it is perhaps easier to see how his writing is part and parcel of his worship. Though not immediately evident to his students, but well known to colleagues, friends and family is Gause's rather prolific collection of more creative literary reflections. Through the years, Gause has offered written worship and prayers first to God, and then as gifts to acquaintances. These poetic offerings are written in the form which Gause calls 'metered prose'. These were written, he says, because they could

---

[146] Alexander and Gause, *Women in Leadership*, p. 62.

[147] See for example Gause's comments on Ephesians 5 and the headship issue. He writes, 'Christ's headship over the church is the pattern by which husbands and wives are to understand their relationship to each other (v. 23); but this pattern is analogy, not exact transfer of meaning' (Alexander and Gause, *Women in Leadership*, p. 88). See also his comments on 1 Tim. 3.1-7: 'When all these things are considered, and when are not bound by a mechanical literalism making language do what it is not intended to do, there does not seem to be adequate scriptural reason to limit the role of bishop to men' (Alexander and Gause, *Women in Leadership*, p. 99).

[148] Alexander and Gause, *Women in Leadership*, p. 107.

not be left unwritten.[149] He describes the process as one in which the reflection or prayer 'swells up inside' and is then put into words with 'balanced sentences', never attempting rhyme. The prose 'crescendos', moving from the least impacting thought to the greatest. They utilize active verbs rather than passive and the language is more emotive than might be found in his more academic work. The subject matter is normally personal experience, whether of crisis, victory or joy.[150]

At least one of these has been published and that in a scholarly journal,[151] evidencing the fact that though these pieces are emotive reflection, the reflection is in light of Gause's scholarly thought. A review of some of this collection reveals that the occasions for writing range from the everyday (table blessings,[152] travel,[153] holidays[154]), formal occasions,[155] international events,[156] or devotional reflection on biblical texts or truths.[157]

One last work should be considered, as much for its personal value to the Gause family as for its theological reflection for the rest of his readers. This work is the book he co-authored with his son, Val, titled *The Emmaus Road*.[158] This work began with a sermon titled 'The Emmaus Road' which was preached at the New Covenant Church of God in Cleveland, Tennessee. When Gause spoke to his son, Val, about the sermon, he made suggestions about how he might approach writing a series of reflections on those who encountered the crucified and risen Jesus. Gause invited his son, a newspaper columnist, to put his own reflections on these figures on paper. Eventually, they produced, together, this collection of reflections. Later developments in the life and relationship of this father and son could not have been known at the time of this collaboration but in reflecting on the process, Gause sees that it was redemptive for his son. He now sees it as the 'highlight of his publishing career'.[159]

---

[149] Interview.

[150] Interview.

[151] R. Hollis Gause, 'The Daystar from on High', *JPT* 11/1 (Oct 2002), pp. 143-44.

[152] R. Hollis Gause, 'A Table Blessing', 30 January 2006.

[153] R. Hollis Gause, 'The Desert Shall Rejoice and Blossom as the Rose', 20 May 2005.

[154] R. Hollis Gause, 'The Lord's Supper (A Christmas Meditation), n.d.

[155] R. Hollis Gause, 'Patten University Graduation, Invocation', 14 May 2004; 'Invocation, General Assembly', 11 August 1996; 'Prayer for Josh and Hope', 21 August 2004.

[156] R. Hollis Gause, '9/11', n.d.

[157] R. Hollis Gause, 'Meditation Based on Psalm 138:1-3', 2006; 'A Prayer Based on Isaiah 58', n.d.

[158] R. Hollis Gause and Val Gause, *The Emmaus Road* (Xulon Press, 2005).

[159] Interview. Val Gause died of cancer in August 2006.

Epilogue

It seems fitting to close this appreciative essay with a brief meditation written by Dr. Gause on December 24, 2000.

Meditation[160]
Psalm 139.1-12

Every road traveled is in His presence
Every rest taken is in His caring.
Every word spoken is in His hearing.
Every thought conceived is in His knowing.
Every deed done is in His seeing.
Every night covering is in His unveiling.
Is this frightening?
Is this comforting?
YES!

---

[160] R. Hollis Gause, *Meditation* (© R. Hollis Gause, 24 December 2000).

2

Tongues of Angels, Words of Prophets: Means of Divine Communication in the Book of Judges

Lee Roy Martin[*]

A. Introduction

The mention of the book of Judges calls forth images of battle between Israel and the Canaanites, tales of murder and intrigue, and stories of extraordinary characters. The topic of divine speech, however, rarely surfaces in discussions of Judges. Although the voice of God is a topic that should resonate with Pentecostals, whose distinctive theology includes the charismatic revelatory gifts, when approaching Judges, they give most of their attention to the Spirit passages. Pentecostals take note of the empowering activity of the Spirit of Yahweh,[1] and they observe the questionable moral character of the judges upon whom the Spirit descends.[2] Like everyone else, however, Pentecostals hardly reflect on the voice of God in Judges.

Notwithstanding its apparent obscurity, the speech of Yahweh figures prominently in nine episodes of Judges, episodes that are crucial to

---

[*] Lee Roy Martin (D.Th., University of South Africa) is Associate Professor of Hebrew and Old Testament at the Pentecostal Theological Seminary in Cleveland, TN.

[1] Pentecostal-Charismatic studies of the Spirit of Yahweh in Judges include: Stanley M. Horton, *What the Bible Says about the Holy Spirit* (Springfield, MO: Gospel Publishing House, 1976), pp. 33-42; George T. Montague, *The Holy Spirit: Growth of a Biblical Tradition* (An Exploration Book; New York: Paulist, 1976), pp. 17-18; John Rea, *The Holy Spirit in the Bible: All the Major Passages about the Spirit: A Commentary* (Lake Mary, FL: Creation House, 1990), pp. 48-55; Wilf Hildebrandt, *An Old Testament Theology of the Spirit of God* (Peabody, MA: Hendrickson, 1995), pp. 112-18; Lee Roy Martin, 'Power to Save!?: The Role of the Spirit of The Lord in the Book of Judges'; *Journal of Pentecostal Theology* 16.2 (2008), pp. 21-50.

[2] E.g., Horton, *Holy Spirit*, p. 35, reveals an awareness of the tension between purity and power when he acknowledges that sometimes God worked 'in spite of' the judges. I have addressed this concern in 'Judging the Judges: Finding Value in these Problematic Characters', *Verbum et Ecclesia* 29.1 (2008), pp. 110-29.

the development of the narrative.[3] In these episodes, Yahweh speaks in response to the priestly inquiry; he speaks through the angel of Yahweh; he speaks through prophets; he speaks through a dream; and he speaks directly, with the means of communication unstated.[4] It is the purpose of this paper to survey the divine communication in Judges by briefly examining each of the nine episodes in which God's speech is reported. I will conclude with a summary of the significance and implications of those divine interventions.

B. The Voice of Yahweh

1. 'Judah shall go up' (1.2)

Divine communication is a significant element in the opening episode of the book of Judges, for as soon as the narrative gets underway, God is invited to speak. After the death of Joshua, the Israelites seek Yahweh's direction for leadership by means of the first recorded priestly inquiry. They ask, 'Who shall go up first for us against the Canaanites, to fight against them?' (Judg. 1.1).[5] In the books of Exodus through Deuteronomy, there is no need for such an inquiry, because Yahweh speaks face to face with Moses. After the death of Moses, Yahweh again takes the initiative to speak to Joshua quite directly.[6] After Joshua's death, however, the Israelites begin to inquire of Yahweh by means of the High Priest.[7]

In response to Israel's inquiry, Yahweh names Judah as the tribe of leadership,[8] saying, 'Judah shall go up. I hereby give the land into his hand' (Judg. 1.2), thus introducing a new structure of leadership for

---

[3] Sections of this paper are dependent upon Lee Roy Martin, *The Unheard Voice of God: A Pentecostal Hearing of the Book of Judges* (JPTS; Blandford Forum, UK: Deo, 2008).

[4] The Hebrew roots אמר (to say) and דבר (to speak) are used 49 times in Judges with God (or one of his agents) as the subject. Also, in reference to the speech of God, the root צוה (to command) is used 4 times and the word קול (voice) is used 3 times. Taken together, in Judges we find 56 references to the speech of God.

[5] Biblical quotations are translations of the author.

[6] It is recorded 14 times that Yahweh spoke to Joshua (Josh. 1.1; 3.7; 4.1, 8, 15; 5.2, 9; 6.2; 7.10; 8.1, 18; 10.8; 11.6; 20.1)

[7] Nosson Scherman, *The Prophe*

ts: *Joshua/Judges. The Early Prophets with a Commentary Anthologized from the Rabbinic Writings* (Artscroll; Brooklyn, NY: Mesorah, 2000), p. 118.

[8] Although ch. 1 does not mention the tabernacle or the priests, the verb שאל (to ask) followed by the preposition ב (in, with, by), signifies the cultic ritual of 'inquiring, consulting'; Francis Brown et al., *The New Brown, Driver, Briggs, Gesenius Hebrew and English Lexicon: With an Appendix Containing the Biblical Aramaic* (trans. Edward Robinson; Peabody, MA: Hendrickson, 1979), p. 982. Inquiring of Yahweh would involve the priest and would occur in the communal setting of the tabernacle. Soggin admits as much, but still wants to see an explicit reference to the tabernacle. Cf. J. Alberto Soggin, *Judges: A Commentary* (OTL; Philadelphia: Westminster, 1981), p. 20. This may have been the first use of the *Urim* and the *Thummim* (Exod. 28.30; Num. 27.21); cf. Scherman, *Joshua/Judges*, p. 118.

Israel. For the first time in the canonical story, the narrative lacks a central character. After the death of Joshua, Yahweh does not choose a single person as national leader. When the Israelites ask Yahweh, 'Who shall go up for us first?', Yahweh names the tribe of Judah as preeminent. The absence of a replacement for Joshua might suggest a 'sense of uncertainty'[9] about Israel's future paradigm of leadership, but the personal guidance of Yahweh appears to be continuing.[10]

This first episode of Judges supplies important narrative indicators, including the temporal setting and the main characters of the story. According to these first two verses: (1) the story of Judges occurs just after the death of Joshua; (2) the main characters are the Israelites and Yahweh; and (3) the story involves the Israelites' continuing struggle to gain control of the land from the Canaanites. Furthermore, the opening verses of Judges suggest that the Israelites were operating purposefully in a unified fashion and were acting faithfully toward God. It is clear, however, that the conquest of the land is not complete, a fact that foreshadows the conflict that escalates throughout the book.

2. 'You have not heard my voice' (2.2)

After Yahweh names Judah as the tribe of leadership (Judg. 1.2), the succeeding verses are devoted to Judah's battles, in which he defeats numerous enemies and claims new cities. Verse 19 records Judah's first defeat, which is followed by a long register of failures that lists the tribes and their lack of success.

Yahweh responds to the failure of the Israelites in Judg. 1 by sending the angel of Yahweh, who brings a passionate message of rebuke from Yahweh (2.1-5). He begins with a reference to the exodus tradition, declaring, 'I brought you up from Egypt and I brought you into the land that I swore to your ancestors' (2.1). The reference to the exodus characterizes Yahweh as their savior and suggests that their future prospects in Canaan are based not upon their commitment to Yahweh but on his commitment to them. The mention of the ancestors affirms God's continuing faithfulness in his relationship with the people of Israel. This is not a new God who speaks; he is the God of Abraham, the God of Isaac, and the God of Jacob.

Yahweh continues his speech with a reaffirmation of his faithfulness: 'I will not break my covenant with you forever' (2.1). Yahweh insists that he is a God who can be trusted, a God of covenant faithfulness –

---

[9] Carolyn Pressler, *Joshua, Judges, and Ruth* (Westminster Bible Companion; Louisville, KY: Westminster John Knox, 2002), p. 130.

[10] The lack of a national leader does not imply an absence of leadership on the tribal level. The hearer of Judges would be aware of earlier texts (such as Josh. 23.2) that indicate the existence of leadership categories that include 'elders' (זקנים), 'heads' (ראשים), 'judges' (שפטים), and 'officers' (שטרים).

forever. The hearer of Judges 2 would understand that Yahweh is the Israelites' great king who has freely chosen to know them as his unique liberated covenant people and who has unconditionally pledged himself to be faithful to them even in the face of their disobedience to the stipulations to which they had agreed.

After insisting upon his own fidelity, Yahweh addresses the Israelites with this accusation: '[I said] you shall make no covenant with the inhabitants of this land; you shall throw down their altars: but ye have not heard (שׁמע) my voice. What is this you have done?' (2.2). Yahweh's indictment of the Israelites suggests the following implications: (1) Unlike the gods of Canaan, Yahweh is the God who speaks. (2) Yahweh's reference to the hearing of his 'voice' rather than to the keeping of his 'commands' suggests a personal relationship, a relational context. (3) The Israelites' failure to hear the voice of Yahweh is their fundamental and underlying error. Israel had vowed eagerly to listen to Yahweh (Josh. 24.24), but now their vows are broken. The crucial point of Judg. 2.1-5 is that while Yahweh has been faithful to his covenant with the Israelites, they have been unfaithful to him.[11] (4) Yahweh's question to Israel, 'What is this you have done?', is an expression of personal injury and emotional vulnerability to human offense. This question, coupled with the terse and laconic style of delivery, indicates that Judg. 2.1-5 is a passionate speech from a God who is invested in his covenant people.

Although Yahweh promises that he will never break his covenant, a covenant that includes his giving of the land, he concludes his speech by declaring that he will discipline Israel by allowing the Canaanites to remain as thorns and snares. Yahweh, however, will not entirely abandon Israel. Yahweh's response to the infidelity of the Israelites is not legalistic or mechanistic; moreover, his response is not altogether predictable; for although the Israelites show signs of repentance by weeping and offering sacrifices, he does not relent in his decision to allow the Canaanites to remain.

Yahweh's speech serves as a dramatic conclusion to the first half of the prologue (Judg. 1.1-2.5). In terms of dramatic structure, Judg. 1.1-31 can be understood as the introduction to the drama and Yahweh's speech (Judg. 2.1-5) is the causal moment (*das erregende Moment*), which signals the beginning of rising action in the drama.[12] In fact it is Yahweh's professed commitment not to break the covenant forever that, together with Israel's recurring violations of the covenant, accounts for the dialectical forces that generate the long acknowledged cyclical mo-

---

[11] Israel's unfaithfulness reaches its consummation at the end of Judges, where it is said, 'they all did what was right in their own eyes' (17.6; 21.25).

[12] Gustav Freytag, *Die Technik des Dramas* (Leipzig: S. Hirzel, 1897), p. 107.

tion of the rest of the book. Thus, Yahweh's speech sets the agenda for the narrative that follows.[13]

3. 'They transgressed my covenant' (2.20)

A second introduction (Judg. 2.6-3.6) retells the death of Joshua and then describes the subsequent apostasy of the Israelites. Like the first introduction, the second introduction concludes with a divine speech. Yahweh's speech (Judg. 2.20-22) restates elements of his earlier speech; but, rather than speaking directly to the Israelites as in Judg. 2.1-5, Yahweh speaks about Israel in the third person. The two speeches may refer to the same event, with the second speech coming in the form of a report that is directed to the hearers of Judges.

In this second rebuke Yahweh comes right to the point by stating the cause of his dissatisfaction with the Israelites. He says, 'Because this nation has transgressed my covenant that I commanded their ancestors, and they have not heard my voice...' (2.20). Earlier in the chapter, the narrator describes the sin of Israel as idolatry, that is, the forsaking of Yahweh and the worshiping of the Baals (Judg. 2.11-13). In his speech, however, Yahweh characterizes the sin of the Israelites in terms of his covenant relationship with them. The hearer of Yahweh's speech may be reminded of Yahweh's earlier word to Moses:

> Behold, you will sleep with your ancestors; and this people will rise up and play the harlot after the gods of the foreigners of the land, where they go to be among them, and they will forsake me, and violate my covenant that I have made with them (Deut. 31.16).

The reference to the Israelites as 'this people' in Deut. 31.16, parallels 'this nation' in Judg. 2.20, and the charges that the Israelites will 'play the harlot' (זנה) after foreign gods and will 'forsake' (עזב) Yahweh find their counterparts in Judg. 2.17 and 13 respectively. Furthermore, the breaking of the 'covenant' is the focus of both Deut. 31.16 and Judg. 2.20.

God's covenant with the Israelites demands their absolute allegiance, and their disloyalty offends God, moving him to act in judgment. In response to Israel's unfaithfulness, Yahweh declares, 'I also will no longer drive out before them any of the nations that Joshua left before he died' (2.21). In spite of the apparent severity of his judgment, Yahweh names a salvific or disciplinary purpose for allowing the Canaanites to remain in the land. The Canaanites will be allowed to remain in the land in order to provide the new generation with the opportuni-

---

[13] For a more extensive discussion of this passage, see Martin, *The Unheard Voice of God*, ch. 5.

ty to prove themselves faithful in the face of severe temptation (2.22) and in the conduct of war (3.1-6).

The dual introduction to Judges (1.1-2.5; 2.6-3.6) prepares the reader for the stories that follow and offers, through the construction of a theological paradigm for the period, a rationale for the cycle of judges. The Israelites fail to vanquish the Canaanites completely and subsequently engage in idolatrous syncretism. According to the introduction, therefore, the Israelites' root problem is their refusal to hear and obey God's word: 'You have not heard (שמע) my voice' (2.2). The charge is repeated three more times in Judges: 'They would not hear the judges' (2.17a); 'They have not heard my voice' (2.20); 'You have not heard my voice' (6.10).

4. 'Go ... I have given Sisera into your hand' (4.6-7)

The first and paradigmatic[14] judge is Othniel who is hailed earlier as a heroic warrior (Judg. 1.13), and the second judge is left-handed Ehud (3.12-30), who defeats King Eglon of Moab.[15] Then, after the brief mention of Shamgar, who saves the Israelites from the Philistines (3.31), Deborah is introduced as a prophet who is 'judging Israel' (4.4-5) in Ephraim. As a judge, the people come to her for justice, and as a prophet, she speaks for Yahweh.[16] It is not insignificant that a woman fills these roles that are traditionally assigned to men. I find it ironic that after the words of Deut. 18.15, 'The Lord will raise up for you a prophet like me from among your brothers', the first person who is called a prophet is not a 'brother' but a 'sister'.[17] Mieke Bal, in reflecting on the role of Deborah, observes that 'the only judge who combines all forms of leadership possible – religious, military, juridical, and poetical – is a woman and calls herself and/or is addressed as "a mother

---

[14] Cf. Block, *Judges, Ruth*, p. 149; and Lawson Grant Stone, 'From Tribal Confederation to Monarchic State: The Editorial Perspective of the Book of Judges' (Ph.D., Yale University, 1988), pp. 260-89, where Stone provides an extended discussion of Othniel's paradigmatic role in Judges.

[15] Ehud, as he approaches King Eglon, declares that he brings to the king 'the word of God' (דבר־אלהים). Ehud's statement suggests a claim of divine endorsement and guidance. Perhaps we could infer that God had spoken to him and provided the strategy for his victory.

[16] I use the term 'prophet' rather than 'prophetess' because the gendered terminology is a manifestation of Hebrew grammatical categories and is not an expression of different roles. In the contemporary Church we would not refer to a woman priest as 'priestess', and neither should we refer to a woman prophet as 'prophetess'.

[17] Her prophetic role is downplayed by John Gray, *Joshua, Judges, and Ruth* (New Century Bible; Greenwood, SC: Attic, rev. edn, 1977), who names the prophet of Judg. 6.7 as the 'first emergence of the prophet in Israel' (p. 171).

in Israel"'.[18] Bal and other interpreters such as Elie Assis are correct to point out the uniqueness of Deborah's judgeship, but in so doing they fail to recognize that each of the judges is unique.[19] Deborah is clearly a judge (4.4-5) who rises up to bring deliverance (5.7-8), and who embodies the programmatic statement in the prologue, which says that Yahweh 'raised up judges, who saved them out of the hand of those who plundered them' (2.16).

As a judge, Deborah stands within the tradition of Moses and the leadership structure attributed to Moses (Exod. 18.13-26). The biblical narrative prior to the book of Judges establishes a system of tribal leadership that includes judges, but the exact structure of leadership is not fully discernable. Like the texts that describe the office of prophet, these texts about judges assume that men will fill the position, but women are not explicitly forbidden from doing so.

As a prophet, Deborah speaks three prophetic words and she utters a song of praise. Her first act is to summon Barak, and by the word of the Lord she commissions him to attack King Jabin of Canaan, who had oppressed the Israelites for twenty years. Her words are not lacking in detail, as she specifies the location where Barak is to encamp, the number of soldiers that he is to recruit, the names of the tribes who

---

[18] Mieke Bal, *Death & Dissymmetry: The Politics of Coherence in the Book of Judges* (Chicago Studies in the History of Judaism; Chicago: University of Chicago Press, 1988), pp. 209-210.

[19] Elie Assis, 'Man, Woman, and God in Judges 4', *Sjot* 20/1 (2006), pp. 110-124 (p. 111). Block, *Judges, Ruth*, pp. 193-97, has expended considerable effort to classify Deborah as different from the other judges. Cf. Daniel I. Block, 'Deborah among the Judges: The Perspective of the Hebrew Historian', in A. Millard, J. Hoffmeier, and D. Baker (eds.), *Faith, Tradition, and History* (Winona Lake, IN: Eisenbrauns, 1994), pp. 229-53; and Daniel I. Block, 'Why Deborah's Different', *BR* 17/3 (2001), pp. 34-40, 49-52. Devotion to a male leadership model is expressed as well by Herbert Wolf, 'Judges', in F.E. Gaebelein (ed.), *The Expositor's Bible Commentary* (Grand Rapids, MI: Zondervan, 1992), III, pp. 375-508, who, incredibly and without any biblical warrant, insists that Deborah's 'prominence implies a lack of qualified and willing men' (p. 404). If God prefers male leaders, then why does he not dispense with Deborah entirely and call Barak directly, as he calls Gideon later? Or why does he not raise up a leader from birth, as he raises up Samson and Samuel? It is not from necessity that God uses Deborah but from his divine choice. It has been argued as well that the ministry of women is an exception that God allows only in times of extreme spiritual chaos. If that were true, we would expect Deborah to be one of the final judges, since the Israelites grow more unfaithful as the book progresses. I would argue that male domination is the aberration, caused by human sinfulness, and that in God's redeemed kingdom there is no domination or subjugation (cf. Gal 3.28). For a recent Pentecostal presentation regarding the leadership role of women, see Kimberly Ervin Alexander & R. Hollis Gause, *Women in Leadership: A Pentecostal Perspective* (Cleveland, TN: Center for Pentecostal Leadership & Care, 2006). I contend that women should be welcomed at all levels of leadership, both civil and ecclesiastical.

will be involved, the name of the enemy general, and the exact location of the battle (4.6-7).

Speaking as the messenger of Yahweh,[20] she assures Barak of victory, declaring, 'I will give him into your hand' (4.7). There is no indication in the text that Barak questions Deborah's credentials or that he is disturbed by her gender; nevertheless, his response is less than enthusiastic. He requires that Deborah accompany him to the battle, and because of his demand that she be physically present, he is deprived of the glory.[21] Consequently, Deborah proclaims that the glory of victory will go to a woman,[22] and at this point in the narrative that woman appears to be Deborah herself.

Deborah escorts Barak to the place of battle, and when the armies have assembled she commands Barak, 'Rise up; for this is the day in which Yahweh has given Sisera into your hand; has not Yahweh gone out before you?' (4.14).[23] In addition to Deborah's first prophetic word that served as the initial command to Barak, she now delivers a second word that specifies the exact timing for Barak's attack on the enemy. Deborah's words sound much like those of Moses, who promises the Israelites, 'It is Yahweh who goes before you; he will be with you; he will not fail you' (Deut. 31.8).[24] Like before, she speaks with no hint of uncertainty, providing Barak with the assurance that he needs to initiate the battle.

Why Deborah does not lead the army is left unstated, but I would suggest that it has something to do with her role as prophet.[25] Deborah's activity seems to parallel that of Moses when the Amalekites attacked Israel in the wilderness (Exod. 17.8-13). Just as Deborah directs Barak to engage in battle, Moses directs Joshua, who serves as com-

---

[20] The phrase 'Has not Yahweh, the God of Israel, commanded' is used to introduce the words of Yahweh, and takes the place of the messenger formula 'Thus says Yahweh'.

[21] It might be inferred that Barak's response arises out of doubt and disobedience, but cf. the words of Moses to God in Exod. 33.15. See Assis, 'Man, Woman, and God in Judges 4', pp. 120-23, who sorts out the implications of Barak's demand that Deborah accompany him.

[22] Some scholars conclude that in the poetic version of the battle (Judg. 5) Deborah is portrayed as the leader of the army. Cf. Susan Ackerman, *Warrior, Dancer, Seductress, Queen: Women in Judges and Biblical Israel* (AB Reference Library; New York: Doubleday, 1998), p. 31.

[23] Cf. the words of Yahweh to Gideon (Judg. 7.9) and David (1 Sam. 23.4).

[24] Cf. Exod. 23.23; 32.34.

[25] Often it is assumed that it is Deborah's gender that prevents her participation in the battle; cf. Assis, 'Man, Woman, and God in Judges 4', p. 119. The relationship between prophecy and warfare is explored, along with its attendant scholarship by Rick Dale Moore, *God Saves: Lessons from the Elisha Stories* (JSOTS 95; Sheffield: JSOT Press, 1990), pp. 128-47, who observes that it is 'Israel's prophet, not its conventional military resources, that represents the true strength and salvation of the nation in its confrontation with foreign military aggression' (pp. 128-29).

mander of the army in the wilderness. Similarly to Deborah, Moses issues the initial command (Exod. 17.9), and he accompanies Joshua to the battle zone, but he does not participate in the battle nor issue orders regarding the conduct of battle. Finally, Moses' recording of the battle story in a scroll (Exod. 17.14) may be compared to Deborah's recounting of her story in song. Assis writes that Deborah's 'act' of deliverance is 'in the act of delivering prophecy'.[26]

The prophecies of Deborah are fulfilled when the Israelites win the battle, and the glory of killing Sisera goes to Jael, a woman who drives a tent peg through the head of the unsuspecting general. The war is followed by a victory song that glorifies Yahweh, Deborah, Barak and Jael, and makes a mockery of Sisera and his defeat.

In light of the connections between prophecy and song (Exod. 15.20, 1 Sam. 10.5; 18.10, 1 Chron. 25), we might classify Deborah's song as prophetic praise; however, the song includes no messenger formula and no direct speech from Yahweh. Nevertheless, the song includes at least one word of divine communication: 'Curse Meroz, says the angel of Yahweh, curse severely its inhabitants, because they did not come to the help of Yahweh, to the help of Yahweh against the mighty ones' (Judg. 5.23).[27] In Judges, the angel of Yahweh brings a word of rebuke to the Israelites (2.1-5), a word of commission to Gideon (6.11-24) and a word of annunciation to Samson's mother (13.2-23). Here, in Deborah's song, the angel appears, as if singing along with Deborah and Barak, and then he breaks in with a solo part. The angel's pronouncement is the concluding word to the section of the song that praises those who fought for Yahweh and condemns those who did not fight (5.9-23). The town of Meroz is singled out for special judgment because it lies within the vicinity of the battlefield[28] and its inhabitants[29] would have heard and ignored Barak's call to arms. The song of victory is longer than the prose narrative, and its placement at the end of the Deborah cycle leaves the hearer quite hopeful concerning Israel's future. The song concludes with these words: 'Thus all your enemies will perish, O Lord; but those who love you are like the rising of the sun in its strength' (5.31).[30]

---

[26] Assis, 'Man, Woman, and God in Judges 4', p. 119.

[27] The phrase 'against the mighty ones' (בגבורים) might be translated instead, 'with the mighty ones', thus signifying the army of Barak.

[28] Cf. Wolf, 'Judges', p. 414.

[29] It has been argued that in this context the Hebrew ישבים (inhabitants) means 'rulers'. See Norman K. Gottwald, *The Tribes of Yahweh: A Sociology of the Religion of Liberated Israel, 1250-1050 B.C.E.* (Maryknoll, NY: Orbis, 1979), pp. 512-34.

[30] This mention of Yahweh worshipers as 'those who love' him is a rare early acknowledgement of the emotional aspect of Israelite religion according to Walther Eichrodt, *Theology of the Old Testament* (2 vols.; Philadelphia: Westminster, 1961), I, p. 251.

5. 'Do not fear the gods of the Amorites' (6.10)

The mood of hope and optimism created by the song of Deborah is replaced immediately by a mood of extreme desperation[31] when the Israelites rebel yet again (6.1), and Yahweh gives them into the hand of the Midianites and Amalekites,[32] who for seven years rob the Israelites of their crops and livestock, leaving the land impoverished and the people helpless. The narrative portrays Israel's suffering as more severe than in earlier cycles, a fact that builds the tension to a higher level, indicating that 'things may be getting worse'.[33] The Midianites are not content to rule or to rob the Israelites; apparently they are intent upon rendering the land uninhabitable for the Israelites, thus displacing them from the land that Yahweh had given them.[34]

As before, the Israelites cry out to Yahweh for help, but the usual cyclical pattern is interrupted when, before he raises up a deliverer, Yahweh sends to them an unnamed prophet.[35] This makes two consecutive cycles in which a prophet has entered the story at precisely the same point, and the reader might anticipate that this prophet would function as a judge, in much the same fashion as Deborah functioned in the previous cycle.[36] This prophet, however, functions differently from Deborah in at least three ways: (1) the nameless prophet addresses the whole people of Israel, whereas Deborah addresses only Barak, an individual; (2) Deborah arises with an encouraging word of victory, but the anonymous prophet brings a stinging word of reprimand;[37] and

---

[31] Cf. Scherman, *Joshua/Judges*, p. 151; Barry G. Webb, *The Book of the Judges: An Integrated Reading* (JSOTS 46; Sheffield: JSOT Press, 1987), p. 144.

[32] Midianites and Amalekites are 'echoes from the past' according to Michael Wilcock, *The Message of Judges: Grace Abounding* (Downers Grove, IL: InterVarsity Press, 1992), p. 76, who points out that Moses' wife was Midianite (Exod. 2.15-22) and that early in the Israelites' wilderness journey they were attacked by the Amalekites (Exod. 17.8). See also Num. 31.1-12; Deut. 25.17-19.

[33] J. Clinton McCann, *Judges* (Interpretation: A Bible Commentary for Teaching and Preaching; Louisville, KY: John Knox, 2002), p. 63.

[34] Cf. David Lieberman, *The Eternal Torah: A New Commentary Utilizing Ancient and Modern Sources in a Grammatical, Historical, and Traditional Explanation of the Text* (River Vale, NJ: Twin Pines Press, 1979), II, p. 116. This is contra Bernon Lee, 'Fragmentation of Reader Focus in the Preamble to Battle in Judges 6:1-7:14', *JSOT* 25 (2002), pp. 65-86 (pp. 71-72), who limits his description of the Midianite threat as a 'series of raids'. Gaining control of the trade route may be the Midianite objective, which requires the removal of the Israelites. Cf. Gottwald, *The Tribes of Yahweh*, p. 432.

[35] Cf. L. Juliana M. Claassens, 'The Character of God in Judges 6-8: the Gideon Narrative as Theological and Moral Resource', *HBT* 23/1 (2001), pp. 51-71 (p. 56). Cf. Dennis Olson, 'Judges', *The New Interpreter's Bible: Numbers-Samuel* (12 vols.; Nashville, TN: Abingdon, 1994), II, pp. 721-888 (p. 792).

[36] See Lillian R. Klein, *The Triumph of Irony in the Book of Judges* (Bible and Literature, 14; Sheffield: Almond, 1988), p. 50, who suggests that the reader may expect this prophet to be even more effective than Deborah, but he is not effective at all.

[37] Cf. Pressler, *Joshua, Judges, and Ruth*, p. 169.

(3) the prophet of ch. 6 interrupts the cyclical pattern while Deborah functions within the pattern, fulfilling the role of judge.[38]

The verb forms in the prophet's message indicate that Yahweh is the primary character within the speech itself. The first six verbs have Yahweh as their subject: (1) 'I myself brought you up (אנכי העליתי) from Egypt'; (2) 'I brought you out (ואציא) from the house of bondage'; (3) 'I delivered you (ואצל) from the hand of Egypt'; (4) 'I dispossessed them (ואגרש) from before you'; (5) I gave to you (ואתנה) their land'; and (6) 'I said to you, "You shall not fear (לא תיראו) the gods of the Amorites"'. By this unbroken series of assertions, Yahweh claims to be Israel's God, Israel's savior, Israel's victor, and Israel's provider. The emphasis upon the person of Yahweh is strengthened further by the emphatic pronoun that precedes the first verb. This combination of pronoun and verb produces a phrase that occurs here for the first time in the Old Testament: 'I myself brought you up (אנכי העליתי) from Egypt'.[39] Yahweh alone is Israel's savior.

Yahweh completes his self-testimony with one more word. He declares, 'I said to you, "I am Yahweh your God; you shall not fear the gods of the Amorites"' (6.10).[40] Yahweh's exclusive claim for the loyalty of Israel stands at the core of the Torah, and when Yahweh says 'you shall not fear the gods of the Amorites' (6.10), his use of the verb 'to fear' is meant to prohibit the 'worship', 'reverence' and 'service' of other gods.[41] On several occasions Yahweh forbids the worship of other gods (Deut. 11.16), the service of other gods (Deut. 13.6) or the pursuit of other gods (Deut. 6.14), and the Decalogue begins with this word: 'I am Yahweh your God, who brought you out of the land of Egypt, out of the house of bondage. You shall have no other gods before me' (Exod. 20.2-3).[42]

When compared to Yahweh's earlier rebuke of the Israelites (2.1-5), this speech suggests that the Israelites have regressed in their covenant relationship to Yahweh although they have not abandoned him alto-

---

[38] Cf. Olson, 'Judges', pp. 795-96.

[39] This combination of pronoun and verb, אנכי העליתי ('I, even I brought up'), is found only in two other OT texts: 1 Sam. 10.18 and Amos 2.10.

[40] The Amorites are well-known in the biblical narrative, being mentioned sixty times in Exodus through Joshua, but the phrase 'the gods of the Amorites' appears in only one other text, in which Joshua challenges the Israelites, 'choose for yourselves today whom you will serve: whether the gods which your fathers served which were beyond the River, or the gods of the Amorites in whose land you are living' (Josh. 24.15).

[41] Cf. Clines, *DCH*, IV, p. 278, who includes the definition 'revere, be in awe of'. See also Köhler, *HALOT*, I, p. 433.

[42] The use of the word 'fear' in Judg. 6.10 foreshadows the Gideon narrative. See Barnabas Lindars, 'Gideon and Kingship', *TS* 16 (1965), p. 317, n. 1, who writes that the prophet's speech is 'incorporated by the narrator to prepare for the dialogue in the call story'.

gether. In the earlier speech, Yahweh scolds the Israelites for their passive failure to tear down the Canaanite altars, but now he scolds them for a more active role in illicit worship.[43] As in his earlier speech (2.1-5), Yahweh here summarizes Israel's entire rebellion in one concise judgment: 'But you did not hear my voice' (6.10). The impact of this singular verdict is made all the more striking by its rude appearance following the long series of verbs that declare Yahweh's faithful deeds. Unlike Yahweh's earlier speech (Judg. 2.1-5), this speech comes abruptly to an end with no pronouncement of penalty, no statement of consequences for the unfaithfulness of the Israelites, and no response from the Israelites. Their lack of response leaves the impression that they are continuing to disregard Yahweh's voice. They have cried out to Yahweh for his aid, but they do not hear when he answers.[44]

The placement of Yahweh's speech in the midst of the cyclical pattern, rather than outside the pattern, makes it an integral part of the Gideon cycle, and themes of the speech are continued later in the Gideon narrative. I conclude that Yahweh's speech foreshadows the Gideon narrative in at least four ways: (1) it highlights the Egypt/exodus tradition;[45] (2) it portrays the Israelites as syncretistic worshipers; (3) it introduces the theme of fear; and (4) it calls attention to the continuing theme of hearing the voice of Yahweh.

Olson argues that this speech marks a transitional point in the narrative of Judges and begins the second major section of the book.[46] In light of the Israelites' repeated idolatry and in light of their unwillingness to hear the voice of Yahweh, Olson suggests further that the prophet's speech may cause the reader to question whether God has reached the limits of his patience.[47] Surprisingly, Yahweh once again demonstrates his mercy; and, in spite of the Israelites' obstinacy, he does not abandon them.[48]

---

[43] Historical, archaeological, and social research on early Israel suggests that the worship of multiple gods was the rule rather than the exception, and that the term 'syncretism' itself must be reconsidered. See Erhard Gerstenberger, *Theologies in the Old Testament* (trans. John Bowden; Minneapolis: Fortress, 2002), pp. 274-81; Goldingay, *OT Theology: Israel's Faith*, pp. 38-40; David Penchansky, *Twilight of the Gods: Polytheism in the Hebrew Bible* (Louisville, KY: Westminster John Knox, 2005), p. 33.

[44] Is it possible that, in a similar fashion, we cry out for the biblical text to speak to us, but we hear what we want to hear and turn a deaf ear to the rest?

[45] Egypt is mentioned in nine verses of Judges: 2.1, 12; 6.8, 9, 13; 10.11; 11.13, 16; 19.30; and the exodus seems to be in the background of Judg. 5.5 and 21. Cf. the language of Ps. 77.14-20, which is similar to Judg. 5.

[46] Olson, 'Judges', pp. 795-96. The third major section of Judges commences with Yahweh's speech in Judg. 10.11-16.

[47] Olson, 'Judges', pp. 795-96.

[48] For a more extensive discussion of this passage, see Martin, *The Unheard Voice of God*, ch. 6.

6. 'Yahweh is with you, mighty warrior' (6.12)

After the prophet's stinging rebuke, the scene shifts suddenly to a man named Gideon, who is threshing his grain in the wine press so that he will not be discovered by the Midianites. He is approached by the angel of Yahweh who commissions him as the next deliverer, and before the story comes to an end, Gideon has received thirteen distinct communications from God in four different episodes.

God's first communication with Gideon comes in the form of a call narrative in which the angel of Yahweh confronts Gideon with a surprising declaration – 'Yahweh is with you, mighty warrior' (6.12). The angel's statement is surprising to the reader, since Gideon has been revealed in the previous verse not as a mighty warrior but as a farmer who is hiding from the Midianites. The angel's statement is surprising to Gideon as well, given his context of constant oppression, which indicates to him that Yahweh is *not* with the Israelites. Gideon, unaware that the messenger is Yahweh, gives voice to his frustration, by recounting Israel's deliverance from Egypt and then lamenting, 'but now Yahweh has forsaken us and given us into the hands of the Midianites' (6.13).[49] Apparently, Gideon's theology does not allow for the possibility that Yahweh might be *with him* even in the midst of suffering.

The angel of Yahweh does not answer Gideon's complaint that Yahweh has not saved them; instead, he points to Gideon himself as Yahweh's instrument of salvation. The angel says, 'Go in this your might, and you shall save Israel from the hand of the Midianites; have I not sent you?' (6.14). Thus Gideon, who charges God with failing to save Israel, is himself charged with the task of salvation. Notwithstanding Gideon's objections, Yahweh promises to 'be with' Gideon, enabling him to defeat the enemy (Judg. 6.16; cf. Exod. 3.12).

This first dialogue between God and Gideon concludes with Gideon's request for a sign and God's gracious performance of that sign. When Gideon brings an offering of meat and bread and places it upon a rock, the angel touches the offering with his staff, and flames burst forth from the rock and consume the sacrifice. The angel vanishes, causing Gideon to fear for his life, because he realizes that he has 'seen the angel of Yahweh face to face' (6.22). Yahweh then speaks a final word of assurance to Gideon: 'Peace be to you; fear not; you will not die' (6.23).

---

[49] Gideon had heard of the exodus and Yahweh's faithfulness in the past but not experienced Yahweh's 'wonders' (נפלאת); cf. the use of the same term in Exod. 3.20; 15.11 and Josh. 3.5. The failure to appreciate Yahweh's former saving acts is reflected as well in Judg. 2.10, '... And there arose a new generation after them who did not know Yahweh nor the works that he had done for Israel'.

Gideon's first encounter with God exhibits numerous similarities to the call narrative of Moses[50] and casts Gideon as a new Moses,[51] invested with divine authority, who will deliver the Israelites from oppression. Gideon's call narrative also provides a setting for his own consecration through his presentation of a sacrifice.

That same night, Yahweh speaks the second time to Gideon, commanding him to destroy his father's altar to Baal and the Asherah beside the altar (cf. Judg. 2.2). Gideon is to build an altar to Yahweh on the site of the razed altar and offer up a whole burnt offering to Yahweh (6.25-26). Gideon obeys, but he works surreptitiously by night because he is 'afraid' (6.27). This is the first and only time in Judges when a judge acts in direct opposition to the Canaanite gods, and the angry response of Gideon's neighbors highlights their thoroughgoing idolatry.

After the Spirit of Yahweh empowers Gideon to muster an army who will resist the Midianites, God graciously answers Gideon's repeated requests for a sign (using the fleece). Yahweh then speaks to Gideon a third time, informing him that the Israelite army is so large that they might be tempted to attribute the victory to their own strength rather than to God's help. In order to reduce the size of the army, Yahweh allows all those who are fearful to return to their homes (7.3). With ten thousand soldiers remaining, Yahweh sifts Gideon's army the second time and chooses only the three hundred who lap water like a dog.[52] The fact that the testing occurs at the Fearful Spring (7.1) leads Lindars to conclude that the test ensures that only the bravest men will be retained in the army.[53]

Before Gideon engages the Midianites in battle, Yahweh speaks to him the fourth and final time, telling Gideon to go down to the Midianite camp where he will 'hear what they say' (7.11). At the camp Gideon overhears a Midianite soldier recounting a dream in which a loaf of bread rolled into the camp and flattened a tent. The soldier

---

[50] Mark S. Smith, 'Remembering God: Collective Memory in Israelite Religion', *CBQ* 64/4 (2002), pp. 634-38. For a list of these similarities, see Martin, *The Unheard Voice of God*, ch. 6.

[51] Lindars, 'Gideon and Kingship', p. 317. Lindars summarizes the conclusions of Walter Beyerlin, 'Geschichte und heilsgeschichtliche Traditionsbildung im Alten Testament: Ein Beitrag zur Traditionsgeschichte von Richter 6-8', *VT* 13 (1963), pp. 1-25.

[52] The use of the word 'dog' (כלב) suggests to me an allusion to Caleb (also כלב), the only person besides Joshua who was unafraid of the Canaanites and who has already been featured prominently in Judges (1.12, 13, 14, 15, 20; 3.9). Earlier allusions to Caleb include Othniel, the first judge, who is the nephew of Caleb; the husband of Jael, hero of Judg. 4-5, who is a relative of Caleb (1 Chron. 2.55); and the name of the site where Jael kills Sisera (קדש, 'Qadesh', cf. Num. 13.26, the location where Caleb speaks to Israelites and enjoins them not to fear the inhabitants of the land).

[53] Lindars, 'Gideon and Kingship', p. 319.

interprets the dream as a prediction of Gideon's victory by the power of Yahweh. As soon as Gideon hears the dream, 'he worshiped' (7.15), and he returned full of confidence to his awaiting army.

The fact that it is Yahweh who directs Gideon to go down into the camp of Midian suggests that Yahweh himself is the source of the prophetic dream. Yahweh's words to Gideon, 'you will hear (שמע) what they say', may convey both the literal sense of Gideon's overhearing the Midianite soldier and the theological sense of Gideon's finally perceiving the authenticity of God's word. Ironically, although Gideon has difficulty hearing the word of the angel of Yahweh and the word of Yahweh himself, he finally hears the voice of Yahweh speaking through an enemy soldier (Judg. 7.9-11).

7. 'I will not save you again' (10.13)

Upon Gideon's death, his son Abimelech[54] claims the kingship of Shechem and rules until he falls to the retribution of Yahweh. Abimelech is followed by two minor judges: Tola and Jair. The Israelites sin once again, and Yahweh gives them into the hands of the Philistines and the Ammonites who oppress them for eighteen years. The Israelites cry out to Yahweh for his aid, but in light of the idolatry of Gideon, the dictatorship of Abimelech, and two more implied cycles of sin and deliverance, Yahweh speaks directly to the Israelites and angrily declares that he is finished with them (10.11-16). He says to them,

> Was it not from the Egyptians and from the Amorites and from the Ammonites and from the Philistines – and when the Sidonians and Amalek and Maon oppressed you, you cried unto me, and I saved you from their power? But you have forsaken me and served other gods; therefore, I will not save you again. Go and call upon the gods that you have chosen. They will save you in the time of your distress (Judg. 10.11-13).

Yahweh reminds the Israelites of the numerous times that he has saved them,[55] yet they continue to forsake him and serve foreign gods. He furiously rebukes them and announces that he will save them no more. The tone of Yahweh's rebuff is quite sarcastic,[56] 'Go and call upon the gods you have chosen', perhaps alluding ironically to Joshua's covenant renewal ceremony where the Israelites 'chose' to serve Yah-

---

[54] Abimelech means in Hebrew 'my father is king'. We are not told whether the name is suggestive of Yahweh's rule or of Abimelech's (or Gideon's?) ambitions.

[55] The list of nations in Judg. 10.11-12 corresponds to previous deliverances: Amorites (Num. 21; Josh. 24.8); Ammonites (Judg. 3.13); Philistines (Judg. 3.31); Sidonians (Josh. 13.6; Judg. 3.3); Amalekites (Judg. 6.3, 33; 7.12); Maon (Josh. 15.55. The LXX has Midian in the place of Maon, which would point to Judg. 6)

[56] Cf. Webb, *Judges: An Integrated Reading*, p. 45.

weh (Josh. 24.22). In response to Yahweh's reprimand, the Israelites, for the first time in Judges, confess their sin, put away the foreign gods, and renew their worship of Yahweh.

In light of the apparent repentance of the Israelites and the previous mercies of Yahweh, the hearer of Judges would likely expect Yahweh to respond by changing his mind (cf. Judg. 2.18) and by raising up a judge who would bring salvation to the Israelites (cf. 3.9; 3.15; 4.4; 6.11). God, however, does not respond as expected. Yahweh's refusal to rescue his people is all the more unexpected given his earlier declaration: 'I will never break my covenant' (2.1). The cycle of sin and salvation that is repeated four times earlier in the book of Judges (3.7-11; 12-30; 4.1-5.31; 6.1–8.28) will not be repeated quite the same again.

Yahweh's speech in ch. 10 discloses several striking features: (1) Verses 6-16 offer details of the longest dialogue between God and Israel within the book of Judges.[57] (2) The dialogue is unmediated. That is, the text does not report the presence of an angel, prophet, or any other messenger. (3) It records the longest list of idols in Judges. (4) It is the only time in Judges that the Israelites are said to have repented and laid aside their idols. (5) It is the only time in Judges that Yahweh refuses to come to the aid of his people when they call upon him. (6) The passage brings into focus the tension between Yahweh's anger and his compassion, a tension that is occasioned by the rebellion of his covenant people.[58]

This speech suggests that the relationship between Yahweh and Israel is fractured and is in danger of irreparable breakage. Since we are familiar with the subsequent biblical narratives of Samuel and Kings, we know that the fracture will be repaired; consequently, it is difficult for us to recognize the significance of Yahweh's impassioned speech and to take seriously his dejection. The voice of Yahweh in Judg. 10.6-16 is angry, injured, frustrated and weary; but it is a voice that must be heard.

8. 'He will begin to save Israel' (13.5)

In the first half of the book of Judges, the role of God is clear – when the Israelites sin, he hands them over to an enemy for discipline; and,

---

[57] Cf. J. Gordon Harris, Cheryl Anne Brown, and Michael S. Moore, *Joshua, Judges, Ruth* (New International Biblical Commentary; Peabody, MA: Hendrickson, 2000), p. 221.

[58] For a more extensive discussion of this passage, see Martin, *The Unheard Voice of God*, ch. 7; Martin, 'God at Risk', pp. 722-40. I address the tension between Yahweh's anger and his compassion in 'Yahweh Conflicted: Unresolved Theological Tension in the Cycle of Judges 10:6-16', *Old Testament Essays* 22.2 (2009), pp. 356-72.

when they cry out to him, he raises up a judge who delivers them. Following Yahweh's withdrawal in Judg. 10.13, however, the role of God is ambiguous, as the tension surrounding the God's anger and his compassion intensifies.[59]

As a result of Yahweh's refusal to offer further aid to the Israelites, the elders of Gilead, by their own initiative, seek out Jephthah to be their leader; and the narrative continues to display the tension between Yahweh's faithfulness and his frustration. The tension is evident in that, although the Spirit of Yahweh comes upon Jephthah, Yahweh does not prevent the sacrifice of Jephthah's daughter, and he does not prevent the intertribal battles that follow Jephthah's victory. Throughout the Jephthah story, Yahweh remains silent.

The tension between Yahweh's anger and his compassion persists and even grows stronger in the Samson cycle. In contrast to earlier cycles, the Israelites do not cry out for God's help, but still he reveals his compassion by appointing Samson from before birth. The angel of Yahweh appears to Samson's mother with a word of promise:

> Although you are barren, having borne no children, you shall conceive and bear a son. Now be careful not to drink wine or strong drink, or to eat anything unclean, for you shall conceive and bear a son. No razor is to come on his head, for the boy shall be a nazirite to God from birth. And he will begin to save Israel from the hand of the Philistines (Judg. 13.3-5).

The angel's revelation to Samson's mother is noteworthy for several reasons. First, Yahweh's breaking of his silence indicates that he may be returning to full engagement with his people. Second, in light of his mother's barrenness, Samson's birth can be understood as a miracle, a fact that might anticipate divine blessings upon Samson's life. Third, the calling of Samson to be a nazirite adds to the sense of purpose and devotion attached to his life. Fourth, the annunciation narrative includes elements that bring to mind the call of Gideon, who was successful in delivering the Israelites from their oppressor; therefore, the angel's visitation to Samson's mother might suggest that he also is destined for victory. Fifth, the ambiguous declaration that Samson will 'begin' to save Israel, might be the single possible portent of Samson's lack of effectiveness.

Although Yahweh speaks to Samson's mother, he never speaks to Samson himself. Throughout the Samson narrative, Yahweh repeatedly gives his Spirit to Samson; and the narrative states that Yahweh is working behind the scenes, directing Samson's actions (14.4) and ans-

---

[59] For an excellent survey of the increasingly ambiguous role of Yahweh in the narrative, see Exum, 'The Centre Cannot Hold', pp. 410-31. While I have focused my attention on the speech of Yahweh, Exum devotes the bulk of her study to his actions.

wering his prayers (15.18-19; 16.28).[60] Although Samson never admits
his errors and never utters words of repentance, Yahweh restores his
strength for his last act of vengeance upon the Philistines. The role of
God in the affairs of Israel continues to be unclear to the hearer of the
Samson story.

9. 'Judah is first' (20.18)

In the epilogue to Judges, Yahweh disappears almost entirely. The
characters invoke the name of Yahweh (17.2, 3, 13), but Yahweh himself is silent. The final chapters of Judges recount unspeakable atrocities
that are enacted while Yahweh remains intentionally uninvolved, allowing the Israelites to 'do what is right' in their own eyes (17.6;
21.25).

When the Israelites decide to go to battle against the Benjaminites,
one of their own tribes, they turn to Yahweh for his direction. In an
episode that recalls Judg. 1.1-2, the Israelites inquire of Yahweh, 'Who
shall go up first to fight the Benjaminites?', and Yahweh replies, 'Judah
is first'[61] (20.18). The Israelites proceed to battle, but are defeated, and
after weeping before Yahweh they inquire of him again, this time asking, 'Shall we go up again to fight the Benjaminites?', and Yahweh
replies in the affirmative (20.22). They fight for a second day, and
again they are defeated. They weep, fast, offer sacrifices and inquire
again. This time, Yahweh not only instructs them to continue the
battle, but he insures the Israelites of victory (20.28). The Israelites
who once fought together against the Canaanites are now warring
against one of their own tribes.

Yahweh's role in the battle is ambiguous, in that, even though he
responds to the inquiries of the Israelites, he causes the war to be prolonged. Perhaps Yahweh's drawing out of the Israelite conflict is a
reflection of his own prolonged inner conflict that he experiences as he
is forced repeatedly to choose his response to the chronic infidelity of
the Israelites.

C. Conclusions

The foregoing discussion of divine communication suggests that the
voice of Yahweh functions as an important narrative element within
the book of Judges. Both the frequency of divine speech and its stra-

---

[60] The silence of Yahweh is continued from Judges into 1 Samuel, where we are told
'the word of Yahweh was rare in those days' (1 Sam. 3.1).

[61] The Hebrew text (יהודה בתחלה) says only 'Judah is the first'; it does not repeat Judg.
1.2, 'Judah shall go up' (יהודה יעלה). Thus, at this point, Yahweh refrains from authorizing
the battle.

tegic location within the narrative point to its importance as a crucial piece of the interpretive puzzle of Judges.

The placement and the content of the divine word in Judges are consistent with other thematic indicators in the book that manifest the spiraling decline of Israel's devotion to Yahweh, the gradual disintegration of the covenant relationship between Yahweh and Israel, and the escalating tension within the passions of Yahweh himself. The first episode of the book of Judges begins with an assuring, guiding word from Yahweh, but that episode concludes with a judging, disciplining word in which Yahweh declares his displeasure with the Israelites. That word of discipline is repeated at the end of the introduction, and Yahweh does not speak again until the beginning of the third cycle of evil, oppression, and salvation, when Deborah arises as a prophet. Deborah's ministry is the culmination, or high point among the stories of the effective judges. Her story is followed immediately by a nameless prophet who introduces the beginning of the transitional period of Gideon and Abimelech. Yahweh's frequent communications with Gideon lend divine authority and expectation to his leadership, and we are quite disappointed when, after his miraculous victory, his foolhardy actions plunge the Israelites anew into the abyss of idolatry. In Yahweh's final speech to the Israelites, his words pour forth a surge of frustration, and he refuses to save them again. He is mostly silent for the second half of the book of Judges, venturing forth only to announce the birth of Samson and to answer the Israelites' final inquiry concerning their intertribal conflict.

Taken together, Yahweh's speeches show that, although the actions of the Israelites are essential to the story, it is Yahweh who decides the course of the narrative. Repeatedly, Yahweh speaks of himself as the God who brought the Israelites out of Egypt. His numerous allusions to the exodus, along with the fact that he saves the Israelites even when they show no sign of repentance, suggest that all of Yahweh's acts of salvation in Judges flow from the paradigm of the exodus.

In my hearing of the voice of Yahweh in Judges, I did not always hear what I expected to hear, and I did not always hear what I wanted to hear. I heard of Yahweh's oath, his covenant, his mighty acts and his faithfulness. However, I did not hear a solution to every conflict or the erasing of every troubling tension. I did not hear the comforting words of closure, for in Judges, the anger of Yahweh seems to be longer than a 'moment' (Ps. 30.5). In the voice of Yahweh, I heard disappointment – 'What is this you have done?' (Judg. 2.2). I heard threat – 'I will not save you again' (10.13). I heard chiding frustration – 'Call on the gods you have chosen; they will save you' (10.14). Finally, I heard nothing but deathly, alienating, disturbing silence – enough to make one ache for another word 'just once more' (16.28).

Abstract

In this survey of divine communication in the book of Judges, I observe that Yahweh speaks through a variety of agents and with a broad array of objectives. Yahweh responds to Israel's inquiries; he speaks through prophets; he speaks through an angel; he speaks directly; and he speaks through a dream that is given to an enemy soldier. Although the voice of Yahweh in Judges is virtually unnoticed by biblical scholars, I argue that divine communication is a prominent feature of the book, and that the speeches of Yahweh register crucial movements in the narrative.

3

'Then they will know that a prophet has been among them': The Source and End of the Call of Ezekiel

Rickie D. Moore[*]

In the early 1970s I was blessed to have R. Hollis Gause as my professor in New Testament studies at Lee College. His gifts and brilliance as a scholar, teacher, and theologian had already become legendary among his students. Consequently, by the time I joined the ranks of the seminary faculty in the early 1980s it seemed altogether too soon for me to think of Dr. Gause as my colleague. It took me years to work my way up to that thought. And so, you can imagine something of how I felt in January of 2006 when Dr. Gause asked if he could visit my Ezekiel course. I thought he might drop in for a single afternoon session or so, but when I opened the door on the first day of class, there sat Dr. Gause beside the other dozen or so students at the seminar table with pen drawn and plans, I soon found out, to take in the whole experience. Suffice it to say that, for me, this gave new meaning to the phrase 'intensive J-term'.

After the initial shock, this actually turned into one of the most enriching classroom experiences of my life. While it is almost tempting to claim that Dr. Gause was once my student, I know better, and so do the other students who, along with me, benefited so richly that week from Dr. Gause's wonderful insights. We were all blessed, and I was honored by the gracious presence and partnership of my esteemed elder and colleague, and I thought it would be appropriate to attempt to honor him through offering this study on the prophet Ezekiel, whose book we enjoyed studying and teaching together.

[*] Rickie D. Moore (Ph.D., Vanderbilt University) is Professor of Old Testament at the Lee University, Cleveland, TN, USA.

Ezekiel was a priest who was called to be a prophet. The source and end of this call, reduced to bare essence, was simply and utterly *God*. Ezekiel was all about God. It is for good reason that scholars often describe Ezekiel as the most radically theocentric of all the Hebrew prophets.[1] The book opens with a vision of God and a prophetic call that springs forth from this vision. As the call takes shape, it has much to do with bearing witness to endings – the end of Israel, the end of Jerusalem, the end of the Temple, and, most fundamentally and radically of all, the end of God as He had previously been known. Indeed, this last ending, which appears first in the book, is the root source of all the other endings. Yet significantly, Ezekiel's call carries him one step further than merely bearing witness to these endings. He embodies an ending within his own person. Specifically, his entry into his commission as a prophet entails a stark and shocking termination of his own identity and function as a priest. Thus, Ezekiel is called both to present and to represent, in his own terminal experience, the end of all things.

The book explicitly voices this emphasis on the theme of the end in its first poetic oracle at the beginning of ch. 7:

> Now you, son of man, thus says the Lord GOD concerning the land of Israel:
> An end! The end has come upon the four corners of the land.
> Now is the end upon you, and I will send my anger upon you,
> and will judge you according to your ways;
> and I will bring upon you all your abominations.
> And my eye shall not spare you,
> neither will I have pity;
> but I will bring your ways upon you,
> and your abominations shall be in the midst of you;
> then you shall know that I am Yahweh.
> Thus says the Lord GOD:
> An evil, a singular evil, behold, it comes.
> An end has come, the end has come;
> it dawns upon you; behold, it comes (7.2-6).[2]

The book obtrusively registers here a primary focus of its entire message by repeating the Hebrew word for 'end', קֵץ (*qṣ*) five times in five verses. It is not that Ezekiel was alone among the prophets in seeing this end.[3] Foreseeing the demise of Israel and its geographical and theological center, Jerusalem, was surely one of the most prominent commonalities among the widely diverse prophets of the pre-exilic

---

[1] See, for example, Christopher J.H. Wright, *The Message of Ezekiel* (Downers Grove, IL: InterVarsity Press, 2001), p. 23; Paul Joyce, *Divine Initiative and Human Responsibility in Ezekiel* (JSOTS 51; Sheffield: JSOT, 1989), ch. 6.

[2] Translations in this paper are my own unless otherwise noted.

[3] In fact, see the similar use of the term קֵץ (*qeṣ*) in Amos 8.2. Cf. Joseph Blenkinsopp, *Ezekiel*, Interpretation (Louisville, KY: John Knox, 1990), pp. 45-46.

period. Yet it is the purpose of this article to show how Ezekiel bears this particular message with an intensity and to an extremity found in no other prophet. Even the language of the above passage reflects this, for in the reference to the end of 'the four corners of the land', land, ארץ (*ereṣ*), could just as well be translated *earth*,[4] registering something on the order of a cosmic ending of what began all the way back in Genesis, with Ezekiel himself taken aback with it as God rewinds his identity, as it were, all the way back to 'son of man' (אדם: *adam*), the primal address that God uses for Ezekiel throughout the entire book. Surely Ezekiel represents the end in a most radical way. While Isaiah plays a leading role in breaking open the prospect of Israel's end and Jeremiah plays the crucial role of carrying Jerusalem across the very threshold of the end, it is Ezekiel who plays the finale role of getting to the bottom of the end.

It is particularly appropriate to speak of Ezekiel in terms of *playing a role,* because to an extent that goes beyond any other OT prophet, even Hosea, Ezekiel is made to *enact* the message he speaks. Thus, leading up to the explicit word on the end in ch. 7, we see God in chs. 4, 5, and 6 directing Ezekiel to perform sign acts that dramatize this message. In ch. 4 Ezekiel acts out the final siege of Jerusalem by making a model of the city on the ground and lying before it with his face set against it behind an iron shield, lying on one side then the other for the number of days that would respectively represent the number of years of captivity to be endured first by the northern kingdom and then by the southern. Ezekiel is even directed to display his restriction to a daily diet of siege rations cooked on an open fire fueled by dung, thereby defiling his sacerdotal qualifications. Thus, the entire scene signifies *the end of the holy city but also the end of the holy priest.*

In ch. 5 God requires Ezekiel to shave off all the hair of his face and head – the ancient world's mark of shame for a freshly conquered captive[5] – and then Ezekiel is told to divide the clippings into multiple piles that are respectively assigned to different means of destruction – all to serve as a sign of *the end of all segments of the people of Israel,* any way you cut it. Ironically, Ezekiel is a *captive* in Babylon pressing *captives* to face their *captivity*. His actions are a sign of *the end of all efforts to avoid facing the end.*

At the fall of Jerusalem, there would be those who would try to escape to the mountains, but in ch. 6 Ezekiel is directed to utter a dramatic soliloquy of judgment against 'the mountains of Israel' (v. 2) with stage

---

[4] Cf. Blenkinsopp, *Ezekiel*, p. 45.

[5] Cf. 2 Sam. 10.4-5. Shaving of head and beard was explicitly prohibited for priests in the Torah (Lev. 21.5), so that this too would have represented a defamation of Ezekiel's priestly office. Cf. Wright, *Message of Ezekiel,* p. 83.

directions to strike his hand and to stamp his foot (v. 11) in order to emphasize the coming termination of those both far and near, of those who flee the siege as well as those who remain behind (v. 12). It is a dramatic signal of *the end of all remaining means of escape from the end*.

Yet even more significantly, in the midst of these sign acts God introduces (5.13) and begins to repeat (6.7, 10, 13, 14) a solemn declaration that reveals this end to be only a means to a more ultimate end. This divine declaration, which becomes the dominant refrain of the entire book, occurring in almost every subsequent chapter, often multiple times in the same chapter, simply declares this more ultimate end and goal to be *'that they will know that I am Yahweh.'*[6] Even as God rewinds Ezekiel's identity back to the primal terms of his Genesis creation, 'son of *adam*', it is as if he is rewinding his own identity back to the primal terms of his Exodus revelation, 'I am that I am'.[7] Thus the end effects a return to first things, putting first things first once again, restoring what was meant to be from the beginning, as far as this most important matter of God's revelation of himself.

For Yahweh to be acting decisively before Israel and the nations to the end *that they would know that he is Yahweh,* presupposes a protest and repudiation, on his part, to how he had come to be and was continuing to be known by them. Thus, all that he now does, according to the book of Ezekiel, he does in order to manifest a new and counteracting revelation of himself. In this light, the revelation of God that comes in the opening chapter of Ezekiel takes on added significance.

One of the most obvious things to be said of the vision of God in the first chapter of Ezekiel is that it manifests God in a way that is not like anything ever seen before. The vision is an unspeakable spectacle too wonderful for Ezekiel's words, featuring something like a mobile throne of indescribable technology, unearthly figures and forms, and inexpressible radiance and movement. This is punctuated by the number of times that Ezekiel's eyewitness account must resort to expressions such as 'it was like' or 'it had the appearance of', and the like. To be constantly reaching in different directions to describe what the vision was like only emphasizes how much it was *un*like anything

---

[6] This so-called 'self-recognition formula' was given extensive form-critical and traditio-historical analysis in the magisterial work of Walther Zimmerli. See his *Ezekiel 1: A Commentary on the Book of the Prophet Ezekiel Chapters 1–24* (Hermeneia; Philadelphia: Fortress, 1979); *Ezekiel 2: A Commentary on the Book of the Prophet Ezekiel Chapters 25–48* (Hermeneia; Philadelphia: Fortress, 1983); *I Am Yahweh* (Atlanta, GA: John Knox, 1982).

[7] Exodus 3, of course, presents God's disclosure of this name to Moses (v. 14) in what is surely the most foundational instance of God's self-revelation in Hebrew Scriptures. Yet the book of Exodus goes on to highlight the name by introducing and repeating the same divine declaration featured in Ezekiel, *'that they will know that I am Yahweh'*, where 'they' refers sometimes to the people of Israel (6.2; 10.2) and sometimes to Pharaoh and the Egyptians (7.5, 17; 9.14; 14.4, 18).

previously known. If it bore some resemblance to the ark of the covenant where God's presence rested, as scholars have assumed, then it is surely an ark that had now morphed into something far beyond what was known on earth. For it was not to be carried; this ark had wheels, indescribable wheels, but even more than that, it hovered and flew by a propulsion system of God's own Spirit. It was quite literally a UFO – an unidentified, even *unidentifiable*, flying object. There could hardly be a stronger, more direct statement in all of Scripture of the revelation that God is not in a box.

Ezekiel's vision of God posed a stunning unsettling of the Hebrew belief that God's presence with the ark had come to a permanent rest and residence in the Temple of Jerusalem. Although many things about this vision were indescribable, one thing was clear: God was on the move and he was no longer settled in Jerusalem. Instead, he was *'there'* (v. 3; שם) in the land of Israel's exile. The Hebrews were again strangers in a strange land, but now there appeared the perfect stranger, the ultimate alien. It was none other than the God of absolute otherness, who was coming to make himself known this time as the unknown and unknowable One, just as he made himself known in Exodus as 'I am that I am' – a name that is like an incomplete sentence that we can never completely complete, because the One so named can never be completely designated and known.

Ezekiel was made to know that God too had gone into exile, but it was a self-imposed exile in order to distance himself from the place and from the ways that he had come to be known. He was taking a trip far enough away to get completely beyond his falsely ascribed identity and to reclaim the name by which he ever insists on being known:

> *I AM that I AM;*
> *I AM* ... not who you think I am;
> *I AM* ... not who you presume that I am,
> *I AM* ... not confined to the places or to the ways you have known
>   me.
> *I AM* ... coming as you have never known me before, so that you
> *will know* that *I AM, Yahweh!*

These implications, which are only intimated in Ezekiel's opening vision, are drawn out fully as the book unfolds. Yet God's first move is to open up Ezekiel's call to be his messenger from this vision in ways that bind him closely to God and to the radical-ness of this vision. One way involves God making a play on Ezekiel's name. Even as God will draw special attention to the meaning of his own name, he here draws out a special significance for the name of Ezekiel. This name, יחזקאל (*yeḥezqel*) in the Hebrew, is typically understood to mean 'God makes strong/God strengthens',[8] yet the verb here, חזק (*ḥazaq*), is fundamentally associated with hardness, thus capable of yielding the sense, 'God makes hard/God hardens'. And in 3.8 and 9 God three times utilizes an adjectival form from the root of this very verb in this very sense as he says to Ezekiel,

> Behold, I have made your face hard (חזק: *ḥazaq*) against their faces, and your forehead hard (חזק: *ḥazaq*) against their foreheads [that is, the faces and foreheads of the people of Israel]. As an adamant stone harder (חזק: *ḥazaq*) than flint I have made your forehead: do not fear them, neither be dismayed at their looks, for they are a rebellious house.

As if to bring this quality of hardness into close association with God himself, the call narrative comes back to this term in a subsequent reference in 3.14 where Ezekiel says,

> So the Spirit lifted me up, and took me away; and I went in bitterness, in the heat of my spirit; and the hand of Yahweh was hard (חזק: *ḥazaq*) upon me.

In this verse we also find the juxtaposition of God's Spirit and Ezekiel's spirit, and not only that, but Ezekiel's spirit is characterized by a term, חמה (*ḥemah*), that is used repeatedly hereafter in the book to characterize the spirit in which God will act against his people (5.13; 6.12; 7.8; 8.18; 9.8; etc.). The term חמה (*ḥemah*) literally means 'heat' and figuratively connotes 'anger' or 'fury', as the KJV prefers to translate it in these subsequent theological references.

The other term used here in 3.14 to characterize Ezekiel's spirit is '*bitterness*' (מר: *mar*). It plainly forms an opposite to the *sweetness* that Ezekiel first tastes (3.3) after he follows God's instruction in 3.1 to 'eat the scroll' extended to him by the hand of God (2.9). The bitterness that settles within him accords with the words he sees written on the scroll, for as 2.10 makes clear, they were 'lamentations, mourning, and woe'.[9] This is an especially graphic indication and manifestation of Ezekiel's complete identification with the message God was calling him to deliver. He was literally embodying the words that spelled the end.

Thus, we see Ezekiel's radical interconnection with God in all God's radicalness. (1) Yahweh was explicating the extreme implications of Ezekiel's name and he would excavate the extreme implications of his own name; (2) Yahweh's hand was hard and he was making Ezekiel hard; (3) Ezekiel was left in the heat of his spirit and Yahweh would

---

[8] Cf. Wright, *Message of Ezekiel*, p. 17.

[9] All this is closely paralleled, of course, much later in Scripture in the experience of John in Rev 10.8-11.

hereafter act in the heat of his Spirit, (4) Yahweh's words were bitter and after consuming their honey coating, Ezekiel too was bitter.

It would appear from reflection upon these opening chapters that the words that Ezekiel was consuming were consuming him. Yet what follows in the next chapter, Ezekiel 4, should leave no doubt. Here Yahweh requires Ezekiel to eat something else.[10] As noted earlier, the meager siege rations would have been unusual in themselves, but it is the cooking method that is most noteworthy. Being commanded to use a fire fueled by human dung elicits shocked protest from Ezekiel:

> Ah Lord Yahweh! Behold, my life has not been defiled; for from my youth even until now I have not eaten anything that died of itself or was torn by animals; nor did any unclean flesh enter my mouth (4.14).

God relents in response to Ezekiel's desperate appeal but not very much. He allows him to use animal dung instead – less shameful but still defiling for this priest, who had just reached the age of his ordination.[11] Ezekiel's priestly ministry was dead on arrival. This constituted nothing less than the end of Ezekiel the priest. Thus, as Yahweh prepares to manifest the end of his own identity, in the sense of how he was then known, he executes the end of Ezekiel's identity.

Yet one divine statement in Ezekiel's call experience stands out starkly over against this cumulative emphasis on the end. As God lays out Ezekiel's hard call to stand as a watchman and declare an unwelcome warning that the people of Israel will not hear, so God declares, 'because they will not hear me' (3.7), Yahweh seems for one instant, in Ezek. 2.5, to look beyond their not hearing and their not knowing to say, *'then they will know that a prophet has been among them'*. In a way that anticipates the refrain that expresses the pre-eminent end and goal of the message of the book, *'that they will know that I am Yahweh'*, God here at the outset links the retrieval of his own identity to that of his prophet, this disqualified priest and mere 'son of *adam*'.

From this radical starting point, featuring a theology-stopping vision and a priesthood-stopping call, a relentless message of the end proceeds to unfold in the book and through the life experience of Ezekiel. Having already noted how the sign acts of chs. 4-6 visually dramatize this message and how ch. 7 verbally highlights it, we now move forward to how the second major vision of God, in chs. 8–11, presents the book's most elaborate and riveting revelation of the end. With spectacular

---

[10] Margaret S. Odell, 'You are What You Eat: Ezekiel and the Scroll', *JBL* 117/2 (1998), pp. 229-48, recently has developed a suggestive argument that this fourth chapter together with ch. 5 should be regarded as part of the call narrative.

[11] This was 'the thirtieth year' of his life, according to the reference in 1.1, as most scholars understand it. For a thorough discussion of the various issues and different theories, see Zimmerli, *Ezekiel*, vol. I, pp. 113-15.

visual effects this vision witnesses to the glory of Yahweh, envisioned in chs. 1–3, now seen to be departing from the temple and the city of Jerusalem.

This vision is a drama that plays out in three stages. First, after being transported in the Spirit to Jerusalem, Ezekiel beholds that *Yahweh's glory* (כבוד: *kabod*) *is 'there'* (שׁם: *sham*) (8.4). Ezekiel notes that this is the same glory he had seen in the plain (3.23) and by the river Chebar (1.28). Yet now God is taking Ezekiel on a sightseeing tour of the *Un*holy Land. Not only is God providing the transportation (3.3), he is serving as omniscient tour guide. The package even includes an excursion to an excavation site where Ezekiel is allowed to participate in a dig – a dig on the temple mount, no less. God says to Ezekiel, 'Son of man, dig now in the wall and when I had dug in the wall, behold a door'. It is a door that opens to the second phase of the three-part vision.

God tells Ezekiel, 'Go in, and see the wicked abominations that they do here' (8.9). Thus Ezekiel is made to see that, although Yahweh's glory was there, *great abominations were also there* (8.6). From here the tour quickly moves on and takes in a dizzying array of sites, but they are not the usual stops featured on the standard tours, for this is *the tour to end all tours*. This tour guide has access to places no one else knows, and he wants Ezekiel to know and now wants us to know that he knows everything – everything that is going on behind closed doors and inside back rooms and within exclusive quarters and even in the recesses of secret chambers. And just what is going on here? Ezekiel is shown 'greater' (8.9) and 'greater' (8.13) and still 'greater abominations' (8.15). In fact, it is more than enough to bring Yahweh to the place of announcing, 'I will go far off from my sanctuary' (8.6). And this announcement points us to the third and final phase of the vision.

Yahweh's glory leaves there. This third phase itself features three movements:

1. The glory of Yahweh lifts up from the cherubim and moves to the threshold of the house of Yahweh (9.3), whereupon God orders a hit on all (9.5) except those who sigh and cry over the abominations (9.4). This execution order prompts Ezekiel to offer up intercession (9.8), to which Yahweh vows that he will have no pity (9.10).

2. The glory of Yahweh goes forth from the threshold (10.18) and stands over the east gate of the house of Yahweh (10.19), whereupon God orders a more focused hit on certain named leaders, who immediately drop dead (11.1-13). This too prompts Ezekiel to intercede (11.13), and this time Yahweh responds by promising to be 'a little sanctuary' to those who will be scattered among the lands and to re-gather a remnant and give them not only the land (11.17) but also a new heart and spirit (11.19).

3. Yet the glory of Yahweh nevertheless goes up from the midst of the Jerusalem and is last seen standing above the mountain on the east of the city (11.23).

Israel's doctrine of eternal security and positional soteriology[12] had affirmed it could never happen, but Ezekiel had now witnessed it: Yahweh's presence in Zion had come to an end.

After this deathly vision of God inhaling, as it were, and withdrawing his breath, his wind, his *ruaḥ* (רוח) from Jerusalem, something akin to a deathwatch transpires in the following sequence of chapters. Though strikingly diverse, they all feature words on various kinds of endings that all lead up to a final end. These different endings could be summarized as follows:

1. Ezek. 12 – A Sign Act of Ezekiel portraying a captive going into captivity: *the end of the prince in Jerusalem and all the house of Israel* (12.1-20) and *the end false visions and flattering divinations* (12.21-28).

2. Ezek. 13 – Prophecies against prophets who whitewash and women who charm with magic: *the end of whitewashing prophets and the wall they whitewash* (13.1-15) and *the end of the business of prophecy-for-profit* (13.16-23).

3. Ezek. 14 – A Word to Elders who come to Ezekiel to inquire of Yahweh with idols in their hearts: *the end of idol-worshipping prophet-seekers and the prophets who respond to them* (14.1-11) and *the end of efficacious intercession* (even if Noah, Daniel & Job were to plead for God to withhold his 'four severe judgments on Jerusalem' (famine, beasts, sword, pestilence) (14.12-21).

4. Ezek. 15 – An Allegory of the Wood of the Vine (good only as fuel for the fire) compared to the inhabitants of Jerusalem: *the end of the inhabitants of Jerusalem* (15.1-8).

5. Ezek. 16 – An Allegory of the orphaned daughter adopted, raised, adorned, turned harlot, and then shamed: *the end of Jerusalem's not knowing her abominations and shame* (cf. 16.2 and 16.63).

6. Ezek. 17 – A Riddle of the Cedar Branch and the two Eagles that respectively re-plant and replenish it (the branch turns to the first eagle [Babylon] but its roots reach to the second [Egypt]: *the end of those in Jerusalem who break the covenant with Babylon [which Yahweh further specifies as 'my covenant' in 17.19] to court the favor of Egypt.*

7. Ezek. 18 – A Refutation of the Proverb of Children Suffering For the Sins of their Fathers: *the end of ducking individual moral responsibility* (18.3).

8. Ezek. 19 – Lamentation for the Princes of Israel, compared to a succession of lions that become trapped, first by Egypt and then by Babylon (19.1-9) and then to a vine that gets plucked up and replanted in the

---

[12] One of the clearest depictions of this popular theology can be found in the so-called temple sermon of Jer. 7.1-15.

wilderness until there is 'no strong branch – a scepter for ruling' (19.10-14): *the end of Israel's royal line.*

9. Ezek. 20 – A Word to Elders who come to Ezekiel to inquire of Yahweh that recalls the abominations of their fathers in Egypt, in the wilderness, and in the promised land – sins they are now doing 'in the manner of their fathers' (20.1-30): *the end of inquiring of Yahweh (20.31), the end of profaning God's holy name (20.39), and the end of forgetting the people's profaning ways and doings (20.43).*

10. Ezek. 21 – A Prophecy of Yahweh's Sword (Babylon) coming against Jerusalem, the sanctuaries, and the land of Israel 'to cut off the righteous and the wicked' to be accompanied by Ezekiel sighing and wailing: *the end of the land of Israel* (21.27 [Heb: 21.32], 'a ruin, a ruin, a ruin will I make it!); *'the time of the iniquity of the end (קֵץ: qeṣ)'* (21.25, 29 [Heb: 21.30, 34].

11. Ezek. 22 – A Word against the Bloody City (Jerusalem) to make her know all her abominations (violations of God's laws, esp. the Decalogue) followed by a picture of coming judgment in terms of Jerusalem becoming a smelting furnace consuming ' with the fire of his wrath' (22.17-31): *the end of Jerusalem.*

12. Ezek. 23 – An Allegory of the Two Harlots (Samaria and Jerusalem) who multiply harlotries with Egypt, then the older with Assyria and the younger with both Assyria and Babylon until God exposes their lewdness and destroys them: *the end of Jerusalem and all her defilements.*

And throughout all of these chapters again and again we hear that these various endings are coming about so *'that they will know that I am Yahweh'*, and again and again we read, so *'that they will know that I am Yahweh'*. If this study seems redundant, make no mistake about it, so is the book of Ezekiel. This would-be priest is a systematician who offers something of a systematic theology of the end. He witnesses to how Yahweh for the sake of his name systematically scrapes off everything that has become associated with it: the land of Yahweh, the people of Yahweh, the city of Yahweh, the temple of Yahweh, the kingdom of Yahweh, even the priesthood of Yahweh.[13] God renders everything *'is not'* in order that everyone will know that *'I am He Is'* indeed *Yahweh*. In a sense this disqualified priest witnesses the ultimate priestly act: God acting as his own priest to sanctify his own holy name, a God who will stop at nothing, a God who will stop everything, indeed bring to an end anything, for God's sake, in order to hallow that name for which

---

[13] See Walter Brueggemann, *Hopeful Imagination: Prophetic Voices in Exile* (Philadelphia: Fortress, 1986), chs. 3–4, where he presents, along similar lines, the most profound and compelling grasp of the heart of Ezekiel's theology that I have read. See especially ch. 4, where Brueggemann discusses what is theologically at stake in God finally acting for the sake of his holy name.

his only begotten Son would one day teach us to pray, 'hallowed be thy name'.[14]

In ch. 24 comes the end, at least the beginning of the end. The announcement comes that Babylon has commenced the siege of Jerusalem. In accord with this grave event, God speaks a word *through* Ezekiel followed by a word *to* Ezekiel: God tells him that 'the desire of (his) eyes' will be 'taken away' and he is not to grieve (24.16). That very evening Ezekiel's wife dies (24.18), and in his silence he is told he is a sign of how the people of Israel will lose 'the desire of their eyes', namely the sanctuary along with their sons and daughters (24.21-25). Ezekiel is further told that on the day this happens to them an escapee will come and report this to him, whereupon his muteness will give way to his mouth being opened again (24.26-27) and 'then they will know', says God yet again, 'that I am Yahweh' (24.27). The intervening chapters (25-32) present a long series of oracles against other nations that seem to function almost like a literary delay that registers Ezekiel's intervening silence before the people of Israel.

Then finally in ch. 33 comes the announcement of the end itself. The escapee arrives and utters the terse message, 'the city has fallen' (33.21). No embellishment, no elaboration is needed. When it finally happens, the end does not need to be hyped. The brevity followed by silence is thunderous. Yet interestingly this chapter immediately goes on to inform us that Ezekiel's mouth had already been opened the evening prior to the morning when the herald arrived (33.22). Then again, Ezekiel was told that his mouth would be opened on the day the news arrived, and does not the day begin for the Hebrews at sundown? The end of our day is the beginning for them, and in this light, it seems altogether significant that this day that would bear the news of the end of Jerusalem would begin on the evening prior with the re-opening of Ezekiel's mouth, a re-activation of his watchman role, and the uttering of one last prophecy of the end (33.23-29) – a prophecy ending yet again with the words, 'that they may know that I am Yahweh' (33.29). However, this time there comes one more word beyond this oft-repeated goal, this relentlessly reiterated end – a word directed to Ezekiel:

> And as for you, son of man, the children of your people speak of you by the walls and in the doors of the houses, and speak one to another, every one to his brother, saying, Come, please, and hear what the word is that comes forth from Yahweh. And they come to you, as people do, and they sit before you as my people, and they hear your words, but do not do them; for with their mouth they show much love, but their heart

---

[14] See Joachim Jeremias, *The Lord's Prayer* (Philadelphia: Fortress, 1964), p. 22; *The Prayers of Jesus* (Philadelphia: Fortress, 1964), p. 99.

goes after their own gain. And, indeed, you are to them as a very lovely song of one who has a pleasant voice, and can play well on an instrument; for they hear your words, but they do not do them. And when this comes to pass, (and behold, it will come) then they will know that a prophet has been among them (33.30-33).

The end of Jerusalem is a means to the end *that they will know that I am Yahweh*, but the reaching of that end now brings the beginning of *their knowing that a prophet has been among them*. The restoration of the identity of God now yields the fruit of further restoration, and the first fruit of that restoration is the identity of God's prophet. This is the first fruit that will lead the way, announce the news, utter the word that will restore the holy land, the holy city, the holy temple, and the holy people.

In a sense the prophet is not given to know that he is a prophet – not yet, not now – but only *then* – that is, afterward, after the end comes, after *his* end comes – then *they* – others, not he – *they* will know that a prophet *has been* – indeed true prophets are only known after they have become 'has beens'. 'Then they will know that a prophet has been among them.' That is enough, for it is not so much about knowing as about being known by the One who knows, the One who knows the answer to the question, 'Can these bones live?' 'O Lord God, thou knowest.' That is where it all finally ends and at last begins.

I conclude with one final comment. From the moment I chose the title for this paper until coming now to these closing lines, I have written with a constant awareness of the affinity, which weighs significantly in my own thinking, between this ancient messenger named Ezekiel and the one in whose honor I have offered this study. It is my view that, in very many ways, what Ezekiel represented to the people of ancient Israel, Hollis Gause has represented to the Church of God in our lifetime. While I do not know what will finally be said by those who come after him, I cannot help but believe that, when that day comes, *then they will know that a prophet has been among them*.

★★★★★★★★★★★★★★★★★

Abstract

Ezekiel's call to be a prophet finds its source in a spectacular revelation of the glory of God beside a river in Babylon. It is a revelation that signals the beginning of the end of many things: the nation of Judah, the city of Jerusalem, the temple of Zion, and even the end of Ezekiel's priesthood, which is itself a sign of the radicalness of the ending. Yet the end of Ezekiel's identity as priest only reflects the even more radical ending of the identity of God as He had previously been known. And all of this, so Ezekiel is commissioned to announce to all the people, is to the ultimate end that 'they will know that I am Yahweh'. This is the oft-repeated refrain that constitutes the theological goal of the book and the end of Ezekiel's call. This study explores and elaborates the profound means by which the book presents the message of the end, particularly through its posing and juxtaposing of the end and reconstitution of Ezekiel's identity and the identity of God.

4

Was the Last Supper a Passover *Seder*?

James M. Beaty[*]

Introduction[1]

There have been various attempts to make John agree with the Synoptics on the date of the Last Supper,[2] although some scholars have preferred

---

[*] James M. Beaty (Ph.D. Vanderbilt University) is Professor Emeritus of New Testament at the Pentecostal Theological Seminary in Cleveland, TN.

[1] Based on the New Testament and on the life and liturgy of the early Church, I accept as confirmed fact that Jesus was crucified on Friday and that the resurrection occurred on Sunday, the first day of the week. All four Gospels say that he died on the day before the Sabbath (Mt. 26:62 ['next day' that followed the 'preparation' = Sabbath cf. 28.1]; Mk 15.42; Lk. 23.56; Jn 19.31) and that the tomb was found empty on the first day of the week (Mt. 28.1; Mk 16:2; Lk. 24.1; Jn 20.1). This eliminates those suggestions, based on 'three days and three nights' (Mt. 12:40) that would shift the crucifixion forward (before Friday). Note however that Mt. 16.4 mentions the 'sign of Jonah' with no reference to 'three days and three nights'.

Biblical time is inclusive, not exclusive, as the West now understands it. This was because Hebrew did not, and neither did Greek or Latin, have a zero in its counting system; therefore, in Jude 14, Enoch is the seventh from Adam, not the sixth; because Adam is 1; Seth, 2; Enos, 3; Cainan, 4; Mahalaleel, 5; Jared, 6, and Enoch, 7 (Gen. 5.1, 5, 9, 12, 15, 18, 21). In 1 Sam. 30 the phrase, 'three day and three nights' (v. 12), is clarified as 'three days ago' (v. 13) or 'today makes three days' ('hoy hace tres días' is the Spanish translation of that text in Reina-Valera). Also Jesus made three predictions of his death and stated that he would be raised from the dead 'on [dative only-no preposition] the third day' (Mt. 16.21; 17.23; 20.19; Lk. 9.22; 18.33; cf. 24.7) and 'after [*meta*] the third day (shall have arrived)' (Mk 8.31; 9.31; 10.34).

See Wikipedia: 'The Hindu numeral system (base 10) reached Europe in the 11th century, via the Iberian Peninsula through Spanish Muslims (the Moors,) together with knowledge of astronomy and instruments like the astrolabe, first imported by Gerbert of Aurillac. So in Europe they came to be known as "Arabic numerals". The Italian mathematician Fibonacci or Leonardo of Pisa was instrumental in bringing the system into European mathematics in 1202.'

In order to move the crucifixion up to Thursday, Roger Rusk has argued that a crucifixion on Friday requires a 'day of silence' about which 'the gospels say nothing' (Roger Rusk, 'The Day He Died', *Christianity Today*, 18.3 [March 29, 1974], pp. 4-6 [4]). But a close reading of John reveals that, following the excitement resulting from the raising of Lazarus, Jesus and the disciples retired to Ephraim (11.54). Then after his entry into Jerusalem and public teaching in the temple we read, 'When Jesus had said this, he departed and hid himself from them' (12.36b).

the chronology of John.[3] But the majority of scholars have concluded that there is no satisfactory way to harmonize the two.[4] After referring to various ways of interpreting the difference, Hagner says, 'Any of these possibilities seems preferable to the Herculean attempt to harmonize the discordant chronologies.'[5] Gilmore gives a good review of the problem as of 1961, and closed with these comments: 'In the present state of our knowledge, therefore, the matter must be left open. More research and discussion are needed. But it should not be forgotten that if any definite conclusions are reached as a result they are likely to be of more than academic interest.'[6]

Concern for History

It is true that the four Gospels are the message of the Church, the proclamation of the Good News that 'God so loved the world that he gave his only begotten Son, so that whoever believes in Him should not perish but have everlasting life.'[7] And it is also true that the proclamation of the Word has power; as Paul puts it, the gospel is 'the power of God unto salvation to everyone who believes' (Rom. 1.16). But it is also equally true that the four Gospels are not history in the modern sense of just satisfying intellectual curiosity about who, when, where, what, why and how. But at the same time the Gospels are rooted in history. As the Apostles Creed puts it, Jesus Christ 'suffered under Pontius Pilate'. Some scholars are satisfied to let John and the Synoptics tell a different story about the night of the Last Supper and

---

[2] So A.T. Robertson, the great conservative, in his *A Harmony of the Gospels* (New York: Harper & Brothers, 1922), pp. 282-83; see also Charles C. Torrey, 'The Date of the Crucifixion According to the Fourth Gospel', *JBL* 50/4 (1931), pp. 227-41; Barry D. Smith, 'The Chronology of the Last Supper', *WTJ* 53 (1991), pp. 29-45; and others. Smith wrote (p. 40), 'And really there are only two verses that give reason to place Jesus' death on Nisan 14: John 18:28; 19:14.' Then he attempts to harmonize John with the Synoptics. I shall attempt to show that there is only one pericope (with its parallel passages) in the Synoptics that stands in the way of harmonizing the Synoptics with John.

[3] V. Taylor, *The Gospel according to St. Mark* (London: Macmillan, 1966), pp. 664-67; F.F. Bruce, *New Testament History* (Garden City, NY: Doubleday, 1972), pp. 191-92; T. Preiss, 'Le dernier repas de Jésus fut-il un repas pascal?' *TZ* 4 (1948), pp. 81-101.

[4] Smith, 'The Chronology of the Last Supper', p. 29. He lists the following as of this opinion: G. Dalman, *Jesus-Jeshoua* (London: SPCK, 1929); I.H. Marshall, *Lord's Supper and Last Supper* (Exeter: Paternoster, 1980), pp. 57-75; R.E. Brown, *The Gospel according to St. John 2* (2 vols.; AB 29-29a; Garden City, NY: Doubleday, 1970), pp. 555-58; C.K. Barrett, *The Gospel according to St. John* (2nd ed.; Philadelphia: Fortress, 1978); R. Schnackenburg, *Commentary on the Gospel of John* (3 vols.; London: Burns & Oates, 1982) pp. 33-47; L. Morris, *The Gospel according to St. John* (NICNT; Grand Rapids: Eerdmans, 1971), pp. 774-85.

[5] Donald A. Hagner, *Matthew 14–18* (WBC; Dallas: Word Books, 1995), p. 764.

[6] Alec Gilmore, 'The Date and Significance of the Last Supper', *SJT* 13.3 (1961), pp. 256-69.

[7] All citations from Scripture are my translations, unless indicated otherwise.

therefore about the day of the crucifixion. But for me I find it hard to affirm at the same time that Jesus died on Nisan 14 in John and on Nisan 15 in Matthew, Mark and Luke.[8]

Procedure in This Study

The first thing that I shall attempt to do in this study is to describe the order of the events for Nisan 14 at the time of Jesus. This is the period from sunset following Nisan 13 to sunset following Nisan 14. The latter sunset was the beginning of Nisan 15 and was the time that the Passover Supper was to be eaten.[9] The location would have been Jerusalem where the temple was located, because the lamb had to be sacrificed in the temple.[10] In the second place, I will look at the Gospel of John, where it is clear that Jesus was crucified on Nisan 14, as the lambs were being slain, and therefore had eaten his last supper on the night following Nisan 13. With this I will look at the patristic evidence, which stands solidly with the Johannine chronology. And in the third place, I will examine the pericope in the synoptic Gospels that, when read in the light of John, proves to be the problem. This is about the disciples going into Jerusalem to make arrangements for the room. These three parallel passages are Mt. 26.17-19; Mk 14.12-16; and Lk. 22.7-12. Then the question of whether the Last Supper was or was not a Passover meal will be looked at in the light of these considerations.[11]

I. The Passover in the Time of Jesus

In the time of Jesus it is variously estimated that the resident population of Jerusalem was from eighty to a hundred thousand and that 'this was more than doubled by the pilgrims who came for the holidays, espe-

---

[8] This concern is sometimes seen as a narrow, sectarian view, tied to one's concern for the integrity of Scripture. And in one sense it is. But such a view would not be tolerated in secular history. Who would ever think of letting any important event be affirmed as happening on two different dates? But of course, many would say, John is right and the Synoptics are wrong, or vice versa. And I am not willing to say that.

[9] I will rely heavily on Jewish scholarship for this picture.

[10] Since 70 CE this has changed and most of the history of the Seder has been formed by rabbinic Judaism without access to the temple. See Baruch M. Bokser, *The Origins of the Seder: The Passover Rite and Early Rabbinic Judaism* (Berkeley: University of California Press, 1984), p. 188.

[11] I will only deal with the question of whether the Last Supper was a Passover Meal (with the sacrificial lamb) or whether it was eaten on the preceding night (without it). Either way, the Supper is deeply influenced by the Passover motif. I will not deal with all the thorny questions of what year it was.

cially at *Pesach*.'[12] Schauss describes how congested it was, 'Every inn was filled to overflowing, and whoever had a bit of room in his house made it available to the visiting pilgrims, never accepting any payment. It was customary, however, for the pilgrims to offer their hosts the skins of the animals they had sacrificed in the Temple (see *Yoma* 12.a).'[13]

Thus Jerusalem, at Passover, became a crowded, noisy, busy city. The need for sacrifices meant that the sheep and cattle markets flourished, but people were also busy, selling everything imaginable: bread, fish, wine, spices, condiments, and even jewelry, clothing, and adornments. Mixed in with these were all kinds of tradespersons: tailors, shoemakers, blacksmiths, and others, each plying his or her respective trade. And this was the scene for days before the high festival itself arrived.

The 14th of Nisan, the day of the slaughter of the lambs, is also the day that all leaven, in whatever form, had to be removed from the house.[14] This was done on the night before, or stated differently, after sunset following the 13th (the point at which the 14th day began).[15] The following morning at a signal given from the temple by the priests, all leaven was burned.[16]

At that time the priests were organized into bands and generally one band or shift was on duty at the temple for a week. But at Passover all 24 bands were on hand because of all the extra activities in the temple. The animal to be sacrificed on the fourteenth of Nisan was to have been selected on the tenth (*m. Pesahim* 9.5).[17]

---

[12] Hayyim Schauss, *The Jewish Festivals, History and Observance* (trans. Samuel Jaffe; New York: Shocken Books, 1938), p. 48. See also Joachim Jeremias, *Jerusalem in the Time of Jesus* (trans. F.H. & C.H. Cave; Philadelphia: Fortress Press, 1969), pp. 58-77.

[13] Schauss, *The Jewish Festivals*, p. 48.

[14] The terms 'unleavened (bread)' or 'the feast of unleavened (bread)' are used in three ways. One, to refer to the seven days following the Passover meal; two, to refer to the seven days plus the Passover meal; and three, to refer to 14th Nisan, the day of the slaying of the Lambs (Mk 14:12; Lk. 22:7), which was also the day that the leaven had to be found, removed and burned.

[15] This is still practiced by religious Jews. Even the small Samaritan sect in Nablus cleans out the leaven on the night before the night of the Passover Meal.

[16] *M. Pesahim* 1-3. Although *Pesahim* is the earliest written Halakah about the procedure of removing leaven before the Passover meal, the practice is as old as Passover itself and goes back to the Torah. I was taught by Rabbi Lou Silberman that, although the writing down of the oral law (Mishnah) occurred about 200 CE (as he put it), it was basically formed by 200 BCE, though this understanding is of course very much in dispute at present.

[17] Bokser gives a scholarly and critical translation of *Pesahim* 10 in the Mishnah and Tosefta, which he calls 'the earliest full description of the Passover evening celebration,' in his book, *The Origins of the Seder*, pp. 29-36.

By noon on the 14th all work has been suspended and multitudes with animals for sacrifice are headed for the temple. The evening sacrifice is offered an hour early and by three o'clock the offering of the Passover sacrifices begin. This is done in three cycles. The court of the temple is filled to capacity with men with their lambs to be offered; the gates are closed and the Levites blow a triple blast on their trumpets to initiate the ceremony and then continue by singing the *Hallel* psalms. Each person slays his own animal, while the priests, standing in rows with their silver and gold basins, catch the blood, pour it at the base of the altar and help with the proceedings (*Pesahim* 5.6). Each lamb is skinned and the fat and kidneys removed for burning on the altar (*Pesahim* 5.9-10; cf. Lev. 3.3-5).[18] The ritual is over in about 40 minutes and is repeated two more times. Each ceremony is done with great dignity and devotion and moves quietly and orderly. And each family-head leaves, carrying on his shoulder the carcass of his Passover lamb, wrapped in its own skin.[19]

In the late afternoon, if it is not raining, portable clay stoves, set up in the courtyards, are fired up with 'fragrant pomegranate wood' for the roasting of the Passover lamb.[20] The meal will be held in the largest room in the house, with the head of the house presiding. All are welcome, family and friends; and all are included, men and women, masters and slaves, poor and rich, without any distinctions. And all are dressed in white, except the women from Babylonia, who wear bright colors.[21]

By the time the Supper begins, the streets are quiet and the full moon is shining overhead.[22] And since the sacrifice had to be consumed during that one night, smaller families combined with neighbors or pilgrims; each celebration generally consisted of ten or more (*b. Pesahim* 64b).[23]

The Passover meal is basically a meal commemorating and celebrating God's mercy and deliverance in the Exodus. In general there is great caution among scholars about specifying the content and form of the Passover Seder before 70 CE.[24] The *Seder*, which means *order*, is

---

[18] Marvin R. Wilson, *Our Father Abraham* (Grand Rapids: Eerdmans, 1989), p. 244.

[19] Wilson, *Our Father Abraham*, p. 244; citing *Pesahim* 65.b.

[20] Wilson, *Our Father Abraham,* p. 244; citing *m. Pesahim* 7.1.

[21] Schauss, *The Jewish Festivals*, p. 54.

[22] By definition Nisan 14 always fell on the full moon of a lunar month.

[23] Wilson, *Our Father Abraham*, p. 243; and J.Z. Lauderbach, 'Passover Sacrifice' in Isidore Singer (ed.), *The Jewish Encyclopedia* IX (New York: Ktav, n.d.), pp. 556-57.

[24] See Jonathan Klawans, 'Was Jesus' Last Supper a Seder?' *BR* 17 (Oct 2001), pp. 24-47. He states: 'Rabban Gamaliel used to say: Whoever does not make mention of the following three things on Passover has not fulfilled his obligation: namely, the Passover sacrifice, unleavened bread (*matzah*) and bitter herbs" (p. 31). The dating is after 70 CE; but all three items are mentioned in Exodus (12.8), which also mandates perpetual obser-

made up of prayers, symbolic acts, explanation-instruction, the meal and the reading or chanting of the Hallel (Pss 115–118). It consists of two types of activities: the eating of the meal and the celebration of its meaning.

The first part begins with the first cup, wine mixed with water, and the corresponding blessing.[25] Then follows the washing of the right hand, the eating of the 'lettuce dipped in a tart liquid',[26] the breaking and hiding of part of a *mazzah,* and the explanation-instruction part called the *Haggadah* (this was celebratory and didactic, in order to pass on the meaning to the next generation).

The second part (this is my division) began with washing the hands and the grace before meals. The eating included (a) the '*matsoh* and bitter herbs, dipped in *charoses,* a mixture of nuts and fruits in wine',[27] (b) the roasted lamb and (3) the hidden piece of *mazza* (the *afikoman*)[28] at the end of the meal. The meal was concluded with the blessing after meals, the singing of the *Hillel* and the 'benediction for redemption.'[29]

Passover was different from most of the other feasts; it was joyful, but also a solemn occasion, although no fun-making activities were permitted. However, after the meal people could visit from house to house to greet and wish each other well.[30] Many of them would go to the Temple Mount, where the doors would be opened at midnight,[31] and 'spend the rest of the night there, praying and singing hymns of praise to God.'[32]

One further note about the relation of the Feast of Unleavened Bread to Passover: in the Mosaic Law Nisan 14 was designated Passover; on that day the lamb was slain and prepared, but the meal was to fol-

vance, with the command to explain the rite 'when your children shall ask, "What does this ritual mean?"' (12.26-27).

[25] 'We should note, however, that at most meals ancients watered down wine at least two parts water to every part wine...in Jewish texts, see *Sifra Shir.* Par. 1.100.1.2; *b. 'Abod. Zar.* 30a; *Num. Rab.* 10.8; Safrai 1974/76b: 748), unless they specifically wished to get drunk ... in the latter case, Greeks may also have added some other intoxicants' (Craig S. Keener, *A Commentary on the Gospel of Matthew* [Grand Rapids: Eerdmans, 1999], p. 625). Wilson thinks the wine and water was heated, based on *Pesahim* 7:13, pp. 244-45.

[26] Louis Jacobs, 'Passover', *Encyclopaedia Judaica* (Jerusalem: Peter, 1971), pp. 167-68, has 'parsley in salt water.'

[27] Schauss, *The Jewish Festivals,* pp. 54-55.

[28] The meaning of the word is not absolutely clear, but may be derived from the Greek τὸν ἐρχόμενον (the coming one).

[29] Schauss, *The Jewish Festivals,* p. 55. The exact order of the Passover is not absolutely verifiable in the first century, but most of these elements formed a part of it.

[30] This was different from the original celebration in Egypt when all had to remain in the room for the duration of the night.

[31] Josephus, *Antiquities* 18.2.2 (29); Wilson, *Our Father Abraham,* p. 245.

[32] Wilson, *Our Father Abraham,* p. 245.

low after sunset, which means that it was actually eaten on Nisan 15. There was to be no leavened bread at the Passover or for the week following (Nisan 15-21). This meant that the leaven would have to be removed on Nisan 14 or before. Thus, the Passover Meal was the first meal of the week of Unleavened Bread.[33]

II. The Chronology of the Passover in John

The Gospels do not record what Jesus did with all the precision that a modern reader has come to expect from a newspaper article. But faith reminds us that 'all things necessary for our salvation' are there. Nevertheless, it is still appropriate to analyze and scrutinize thoroughly what we do have in order not to draw wrong conclusions from it.

As already mentioned the Gospel of John, as generally interpreted, places the Last Supper on the night before the Passover. Baruch M. Bokser, concludes 'John is presenting Jesus as a Passover offering' that is 'slain at the time the lambs are slain'.[34] So let us look at John.

Just before the triumphal entry of Jesus into Jerusalem, John relates the raising of Lazarus from the dead (11.1-44).[35] This took place at Bethany, a village adjoining Jerusalem, and provoked the attention of the religious authorities (11.45-53), causing Jesus to retire to Ephraim in the desert (11.54). John then added the following: 'Now the Passover of the Jews was approaching (near), and many from the country went up to Jerusalem before the Passover in order to purify themselves (v. 55).' The pilgrims that had gone up for the feast began to look for Jesus and to wonder if he would be there. And the authorities were anxiously seeking to arrest him in order to avoid trouble during the feast (11.56).

In this Gospel the Last Supper begins with ch. 13. John opens with these words, πρὸ δὲ τῆς ἑορτῆς τοῦ πάσχα ('before the Feast of Passover'). This is the night before the Passover meal.[36] Both the text

---

[33] The feast has been extended to eight days in certain times and places.

[34] Baruch M. Bokser, 'Was the Last Supper a Passover Seder?' *Bible Review* 3.2 (Summer, 1987), p. 33. So did Solomon Zeitlin, 'The Last Supper as an Ordinary Meal in the Fourth Gospel', *JQR* 42/3 (1952), pp. 251-60. In reference to buying what was needed for the feast he said, 'From this it is evident that the arrest of Jesus took place on an ordinary night, the thirteenth of Nisan, and not on the Passover night because on a holiday no transactions were possible in Jerusalem. (and) The Paschal lamb was purposely omitted because Jesus was personifying himself as the Paschal lamb who was supposed to redeem his believers' (pp. 259-60).

[35] Was this intended to be an 'action-parable' of his own resurrection?

[36] Cf. F. Blass & A. Debrunner, *A Greek Grammar of the New Testament and Other Early Christian Literature* (Chicago: University of Chicago Press, 1961), p. 114: 'The peculiar construction πρὸ ἓξ ἡμερῶν τοῦ πάσχα '6 days before the passover' is Hellenistic (properly '6

and the context make it clear that this is not the Passover meal itself. This becomes clear when Jesus told Judas to do quickly what he was going to do and the other disciples thought that, since Judas handled the money, Jesus was telling him to 'buy the things that we need for the feast' (13.29), which would have been the following night.

After three chapters of teaching (14-16) and Christ's Prayer (17), the story continues: the garden, the arrest, the house of the High Priest, Peter's denial, and the interrogation by the High Priest before being sent to Pilate. At that point, another clue: 'Then they led Jesus from the residence of Caiaphas into the praetorium: it was early; but they themselves did not go into the praetorium, so as not to be defiled, but be able to eat the Passover' (18.28).[37]

After the investigation before Pilate and his reluctant sentence, John informs us that 'it was Passover Eve,[38] about six o'clock in the morning' (19.14, by Roman reckoning), when Pilate presented Jesus before the people. John does not specify the hours, but Jesus was crucified on Golgotha and in the course of time 'gave up the ghost' (v. 30, KJV). Persons that were crucified would sometimes linger on for many hours; and since the Sabbath, which, in this particular year, was also the Passover, was rapidly approaching, the religious authorities petitioned Pilate that the soldiers be ordered to break the legs of those crucified in order to hasten death (19.31). This was done on the other two who were crucified with Jesus, but when they found that Jesus had already died, they did not break his legs. So not only was Jesus offered at the same time as the Passover lambs, but, as specified concerning the lambs, 'Not a bone was broken' (19.32-33). But one of the soldiers did pierce his side with a lance, and blood and water came out (19.34).

Through the intervention of two influential Jewish leaders, Joseph of Arimathea and Nicodemus, who had been touched by the ministry of Jesus, his body was buried in a near-by tomb, belonging to Joseph, because the Passover-Sabbath was rapidly approaching (19.42).[39] His body was in the tomb part of Friday, all day Saturday and part of Sun-

---

days ago, reckoned from the Passover') Jn 12.1.' See also James Hope Moulton, *A Grammar of New Testament Greek*, I (Edinburgh: T. & T. Clark, 3rd edn, 1900), pp. 100-101.

[37] 'Be defiled' and 'eat' are both in the subjunctive: 'in order that they might not be defiled' and 'in order that they might eat.' The latter is conditioned on the first.

[38] My translation of 'the Preparation of the Passover.'

[39] Alfred Plummer, *An Exegetical Commentary on the Gospel according to St. Matthew* (repr.: Grand Rapids: Baker Book House, 1982): 'The Passover coincided with the Sabbath, which began on the Friday evening. Our Lord, knowing that He would be unable to celebrate it at the proper time, had a representative supper on the Thursday evening' (p. 357).

day, but early Sunday morning before dawn, Mary Magdalene found an empty tomb, because the Master had risen from the dead.

The writer of the Fourth Gospel, after the magnificent prologue with which he opens his Gospel, presents the testimony of John the Baptist about Jesus in these words: 'Behold the Lamb of God, who takes away the sin of the world' (1.29). And he repeats that same testimony the following day (1.36). So John the writer saw Jesus through the lens of the paschal lamb whose blood on the doorposts meant salvation for the people of God in Egypt and was instrumental in their deliverance from Egypt.

Now God's Eternal Word made flesh suffers and dies on the same day and at the same time that the paschal lambs are being slaughtered for Passover. Only John tells of the order of Pilate to the soldiers to break the legs of the three who were crucified that day. But he also noted that since Jesus had already died, this was not done, so that the Scripture could be fulfilled that no bone of his body was broken (19.36). This also identifies Jesus, in his mind, as the Lamb of God, since the Law specified, concerning the lamb for the Passover, that 'neither shall you break any bone of it' (Exod. 12.46; Num. 9.12; cf. Ps. 34.20).

Historical Witnesses to the Johannine Chronology

The earliest Christians were Jews or Jewish proselytes in Jerusalem and Judaism was their thought-world. They believed that Jesus was the long-expected Messiah of the Jews. They were 'Jewish' people who believed in Jesus as the Messiah, but also they had been transformed by the regenerating power of the resurrection and had been baptized in the Holy Spirit. This meant that they continued to participate in the structures of Jewish religious life, like temple worship (Acts 3.1-10), Sabbath-keeping and the annual festivals, two of which, Passover (Acts 20.6, 16; cf. 1 Cor. 5.6-8) and Pentecost (Acts 20.16), had taken on drastically new dimensions and in time became the anchor points of the liturgical year for the Christian church.[40]

However, the celebration of the resurrection on the first day of the week began to displace Sabbath observance, especially in the Diaspora. And the annual feast of Passover, which at first continued to be observed on Nisan 14, with time shifted to the Sunday following Nisan 14. In the second century the Quartodecimans[41] of Asia Minor were still keeping Passover on the 14th of Nisan according to the Jewish calendar, while the West held the annual celebration of the Resurrec-

---

[40] H. Leclercq, 'Paques', col. 1524, n. 2.
[41] From Latin 'quartusdecimus' = the fourteenth. E.P. Leverett, ed., *A New and Copious Lexicon of the Latin Language* (Boston: Wilkins, Carter, & Co., 1859), p. 733.

tion on Sunday and correspondingly the last supper on Thursday night. But although the Quartodecimans observed Nisan 14, they followed the Johannine chronology and ate the meal on the evening before the Jews observed Passover and fasted until 3:00 pm the following day (the same day by Jewish reckoning). This calendar problem was dealt with at Nicaea (325 CE), but then the focus of the problem was in the churches in Syria, Cilicia and Mesopotamia.

In the church fathers of the early centuries there seems to have been a general consensus on the Johannine chronology of the Last Supper. Tertullian (c. 155-225) in his *Answer to the* Jews [8] says that Jesus was crucified 'on the first day of unleavened bread, on which they slew the lamb at even.'[42] Clement of Alexandria (c. 150-220) wrote that, on the thirteenth, the disciples asked Jesus where they should go and prepare the room and that, on the fourteenth, Jesus suffered. Then he added: 'With this precise determination of the days both the whole Scriptures agree, and the Gospels harmonize.'[43] The last clause, 'And the Gospels harmonize', means that Clement, who spoke Greek from birth, was educated in Greek and was writing in Greek, read Matthew, Mark and Luke as agreeing with John.

Hippolytus of Rome (c. 170-235), in his *Philosophoumena*, wrote (also in Greek), 'At the time of his passion, the Christ did not eat the legal Passover; it is He who was the Passover, pre-announced and fulfilled on the day specified.'[44] In his book on the Passover Hippolytus also wrote, 'After having said: I will eat no more the Passover, the Savior did, in fact, eat supper before the Passover, but he did not eat the Passover, he suffered it: for the time to eat it had not yet come.'[45]

---

[42] Jack Finegan, *Handbook of Biblical Chronology*, Revelation (Peabody: Hendrickson, 1998), p. 365. See also Alexander Roberts & James Donaldson, eds., *The Ante-Nicene Fathers* (Grand Rapids: Eerdmans, 1951), vol. III, p. 167.

[43] Fragments found in Greek only in the Oxford Edition, quoted from the *Pascal Chronicle* in Alexander Roberts & James Donaldson, eds., *The Ante-Nicene Fathers* (Grand Rapids: Eerdmans, 1951), vol. II, p. 581.

[44] H. Leclercq, 'Pâques', *Dictionnaire d'archéologie chrétienne et de liturgie* (ed. Fernand Cabrol; Paris: Librairie Letouzey et Anê, 1938), vol. XIII, Part 2, cols. 1521-74 (col. 1527). Original: 'au temps de sa Passion, le Christ ne mangea pas la Pâque légale, c'est lui qui était la Pâque annoncée et réalisée au jour marqué.' All translations from this dictionary are my own.

[45] H. Leclercq, 'Pâques', col. 1527. For an exhaustive listing of patristique references to the texts involved see Centre d'analyse et de documentation patristiques, *Biblia Patristica, index des citations et allusions bibliques dans la littérature patristique* (vols. I-VI) (Paris: Editions du Centre National de la Recherche Scientifique), 1975-87.

III. The Chronology in the Synoptic Gospels

Now let us look at the Synoptic Gospels. The first three Gospels in canonical order are referred to as the 'synoptic' Gospels, because they 'see' things 'together' or from the same perspective. Each, of course, has its own point of view, style and form. Today it is generally considered that the first three Gospels present the Last Supper as a Passover meal. But Duchesne pointed out, over 100 years ago, 'This interpretation, which many commentators still maintain, was not admitted, in the second century, by any church, or at least, it would be impossible to cite a single witness in its favor, while there is no lack of important texts to the contrary.'[46]

But it is also generally recognized that this interpretation (that in the Synoptics Jesus ate the Passover) is not without its difficulties. R.S. Wallace, for example, mentions several of these.[47] (1) There is no mention of the paschal lamb in any of the five accounts of the Supper (including 1 Cor. 11.23-26). (2) The bread is apparently ordinary bread; none of the accounts states that the bread used was unleavened. (3) How could Jesus be arrested after the Passover had begun? (4) How could the linen cloth used to envelop the body of Jesus have been purchased on the day of Passover, which was also a Sabbath? (5) And how could Simon of Cyrene have been 'coming in from work in the fields' on a day that was the Sabbath?[48]

The Key to the Date in the Synoptic Gospels

Now let us ask, is there a key that will help us to interpret the synoptic Gospels in harmony with the Gospel of John? Or should we ask, why did the Greek-speaking fathers of the church find no difficulty in the chronology of the Last Supper in reading the Greek text of the four Gospels? I believe that the key to the date of the Lord's Supper as reported in the synoptic Gospels depends on two things. The first thing

---

[46] Louis Marie Olivier Duchesne, 'La Question de la Pâque au Concile de Nicée', *Revue des Questions Historiques* XXVIII (1880), pp. 5-42 (8). Translation mine. French original: 'Cette interprétation, que beaucoup de commentateurs maintiennent encore, n'était, au second siècle, admise par aucune église, ou de moins il serait impossible de citer un seul témoignage en sa faveur, tandis qu'il ne manque pas de textes importants en sens contraire.' H. Leclercq, 'Pâques', col. 1524, also writes, 'One cannot bring forth any proof that in the second century a single church admitted this interpretation (viz., that Jesus ate the Passover on Nisan 14 and died on Nisan 15).' ('On ne peut apporter aucune preuve qu'au IIᵉ siècle, une seule Eglise admit cette interprétation.')

[47] R.S. Wallace, 'Lord's Supper (Eucharist)', *The International Standard Bible Encyclopedia*, III (ed. Geoffrey W. Bromiley; Grand Rapids: Eerdmans, 1980), p. 164.

[48] The Law specified that no 'servile work' be done (Num 28.18).

is a clear understanding of what had to be done on Nisan 14.[49] I am referring to collecting the leaven, burning the leaven, and offering the lamb, all of which had to be done before the meal began. The second thing is a correct interpretation of the three parallel passages in the Synoptics about the disciples making the necessary arrangements for the Passover celebration. These passages, as already mentioned, are Mt. 26.17-19; Mk 14.12-16; Lk. 22.7-12.[50]

M'Niele, in commenting on Mt. 26.17, says, 'Here is the crux of the chronology.... The discrepancy between the syn. and the 4th Gosp, mainly lies in the present verse.'[51] And although he accepts the traditional interpretation that the Synoptics are different from John, he goes on to assert why that interpretation is extremely difficult.

> But the chronology of the 4th Gosp. is to be preferred, according to which the Lord died at the time that the lambs were being killed. For (1) the two disciples would hardly have had time to make the preparations on the 14th. (2) Apart from this verse there is nothing in the present section which demands that date. (3) Details of the Last Supper make its identity with the Passover very doubtful.[52] (4) The Sanhedrin had determined to arrest Jesus before the festival, yet according to the synoptic chronology they arrested Him *on* the festival (5) No Jew would carry arms on the festival (v. 51, Mk, Lk.), nor would Joseph have bought linen (Mk xv. 46).... (6) Mk xv. 42 can only mean that Joseph buried the Body at once, because it was Friday afternoon, and the hour when the Sabbath would begin (6 p.m.) was near. Hence (Lk. xxiii. 56) the women could not embalm it at once, but were obliged to wait till the Sabbath was over.[53]

---

[49] One needs to be versed in law to translate a legal text and in medicine to translate a medical text. One always needs to know something of the subject (and the more the better) when translating.

[50] The reason why Jesus sent Peter and John to make the arrangements, rather that going himself with the twelve, is probably related to the opposition and hostility already generated against his person. M'Neile suggests: 'The sending of the two disciples perhaps suggests that secrecy was necessary. Jesus did not enter the city until dark.' Alan Hugh M'Neile, *The Gospel according to St. Matthew* (New York: Macmillan, 1955), p. 379. The authorities were looking for an occasion to arrest him and Judas was looking for one to betray him in some clandestine way.

[51] M'Neile, *The Gospel According to St. Matthew*, pp. 377-78.

[52] See also Ulrich Luz, *Matthew 21–28, a Commentary* (trans. James E. Crouch; Minneapolis: Fortress, 2005), p. 355.

[53] M'Neile, *The Gospel According to St. Matthew*, pp. 377-78. See also Luz, *Matthew 21–28*, 'Apollinaris of Laodicea emphasized that Jesus' last meal was a 'supper...and not yet the Passover food' (δεῖπνον ... καὶ οὕτω πάσχα βρῶμα)' (p. 355). He cites Theophylactus (441) as saying, 'In that year the Lord did not eat a Passover' [and then notes that] 'The Orthodox churches use leavened bread in the Eucharist rather than unleavened bread as in the West' (p. 355).

The Day the Disciples (Peter and John) Made the Arrangements[54]
First, a question: Was the day that the apostles made the arrangements the same day as 'the day of preparation', which is mentioned in Mt. 27.62; Mk 15.42; Lk. 23.54; Jn 19.14, 31, 42? My conclusion is that it is not. Therefore, I have used the phrase 'make the arrangements' because the Greek word for *prepare* in this passage in all of the Synoptics is ἑτοιμίζω, which means to *put or keep in readiness, prepare* (BAG). The word used in the 'day of preparation' is παρασκευή, a noun, from the verb, παρασκευάζω, and means to *prepare oneself for something*.[55] The noun is used in two contexts: (1) for the day before the Sabbath and (2) the day before the Passover. Since the day before the Sabbath (the seventh day) is always Friday (the sixth day), the word, when it referred to Friday, could have two connotations: (1) as the day of preparation for the Sabbath and (2) as the name for the sixth day of the week. In connection with Passover it was Nisan 14, the day when the leaven is collected and destroyed and the lamb sacrificed and roasted, and that day could fall on any day of the week. παρασκευάζω is not used in the three passages mentioned about the apostles making arrangements for the Passover.

So the question is – What had to be arranged in preparation for Passover? Apart from, and before, what was mandated by Scripture to be done on Nisan 14, there was the matter of having a place in which to celebrate the Passover. This is the focus of these three passages. The question then arises: Were they sent on this mission on the morning of Nisan 14, which had already begun at sunset the night before, or were they sent the day before, on Nisan 13?

Things That Had To Be Done on Nisan 14
In the Law two things are specified for Nisan 14: the removal of all leaven from the house (Exod. 12.15, 19; 34.18; Lev. 23.6; Num. 28.17; Deut. 16.3) and the slaying and offering of the sacrificial lamb (Exod. 12.3-6). In the Jewish calendar the Feast of Unleavened Bread followed the Feast of Passover (Lev. 23.5-6; Num. 28.16-17).[56] But since unleavened bread was also mandated for Passover, it was necessary to remove the leaven on the 14th of Nisan, which was also the

---

[54] Matthew (26:19) has 'the disciples'; Mark (14:13) has 'two of his disciples'; and Luke (22:8) has 'Peter and John.'

[55] Solomon Zeitlin, 'The Last Supper as an Ordinary Meal in the Fourth Gospel', p. 252, points out that παρασκεῖν did not come from Aramaic (*contra* Torrey), but had been used by Augustus Caesar in a 'decree that the Jews should not be summoned to appear before the judge on the Sabbath, or on the day before the Sabbath' (p. 252) and that 'The Hellenized Jews did not use the word παρασκεῖν but προ σαββάτων (*sic*), comp. *Ant.* 3.10, 7; Judith, 8.6; II Macc. 8.26' (p. 252, n.3).

[56] Cf. Ex 12:19, 'For seven days no leaven shall be found in your houses.'

day the lambs were to be sacrificed. The Passover meal followed that night. The point of the inquiry of the disciples and the purpose of going into the city was first, to assure a place to celebrate the feast, although this was probably more of a reconfirming, since Jesus told them to go to so-and-so's place (26.18).[57]

IV. The Chronology of the Passover in Mark

The plot to silence Jesus as given by Mark (14.1-2) is very similar to the accounts in Matthew and Luke.

> [1]Now Passover and Unleavened Bread were to begin after two days. The high priests and the scribes were seeking a way to lay hands on him through deception in order to kill him. [2]Because, they were saying, 'It must not be done during the Feast, or there will be a public uproar.'

Then Mark gives the account of the anointing at Bethany (14.3-9) and the story of Judas agreeing to betray Jesus (14.10-11). At that point he relates the account of the disciples going into Jerusalem to make arrangement for their accommodations during the festival (14.12-16).

Exegesis of Mark 14.12

Καὶ	conjunction
τῇ πρώτῃ ἡμέρᾳ	adverbial phrase in the dative, modifying the verb
τῶν ἀζύμων,[58]	adjectival phrase in the gen. pl. modifying *day*
ὅτε τὸ πάσχα ἔθυον,	adjectival clause modifying *day*
λέγουσιν αὐτῷ	verb + indirect object
οἱ μαθηταὶ αὐτοῦ	subject
ποῦ θέλεις ἀπελθόντες ἑτοιμάσωμεν	question
ἵνα φάγῃς τὸ πάσχα	adverbial (purpose) clause

Here it is made clear that 'the first day of ἀζύμων' was the day that the Passover lambs were to be offered. The Law specified Nisan 14 as the day of the slaughter, with Passover following after dark (therefore, on the beginning of Nisan 15). The 15th was also a day of holy convocation with no servile labor and also the first of seven days of unleavened bread, with the seventh also a holy convocation. If one was going to have the house freed from leaven, it had to be done no later that the 14th, before the Passover meal began after dark that day. Thus it seems

---

[57] Luz, *Matthew 21-28*, p. 352.

[58] Since ἀζύμων is a genitive, plural modifier, it probably has an implied substantive and means 'of the days of unleavened bread'. So Nisan 14 was called the 'the first day of the days of unleavened bread'.

that, in the time of Jesus, Nisan 14 had come to be referred to as the first day of unleavened bread (ἀζύμων).

At the supper there is no mention, by Mark or any of the other Gospels, of it being Passover; no mention is made of a lamb, or the bitter herbs, or unleavened bread (ἄρτος, not ἀζύμων, is used in referring to the bread).[59] And when apprehended (14.53), Jesus is taken from the Garden to the residence of the High Priest. Would the high priest have been available if he had been involved in a Passover Meal that very night? Early on Friday, the fourteenth, Jesus appears briefly before the Sanhedrin and is then sent to Pilate. By 9:00 am he is crucified (15.24); at noon there is a great darkness (15.33); and Jesus dies at 3:00 pm, while the lambs are being slaughtered in the temple. He is hurriedly buried and is in the tomb during the Passover meal.

Now for a closer look at the grammar. Following the conjunction, καί, we have what could be called a prepositional phrase without a preposition: τῇ πρώτῃ ἡμέρα τῶν ἀζύμων ('the first day of unleavened [bread]'). This phrase is used as an adverb of time, since it modifies the verb. And the word 'day' in this phrase is also modified by adjectival clause that follows, viz., ὅτε τὸ πάσχα ἔθυον ('when the Passover [lambs] were killed/sacrificed').[60] The day being referred to can only be Nisan 14, the day designated for the slaying of the lambs and the removal of the leaven.[61]

At this point we have a reflection of a first-century understanding and designation of this phrase, since in a strict sense, the Feast of Unleavened Bread followed Passover and was to be observed from Nisan 15 to 21 (Exod. 12.18; Lev. 23.6-7; Num. 28.17; Deut. 16.3). But it also reflects a logical and practical interpretation of the Law. If Passover was to be eaten on the night following the 14th, then the leaven had to be removed no later than the 14th. Since it was the practice to remove the leaven at the beginning of Nisan 14, the day itself could properly be called the first day of unleavened bread.

Then the verb follows, with its indirect object (λέγουσιν αὐτῷ ['they speak with him or say to him']), and the subject with a pronominal adjective, οἱ μαθηταὶ αὐτοῦ, 'his disciples'). The simplest subject-verb sequence in English is 'His disciples speak to/with him (or say to him).'

---

[59] Alberto Mello, *Evangile selon Saint Matthieu, Commentaire midrashique et narratif* (translation from Italian by Aimée Chevillon; Paris: Les Editions du Cerf, 1999), p. 450. However, Deuteronomy calls unleavened bread 'the bread of affliction' and in the latter uses the ordinary word for bread (16.3). Klawans, 'Was Jesus' Last Supper a Seder?', p. 47, n. a.

[60] Thus, 'the day' (apart from the definite article) has three modifiers: (1) it is the 'first' day; (2) it is the day 'of unleavened (bread)'; and (3) it is the day 'when the Passover is offered.'

[61] In this context it could not refer to the first of the seven days of unleavened bread that followed the Passover meal.

The adverbial phrase, τῇ πρώτῃ ἡμέρᾳ, modifies the verb λέγω[62] and can be translated as a dative of time, as it generally is (meaning the time of the speaking), or as a dative of reference, as I think it should be (meaning that about which the disciples spoke).[63] By reading it as a dative of reference we get, 'The disciples speak (historical present) to Jesus about the first day of unleavened bread, *the day* when the Passover [lambs] were [accustomed to be] killed/sacrificed.'

In the first century the removal of the leaven had already been institutionalized and was to be carried out on the night before the slaying of the lambs.[64] But this would still have been on the fourteenth, because the day began at sundown of the preceding day. The leaven was collected and put into a container on the night following the thirteenth and then was ceremonially burned on the morning of the fourteenth. This makes Nisan thirteen the last day that one could arrange for a room and have it ready for the removal of the leaven that night.

V. The Chronology of the Passover in Matthew

Matthew opens his final narrative section (after the discourses of chs. 24 and 25) with an announcement made by Jesus: 'After two days Passover is here; and the Son of Man is betrayed to be crucified.' Matthew then mentions the intention of the religious authorities to make the arrest before Passover. Following the anointing of the head of Jesus by an unnamed woman in the house of Simon the leper, he records the agreement that Judas Iscariot made to lead the authorities to Jesus.

Then Matthew opens his account of the Last Supper (26.17-30) very much as Mark did. The Greek text of the first verse is:

τῇ δὲ πρώτῃ τῶν ἀζύμων	(adverbial phrase, dative of reference, modifying the verb *approached*)
προσῆλθον οἱ μαθηταὶ τῷ Ἰησοῦ λέγοντες,	(verb [2nd aorist] + subject + indirect object + present participle)
ποῦ θέλεις ἑτοιμάσωμέν	(adverb + verb [pres. ind.] + verb [1st aorist subj. act.])

---

[62] BAG: *utter in words, say, tell, give expression to.*

[63] J. Harold Greenlee, *A Concise Exegetical Grammar of New Testament Greek* (Grand Rapids: Eerdmans, 1953), p. 32. Also Corey Keating at http://www.ntgreek.org/. 'Dative of Reference - Shows interest in a way that is similar but more remote than that of the indirect object.... It acts to give a frame of reference or context to the statement.... It can be translated with the phrases *with reference to, concerning, about*, or *in regard to.*'

[64] Cf. *Pesahim* 1.3 (Jacob Neusner, trans., *The Mishnah: A New Translation* (New Haven: Yale University Press, 1988), p. 230. [A] 'R. Judah says, "They seek out [leaven] (1) on the night of the fourteenth, (2) on the fourteenth in the morning, and (3) at the time of removal".' Although this was written long after the Last Supper, Rabbi Judah Ha-Nasi (c. 135-219 CE) is not giving a new regulation, but one that had been in effect for generations.

σοι φαγεῖν τὸ πάσχα   (indirect object + verb [present infini-
                                       tive] + object)

Diagram of the Structure of the First Half of the Verse
The disciples | approached
                \ Jesus
                \concerning the first (day) of Unleavened Bread
                \saying
['Where do you want us to prepare for you to eat the Passover?']⁶⁵

If Matthew used Mark, he dropped the καὶ and added the δὲ; dropped the word *day* and the clause *when the Passover was offered*; and reworded part of the rest. I translate: 'The disciples approached Jesus concerning the first (day) of Unleavened Bread, saying, "Where do you want us to prepare for you to eat Passover?"' A smoother translation would be: 'The disciples came to Jesus with a question about the first day of unleavened bread, saying to him, "Where do you want us to prepare for you to eat the Passover?"' For all practical purposes, what the disciples were saying is this. 'Today is Nisan 13, and at sundown the first day of ἀζύμων begins. What are your instructions?'

Albright and Mann came to the conclusion that 'It is possible to translate the Greek by "With reference to the first day of Unleavened Bread."'⁶⁶ But because they did not take into account the time for removing the leaven, they failed to understand that the conversation and the 'arrangements' were made on Nisan 13 and thus, they left the Last Supper on the night following Nisan 14, although they mention as a possible option Jaubert's suggestion 'that Jesus and his disciples followed the old solar calendar, and so kept Passover on a fixed day, Tuesday.'⁶⁷ But as Finegan points out,

> Qumran did not intercalate its calendar but simply allowed the discrepancy to accumulate ... if the calendar was in use from, say, around 124 BC, the discrepancy would have amounted to ... seven or eight

---

⁶⁵ A suggestion for further research: explore other usages of the dative of reference in Greek, how this construction in Matthew and Mark was translated into other languages, like Syriac, Latin, etc., and how it was understood in the writings and liturgy of the Eastern Church.

⁶⁶ W.F. Albright and C.S. Mann, *Matthew, Introduction, Translation and Notes* (*The Anchor Bible*; Garden City: Doubleday, 1971), p. 319:

17. *On the first day of Unleavened Bread.* This would be Nisan 15, the day after the Passover, but Matthew certainly means to indicate that the preparations were being made on the day *before* Passover.... Perhaps the expression as we have it here is not as simple as it appears. It is possible to translate the Greek by 'With reference to the first day of Unleavened Bread ... ' – i.e., the disciples were asking Jesus for guidance as to the procedures to be followed for the next day.

⁶⁷ Albright and Mann, *Matthew*, p. 319.

months by the time of the crucifixion of Jesus, and this in itself provides a difficulty for the theory that the Last Supper was observed in
terms of the Qumran calendar.[68]

R.T. France, who concluded that the Last Supper was held the night
before Passover, comments on the phrase 'the first day of Unleavened
Bread' as follows:

> Properly speaking the feast of *Unleavened Bread* ran from Nisan 15 to
> 21, but Passover day itself, Nisan 14, was loosely included in that pe-
> riod (in fact it was on the evening which began Nisan 14 that leaven
> began to be removed from the houses: Mishnah *Pesahim* 1.1-3), and so
> it is referred to here as *the first day of Unleavened Bread*.[69]

Alfred Plummer also concluded that the Last Supper was held on the
night before Passover, however without clarifying the textual basis. He
said, 'It is best to hold fast to the very clear and thoroughly consistent
statements in the Fourth Gospel, and correct the confused and incon-
sistent Synoptic narratives by them.'[70]

Then the text of Matthew continues,

> [18]And he (Jesus) says, 'Go into the city, to so-and-so's place,[71] and say
> to him, "The Teacher says, 'My time is near; may I, with my disciples,
> do the Passover at your place?'"[72] [19]And the disciples did as Jesus com-
> manded them, and prepared (for) the Passover.[73]

---

[68] Finegan, *Handbook of Biblical Chronology*, p. 49. So also Klawans, 'Was Jesus' Last
Supper a Seder?', p. 47, n.5, where he points out that this calendar had no intercalation,
'And without intercalation, by Jesus' time, Jubilee's 364-day solar calendar would be off
not just by days, but by months.'

[69] R.T. France, *The Gospel according to Matthew, an Introduction and Commentary* (Grand
Rapids: Eerdmans, 1985), pp. 364-65. He also points out, citing J. Finegan, *Handbook of
Biblical Chronology*, pp. 292-296, 'that according to astronomical calculations Nisan 15
never fell on a Friday between AD 27 and 34.'

[70] Plummer, Alfred, *An Exegetical Commentary on the Gospel according to St. Matthew*
(Grand Rapids: Baker Book House, 1982), p. 357.

[71] Hagner (*Matthew 14-18*, p. 764) comments, 'to someone known but not identified'.

[72] By taking 'ποιως' as a present subjunctive rather than a present indicative, it seems
to me to make a question. The place may have been, and probably was, the same 'upper
room' that we know about in Acts 1 and 2, which was the home of the family of John
Mark, whose mother was named Mary. The present indicative (with a future meaning),
viz. 'I am [will be] doing or celebrating the Passover at your place, with my disciples,'
seems rather blunt. See Percy J. Heawood, 'The Time of the Last Supper', *JQR* 42
(1951), pp. 37-44. He pointed out that 'עשׂה (LXX ποιως)' is used, in connection with the
Passover, 32 times in the OT; also 'compare πεποίηκεν τὸ πάσχα, of Moses, in Heb.
11.28' (pp. 43-44).

[73] See Alberto Mello, *Evangile selon Saint Matthieu,* p. 449. The French text of Mt.
26.18 used by Aimee Chevillon in translating Mello (from the Italian original) is as fol-

As is known from many sources, pilgrims came from near and far and made arrangements for accommodation in Jerusalem. Jesus and his disciples had been nearby at Bethany for several days, but at this time they are about to move to a location in Jerusalem, as required by the Law of Moses. The two Greek phrases πρὸς τὸν δεῖνα and προς σε are equivalent in French, respectively, to *chez un tel* (at so-and-so's place) and *chez vous* (at your place or in your home).

Then Matthew records the Last Supper and no mention is made to any thing that would identify the supper with the Passover meal itself. Jesus had, of course, made mention of his intention to 'do the Passover', which very well may have been a code term for his death, which he was announcing as imminent. It could have had a double meaning. To the disciples and to the owner of the house, it was probably understood to refer to using the facility for a week or more. For Jesus it was about the fulfillment of his mission.

After the supper, the teaching and the prayer in Gethsemane, he is arrested and tried before the religious authorities and then sent to the Roman Governor because only he could give the death penalty, which was what was being sought. All the activity on the part of the religious establishment during Thursday night and the day Friday is really strange if this is the solemn night of the Passover meal and Friday is the Day of Holy Convocation, when no servile labor was to be done.

Why the traditional interpretation?

One might ask why these two constructions in Mark and Matthew came to be understood in the way they are commonly understood, viz., as 'on the first day'. I believe there are two main reasons. First, the phrase, even in the nominative, speaks about a specific time, viz., the first day (or the first) of unleavened (bread). And second, the dative case is often used for 'on or at the time indicated.'[74] However this is not the only usage of the dative; it also means 'about or concerning' something and 'to or for' someone, as well as the meanings it carries as instrumental and locative.[75] But the question that is posed by the disciples is specifically focused on the time referred to in the dative, and this fact points towards a solution.

---

lows: 'Il dit: "Allez en ville chez un tel et dites-lui: 'Le Maitre dit: Mon temps est proche; je fais la Pâque chez toi avec mes disciples".'

[74] Note that no preposition is used by either writer; the meaning rests solely on the interpretation of the case.

[75] And of course, the same form in the Koine is also instrumental and locative.

VI. The Chronology of the Passover in Luke

Luke opens the story of the passion (22.1-6), much as Mathew and Mark do.

> ¹Now the Feast of Unleavened Bread (ἀζύμων), which is called Passover, was getting near. ²And the high priests and the scribes were looking for a way to put him to death, for they feared the people. ³Then Satan entered into Judas, called Iscariot, who was one of the Twelve. ⁴So he went to the chief priests and temple guards and discussed how to betray him to them. ⁵They were glad and agreed to give him money. ⁶And he consented and was looking for an opportunity to betray him without public notice.

Luke opens the story of making the arrangements for a room (22.7-13) by saying, 'The day of ἀζύμων came, in which it was necessary to offer the Passover (Lambs).[76] And he sent Peter and John saying, "Go and prepare for us, so that we may eat the Passover".'[77] The day is specified as the day of the slaughter (Nisan 14), which began at sunset following the 13th.

The verb used in the first sentence is 'came' (ἦλθεν, 2 aorist of ἔρχομαι) and the question of time arises. Is the morning of Nisan 13 too soon to say that the day for the removal of the leaven and for the slaughter of the Lambs has come? Nisan 14 begins at six o'clock tonight, soon thereafter the leaven must be removed, and the final arrangements for the room have not been made! Unless one dismisses completely the activity of removing the leaven, one must understand that the only time for preparing a room before the 14th began at sundown was during the day of the 13th. Even on the morning of the 13th, one was only hours away from the prescribed time for collecting the leaven.[78] So Peter and John go, follow their instructions, and make the necessary preparations.

Then Luke continues (vv. 14-15), 'And when it was supper-time, he sat down with his apostles and said to them, "Oh! How much I have wanted to eat this Passover with you before I suffer. [But this can not be,][79] for I tell you that I will not eat of it at all until it be fulfilled

---

[76] ἦλθεν (verb) δὲ, (postpositive enclitic)

ἡ ἡμέρα τῶν ἀζύμων (subject),

[ἐν] (preposition) ᾗ (relative pronoun)

ἔδει θύεσθαι (finite verb + infinitive) τὸ πάσχα (direct object).

[77] καὶ ἀπέστειλεν Πέτρον καὶ Ἰωάννην εἰπών   conjunction + verb + direct objects + participle

πορευθέντες ἑτοιμάσατε ἡμῖν   participle + imperative + indirect object + direct object

τὸ πάσχα ἵνα φάγωμεν   conjunction + subj. verb

[78] It is like saying on the morning of Christmas eve (with respect to dinner the next day), 'Well, Christmas is here; what is left to be done?'

[79] See BAG 151, 1.e.

in the kingdom of God".'[80] This, in itself, shows that Jesus is speaking before the time of eating the Passover meal.

He then takes a cup and says, 'Take this and share it with each other! For I tell you, I shall not drink of the fruit of the vine any more until the Kingdom of God shall have come.'

And How about the Leaven?

As one reads the different accounts of the Last Supper, is there any mention of leaven? Well, no, not explicitly. But so much of what Jesus did was symbolic and one could say, almost 'in parables'. All three of the Synoptics record the saying of Jesus about 'the leaven of the Pharisees' (Mt. 16.6; Mk 8.15; Lk. 12.1). In that context he is referring to their ill intent and hypocrisy in trying to entrap him and silence him. In the light of this statement, it is interesting to note that Judas had yielded to such a temptation and had made a deal with the authorities before the meeting that night in the upper room. And that night Jesus revealed that Judas was the one who would betray him.[81] See the following chart.

Activity	Matthew	Mark	Luke
1. Judas Contacted Priests	26.14-16	14.10-11	22.3-6
2. The Preparation	26.17-19	14.12-16	22.7-13
3. LS: Jesus Announces Betrayal	26.20-25	14.17-21	22.21-23 ↓
4. Last Supper: Institution	26.26-29	14.22-25	22.14-20 ↑
5. Who is the greatest?	———	———	22.24-30
6. Denial of Peter	26.30-35	14.26-31	22.31-34

The Removal of the Leaven

How Jesus went about the ceremonial removal of the leaven that night is anyone's guess. Mine is that it was in the traditional way, in order to fulfill all the requirements of the Law. Following that he dealt with the more spiritual dimensions of things, including, not only his betrayal by Judas, but also his denial by Peter and the carnal argument among all of them about 'Who would be the greatest?'

This may be reflected in the early Christian attitude revealed in what Paul wrote in his first letter to the Corinthians (1 Cor. 5.6b-8):

---

[80] Cf. translation of Ferrar Fenton: "[15]And He said to them: I have longingly desired [*epithumia epethumesa*] to eat this Passover with you before My suffering; [16]however, I tell you that I shall not eat of it, until it can be administered in the kingdom of God.' (*The Holy Bible in Modern English*).

[81] παραδίδωμι is translated *betrayed* because that is how it was remembered in what was passed on to Paul (1 Cor. 11.23). Theologically I interpret that to mean that we all betrayed him.

Do you not know that a little leaven leavens the whole batch of dough? Clean out the old leaven, so that the batch may be new, since it is unleavened. For Christ our Passover Lamb was already offered in sacrifice. So, let us celebrate the feast, not with the old leaven, and not with the leaven of ill-will and wickedness, but with the unleavened bread of sincerity and truth.

In fact Paul's agenda with the Corinthians could almost be stated in terms of removing the leaven from the church: e.g. false understanding and veneration of leaders (1.10–4.21); tolerance and approval of fornication (5.1-13); settling disputes in secular courts (6.1-20); misunderstanding of and misguided teaching on sex and marriage (7.1-40); pushing the limits of one's rights vis-à-vis idolatry (8.1-11.1); misunderstanding their cultural liberation (11.1-16); and even disorder with inappropriate attitude and behavior at the Lord's Supper (11.17-34). Also I would suggest that Paul's exhortation to 'examine oneself' before approaching the Table of the Lord echoes the removal of the leaven before the feast. It also has to do with holiness and holy living.

VI. Other Support for this Interpretation

The History of the Church

Several things in the history of the Church point to the fact that the Last Supper was not a Passover Meal. Various church fathers, as already mentioned, make explicit statements that confirm this thesis. Also the fact that the Eastern Orthodox Church uses leavened and not unleavened bread for the Eucharist points in the same direction.[82] And it is very interesting that most of Christian art, especially the earliest, does not represent the Last Supper as a Passover.[83]

Conclusion

Almost all scholars recognize that there is a problem in the Synoptics vis-à-vis John; several, who feel compelled to follow the Synoptics, even think that the chronology of John is correct, and suggest that, either the Synoptic writers got it wrong or there was a corruption in

[82] Although Luz holds that the Last Supper was a Passover (as against the Gospel of John), he gives a good documentation of the position of the Eastern Orthodox Church, which follows the Johannine dating (pp. 355-57).

[83] A mosaic of the 6th century in S. Appolinare Nuovo, Ravenna, shows Jesus and the apostles at the table with a round platter containing two fish. The symbolism probably reflects the anagram, ΙΧΘΥΣ (Jesus Christ, Son of God and Savior). See also V. Denis, 'Iconography of Last Supper', *New Catholic Encyclopedia* (New York: McGraw-Hill Book Company, 1967), Vol. VIII, p. 399-401; and H. Leclercq, 'Cène', *Dictionnaire d'archéologie chrétienne et de liturgie*, Vol. VI, cols. 3045-3047.

the sources they used. Regrettably, the paragraph titles that are assigned to the pericopes in Matthew and Mark by UBS Greek New Testament take the side of the generally understood (or I would say, misunderstood) interpretation of the Synoptics.[84]

Carr, in his commentary on Matthew,[85] came to the same basic chronology that is proposed in this paper, while, at the same time, acknowledging that 'the events of the Passover are full of difficulty for the harmonist.'[86] He sees the character of the Last Supper as 'paschal' and suggests that it followed 'the paschal ceremonial'; however without the Passover lamb. But he did not propose a way of reading the text of the Synoptics that would harmonize with John, as I have endeavored to do.

I find Carr to be very suggestive in the points of correlation that he points out between the Passover ritual and what Jesus did that night:

(a) The meal began with a cup of red wine mixed with water; this is the *first* cup mentioned, Luke xxii. 17. After this the guests washed their hands. Here probably must be placed the washing of the disciples' feet, John xiii.

(b) The bitter herbs ... were then brought in together with the unleavened cakes and a sauce called *charoseth*, made of fruits and vinegar, into which the unleavened bread and bitter herbs are dipped. This explains 'He it is, to whom I shall give a *sop*,' John xiii. 26.

(c) The *second* cup was then mixed and blessed like the first. The father then explained the meaning of the rite (Ex xiii. 8). This was the *haggadah* or 'shewing forth,' a term transferred by St Paul to the Christian meaning of the rite (1 Cor. xi. 26). The first part of the '*hallel*' (Psalms cxiii. and cxiv.) was then chanted by the company.

(d) After this the paschal lamb was placed before the guests.... But at the Last Supper there was no paschal lamb.... At this point, Jesus 'took bread and blessed it, and gave it to his disciples' (v. 26).

(e) The *third* cup, or the cup of blessing, so called because a special blessing was pronounced upon it, followed: 'after *supper* he took the cup' (Luke). 'He took the cup *when he had supped*' (Paul). This is the 'cup' named in v. 27.

(f) After a *fourth* cup the company chanted (see v. 30) the second part of the *hallel* (Psalms cxv-cxviii).[87]

[84] 'The Passover with the Disciples' [Mt. 26.17; Mk 14.12; the parallel in Luke (22.14) is 'The Institution of the Lord's Supper'], while the previous paragraph is 'The Preparation of the Passover'. In John there is no reference to the Passover in the titles.

[85] A. Carr, *The Gospel according to St. Matthew* (Cambridge: University Press, 1896).

[86] Carr, *The Gospel according to St. Matthew*, p. 201.

[87] Carr, *The Gospel according to St. Matthew*, pp. 202-203. The words of Jesus in Matthew (26.18) would seem to confirm such an understanding. Note that the disciples had asked, 'Where do you want us to prepare for you to *eat* the Passover?' But the answer of Jesus, giving words to the master of the house, was, 'I will *do* (not *eat*) the Passover at your house.'

I would suggest that the last supper was a concluding farewell, al-most like a 'graduation-commencement' event, deeply imbued with the theme of Passover. In it the Master is giving his final, in-the-flesh teaching; and at the same time, he is encouraging, and warning, his chosen few. It was held on Thursday night, the beginning of Nisan 14, before the Passover Meal that would follow on Friday night, Nisan 15. The theme of the removal of the leaven was dealt with in the ways suggested, but there was no lamb on the table. The Lamb was at the table and offered himself in parabolic action, which was to be fulfilled the following day in literal terms. 'This is my body!' 'This is my blood!'

★★★★★★★★★★★★★★★★★★

Abstract

The Last Supper, as presented in the synoptic Gospels, is generally interpreted as a Passover *Seder*. John, on the other hand, clearly presents it as occurring on the night before Passover. The purpose of this paper is to suggest a solution to this tension: first, by noting what was required to be done to prepare for the Passover meal, as this was celebrated in the first century, and second: by look-ing carefully at the key passage to the chronology in the Synoptics, viz., the one about making arrangements for the room in Jerusalem. The conclusion of this paper is that the Last Supper occurred the night before the Passover and that it was not a Passover *Seder*. Therefore, when Jesus was crucified on Friday (Nisan 14), it was at the time of the offering of the lambs in the temple.

5

Paul, Crucifixion, and Sanctification in Galatians

J. Ayodeji Adewuya[*]

> ... justification demands holiness of life. God does not justify in order
> to allow a person to continue in sin. To be justified anticipates the pur-
> suit of holiness or sanctification; this is also essential to the saved expe-
> rience (Hebrews 12:14) – R. Hollis Gause. [1]

Sanctification – What's that?

It's amazing how quickly things come in and out of fashion. From
music to fashion, from philosophies to personalities, we live in an ever-
changing world and the Church is not immune to such changes. It is
unfortunate, however, when such changes pertain to important beliefs
such as holiness. Although it is both generally recognized and widely
accepted that Christians ought to be holy, there continues to be a
strong disagreement as to whether holiness on some real and recogniz-
able level is possible in this life. Yet the New Testament has much to
say about holiness or sanctification.

The Pauline writings, in particular, clearly show that believers can
be holy in a greater sense of not just being separated for God but also
living a life of moral purity, ethical righteousness, and spiritual victory
day by day.[2] As the study of Paul's letters reveals, it is unmistakably
clear that one of his overriding or primary concerns is the moral implications of the faith of a person *in Christ*, something which, in theology,
is generally termed sanctification.

As a pastor-missionary-theologian, Paul's concern for sanctification
is evident in his paraenesis and prayers (cf. Rom. 12.1-2; 1 Cor. 5.1-
13; Phil. 1.9-11; 1 Thess. 4.1-7; 5.23-24; 2 Cor. 6.14–7.1). When
addressing the issue of sanctification in different contexts, Paul, as part

---

[*] J. Ayodeji Adewuya (Ph.D., University of Manchester) is Professor of Greek and
New Testament at the Pentecostal Theological Seminary, Cleveland, TN.
[1] R. Hollis Gause, *The Preaching of Paul: A Study of Romans* (Cleveland, TN: Church
of God Department of General Education, 1986), p. 74 n. 16.
[2] J. Harold Greenlee, *What the New Testament Says about Holiness* (Ohio: Schmul,
1994), p. 18.

of his rhetorical strategy, employs different metaphors such as cleansing, crucifixion, purification, yielding to God, etc., both to define sanctification as well as describe its experiential reality/ies in the believer's life. This study is a brief examination of the life of holiness that is required of the saved person beyond the initial experience of justification. The primary attention will be focused on Paul's use of the crucifixion metaphor for the understanding of holiness in the letter. It is a metaphor that, curiously, with various nuances, appears most in Paul's letter to the Galatians, occurring in Gal. 2.20; 5.24; 6.14, three important texts that will be examined in their respective contexts later below. Evidently, Paul maintains a close connection between the believer's justification and sanctification, the latter presuming the former. As Vincent Taylor rightly states, 'the reconciling work of God is itself a sanctifying activity, in the sense that the believer is set apart and consecrated to holy ends and purposes; but in the Christian experience, both in its personal and communal aspects, this divine separation remains and needs to be worked out in a life of ethical and spiritual progress.'[3]

How then should we live?
Through the medium of his letters, Paul continued to serve as a pastor. He dealt with the problems facing real people in the mid-first century as they struggled to understand their identity as Christians. Paul carried out his pastoral task, however, as a theologian also. He appealed to authoritative formulas of faith (see Rom. 1.3-4; 1 Cor. 15.3-5; Phil. 2.6-11; etc.) and the Scriptures. He reflected on the implications of Jesus' death and resurrection, drawing consequences for Christians' conduct and behavior. Paul resolved disputes on theological principles. It is thus clear that Paul's letters are the work of a pastoral theologian.

Reading Paul's letters to various congregations, one cannot but notice that a significant struggle most of the Pauline churches faced was that of identity. The Pauline churches struggled with the issue of identity in two ways. First is the problem of identity in relation to the Jews, and particularly the rite of circumcision. In this regard, the question that needs to be answered relates to the conditions a person would need to fulfill in order to become part of God's people? The issue of Gentile-Christian identity vis-à-vis Jewish Christianity and Judaism was among the most pressing matters that Paul treated in Galatians. Paul sought to explain to Gentiles why they did not have to take up circumcision and Torah observances to become Christians. He tried to make clear to Jewish Christians that they should not impose their kind

---

[3] Vincent Taylor, *Forgiveness and Reconciliation: A Study in New Testament Theology* (London: Macmillan, 1946), p. 144.

of Christianity upon Gentiles. He wanted both Christian groups to live in harmony and mutual respect.

For Paul, the Galatians, although gentiles by birth, have, through their belief in Jesus Christ – his death by crucifixion and resurrection, become part of God's holy people. Moreover, the Spirit has been poured out. They need nothing in addition to these. Second is the problem of how the churches were to relate to the wider Greco-Roman society in which they were situated. This essentially is the issue of lifestyle, that is, how, having become the people of God, believers should live both in a hostile society whose values and principles are often opposed to theirs. Inseparably connected with this is how the members of the believing community were to relate with one another as the holy people of God. In short, Paul has to set out the implications of the gospel for the life of the community.

In addressing these issues, one must note two important strategies that Paul consistently employs. First, when Paul addresses moral or behavioral issues both in his life and those of his converts, he does so with reference to the legacy of his and their past. Hence, his frequent formula, "once you were … now you are" (cf. 1 Cor. 6.9-11; Eph. 2.1-10; Phil. 3.5-10; 1 Tim. 2.15) which he uses both to impress upon and remind them of their new status – who they were, whose they were, and the ethical responsibility that goes with it. Second, as part of his rhetorical strategy, Paul always *shares a testimony*. He often refers to himself not only for apologetic purposes such as one finds in many of his letters, but also as a powerful tool of showing the transforming power of the Gospel that he proclaims. In doing so he also presents himself as a worthy example to be emulated. Hence, he could confidently admonish his converts to imitate him (1 Cor. 11.1). Attention must now be turned to an examination of the relevant passages.

Galatians 2.19-20

> For through the law I died to the law in order that I might live unto God. I have been crucified with Christ. [20]I no longer live but Christ lives in me. And the life which I now live in the flesh, I live by faith in the Son of God, who loved me and gave Himself for me.

Galatians 2.19-20 is one of the most known and significant Pauline texts, a passage that, as earlier said, needs to be examined in context for its proper understanding. It comes at the end of the autobiographical section of the book (Gal. 2.11-20) where Paul writes about the truth of justification by faith, the central gospel truth of the letter. Paul has made it clear that one is not justified by works of the law but through faith in Jesus Christ (2.16).

For the opponents of Paul, to preach justification by faith and not by the works of the law is to make Christians no better than 'Gentile sinners' (2.15), since such preaching would have led the Gentiles to ignore the ethical demands of the law (2.17). Such reasoning, as advanced by Paul's opponents would have meant that the Gentile converts of Paul are 'found to be sinners', further leading to the wrong conclusion that Christ is an 'agent of sin' (2.17). Paul refutes their conclusion in a forceful manner and goes on to turn their arguments back upon them, arguing that if the Galatians were to turn back to the works of the law as the opponents of Paul urged, then believers (both Paul and his converts), would have become again transgressors (2.18). Arguing this way, Paul shows the radical nature of the gospel which he proclaimed and which he is now defending.

For Paul, any attempt to secure acceptance by God on the basis of the works of the law puts a person in direct opposition to what God has revealed and provided for in Christ Jesus, namely justification by faith. As Ziesler rightly notes, 'the real sin is not infringing the law, but in disloyalty to Christ and the new way of acceptability in and through him.'[4] Hence, as Hansen suggests, 'Paul refuses to reconstruct the barrier of the law between Jews and Gentiles because he had died to the law in his experience of the cross of Christ.'[5] As such, the theological basis of Christian ethics will have to be redefined.[6] In order to seal his argument and further explicate the meaning of what he has just said, Paul makes a startling statement, giving a personal testimony: 'For through the law I died to the law' (Gal. 2.19). He does not only present himself as a paradigm for his converts specifically, and believers in general, but he also presents, in a nutshell, the essence of his own theology. He talks about his own death to the law in a manner reminiscent of Rom. 7.1-6. Although the word 'I' may be taken either in a strict personal sense or paradigmatically,[7] it seems inconceivable to see the word as completely devoid of personal overtone or lacking reference to a personal concrete experience. However, one should be careful not to limit what Paul was saying to his personal experience, since

[4] J. Ziesler, *The Meaning of Righteousness in Paul: A Linguistic and Theological Inquiry* (SNTMS 20; Cambridge: Cambridge University Press, 1972), p. 173.

[5] G. Walter Hansen, 'A Paradigm of the Apocalypse: The Gospel in the Light of Epistolary Analysis' in *The Galatians Debate* (ed. Mark Nanos; Peabody, MA: Hendrickson, 2002), p. 148.

[6] B.C. Lategan, 'Is Paul Defending His Apostleship in Galatians? The Function of Galatians 1:11-12 and 2:19-20 in the Development of Paul's Argument', *NTS* 34 (1988), p. 429.

[7] So Richard N. Longenecker, *Galatians* (WBC 41; Dallas: Word Books, 1990), p. 91; Robert Tannehill, *Dying and Rising with Christ: A Study in Pauline Theology* (Berlin: Töpelmann, 1967), p. 55.

what he is saying is valid for every Christian.[8] Here, 'to the law' and 'for God' (cf. Rom. 6.2, 10-11), are placed over against each other to indicate to whom the believer belongs and is subject to. Paul once again reveals his thought of the law as a power that is hostile to (sinful) humans, which brings humans under its jurisdiction, which obstructs the way to life. To this law Paul has now died. His death with Christ (crucifixion with Christ), which he goes on to discuss in the latter part of the verse, results in death to the law and its slavish control.

Christ's death satisfied the demands of the law and nullified its lord-ship both over him and over those who are bound in solidarity with him, those who, like him, have died to sin. Believers, of whom Paul was representative, have been crucified with Christ as a result of which they had become free from the bondage of the law. They are now free to live a mode of existence that is no longer dominated by law. The thought here is that, as in Christ's death on the cross, the believer has died to the powers of sin, world and law, so also in the resurrection of Christ he has been set at liberty for God, in order to live for him, un-der his control. The demands of the law have been fully satisfied and therefore, the law has no more hold on the believer.

The positive side of dying to the law is indicated in the subordinate clause, 'that I may live for God' (Gal. 2.19). The affinity of these verses with the passage in Rom. 6.3-7 is quite striking. A personal appropria-tion of Christ's death and identification with his crucifixion takes place at conversion-baptism. Through faith Christ's death becomes one's own death. For Paul, freedom means transfer from one dominion to another: from law to grace (Rom. 6.14), from sin to righteousness (Rom. 6.18), from death to life (Rom. 6.21-23), and in this place, from self to Christ. This is the very essence of the believer's faith-union relationship with God, a relationship which although could be understood in terms of discipleship, certainly means more. The phrase is reminiscent of Rom. 6.10 and it portrays the believer's faith relation-ship with Christ. When Paul speaks of the believer's past resurrection with Christ, he has in view as well an experience in the actual life his-tory of the believer. Paul is talking in terms of a faith-union relation-ship with Christ, which begins at conversion-baptism. Being raised with Christ is an aspect of being joined with him existentially.

Paul's death to the law was inseparably connected to the person and mission of the crucified Jesus. Thus he proclaims, 'I have been cruci-fied with Christ.' What does Paul mean? Does this refer to self-crucifixion or is it to be construed as merely a reference to self-denial? Or, does it mean more? The passive form of the Greek verb crucify

---

[8] Tannehill, *Dying and Rising*, p. 57.

(συνεσταύρωμαι – 'I have been crucified') suggests that crucifixion in the text is done to the believer. Hence, at first sight, the statement could be understood in a forensic or juridical sense. However, the perfect tense points to a completed action, an indication that, while on the one hand it is not a repeated act that is to be re-enacted in the Christian's life, on the other hand, it has a continuous experiential effect. As such it could be said that the believer, having died according to God's reckoning at Calvary, continues to experience Christ's crucifixion and its attendant benefits. This is the import of the preposition σύν, which in most cases, connotes the believer's 'with-ness' or participation in the event of Christ's crucifixion. This preposition suggests that by crucifixion with Christ, Paul meant more than a positional identification with the Cross. It includes an existential reality by which he personally experienced a crucifixion. When it is suggested that believers are crucified with Christ, it needs to be understood as being more than a figure of speech describing a psychological separation or deliverance from sin. The death and resurrection of Christ are not only historical events but events in which, through faith-union with him, His people have come to share. The point is that death with Christ is the only way that those enslaved by the law can find freedom.

What one finds in Gal. 2.20 is a greater detail of what Paul has stated more generally in v. 19. The counterpart of death with Christ is always resurrection and a new life in Him. Crucifixion with Christ is significant only because it made the new life possible. For Paul, the resurrection forms an integral part of God's redeeming operation. Not only may such an impression be drawn from the present context, but also such a conclusion may be drawn from passages where Paul plainly connects the resurrection with the redemption of humanity.[9] The death and resurrection of Christ are regarded as inseparable coefficients of the same mighty achievement. For Paul, the cross is unintelligible apart from the resurrection.[10] Here Paul interprets the death of Christ from his experience of the risen Lord. This he does by linking 'dying to the law' and 'crucifixion with Christ' to living for God. There is, here, an unmistakable affinity to Rom. 7.4, 6. The death to the law spoken of (v. 19a) is correlative with death to sin (cf. Rom. 7.4, 6; 6.6, 18, 22). Therefore, since this death is described in terms of solidarity with Christ in his crucifixion, the life, which forms its pointed contrast, should be understood in terms of solidarity in his resurrection. Moreover, since this life is obviously life in the individual, existential

---

[9] Phil. 3.10; Gal. 1.1-4.

[10] H.A.A. Kennedy, *The Theology of the Epistles* (Edinburgh: University Press, 1919), p. 71.

union with Christ ('Christ in me'), the co-crucifixion and the co-
resurrection in view must also be primarily experiential in nature.

Paul goes on to describe the result of the union with Christ that
started at conversion (justification) as a life that is lived by faith while
still 'in the flesh' (ἐν σαρκί). The reference to flesh in this verse does
not carry the negative ethical connotations that one sees later in the
letter. Although the emphatic personal pronoun could simply be a
reflexive emphatic construction thus suggesting the translation as: 'I
myself no longer live', the result of Paul's crucifixion with Christ is
particularly striking if one were translate the statement literally as: 'I no
longer I, but lives in me Christ.' This is very significant in light of what
follows. Paul is simply saying, 'I do not live any longer as I once did,
but in a new way – *no longer I*, now Christ lives in me – He is the Lord
of my new life.' Paul has surrendered his sovereignty to Christ. The
word 'flesh' as used here is to be understood as the human body without any ethical connotation. The statement is a contrast between life
'under the law' and the 'life under grace' that becomes a reality when a
person is converted. It is a new life, the reality of which is known and
experienced by faith.[11] It means that by faith, a person makes Christ's
death his/her own with the present benefit of the power of sin having
been broken in his/her life and leading to a new life that is described in
v. 20. Paul lives in the eschatological tension of already/not yet. While
on the one hand the life of the new age which is designated as 'in
Christ' has begun, on the other hand he continues to live in the flesh.
Believers are left with an inevitable tension between the datable, historical and unrepeatable acts of Christ's death and resurrection on the
one hand and the application and realization of those acts in the believer's life on the other.

Summarizing what has been argued thus far, it is clear that Paul's
main emphasis in Gal. 2.19-20 is a concern with the believer's ethical
life that results from his/her relationship with Christ that begins at
justification. As Lategan rightly states, 'it is a life in faith and a life for
God, of which the ethical "style" is at the same time exemplified by
the event of the cross.... Theology and ethics remain inseparable in
Paul's thinking.'[12] Paul was talking about a faith-union relationship
with the crucified and risen Lord. His testimony illustrates that the
gospel's call is that to a holy life that is characterized by a person's self-

---

[11] This faith denotes a personal relationship with Christ. The relative pronoun 'which'
(ὅ) is an accusative of content and is probably to be taken as a substantival synonym for
life (cf. Longenecker, *Galatians*, p. 93).

[12] B.C. Lategan, 'The Argumentative Situation of Galatians', in *The Galatians Debate*,
p. 393.

abandoning surrender of one's former way of life. Furthermore, Gal. 2.20 holds out the prospect of God's enablement to live a sanctified life, one that is received and appropriated by faith.

For Paul, believers now have a new mode of existence. It is not just an existence dominated by a new psychological motivation. As Cauthron succinctly states, 'the motivating principle of Christian living is no longer the self-centered attempt to be worthy of God's favor. It is rather the selfless giving of gratitude and profound appreciation for all that God has done for us and in us by His grace.'[13] As a result of the indwelling Christ, the believer is supplied with a new principle of activity on the ontological level of his/her very being. Paul does not leave the reader in doubt that he has in mind his initial conversion experience and more. It involves a dynamic, ongoing and intimate relationship with the Lord that is grounded in a life of holiness. It should also be noted that whatever holds true for Paul in these verses, also holds true for all believers.

Galatians 5.24

> But those who belong to Christ Jesus have crucified the flesh with its passions and desires.

Galatians 5.24 is the climax of the first unit (Gal. 5.13-24) of the paraenetic section of the letter (5.13–6.10). It is helpful to examine briefly how Paul builds up his argument to that point. In this verse, Paul more or less repeats what he has already said in v. 1a: 'For freedom Christ has set us free'. In v. 1 he had continued: 'Stand fast, therefore, and do not submit again to a yoke of slavery', that is, do not become subject to the law (cf. 4.21). The continuation in v. 13, however, is different, although the freedom's opposite, the theme of 'slavery', is likewise repeated: 'only do not use your freedom as an opportunity for the flesh, but through love become slaves to one another'. Paul recognizes that freedom can be bent to justify harmful behavior. As such, the believer's liberty is seen as freedom from restraints even of the moral law. Paul suggests otherwise. Such a way of interpreting freedom should and could not be. Instead, he forcefully asserts, freedom must not be used as a means of self-indulgence. For Paul, mutual service and love of neighbor is seen as a curb on any kind of wrongly understood freedom. In vv. 14-15, then, this love of neighbor is further inculcated.

---

[13] Hal A. Cauthron, 'Holiness – a Matter of Dying', in *Biblical Resources for Holiness Preaching: From Text to Sermon* (ed. H. Ray Dunning and Neil B. Wiseman; Kansas City: Beacon Hill, 1990), p. 248.

But how could the Galatians live that life of love? Paul provides the answer in v. 16. They must continue living by the Spirit. Thus, Paul sets the stage for the following contrast of the two ways of living – living by the flesh and living by the Spirit. As Howard suggests, '... Spirit is neither the human spirit nor the divine Spirit considered independently of each other, but the divine Spirit as He indwells the human spirit'.[14]

As it is often in Paul's thought, one discovers the significance of a concept by first understanding its opposite. So, before giving further explanation on how living by the Spirit is to be manifested, he describes the opposite, 'life in the flesh', an indication that all was not well in the Galatian church. A brief discussion of Paul's use of the term 'flesh' is necessary at this juncture particularly as a misunderstanding of its usage by Paul has greatly contributed to an attitude of defeatism among some believers. Such people opine that as long as one is in the 'flesh' there is no possibility of victory over sin. Furthermore, in scholarship, Paul's use of flesh has been variously understood. For example, Bultmann understands flesh as human total mode of existence and equates sin with 'flesh'.[15] Bultmann's analysis of the idea of 'flesh' is dominated by a dualistic conception of humans, which in the final analysis is not ethical but natural, and for which in the whole of his theology he wrongly appeals to Paul. Bultmann, however, is compelled to acknowledge that sometimes 'flesh' is personified and as such practically becomes equivalent to 'I'.[16] On Gal. 5.19-21, he argues that the 'works of the flesh' do not primarily have their orientation towards externality and the outward realm of the earthly-natural. Such sins as enmity, jealousy, selfishness may or may not have their manifestation in the realm of external relationships. They are self-centered rather than God-centered. Hence, the flesh is a person seeking his/her own ends in opposition to the Spirit of God. Thus, Bultmann is forced to exegete some phrases e.g. 'when we were in the flesh' (Rom. 7.5) and 'you are not in the flesh, you are in the Spirit' (Rom. 8.9) proleptically to refer in a promissory manner to the glorified state.[17] This does injus-

---

[14] Cf. Richard E. Howard, *Galatians*, vol. I (Beacon Bible Commentary; Kansas City: Beacon Hill Press, 1965), p. 93.

[15] Cf. R. Bultmann, *Theology of the New Testament*, vol. I (trans. Kendrick Grobel; New York: Charles Scribner, 1955), pp. 232-39. Hermann Ridderbos, *Paul: An Outline of His Theology* (trans. John R. de Witt; Grand Rapids: Eerdmans, 1975), 101, criticizes Bultmann's views. He states: 'What is deceptive in Bultmann's interpretation is that with the idea of sin as "flesh" he starts once again from the flesh as humanly limited, etc., as though it were especially therein that the point of contact for sin lay; whereas for Paul "flesh" denotes sin in the whole of its purport as turned away from and averse to God'.

[16] Bultmann, *Theology*, vol. I, p. 245.

[17] Bultmann, *Theology*, vol. I, p. 236.

tice to Paul's meaning. Paul could talk about a person who is 'in the Spirit' and yet lives 'in the flesh' (Gal. 2.20). At the same time, while this person continues to live in the body and in the natural world, he/she is no longer in the flesh but in the Spirit because the Spirit of God dwells within him. Another example is Whiteley who understands flesh as a reference to the 'lower nature'.[18] He argues that, when used in a moral sense, 'flesh' does not necessarily have any physical meaning, since most of the sins ascribed (cf. Gal. 5.19-21) to the lower nature (flesh) could well be practiced by a disembodied spirit. He then went on to say that flesh sometimes means 'sin'.[19] Whiteley's usage of lower nature, which he sometimes interchanges with 'flesh', is not only unclear but confusing. The definition is imprecise. To conceive of the flesh as the lower nature (undefined) implies that there is a nature in humans that is capable of goodness, and, in a similar manner, that there is a nature which is doomed to evil.[20] To apply such a conclusion to our context also implies that the believer is made up of two natures. As a result, a believer lives two lives – serving God with higher (or new) nature and serving sin with lower (old) nature. Such a bifurcation does serious violence to the thought of Paul and entirely misses his point.[21] He does not suggest that there are two opposing, warring factions within the life of the Christian, with either opponent seeking supremacy over the other. Paul does not paint the picture of the believer here as that of a schizophrenic, or a split personality. Paul could talk about a person who is 'in the Spirit' and yet lives 'in the flesh' (Gal. 2.20). He does not allow an idea for constitutional sinfulness – that is, locating sin in the physical body and leaving no room for deliverance from sin until physical death.

Without doubt Paul uses the word flesh in quite a number of ways. However, two distinct meanings are present, 'ethical' and 'non-ethical'. Hence, it requires some care in determining what 'flesh' means in a particular context. What is provided here is a summary.[22] It

[18] D.E.H. Whiteley, *The Theology of St. Paul* (Philadelphia: Fortress, 1964), p. 39. He himself notes that the language he used is dualistic. However, he rightly maintains that Paul presents a 'modified' monistic (unitary) view of the person. He states: 'St. Paul's anthropology is "close-knit" and may reasonably be called "monistic". But on rare occasions, when dealing with non-normal situations, such as death and a possible out of the body experience, he employs a dualistic language.'

[19] Whiteley, *Theology*, p. 39.

[20] William Barclay, *Flesh and Spirit* (Grand Rapids: Baker, 1976), p. 21. He also comments: 'The trouble about such a view is that the rot … is all through human nature; the entire structure is tainted'.

[21] Howard, *Galatians*, p. 95.

[22] For further discussions on Paul's use of 'flesh', the reader may consult any standard scholarly work on the theology of Paul.

helps to realize that, whenever Paul uses the word, he does so in his description of humanity's actual situation. For example, having described the Corinthians as fleshly he goes on to explicate what that means by saying that they were walking like '*mere humans*', that is a *human living like a human* (1 Cor. 3.1-5). The term flesh, with its basic meaning of '*human*' can be seen in three significant relationships to humans. First, it is descriptive of a person as a human being. As such, it is a person's *basis of existence*. Humans exist as flesh. This is in keeping with similar usages in the New Testament (cf. Rom. 3.20; John 3.6; Rom. 8.3; 1 Cor. 1.29). Second, it is humanity's *sphere of existence* or where one (*inner*) lives, in which case it is synonymous with the human body (cf. 2 Cor. 4.10-11). Third, the flesh represents *something that a person uses*, that is the means or basis for living, revealing *how a person lives* (cf. Gal. 3.3). This is often expressed by the phrase 'according to the flesh' (κατὰ σάρκα), a phrase which can also be interpreted in many ways.[23] For instance, in 2 Cor 10.3, Paul draws a distinction between the two.[24] The flesh is still the sphere of the Christian's activity but it is no longer the dominant pattern or motivating power for his/her actions.[25] From the foregoing, it is clear that Paul uses *sarx* in two different senses – sometimes physical and sometimes in the sense of proclivity to sin. For Paul, to live in the flesh is sometimes equivalent to living in sin. However, this is true only as we understand that in such case, one has made the flesh the basis of his/her existence. When Paul thought and spoke of the human situation, he had in mind the human predicament. For Paul, our humanness is not morally neutral. Because of what sin has done to us, our human desires, which were once morally neutral,[26] are perverted, twisted, and slanted toward evil. Thus, to live *by* the flesh results in sinful living, not because the flesh is our sinful nature, but because our *human nature* is no match for sin.

Paul continues in Gal. 5.22 to explain what it means to live a life filled with love. It is a life by the Spirit – a life that issues in the fruit of the Spirit. In discussing the fruit of the Spirit, three important observa-

---

[23] Cf. Howard, *Newness of Life*, pp. 28-33.

[24] Cf. P.E. Hughes, *The Second Epistle to the Corinthians* (NICNT; Grand Rapids: Eerdmans, 1962), p. 348. There is a strong difference between the two uses, one expressing human frailty and the other a principle of life dominated by wrong moral standards.

[25] Cf. C.E.B. Cranfield, *A Critical and Exegetical Commentary on the Epistle to the Romans* (ICC; Edinburgh: T & T Clark, 1979), p. 337. 'They (Christians) are no longer in the flesh in the sense of having the basic direction of their lives determined and controlled by their fallen nature.'

[26] Cf. Howard, 'Two Ways to Live' in *Biblical Resources for Holiness Preaching: From Text to Sermon*, vol. II (ed. H. Ray Dunning; Kansas City: Beacon Hill Press, 1990), p. 201: 'That they were once morally neutral is seen in the fact that every one of the works of the flesh (5:19-21) has a potential right and good fulfillment.'

tions must be made. First, it needs be stressed that Paul does not see the items listed on the fruit of the Spirit as human virtues that can be cultivated, watered or fertilized as if they grew on a tree. They originate from God and their growth and development occur only as believers continue to live by the Spirit and be guided by him. Second, as helpful as an analysis of each item on the list of the fruit of the Spirit may be, such analysis fails to capture Paul's point. What is important to note is that each item is not only related to the other, but also is best understood in the context of social relationship, rather than existing or describing personal virtues that exist apart from the well-being of the community. Third, we need to remember that the word 'fruit' is one of those words that not only can be used both as singular and plural, but also has a collective sense. It may therefore be argued that by using the collective sense, Paul intends all of the qualities he mentioned to exist, at least to a certain degree, in every believer, not distributed among the body of believers as are the spiritual gifts (cf. 1 Cor. 12.4-12; Rom. 14.3-5).

What makes possible Paul's imperative to live by the Spirit? The answer is provided in v. 24: 'Those who belong to Christ Jesus have crucified the flesh'.[27] To belong to Christ is to participate in the life of Christ.[28] Here, Paul expresses the fact of the believer's crucifixion in the active rather than in the passive voice (cf. Gal. 2.19; Rom. 6.6). In the former sense, crucifixion is what the believer does while, the latter implies what is done to the believer, namely, he or she is crucified. Believers are the agents of crucifixion.[29] It has been sometimes suggested that Gal. 5.24 is similar in thought to Gal. 2.20. In this wise, it can be said that believers have crucified the flesh because of the presence of the crucified and risen Christ in them. It is this overwhelming presence of Christ, the crucified and resurrected Lord, his Spirit, the 'fruit of the Spirit' which prevents the intentions of the flesh from discharging the works of the flesh. Therefore, Paul can say that the flesh has been crucified.[30] However, this interpretation is unlikely. In the immediate preceding context, Paul has presented the catalogue of vices

---

[27] The possessive genitive leaves no question as to Paul's meaning--those who belong to Christ. However, as Ben Witherington suggests, it probably also implies those who are in Christ Jesus. Cf. Ben Witherington III, *Grace in Galatia: A Commentary on Paul's Letter to the Galatians* (Grand Rapids: Eerdmans, 1998), p. 412.

[28] Cf. Frank J. Matera, *Galatians* (Sacra Pagina 9; Collegeville, MN: Liturgical Press, 1992), p. 204.

[29] Cf. J.M.G. Barclay, *Obeying the Truth* (Edinburgh: T. & T. Clark, 1988), p. 117.

[30] Hans Dieter Betz, *Galatians* (Hermeneia Commentary Series; Philadelphia: Fortress, 1979), p. 289.

and virtues. He described the former as the manifestation of 'the works of the flesh', and the latter as the 'fruit of the spirit' (cf. v. 22).

In Gal. 5.24, Paul apparently links the crucifixion of the flesh with the belonging-ness to Christ. It is, therefore, conceivable to think about the crucifixion of the flesh and its desires with the crucifixion of Christ. Paul is expressing the same idea as in Rom 6.6. Our 'old man' (the 'person' we once were) has been crucified with Christ. This views a change that has already taken place. The death of the flesh, is not, however, something that works automatically. It is an event that must be appropriated by faith. It is probably no accident, nor is without significance, therefore, that here Paul states in the active voice what elsewhere he puts in the passive. The aorist points to a completed action in the past and might most naturally refer to conversion.[31] He is speaking of an act of will on the part of those who belong to Christ. It is therefore not correct to see this just as a theological statement referring to one's position in Christ[32] but as something that occurs in the Christian consciousness. They have renounced fellowship with sin whose seat is the 'flesh'. Interpreted this way, both the force of the active voice as well as the distinctive Pauline usage of the metaphor are preserved. While, on the one hand, the temptation of forcing a juridical interpretation is avoided, on the other it clearly goes against the view that crucifixion in this verse is a reference to a continuous self-denial, a daily carrying of the cross, a usage that is more noticeable in the Gospels.

Paul probably has in view the free moral decision by believers who belong to Christ. In conversion, they have made a conscious decision to follow the Lord. They have responded to God's saving grace in Christ. They have been regenerated, and now, they say a radical 'No' to sin and thus pass judgment on the whole of their previous life. Hence Gal. 5.24 refers, not to the mystery of baptism, but to an ethical act on the part of Christians.[33] Therefore, in this present context Paul is evidently thinking of the believers' past decision which should form the basis of present action.

---

[31] Longenecker is probably right in his observation that, 'the aorist verb ... , since it identifies the crucifixion of the flesh in the believer's experience as being a past event but assigns that event to no specific time in the past is best translated as a perfect, "they have crucified"'. Cf. *Galatians*, p. 264.

[32] So G.E. Ladd, *A Theology of the New Testament* (Grand Rapids: Eerdmans, 1974), p. 485.

[33] J. Schneider, *s.v.* 'σταυρόω', *TDNT*, VII, pp. 583-84.

Galatians 6.14

> But may it never happen that I should boast except in the cross of our
> Lord Jesus Christ through whom the world has been crucified to me
> and I to the world.

Here, Paul once again employs the language of crucifixion in his description of himself. He had previously talked about 'crucifixion with
Christ', and the 'crucifixion of the flesh'. In the present context, he
talks about 'crucifixion to the world'. It needs to be restated that
though Paul employs a personal language, by extension, what he said
of himself could be said or regarded as true of believers in general. By
now, as has been constantly maintained in this study, crucifixion for
Paul is more than a mere figure of speech. It usually depicts an identification with Christ.

To what reality does crucifixion to the world point? A look at the
context leads in the direction of the conversion or baptism experience.
Paul, in the context, was discussing what constitutes appropriate boasting, in contrast to his opponents who boasted in circumcision and the
law (cf. vv. 12-13). For Paul, there was no other ground for boasting
except the cross. Although 'cosmos' is often used in a general sense,
e.g., as created world (Rom. 1.20), as human living space (Rom. 4.13),
it usually means the human situation qualified by sin, or humankind
itself. As such 'cosmos' is the world (humanity) turned away from God,
rebellious and hostile toward Him, and is depraved humankind that is
headed for judgment. However, in the context, it seems appropriate to
see the world to which Paul refers here not merely as a life of out-
broken sin, but also including his Jewish heritage. For on such heritage
(circumcision and Pharisaical righteousness), Paul had once hung all his
hopes, lived, and served as a slave and even was willing to die.[34]

Further, this 'world' denotes all that stands at enmity with God, the
sphere of pleasure and ambition related to the flesh in which the Ju-
daizers find their boast. It could therefore be seen as representative of
everything in which a person would wish to boast. That is to say, in a
religious sense, he would suppose himself able to depend, for example,
on the law and circumcision (cf. v. 13).[35] It is not just the physical
world, the world of sinful humanity alienated from God, but as Burton
aptly puts it, 'the mode of life which is characterised by earthly advan-

---

[34] Howard, *Galatians*, p. 122.
[35] Cf. Ridderbos, *Paul*, 210; Joseph A. Fitzmyer, S.J., 'The Letter to the Galatians',
The New Jerome Biblical Commentary (ed. Raymond E Brown, Joseph A. Fitzmyer, and
Roland E. Murphy; Englewood Cliffs: Prentice Hall, 1990), p. 788.

tages, viewed as obstacles to righteousness'.[36] 'This world was once to
him a living, vast and tremendous reality … he was the world's servant
and slave, and the world was his absolute, imperious and cruel lord.
This service was hopeless and degrading bondage. But now, through
the death of Christ upon the cross, it had utterly and forever passed
away.'[37]

Through the cross of Christ, the world is crucified to him and he to
the world. What does this mean for Paul? Paul has died to the world,
not by some interior psychological or mystical experience, but through
the historic event at Calvary, which is the realization of the Father's
plan of salvation for humanity.

Certainly Paul does not wish to give the impression that identification with the cross of Christ means an end to a person's relationship to
the physical world or humanity generally. For Paul 'the world' in its
self-sufficiency as well as its legalistic righteousness has received its
judgment and has been done away with in the cross of Christ. Hence,
Paul himself is no longer for the world, insofar as he must love or accept it outside Christ. His relationship to the world is to be determined
by his faith-union relationship to Christ.[38] It seems to me that the conclusion is inescapable that the focus of Paul's preaching was on the
believer's participation in the redemptive significance of Christ's
work.[39] Therefore, the believer can be said to have been crucified to
the world in the same sense that he/she died to sin and the law. It was
both positional and provisional. The perfect indicative passive 'I have
been crucified' (ἐσταύρωται) expresses the fact that this is an event that
has enduring effects. It expresses the condition in which Paul finds
himself through his share in the Christ-event by faith, of which baptism is an expression (cf. Rom. 6.3-11). Paul discovers that the cross is
precisely where his link with the world is severed, since he has come
to share in that fundamental salvation-event by death to sin and baptism into Christ (Romans 6).

Pulling it all together

The argument above could be summed up as follows. Though the
indicative concepts that talk about the believer's crucifixion are formulated differently, they point to the same experiential reality. Paul was

[36] E. de W. Burton, *A Critical and Exegetical Commentary on the Epistle to the Galatians* (ICC; Edinburgh: T & T Clark, 1921), p. 354.

[37] J.A. Beet, *A Commentary on St. Paul's Epistle to the Galatians* (London: Hodder & Stoughton, 1885), p. 176.

[38] Ridderbos, *Paul*, p. 304.

[39] Richard Longenecker, *The Ministry and Message of Paul* (Grand Rapids: Baker, 1971), p. 90.

describing what happens to the believer at the time of the new birth or conversion, that is, the initial moment of putting his faith in the redemptive work of Christ on the cross. The Christian, crucified with Christ, has died not only to the law (cf. 2.19) but also to self (cf. 5.24), and to its earthbound degrading tendencies (cf. 6.14).

As far as Paul is concerned, since the death and resurrection of Jesus and the outpouring of the Spirit, the new people of God are identified, not by the rite of circumcision, but by the Spirit in their midst. The key criterion for being a part of the new people of God is the presence of the Spirit – the circumcision of the heart he calls it elsewhere. The sanctified life is one that is both energized and lived by the power of the Spirit. It is based on more than just a sacred memory. It is a dynamic, life-shaping relationship, walking by the Spirit with lives controlled by the Spirit. It is a journey in which the orientation of the whole being is towards God and his purposes. Expressed in theological terms, Paul presents a picture of sanctification as an experience that is both instantaneous and on going. While the former is present in Gal 2.20, the former is portrayed in Gal. 5.24.

Sanctification comprises a dynamic relationship with God made possible through Christ's crucifixion and resurrection as well as the believer's participation with him in those events. Yet, it is a life to be lived on daily basis in a real world. Paul does not shy away from articulating his other-worldliness as a believer. Though in the world, he is not of the world. In the same manner as Paul, the believer's hopes and aspirations are no longer based on his or her national and religious heritage. Instead, it is his or her being 'in Christ' that determines every course of action.

★★★★★★★★★★★★★★★★★★

Abstract
One of the overriding or primary concerns of Paul's letters is the moral implications of the faith of a person *in Christ*, something which, in theology, is generally termed sanctification. Paul's concern for sanctification is evident in his paraenesis and prayers (cf. Rom. 12.1-2; 1 Cor. 5.1-13; Phil. 1.9-11; 1 Thess. 4.1-7; 5.23-24; 2 Cor. 6.14–7:1) as well as the employment of different metaphors such as cleansing, crucifixion, purification, yielding to God, etc., both to define sanctification as well as describe its experiential reality/ies in the believer's life. This study focuses on Paul's use of the language of crucifixion in his description of sanctification.

6

Pneumatic Discernment: The Image of the Beast and His Number – Revelation 13.11-18

John Christopher Thomas[*]

While numerous aspects of the Apocalypse have been subject to extensive study, little work has been done to this point on the topic of pneumatic discernment. Yet, one does not have to read far into the Apocalypse before encountering divine assistance in the interpretive task (Rev. 1.20) and the oft-repeated call for pneumatic discernment (2.7, 11, 17, 29; 3.6, 13, 22). This study offers a detailed reading of a specific text from the Apocalypse of special significance for this topic. By this means, I hope to make a small contribution toward a greater understanding of the theme of pneumatic discernment in the book of Revelation.[1]

Located in the midst of Revelation 12-14, a section of the book that reveals the content of the unsealed scroll in greater detail, Rev. 13.11-18 follows descriptions of the great red dragon and the beast from the sea, both of whom seek to make war against the rest of the seed of the woman clothed with the sun. This passage also immediately follows a clear call for pneumatic discernment in 13.9-10. Without any words of transition, the narrative of the Apocalypse picks up where it left off before the call to pneumatic discernment in 13.8.

In Rev. 13.11 the hearers learn of yet another beast, 'And I saw another beast coming up out of the earth, and he had two horns as a lamb and he spoke as a dragon'. Each of the details revealed in this verse would be of significance for the hearers. First, they are now introduced, for the first time, to the third member of the triumvirate of

[*] John Christopher Thomas (Ph.D., University of Sheffield) is Clarence J. Abbott Professor of Biblical Studies at the Pentecostal Theological Seminary in Cleveland, TN.

[1] Methodologically, this presentation employs a combination of narrative and intertextual analyses, which seeks to determine, as nearly as possible, the effect of the text upon the hearers. By this means I seek to honor both the visionary nature of the book and the clear priority given in the book itself to hearing the words of this prophecy (1.3).

evil, who comes alongside the dragon and the beast with seven heads to oppose God and make war upon his people. The beast's mere existence is enough to suggest to the hearers that the parody of God and the Lamb continues, only here it appears that the parody extends beyond God and the Lamb to include the Spirit. Second, the fact that this beast's place of origin is identified as the earth makes clear to the hearers the comprehensive nature of this triumvirate's opposition, as they come from heaven (the dragon), the sea (the beast with seven heads), and the earth (the beast introduced here).[2] They might also see in this place of origin a fulfillment of the woe of warning spoken to the earth and sea from the great voice in heaven in 12.12. Third, the fact that the beast is described as having two horns like a lamb would be especially intriguing to the hearers, for they would know full well that lambs do not have horns![3] Thus, while reference to a lamb would no doubt remind them of the lamb language used for Jesus in the Apocalypse, at the same time, the emphasis here is placed not so much upon the lamb language, but upon the two horns, like those belonging to a lamb. While the hearers might possibly think of the ram with two horns in Dan. 8.3 as an analogy,[4] it is much more likely that the two horns (like those of a lamb) would be taken as a reference to the Lamb's two prophetic witnesses, in whom all prophetic abilities appear to converge (Rev. 11.3-13).[5] Therefore, it would seem that in the triumvirate of evil, this beast would be a parody of the Spirit.[6] Fourth, the hearers learn that despite this beast's appearance, having two horns like a lamb, his speech indicates a more sinister relationship, for 'he speaks as a dragon'. While the beast with seven heads bears a physical resemblance to the dragon, this beast speaks as a dragon. Speaking as a dragon would remind the hearers that despite this beast's appearance, he is in league with the dragon, and his words are those of the dragon, just as the words of the Spirit, spoken through prophetic witnesses, are the words of God.

Having learned of this beast's relationship to the dragon, the hearers now become aware of his relationship to the first beast, 'And he exercises (lit. 'does') all the authority of the first beast before him, and he makes the earth and those who are inhabitants in it worship the first beast, whose plague of death was healed'. The emphasis of this sentence is revealed by the first few words of the Greek text, translated

[2] M. Kiddle, *The Revelation of Saint John* (London: Hodder & Stoughton, 1940), p. 253.

[3] D.E. Aune, *Revelation 6-16* (Nashville: Nelson, 1998), p. 757.

[4] Aune, *Revelation 6-16*, p. 757.

[5] J. Sweet, *Revelation* (London: SCM, 1979), p. 215

[6] R.H. Gause, *Revelation: God's Stamp of Sovereignty on History* (Cleveland, TN: Pathway, 1983), p. 183.

somewhat literally as, 'and the authority of the first beast'. Thus, before
attention is devoted to the second beast's activity, focus is already
placed upon the authority of the first beast. The attentive hearers
would hardly miss the fact that the authority exercised by this beast is
the same authority originally derived by the first beast from the dragon
himself (13.2, 4, 5, 7). While not stated explicitly, the hearers may
suspect that this beast's exercising of all the authority of the first beast
may very well include the waging of war, as it is this specific attribute
for which the first beast is praised by the whole earth (13.5). It might
strike the hearers as significant that with the mention of this beast's
activity the verb tense shifts from past to present, perhaps suggesting
that the activity of this beast is an ongoing reality for John and his
church. It should perhaps be noted that the verb found here is ποιεῖ
(*poiei*, 'he exercises' or 'he does'), the first of several occurrences of a
form of this verb in the next six verses. Just as reference to the first
beast's authority precedes the mention of this beast's activity, so reference to the first beast follows mention of this beast's activity, as the
hearers learn that the exercising of this authority is done 'before him'
or 'in his presence'. Thus, in the Greek sentence, references to the first
beast form an inclusio around the mention of this beast, making clear
the dependency of the latter upon the former. For the action of this
beast to be described as ἐνώπιον αὐτοῦ (*enopion autou,* 'before him')
would be yet another way in which the hearers would detect a parody
of God and his work, as to this point in the Apocalypse with few ex-
ceptions (2.14; 3.8, 9; 12.4) the term ἐνώπιον (*enopion*, 'before') rather
consistently occurs with reference to God (1.4; 3.2, 5; 4.5, 6, 10 [2x];
7.9, 11, 15; 8.2, 3, 4; 9.13; 11.4, 16; 12.10) or Jesus (5.8; 7.9)! As such,
it also reminds of those OT texts that use this language to denote 'serving before the Lord' as a faithful servant (1 Kgs 17.1; 18.15).[7] The parallel between this word's usage to describe the relationship between
this beast and the first beast, on the one hand, and its usage to describe
the relationship of the two lampstands (who are the two prophetic
witnesses) and the Lord of the earth (Rev. 11.4), on the other hand,
would be additional reason for the hearers to see in this beast a parody
of the Spirit. However, the exercising of such authority, as the servant
of the first beast, is not an end in itself. Rather this authority is exercised in order that the earth and those who are inhabitants in it might
worship the first beast, a point which the second appearance of the
verb ποιεῖ (*poiei*, 'he makes') in this verse makes clear. Such information helps explain how it is that the whole earth comes to worship the
dragon and the beast (12.4). Such worship is the result of the activity of
this beast. Here the hearers learn that the implicit connection made

[7] Kiddle, *The Revelation of St. John*, p. 254.

earlier between the healing of the first beast's plague of death and his worship by the world (12.3, 4) is made explicit in this verse (13.12).[8]

The words that follow begin to reveal the way this beast accomplishes his task, 'And he does great signs, in order that he even makes fire to come down unto the earth before men'. Owing to the Christologically conditioned nature of 'signs' within the Johannine community, the doing of great signs by this beast again underscores the way in which he continues to parody the activity of Spirit. The extent of this beast's ability is demonstrated by the fact that he is even able to make 'fire fall from heaven unto the earth before men'. The mention of fire from heaven would no doubt remind the hearers especially of Elijah, whose sacrifice was consumed by fire that fell from the Lord (1 Kgs 18.38). Thus, this beast is able to do what the prophets of Baal could not do,[9] in imitation of Elijah. At the same time, mention of fire could not help but remind the hearers of the two prophetic witnesses from whose mouth fire came to devour their enemies. As such, the actions of this beast reveal his continued parody of the work of the Spirit. The attribution of many great signs to this beast also likely calls to the mind of the hearers the words of Deut. 13.1-5, which warn of a 'prophet' who performs signs or wonders and leads the people to worship other gods. These signs, especially the calling down of fire from heaven unto the earth, were specifically done 'before men'.

The purpose of these great signs, and the fire falling from heaven in particular, is made explicit in the next words encountered by the hearers, 'and that he might deceive those who dwell upon the earth by means of the signs which had been given to him to do before the beast, saying to those who dwell upon the earth to make an icon/image to the beast, who has the plague of the sword and lived'. For Johannine hearers 'deceive' language reminds of those who would deceive themselves (Jn 7.47; 1 Jn 1.8; 2 Jn 7) or others (Jn 7.12; 1 Jn 2.26; 3.7), the false prophetess (called Jezebel by Jesus), who 'teaches and deceives my servants to commit sexual immorality and to eat food sacrificed to idols' (Rev. 2.20), and most recently the agent of deception *par excellence*, the great dragon, the one who stands behind all the human agents of deception (Rev. 12.9). For the hearers to discover that this beast is also one of those who deceives others, makes clear to them his relationship, not only to the dragon, but also to the false prophetess 'Jezebel', and may even indicate that he himself should be considered the archetypal false prophet, a suspicion that will be confirmed later in the book (19.20). At any rate, the contrast between this beast and the two prophetic witnesses continues to become clear. The intended audience

---

[8] E.-B. Allo, *L'Apocalypse* (Paris: Gabalda, 1921), p. 190.
[9] G.R. Beasley-Murray, *Book of Revelation* (Grand Rapids: Eerdmans, 1981), p. 217.

of these signs are 'those who dwell upon the earth', those earlier described as worshipping the first beast (13.8), explaining in part the reason for the first beast's worship. At the same time, it is made clear to the hearers that the signs that this beast performed came from an ability given to him, presumably by means of the authority derived from the first beast (13.12). For these signs, like the exercising of authority, were done 'before the beast', a phrase that again parodies the relationship of God to his servants, especially the two prophetic witnesses (11.4). Part of this beast's activity of deception is his 'prophetic' words to those who are inhabitants upon the earth ποιῆσαι εἰκόναι (*poiesai eikonai*, 'to make an image') to the beast. It is significant that this beast seeks to encourage the worship of the first beast by instructing those who are inhabitants upon the earth to make an image of the beast themselves. Discerning hearers could not help but to find in this instruction a violation of the divine prohibition against the making of such images (Deut. 4.16). The fact that this beast does not make the image himself, but encourages the inhabitants of the earth to do so is indeed telling, for the hearers would likely understand such an act as constituting a tangible step on the part of the inhabitants upon the earth in the direction of worshipping the first beast. As revealed earlier in 13.3-4, there is a concrete connection between the worship of the first beast and the fact that he had survived a mortal wound, as the beast is identified with the words, 'who has the plague of the sword and lived'. For the first time it is revealed that the plague, or wound, suffered by the beast, was one inflicted by a sword. While it is possible that the hearers would take this detail as a subtle reference to the death of Nero, who took his own life with a dagger (Suetonius, *Nero* 49), it is possible that the reference to the sword would be taken as indicating the severity of the wound and the dangerous nature of the instrument that inflicted it. If this wound suffered by the beast is in any way to be identified with the activity of the two prophetic witnesses, it is possible that the hearers would understand in these words the irony of the fact that those destined to be put to death by the sword (13.10) may themselves inflict a mortal wound upon the beast, perhaps with the very sword which he wields. Their death by the sword would in reality be a wound inflicted upon the beast by that very sword. Again, the way in which the beast parodies the Lamb is seen by the fact that even though the beast suffered a mortal wound, 'he lived', just as Jesus lived after his death!

The construction of the image is not an end in itself, for as the hearers discover, 'and it was given to him to give life to the image of the beast, in order that the image of the beast might even speak, and he acted in order that whoever did not worship the image of the beast might be killed'. Again, the hearers would be alert to the fact of the derived nature of this beast's authority by the way in which the passive ἐδόθη (*edothe*, 'it was given') precedes the description of his activities. There may be more than a slight chance that the passive form of this verb would underscore for the hearers the extent to which divine activity is being parodied by the evil triumvirate. The fact that this beast was given the authority to give πνεῦμα (*pneuma*, 'life' or 'spirit') to the image would convey at least two things to the hearers. First, they would perhaps be struck by the fact that this beast would be able to give life to the image of the first beast. While numerous examples from antiquity can be assembled with regard to the way in which statues and/or images could be made to appear alive, some with which the hearers may be familiar,[10] there is no indication in the text itself that this or other activities of this beast are achieved by trickery.[11] Second, the hearers would likely pick up on the fact that by means of his derived authority this beast gives the spirit of life, in a way that mimics God's gift of the Spirit of Life to his two prophetic witnesses earlier (11.11). Perhaps the discerning hearers would also understand this great sign as a parody of Ezekiel's prophetic activity where dead bones live (Ezek. 37).[12] If so, the way in which this beast's prophetic activity rivals that of the two prophetic witnesses found in ch. 11 would continue to build. The activity of this living image even includes speaking, a detail that signifies much more than the effect of such a phenomenon, but would be understood as oracular in nature. In other words, the hearers would understand the speech that comes from the image of the beast to be the words of the first beast himself.[13] The result of such 'prophetic' speech is that all who do not worship the beast might be killed. It appears from the context that the oracular words coming from the beast's image insist both on the universal worship of the image of the beast, i.e., worship of the first beast himself, and the putting to death of anyone who does not participate in such worship.[14] Perhaps such oracular speech further defines for the hearers the great and blasphemous things the first beast is described earlier as having uttered (13.5-6). Thus, it here becomes clear that in the war waged by the dragon, the first beast, and now this second beast, those who withstand the onslaughts of this triumvirate face certain death. But, who are these who would oppose such universal worship of the beast and his image? These are the ones

[10] Cf. G.B. Caird, *The Revelation of Saint John* (Peabody, MA: Hendrickson, 1999), p. 173.

[11] F.J. Murphy, *Fallen Is Babylon: The Revelation to John* (Harrisburg, PA: Trinity Press International, 1998), p. 310.

[12] Sweet, *Revelation*, p. 214.

[13] Aune, *Revelation 6-16*, pp. 762-64. Lucian's account in *Alexander the False Prophet* (24) is perhaps the best-known example of this phenomenon and its oracular significance.

[14] Aune, *Revelation 6-16*, p. 765.

who keep the commands of God and have the testimony of Jesus (12.17), whose names are written in the book of life of the Lamb slaughtered from the foundation of the world (13.8), and who face captivity and sword (13.10). Could they be other than the souls under the altar – those who had been slaughtered on account of the word of God and the witness that they had (6.9), or those coming out of the great tribulation who have washed their garments in the blood of the Lamb (7.14)? If the hearers have not understood before, they certainly do now. The battle in which they will engage, and are already engaging, is one that requires a patient endurance that is faithful unto death (13.10). In this, they stand in solidarity with Jesus, Antipas, and the two prophetic witnesses. Perhaps they, better than modern hearers, understand how the present assaults of the dragon are very tightly connected to the assaults that loom in their future. Perhaps they understand that the war in which they now engage is the same war that lies still in the future. Perhaps they understand that their present responses are no less crucial than those they will make tomorrow. Perhaps they understand the way in which the present and future converge. For the lines of demarcation are clearly drawn; the hearers must either align fully with God or the dragon. There is no middle ground; there is no room for compromise.

Additional oracular words from the image appear to follow in the next statement encountered by the hearers, 'And he makes all, the small and great, and the rich and the poor, and the free and the slaves, in order that there be given to them a mark upon their right hand or upon their forehead'. These words, amongst which the term ποιεῖ (*poiei*, 'he makes') again appears, seem to reveal the means by which those who worship the image of the beast are to be identified. Conversely, this same means, the presence or absence of the beast's mark, would be the way in which those who do not worship the image of the beast could be identified as well. The intended audience is universal and, thus, the results inescapable.[15] The comprehensive list of categories makes clear the universal intent of this oracle. The hearers have earlier encountered a similar, though not identical, listing of humanity (6.15), suggesting that the meaning of this listing would not be lost on them. There is absolutely no one who can expect to be exempt from this demand. All, it seems, are expected to receive a mark in one of two prominent places on their bodies; either upon their right hand, the hand of honor, oaths, and business transactions, or upon their forehead, the place where religious articles were sometimes worn bearing the name of a particular deity indicating to which god or goddess one belonged. Clearly, the hearers would understand that the purpose of such

---

[15] Kiddle, *The Revelation of St. John*, p. 258.

a mark is identity, so that by this means, those who worship the image of the beast could be easily identified. What would the hearers make of such a specific command? How would they likely understand this particular χάραγμα (*charagma*, 'mark' or 'brand')? It is possible that they would see in it a practice similar to that of the branding or tattooing of fugitive slaves, or the sign of a conquering people that was sometimes placed upon the vanquished (Plutarch, *Nicias*, 29), or a religious symbol branded upon a subject people (3 Macc 2.28-30). While any or all of these ideas might be present as the hearers encounter these words, it would not be lost on any of them that the 144,000 have earlier been sealed by God upon their foreheads as a sign of his protection and ownership (7.3; 9.4). Consequently, it is hard to imagine that the hearers would not see in this mark of the beast yet another parody of God and his people. As the seal of God signifies ownership by him, so this beast's mark would signify ownership by the beast. As God's seal signifies protection for his people against the events that accompany the sounding of the trumpets, so the beast's seal signifies protection for those who worship him from death inflicted by him. This mark, then, comes to represent the opposite of that represented by the seal of God. Thus, it becomes unquestionably clear to the hearers that the lines of demarcation between God and the dragon have been drawn absolutely and definitively. To bear the seal of God or the mark of the beast reveals the identity of the worshipper, as well as the identity of the one worshipped. Despite the temptations to the contrary, there is absolutely no middle ground. One either worships God or the beast. Therefore, the hearers' temptations to accommodate themselves to the beast and his system are not to be viewed as minor points of non-conformity to God and his Lamb, but carry in themselves the seeds of identification with the beast. They lead one to the worship of the beast and the receiving of his mark!

But there is more, for the hearers learn that the image of the beast acts 'in order that no one might be able to buy or sell except the one who has the mark, the name of the beast, or the number of his name'. These words reveal that a close connection exists between the worship of the image of the beast, the bearing of his mark, and participation in commercial and economic life. One of the implications of such words is that the scope of the beast's authority, earlier described as extending over all human categories (13.7, 12), is now understood to encompass all economic categories as well. So much so that failure to worship the beast and bear his mark bars one from entry into the commercial and economic systems upon which life depends. Part of the implications of these words for the hearers would be that even if it were possible for one to refuse to receive the beast's mark, and somehow escape death at the moment of refusal, one cannot escape death altogether. For one who does not bear the beast's mark would be excluded from the very agencies to which one normally looks in order to sustain physical life. Such a realization would affect the hearers in several ways. First, their understanding of the beast's authority and stature would be even higher than before, as they now understand that there is nothing or no one on earth beyond his control. Second, in the light of the relationship between worship of the beast's image and access to commercial and economic life, the hearers might now see the words of the resurrected Jesus' with regard to eating food sacrificed to idols (2.14, 20) in a more comprehensive light. Perhaps such retrospective understanding would cause them to examine more carefully their own current involvement with commercial and economic entities, especially those connected to eating meat sacrificed to idols. Is it possible, they might wonder, that they could already be facing the temptation to worship the beast and bear his mark by their participation in various commercial and economic systems? Third, these ominous words of warning would reveal that too much attachment to and/or dependence upon a world order, or its systems, that may be connected to the beast is futile. Eventually, all who do not enter fully into participation and cooperation with the beast will be excluded from them and ultimately put to death. Thus, any temptation to compromise with this world and its systems is seen for the false choice that it is. Specifically, the beast and his system are to be viewed as in diametric opposition to those who keep the commands of God and the witness of Jesus. Not only do the hearers learn about the extent of the beast's authority in the commercial and economic realms, but they also discover more about the nature of the beast's mark, for it is described as 'the mark, the name of the beast or the number of his name'. These enigmatic words serve both to inform, as well as intrigue, the hearers. One the one hand, if they earlier wondered as to the nature of the mark that those who worship the beast are to receive, they now know that, by receiving it, his worshippers bear his name, signifying that they belong to him. They are identified by the fact that they bear in their bodies his mark, his name, and/or the number of his name. On the other hand, they may be intrigued by the fact that the beast's name is not explicitly given as such, though they may be safe in assuming that it may be the same blasphemous name that appears upon his heads, but rather they seem to be given a kind of numerical punning.[16]

As the hearers ponder such mixed hints, they are directly addressed in a way now familiar to them, as they encounter the formula 'Here is ...' Specifically they are told, 'Here is wisdom. Let the one who has understanding calculate the number of the beast, for it is the number of

[16] Sweet, *Revelation*, p. 217.

man, and his number is 666.' The last time the hearers encountered the 'Here is ...' formula, it followed words that appear to have come from the resurrected Jesus and/or the Spirit (13.10). Following the call, 'if any one has an ear let that one hear', prophetic words about captivity and sword are given and the following statement, 'Here is the patient endurance and faith of the saints', helps to unfold the mystery of the previous words. Owing to the close proximity of these words to those that occur in 13.18, it is likely that the reappearance of the formula, 'Here is ...', would carry with it a similar sense of prophetic, pneumatic instruction as had those in 13.10. If so, these words may be yet another example of the pneumatic discernment to which the hearers have been called, time and again in the Apocalypse. The specific phrase, 'Here is wisdom', would be an especially potent one for the hearers, for to this point in the book, wisdom has been ascribed only to the Lamb (5.12) and to God (7.12). Thus, it appears that the wisdom here invoked has divine associations and, consequently, is entirely appropriate in an appeal for pneumatic discernment.[17] Earlier the hearers had been instructed, 'If anyone has an ear let that one hear'. Now they are instructed, 'Let the one who has understanding calculate the number of the beast'. What would 'understanding' likely mean to the hearers? Given its context, it could hardly have reference to mere human intellect. Rather, it would appear to be closely associated with 'wisdom', a suspicion that will be confirmed later in the book when both terms are used side by side in yet another 'Here is ... ' formula (17.9)! Owing to this close association, the hearers might well be wondering whether the term νοῦν (*noun*, 'understanding') would not carry with it a similar sense of divine endowment. Interestingly enough, a similar idea is found near the close of 1 John where the readers are assured that they 'have been given the ability to understand' (1 Jn 5.19). On that occasion, the Greek word διάνοιαν (*dianoian*, 'the ability to understand') occurs with reference to the process by which understanding comes, rather than to 'knowledge' or 'understanding' proper. As such, it bears a striking resemblance to the idea of 'the anointing', which the readers have received from him, an anointing that teaches them all things and makes the need for human teachers superfluous (1 Jn 2.20, 27).[18] Such an interpretation of 'understanding' fits nicely with the occurrence of νοῦν (*noun*, 'understanding') found in the call to pneumatic discernment in Rev. 13.18. Specifically, those who have such understanding are encouraged to 'calculate the number of the beast'. On one level, the hearers would be familiar with various ways by which the number

---

[17] *Contra* Aune (*Revelation 6-16*, p. 769), who sees no explicit mention of a need for divine help in order to understand.

[18] J.C. Thomas, *1 John, 2 John, 3 John* (Cleveland, OH: Pilgrim, 2004), p. 278.

of a person or thing could be calculated. And yet, the hearers would know full well that the calculation to which they are called is no mere parlor game, or a calculation that may be completed owing to one's own ingenuity. Rather, this calculation must take place in the Spirit! That is to say this calculation must be undertaken in the Spirit of pneumatic discernment.

To this point, then, the hearers understand that they must continue to follow the leads that the Spirit makes available to them. As it turns out, they do not have to wait for long before receiving their next hint by means of divine assistance, for of the beast's number it is said, 'and this is the number of man'. Such a statement must come as a bit startling to the hearers, for to this point there is little in the description of the beast that would have encouraged them to view the beast in human terms! In point of fact, most things said about the beast would seem to evoke animal-like images, especially the graphic description of his physical appearance. And yet, as the hearers reflect upon what has come before, perhaps these words bring a growing realization that the beast is more like a human than first thought. For example, the beast wears diadems (13.1), he receives and gives authority (13.2, 12), is wounded and healed (13.3), is worshipped owing to his abilities to make war (13.4), and even speaks (13.6). Thus, despite the beast's larger-than-life quality, the first part in the calculation of his number is to understand that it is 'the number of man'. Therefore, there is an explicit identification of the number and name of the beast with that of a 'man', though the anarthrous construction 'of a man' underscores the fact that the number is that of a human being, not necessarily that of a specific individual. But that is not the only assistance, for the hearers next learn the specific number of the beast, 'and his number is 666'. How would the hearers likely calculate this number? It seems reasonable to assume that, owing to the way in which other numbers in the Apocalypse function, this number too would be taken as having a symbolic or figurative quality.[19] That is to say that the number itself would generate echoes of various ideas and themes that converge in the intertext that is the number 666. So what the hearers are likely to discover is that the number of the beast generates a whole matrix of meaning, not a simple identification of a specific figure, and yet it may do that as well.

Perhaps the first thing to catch the attention of the hearers is the fact that this very number, 666, appears on at least one occasion in the OT, where it is used to designate the weight of gold talents that came to

---

[19] S.S. Smalley, *The Revelation to John: A Commentary on the Greek Text of the Apocalypse* (Downers Grove, IL: IVP, 2005), p. 352.

King Solomon on an annual basis (1 Kgs 10.14).[20] If such a detail was thought by the hearers to be echoed in the number of the beast, it might suggest that such kingly associations reveal something of the kingly aspirations of the beast. At the same time, the implications of such monetary associations would not be lost on hearers who have recently learned that without the beast's mark or number, one is denied access to commercial and economic life. Such an intertextual detail would be enough to give the hearers pause before proceeding to their pneumatic calculations proper.

As they begin to calculate in the Spirit, perhaps the first hint given, that the beast's number is the number of man, alerts the hearers to the fact that despite the beast's mythological-like qualities he is to be calculated in human terms. In other words, the beast himself will be manifested in some way in human form, a realization that might cause the hearers to suspect that there are ways in which they already are encountering the beast in a variety of human forms around them, even as they await the kind of manifestation described in 11.7 and 13.1-18. Thus the realization that the number of the beast is the number of man speaks to genre, the kind of beast that the hearers are to calculate or discern. At the same time, it is very difficult to imagine that the call for pneumatic discernment to calculate the number of the beast would not bring the idea of gematria to the hearers' minds. For at the time in which the Apocalypse was written, letters in the Greek and Hebrew alphabets served a dual function as both letters and numbers. Specifically, Greek letters were assigned the following numerical values.

α'	=	1		$\iota\beta'$	=	12 etc.		σ'	=	200
β'	=	2		$\varkappa'$	=	20		τ'	=	300
γ'	=	3		$\varkappa\alpha'$	=	21 etc.		υ'	=	400
δ'	=	4		λ'	=	30		φ'	=	500
ε'	=	5		μ'	=	40		χ'	=	600
ς'	=	6		ν'	=	50		ψ'	=	700
ζ'	=	7		ξ'	=	60		ω'	=	800
η'	=	8		o'	=	70		λ'	=	900
ϑ'	=	9		π'	=	80		$,\alpha$	=	1000
ι'	=	10		h'	=	90		$,\beta$	=	2000
$\iota\alpha'$	=	11		ρ'	=	100		$,\gamma$	=	3000 etc.[21]

---

[20] A suggestion made by John Sweet to the author in private conversation.

[21] For a concise discussion of this use of the Greek alphabet cf. B.M. Metzger and B.D. Ehrman, *The Text of the New Testament: Its Transmission, Corruption, and Restoration* (4th ed.; Oxford: Oxford University Press, 2005), p. 254 n. 7.

Therefore, it was possible to count up the numerical value of the Greek letters in any name or thing. The practice was popular and widespread, even being found in graffiti written on the walls of various structures. Perhaps the most famous, and certainly most oft-cited, is the piece of graffiti found in Pompeii from sometime before 79 CE, which reads, 'I love her whose number is 545.'[22] The meaning of such a statement would be understandable to the person who wrote it and perhaps to the one 'whose number is 545', but probably not to too wide a circle. In addition to gematria, it was also possible at this time to create a pun out of the numerical value of the letters contained in certain words and names, a method known as isopsephism.[23] According to Suetonius (*Nero* 39), even the emperor Nero was subjected to such sport. One pun reads:

> Nero, Orestes, Alcmeon their mothers slew.
> A calculation new.
> Nero his mother slew.[24]

This isopsephism is based on two things. First, it is based on the well-known fact that Nero had killed his own mother. Second, the numerical value of the name Nero in Greek (1005) is, conveniently or inconveniently enough, the equivalent to the numerical value of the Greek words translated 'the slayer of one's own mother'.

So, as the hearers begin to 'calculate', it would seem safe to assume that they would likely make use of gematria as they proceed.[25] If so, and if some of the hearers are familiar with Hebrew, a possibility suggested by their earlier encounter with the name Abbadon (9.11), which is explicitly identified as a Hebrew name, then perhaps they discern their way to the fact that the numerical value of the Greek word θήριον (*therion*, 'beast') is 666 when transliterated into Hebrew characters.[26] The following Hebrew letters were assigned the following numerical value:

---

[22] As cited in A. Deissmann, *Light from the Ancient East* (trans. L.R.M. Strachan; Grand Rapids: Baker, 1978), p. 277.

[23] R. Bauckham, *The Climax of Prophecy: Studies on the Book of Revelation* (Edinburgh: T&T Clark, 1993), p. 386.

[24] Cited according to the translation of J.C. Rolfe, *Suetonius, II* (London: Heinemann, 1965), pp. 156-59.

[25] It should, of course, be apparent that it would be much easier to discern the practice of gematria if one starts with the name and arrives at the number, rather than beginning with the number and arriving at the name, for in the latter case, one would think the possibilities limitless, as they seem to be with 666!

[26] Cf. W. Hadorn ('Die Zahl 666, ein Hinweis auf Trajan', *ZNW* 19 [1919-20], p. 23), who identifies the numerical value of the transliterated word תריון as ת = 400 + ר = 200 + י = 10 + ו = 6 + ן = 50 for a total of 666 [pp. 11-29].

א	=	1	ל	=	30
ב	=	2	מ	=	40
ג	=	3	נ	=	50
ד	=	4	ס	=	60
ה	=	5	ע	=	70
ו	=	6	פ	=	80
ז	=	7	צ	=	90
ח	=	8	ק	=	100
ט	=	9	ר	=	200
י	=	10	ש	=	300
כ	=	20	ת	=	400

Such a calculation would serve to confirm that the number of the beast is indeed 666, as earlier stated, and that the hearers are calculating in the right way. But such an initial calculation would not likely exhaust their efforts on this score, for the call for pneumatic discernment in 13.18 seems to entail much more. Thus, it is likely that the hearers would continue to calculate perhaps with the hope of identifying a specific individual, the number of whose name is 666. Following the calculations used in arriving at the conclusion that the Hebrew transliteration of the Greek word for beast calculates to 666, perhaps the hearers would discern that when the Greek name Νέρων Καῖσαρ (*Neron Caesar,* 'Nero Caesar') is transliterated into Hebrew, it too calculates to 666.[27] If the hearers' initial calculations point in the direction of Nero, what would be the implications of such a pneumatic discerning? Perhaps that in the person of Nero, whose excesses were widely known and who seems to have embodied many of the characteristics of the beast, the hearers would be able to see how the larger-than-life beast could be manifested in human form. Thus, if for the hearers the beast now has a face, Nero appears to have sat for the portrait.[28] And if the beast has the face of Nero, what are the implications for other details of the beast's description, for example, the fact that he has seven heads? Perhaps the hearers would begin to discern ways in which the beast and the empire were related (and this 'head' to the others?). At

[27] Cf. Bauckham (*The Climax of Prophecy*, p. 387), who identifies the numerical value of the transliterated name נרון קסר as נ = 50 + ר = 200 + ו = 6 + ן = 50 + ק = 100 + ס = 60 + ר = 200 for a total of 666. It is significant that when the final 'ן' is left off the Hebrew transliteration, following the Latin name rather than the Greek, the name calculates to 616, which might go some way toward explaining an early variant reading found in a few manuscripts of the New Testament that read 616 instead of 666 at this point.

[28] C.R. Koester, *Revelation and the End of All Things* (Grand Rapids: Eerdmans, 2001), p. 130.

the same time, it does not seem likely that the hearers would have equated the beast with Nero full stop and ceased their calculations, for there are several ways in which the image of the beast is at odds with what is known of Nero.[29] For one thing, there are differences in the way the death of both are described. One of the beast's heads is said to have suffered the plague of death by the sword, while Nero's own self-inflicted death was not a wound to the head with a sword but inflicted to his body with a dagger. There is also the fact that by the time of the Apocalypse, Nero is surely dead, and despite arguments to the contrary, there is no evidence that the tradition of Nero's return included the idea of his death and resurrection, an idea that is clearly present in the description of the beast in Revelation 13.[30] Perhaps on this understanding, the hearers would think of their initial calculations of the beast, 'It is Nero all over again'.[31] Based on the calculation by means of gematria, it appears that, on the one hand, the hearers would likely see the face of Nero as intimately connected to the face of the beast, but, on the other hand, they would not likely confine the identity of the beast to Nero alone, for there would be still other means of calculation available to the hearers in their attempts at pneumatic discernment.

Specifically, discerning Johannine hearers would likely be familiar with another form of calculation that involves 'triangular numbers', a knowledge that is illustrated in Jn 21.11 where reference is made to the catch of 153 fish. As early as the time of Augustine (*Homilies on the Gospel of John* 122.9), it was noted that 153 is the sum of every number from 1 to 17, indicating that it is a most important number indeed. Yet, in some ways its significance pales when it is compared to the number of the beast, 666, which is the sum of every number between 1 and 36. When arranged in order, as if placing a corresponding number of beads from top to bottom, the number 666 would resemble a triangle. It can be illustrated in this way:

---

[29] In point of fact, it appears that by the time of Irenaeus, Nero was not even considered to be one of the possible solutions to the calculation, as his name does not appear as one of the three proposals suggested by Irenaeus (*Against Heresies* 5.30.3).

[30] Bauckham, *The Climax of Prophecy*, pp. 407-23.

[31] Koester, *Revelation and the End of All Things*, p. 133.

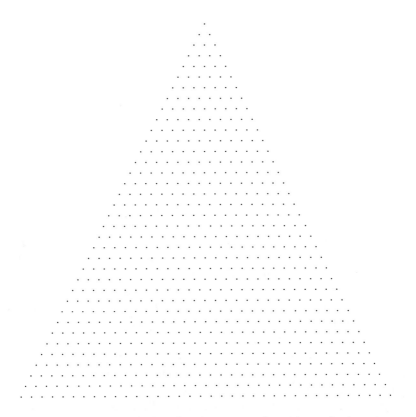

As can be observed, this illustrated version of 666 is perfectly symmetrical and complete in that fashion. What is more, 666 also has the added distinction of being a doubly triangular number, as 36, the last line of numbers, is itself a triangular number being the sum of the numbers from 1 to 8 as illustrated below:

Part of the significance of all this is the fact that doubly triangular numbers (triangular numbers that are built on another triangular number) are quite rare, with 666 being only the eighth such number to occur in the series 1, 6, 21, 55, 120, 231, 406, 666. The significance of the number becomes even more apparent when it is realized that 36 is the only number that is both triangular and square, which may be illustrated in the following way:

```
.   .   .   .   .   .
.   .   .   .   .   .
.   .   .   .   .   .
.   .   .   .   .   .
.   .   .   .   .   .
.   .   .   .   .   .
```

What is the significance of all this for the meaning of the number of the beast? Although the full implications of the hearer's calculations in this regard may not be realized until later in the book, owing to the significance of 36, which was especially honored among the ancients,[32] and the fact that 666 is the triangular number of that triangular number, it might not be going too far to see in the number of the beast, a number that would be understood as of cosmic proportions; perhaps a king amongst numbers![33] That is to say that this calculation of the number 666, along with the calculations by means of gematria, also reveals something of the identity of the beast, who not only exercises unrestrained authority on earth, but appears and acts as a king by the wearing of the ten diadems (13.1). Perhaps, then, in the number 666, the hearers discern a cosmic number, a king of a number for a beast who would himself be a divine king and control the cosmos! Thus, as a result of their calculations in the Spirit, the hearers have discerned two primary things. First, by means of gematria, they have discovered something about his identity. Specifically, they have come to know that the number of the beast is indeed 666 and have gone so far as even to peer into his face. And though his resemblance to Nero is remarkable, they know that he is not simply to be equated with Nero full stop, for Nero is dead, but the beast is not. Second, by means of calculations involving triangular numbers the hearers now have a better sense as to the kind of beast he is. Through their reflection on the number 666 they have discovered things about his aspirations, character, and power. He sees himself as enveloping in himself the cosmos (36) and even fancies himself as the divine king of all, traits consistent with the de-

---

[32] Plutarch (*De Iside et Osiride* 75) notes that the number 36 was held to be particularly sacred by the Pythagoreans. 'The so-called *tetraktys*, namely thirty-six, was the greatest oath, as is well known, and was called the Cosmos (or 'and Cosmos was its name'); it was made up by the sum of the first four even (on the one hand) and (first four) uneven numbers (on the other hand).' Cited according to the translation, with certain modifications, of J.G. Griffiths, *Plutarch's De Iside et Osiride* (Cambridge: University of Wales Press, 1970), p. 239. On this whole issue cf. F.H. Colson, 'Triangular Numbers in the New Testament', *JTS* 16 (1915), p. 70 (pp. 67-76).

[33] Colson ('Triangular Numbers in the New Testament', pp. 70-71) observes, 'When we take into account the identity of what we call digits in 666, it seems likely that in Pythagorean or Nicomachean circles 666 would be a very king amongst numbers'.

scription of his actions encountered earlier in ch. 13. Consequently, the hearers' pneumatic calculations do not serve to satisfy a sense of curiosity to understand history written in advance, but rather they arm them with discerning wisdom to prepare them for their next encounter(s) with him, both now and in the future.

What then are the implications of this reading of Rev. 13.11-18 for the broader topic of pneumatic discernment?

First, this reading suggests that the issue of pneumatic discernment is one that extends well beyond the confines of the first few chapters of the Apocalypse and is indeed part of the very fabric of the book, as numerous details in this passage reveal that not only are the hearers called upon to discern pneumatically but also they are expected to participate in such an interpretative task.

Second, in this passage one of the hearers' primary challenges is to discern the nature and identity of the beast from the earth, who functions as a parody of the Spirit and as a counterpart to the prophetic activity of the two prophetic witnesses. Such a challenge would seem to continue to be faced by the contemporary hearers of the Apocalypse as well.

Third, part of the hearers' task is to discern pneumatically their relationship to economic and commercial systems with which they find themselves involved to determine if such involvement compromises their prophetic witness. Such economic discernment would seem to be no less needed today where the church finds an increasingly complicated economic and interdependent world.

Finally, one of the primary ways in which the hearers are called upon to engage in pneumatic discernment is to exercise the divine wisdom necessary to calculate the number of the beast 'in the Spirit'. As seen in this reading, such spiritual calculation is to take its clues from the pneumatic insights provided in the text itself and is an exercise in pneumatic discernment that reflects prophetically upon the contexts, both present and future, which the church faces.

May this study make a small contribution to the task of pneumatic discernment to which the Apocalypse calls us.[34]

★★★★★★★★★★★★★★★★★

[34] It is an extraordinary privilege for me to offer this study to a volume celebrating the life and ministry of R. Hollis Gause, honored teacher, esteemed colleague, and trusted friend. His pioneering work on the Apocalypse cleared much ground making possible a more authentically Pentecostal reading of this most significant book. For this and numerous other gifts, I offer this study as thanks.

Abstract

This study offers a detailed reading of a specific text from the Apocalypse, 13.11-18, of special significance for the topic of pneumatic discernment. Methodologically, this presentation employs a combination of narrative and intertextual analyses, which seeks to determine, as nearly as possible, the effect of the text upon the hearers. By this means I seek to honor both the visionary nature of the book and the clear priority given in the book itself to hearing the words of this prophecy (1.3).

7

A Theology of the Word ... and That's the Point[1]

Kenneth J. Archer[*]

In various classes and contexts, Hollis Gause often states passionately and emphatically that 'Pentecostal theology is not only a theology of worship, but it is also a theology of witness.'[2] Pentecostal worship is not a means to an end but an end in itself. Witness is the responsibility of the community in ministry to the world which flows out of the worship of God. Witness is not so much a pragmatic activity but rather an ontological existence in the world. These acts are doxological because they are reciprocal and inseparable 'relational' privileges of the Pentecostal community – responsibilities made possible through divine revelation.[3]

In order to grasp R. Hollis Gause's Pentecostal theology of worship and witness one must address his understanding of divine revelation. Divine revelation is the key to his theological method, which opens the door of understanding to his theology. 'Theology of the Word' is the strand that brings coherence to his theological work. If one does not understand his 'Theology of the Word' then one will not grasp the overarching coherence of his theological works, for divine revelation is the beginning and the end. And that's the point!

---

[1] In the classroom, Hollis would pause to take questions and summarize the section of his lecture. During these times he often punctuated crucial concepts with the emphatic statement, 'and that's the point!' The profundity yet clarity of his thought and his saturation in Scripture were most evident during these times of interaction with the students.

[*] Kenneth J. Archer (Ph.D., University of St Andrews, Scotland) is Associate Professor of Theology at the Pentecostal Theological Seminary, Cleveland, TN.

[2] Homer G. Rhea (ed.), *Living the Faith* (Cleveland, TN: Church of God School of Ministry, 2001). This work is a slightly edited transcription based upon the oral video lectures presented by Steven J. Land and R. Hollis Gause. Although the monograph is attributed to both Land and Gause as contributors with no distinction in the text as to who says what, I attribute this statement to Hollis Gause. Furthermore I would attribute ch. 2, 'Doctrine of Divine Revelation: Part One' to Gause. This is based upon my six years of team-teaching Pentecostal theology and hermeneutics with him.

[3] The author's expansion and summarization on Gause's thought.

Divine Revelation: A Theology of the Word

This essay is not an attempt to codify R. Hollis Gause's theology but to guide the reader into his theological posture and pattern of thought by means of his accessible primary writings. I hope to provide a fair and accurate presentation of his understanding of divine revelation. Therefore, I have placed my comments concerning his thought in the footnotes.[4]

Divine revelation is the means by which the triune God reveals himself to humanity.[5] Divine revelation has its origin in heaven and cannot be grasped by humanity. '[R]evelation is always God's act and is not inherent in anything material' whether in creation or in human conscience.[6] 'God as personal God makes himself known; He uses various devices as instruments of his voice, but revelation is always a direct act of God. It is always an encounter with God for salvation or judgment.'[7] The divine utterance of Word is the actualization of divine presence and demonstration of divine power, which includes explanations of his acts and utterances.[8] Therefore, revelation is not just about information concerning the character and conduct of God in history, as attested to by Scripture, but more importantly, it is about encountering God ontologically. Hence, revelation is nothing less than the unveiling of God by his Word. Revelation cannot be discovered by humans because 'revelation is God's gift and it is always His personal act of self disclosure.'[9] The self disclosure of God involves the act of self expo-

---

[4] This essay follows a synchronic approach, but this is not to suggest that Gause's thought has not developed and changed over the years on certain theological topics. Concerning divine revelation, he has remained fairly constant in his position.

[5] R. Hollis Gause, 'Our Heritage of Faith in the Verbal Inspiration of the Bible', in R. Hollis Gause and Steven Jack Land (eds.), *Centennial Heritage Papers 1986: Presented at the 61st General Assembly of the Church of God* (Cleveland, TN: Pathway, 1989), pp. 33-38 (p. 33).

[6] See the theological exposition of Romans 1 by R. Hollis Gause, *The Preaching of Paul: A Study of Romans* (Cleveland, TN: Pathway, 1986), pp. 29-39 (p. 29).

[7] Gause, *Preaching of Paul*, p. 29.

[8] Gause, *Living the Faith*, p. 52.

[9] Gause, *Preaching of Paul*, p. 40. Gause, in various lectures, argues that 'there are two modes of the acquisition of knowledge; investigation and revelation.' Concerning our knowledge of God the only appropriate mode is that of revelation, because revelation is the reversal of epistemological and empirical forms of human investigation. Investigation is an anthropological endeavor which places the investigator/learner 'over the object of his study and elicits from it his information'. The student, then, becomes master of his or her object of study. Revelation is theologically grounded, that is, it is the sole activity of God which places the recipient under and not above God. God is subject not object and confronts humans as such. (This information was taken from my personal copy of his unpublished lecture, 'Inerrancy', pp. 1-19 [pp. 3-4].)

sure.[10] God's revelation allows for one personally to accept him or re-ject him, thus in the self-revealing encounter of God comes redemp-tion or damnation. Furthermore, God opens himself up to the agony of human sinfulness through the cross and the pain of personal rejec-tion of his gracious activity to redeem humanity.[11]

When a person encounters God, she or he encounters his Word.[12] God reveals himself to humanity through the agency of his Word and through the agency of the Holy Spirit.

> The agents of this revelation, according to the Word of God [Scrip-ture], are first of all divine Word, and secondly, the divine Spirit. In John 1:1, the divine Word is the eternal being of the Word or Son of God. So the divine Word is the person of Jesus Christ, God's own Son.[13]

The Word of God, Jesus Christ, 'is the infinite Presentation of the personal character of God, so much so that His Name is Emmanuel, God with us' (Mt. 1.23). Jesus is the incarnate Son of God by the agency of the Holy Spirit. Jesus is the supreme revealer and revelation of God in 'knowing, being and doing' (Col. 2.9) because 'He is equal to God'. The Son is the only begotten of the Father, God of God, from all eternity.[14] By this divine Word every human is immediately enlightened because the Son is the light and life of every human who comes into the world (Jn 1.5, 9).[15] The Word of God, then, is not

---

[10] Gause acknowledges Buber's influence upon his understanding of revelation. See Martin Buber, *I and Thou* (trans. R.G. Smith; New York: Scribner's Sons, 1958). How-ever, Gause modifies Buber's paradigm in a Trinitarian manner. Gause writes, 'he [Buber] leaves the concept of personhood truncated. The three dimensional pattern of I-Thou-He/She provides the essentials of knowing, communing and reciprocating.' God does not define himself but reveals himself by his Names and his acts. We know him as per-sonal because he exists and reveals himself in relationships of personal communion. 'We identify these by the personal pronouns "I, You and He." God is always subject and never an object.' Personal copy of R. Hollis Gause's unpublished lecture notes titled, 'Distinctives of a Pentecostal Theology' (9/2003), pp. 1-44 (p. 9).

[11] See Gause, *Living the Faith*, p. 33.

[12] In Gause, *Living the Faith* we read, 'God does not have to reveal Himself. God re-veals Himself as an expression of His own nature and freedom.' Therefore we can be assured that God did and does reveal himself to humanity because it is God's nature to reveal himself. See also *Preaching of Paul*, pp. 27-31, especially p. 30.

[13] Gause, *Living the Faith*, p. 34.

[14] R. Hollis Gause, distributed lecture notes for the course, 'Pentecostal Theology 601', titled 'The Revelation of God' (September, 2006), pp. 35-42, citation from pp. 40-41. See also Gause, *Living the Faith*, p. 189, where he states that 'the Son exists by eternal begottenness, the Holy Spirit exists by eternal procession.' Thus Gause affirms the classical understanding of the sociality of the immanent Trinity.

[15] Gause, *Living the Faith*, p. 51. See also *The Preaching of Paul*, p. 31, where he argues that people have revelatory experience(s) with God that may not be a 'full revelation of God.' However, this revelation does mean they had an encounter with God for 'they knew God as God not as myth or idol.' Revelation then is not just information derived

primarily a book [Scripture] but a person, Jesus Christ (Jn 1.1, 1-4, 14).[16] The incarnation of divine Word was not a result of the fall of humanity (Gen. 3), even though Jesus is our atonement,[17] but instead the Son from eternity was God's intended personal means to reveal himself fully to humanity.[18] Thus it is proper that '[H]e along with his Father is called the Beginning and the End – the Alpha and the Omega.'[19]

The Holy Spirit is the agent of the divine Word, personally spoken, inscripturated, incarnated and sacramental.[20] The Word of God is divine Word, because it comes by the breath of God, and this breath is the Holy Spirit, which proceeds from the Father. With God 'there is an integral personal identity between word and person.' Word is ontological to personal existence, because 'word is the overflow of one's

---

from human observation of nature that God exists but is a real disclosure of God through his divine Word. Gause emphatically rejects any notion of 'general revelation.'

[16] Gause, 'Revelation of God', p. 40.

[17] In his lecture concerning divine decree, which for Gause is an important aspect of divine Word and the work of Christ, Gause always affirms the totality of Jesus' existence as necessary for atonement. For example, in his lecture handout on 'Divine Providence' distributed September 2006, he writes that the doctrine of decree is a christological issue because 'the work of Christ is a redemptive recapitulation of creation, a microcosm of divine providence and proleptic of the eschaton. The manner in which God governs history is a prediction of the consummation. The life of Christ is teleological from conception to ascension and anticipates the Parousia', which enables 'the redemptive restoration of the original created order', p. 16. See also Gause, *Living the Faith*, ch. 13: 'The Doctrine of Christ: Part Two', pp. 153-64, which I attribute to R. Hollis Gause. On p. 153 Gause writes, 'Jesus' entire life was an offering up of himself unto the Father by the Spirit and offering of Himself in service to man in service and in ministry.' See also his distributed lecture 'Atonement' (Fall 2006), where he defines atonement as reconciliation of the relationship that is broken due to the sin of humanity against God. Atonement is the means of reestablishing the broken relationship between the Holy God and sinful people. 'God's redemptive provision – the atonement – is singular. It is singular as to its reality in the person of Jesus Christ. Jesus is our propitiation or atonement (John 2:1, 2; Romans 3:24, 25; 1 Corinthians 5:7)', p. 7. It is not just the cross and the resurrection but the totality of Jesus' existence that provides atonement for us (p. 15).

[18] Here, Gause draws upon his favorite and most quoted patristic theologian, Irenaeus, for insights into the non-necessity of the Fall as the necessary cause for the incarnation. The incarnation of the Son should be understood first as God's loving and gracious desire to reveal himself fully to humanity in order to draw humanity into the fullness of God's triune fellowship. Second, as a result of the Fall, the Son, in a substitutionary recapitulating manner, also takes on the sin, death and judgment of humanity in order to redeem humanity and creation. The incarnation is the beginning of the fulfillment of Old Testament proleptic types of atonement which anticipate the first coming of the Messiah to save his people. Thus, to discuss Gause's understanding of divine revelation one must logically discuss his understanding of redemption. As a result of human rebellion, divine revelation and redemption are inseparably bound up in each other.

[19] Gause, 'Revelation of God', p. 41.

[20] R. Hollis Gause's lecture handout, 'Perils and Prospects' (Sept 2004), p. 46.

innermost being and exact representation of character.'[21] Speech, then, is an appropriate mode of self-revealing, because through personal speech one exposes oneself to the other. The Holy Spirit knows the depth of God's being and speaks forth the deep things of God (1Cor. 2.9, 10). The divine Word breathed through the prophets (1 Pet. 1.10-12) became incarnate by the action of the Holy Spirit in the womb of Mary (Mt. 1.20; Lk. 1.35).[22]

The divine Word is Spirit and Truth. Jesus said that the Father seeks true worshippers who will worship in 'Spirit and Truth' (Jn 4.23-24). Later in the Fourth Gospel[23] Jesus declares that his words are 'spirit and life' (Jn 6.33). Gause argues that in the Fourth Gospel, Spirit refers to the Holy Spirit and Truth refers to Jesus Christ. Therefore there is a real union and integration of divine Word and divine Spirit without confusing the two divine Persons. This enables the revelatory activity of God by means of Word and Spirit. Furthermore, this union of Spirit and Word is the ground upon which the Apostle Paul describes the revealing work of the Holy Spirit (1 Cor. 2.6-16).[24] However, divine Word is first and foremost the person of Jesus Christ.

As 2 Tim. 3.16 says, 'All Scripture is God-breathed.' This verse is not a proof text for the rationalistic argument of verbal inspiration but instead it serves as an affirmation of the character of the Word of God. All Scripture is inspired because it is the breathing out of God's breath. The breath of God is the Holy Spirit. Therefore, Scripture, both the Old and New Testaments, is also Word of God because it is the in-scripturated breath of divine Word. 'The agent of inspiration is the Holy Spirit, who is divine Person – the third person of the Trinity.'[25]

---

[21] Gause, 'Revelation of God', p. 39.

[22] Gause, 'Revelation of God', p. 41. In his lectures on pneumatology, Gause points out how the Holy Spirit anointed Jesus at his water baptism, commissioned him by empowering him for powerful mission and preaching, and raised him from the dead. A favorite verse for Gause is Heb. 9.14: 'How much more shall the blood of Christ, who through the eternal Spirit offered himself without spot to God, purge your conscience from dead works to serve the living God?' (KJV). Furthermore, the Holy Spirit applies all the redemptive benefits of Christ to the repentant believer; see Gause, *Living in the Spirit: The Way of Salvation* (Cleveland, TN: Pathway, 1980), p. 12.

[23] Gause develops his doctrine of divine Word concerning Jesus and the Spirit primarily, but not exclusively, from John's Gospel and Revelation.

[24] Personal notes taken during his lecture on divine Revelation delivered, September 2006, and not included on the abbreviated notes of the lecture handout, 'The Revelation of God'.

[25] Gause, 'Verbal Inspiration of Scripture', p. 33. Conceiving the Trinity, the designations of God the Father as First, God the Son as Second and God the Holy Spirit as Third are not to be understood as implying hierarchy or subordination of persons within the immanent Trinity but instead refer to the historical progressive revealing of the Triune God to humanity, according to Scripture.

As already stated, the role of the Spirit is to reveal the deep things of God; thus Scripture testifies to the revelation of the triune God to humanity. 'At the center of this is the living Word, Jesus Christ.' Therefore the so-called 'scriptures' of other religions cannot be embraced as Holy Scripture because they do not testify of Jesus Christ or His Word. However, Scripture is more than an authoritative testimony of the Father and Son (Jn 14.15-31) or as Gause would say, 'the historical record of divine revelation.' More importantly Scripture mediates God's revelation because it is the divine voice of God. The Scripture is divine word that cannot be resisted by humans – they may reject it and thus be dammed or receive it and thus be saved, but they cannot ignore or resist God's revelation.[26]

When discussing inscripturated Word (Holy Scripture), one should keep in mind two essentials.[27] First, 'the Scriptures are the voice of God himself, and they are the presence of God.' 'God's Word creates, heals, raises the dead, takes away sin, gives salvation, and executes judgment.' 'Where His speech is heard, He is, and His power is fulfilled.' Because Scripture is Word of God, 'it is always divine encounter.'[28] Second, 'The Word of God [Scripture] is self-authenticating.'[29] The authority and credibility of God's Word is its own integrity, which 'occurs in the fulfillment of divine presence and power by effecting salvation and damnation.'[30] If one sets out to prove or disprove the Bible by a particular epistemological method or science, then one is granting greater authority to a human system that stands in judgment over God's Word – divine revelation. The Word of God judges all

---

[26] Gause, *Living the Faith*, p. 56.

[27] In his opening lecture on biblical Hermeneutics, Gause would affirm the following four presuppositions: (1) The authority and inerrancy of Scripture. (His view of inerrancy does not result from a mechanical fundamentalist understanding of inspiration. It is connected to his understanding of the truth and perfection of God's nature – thus God cannot contradict himself nor will he speak erroneously of salvation and judgment. See 'Verbal Inspiration of Scripture', p. 36. However, early in his teaching ministry, his primary dialogue partners were conservative and moderate Reformed Evangelicals). (2) Scripture is defined as the 66 canonical books of Old and New Testament (which he also identifies as canonical prophecy). (3) The harmony and unity of Scripture are affirmed (which negatively can minimize the diversity of Scripture but positively affirms the inner coherence of Scripture. The inner coherence is what Gause emphasizes). (4) The historical reliability and literal meaning of Scripture are affirmed (meaning is rooted in the literal meaning, but Gause affirms the importance and necessity of figurative language). This information came from my personal copy of his unpublished lecture, 'Pentecostal Hermeneutics' (Fall 2002), which was not distributed to the students in the course. It must be pointed out that Gause's understanding of Scripture is more in line with Wesleyan evangelical tradition than with conservative Evangelicals influenced by Warfield and Hodge.

[28] Gause, 'Verbal Inspiration of Scripture', pp. 35-36.

[29] Gause, 'Verbal Inspiration of Scripture', p. 36.

[30] Gause, 'Verbal Inspiration of Scripture', p. 36.

human systems and 'has about it the ability to demonstrate its own integrity. It is self-affirming in character and quality' as Word of God (Rom. 1.16).[31]

The Word of God is the outflow of the nature of the Father, the person of the Son and the revealing work of the Holy Spirit. The integrity of the triune God is fulfilled in the integrity of the Scriptures.[32] Authority and integrity of Scripture rests in the character of God.

> This shows up in the harmony between the God who speaks, and the God who is Word and the God who is agent of that Word. So, there exists a triune unity and harmony in the oneness of God and the sameness of divine Word, and a sameness of divine character. So, the accuracy of this Word then rests in its agreement with, and reflection of divine nature, especially in a Trinitarian communion and revelation.[33]

Gause, therefore, rejects philosophically grounded rationalistic arguments concerning the infallibility/inerrancy of Scripture. By affirming the self-authenticating nature of Scripture he stands in the tradition of the two great luminaries of the Protestant Reformation, Luther and Calvin.[34] Gause, like Karl Barth, would be considered a fideistic revelationalist.[35] Gause's view is slightly different than that of Luther and Calvin, and unlike Barth, Gause does affirm both 'verbal' inspiration and the 'inerrancy' of Scripture.[36] Scripture is self-authenticating be-

---

[31] Gause, *Living the Faith*, p. 57.

[32] Gause, 'Verbal Inspiration of Scripture', p. 36.

[33] Gause, *Living the Faith*, p. 56.

[34] For the Protestant reformers view of Scripture, see Alister E. McGrath, *Reformation Thought: An Introduction* (Malden, MA and Oxford, UK: Blackwell, 3rd edn, 1999), pp. 150-64.

[35] A fideistic revelationalist is a Christian theologian who rejects attempts to rebut atheism/agnosticism through the use of reasoned philosophical argumentation that does not begin with 'divine revelation' as foundational. These theologians will affirm that Scripture is anchored in real historical-cultural reality (a biblical realism) but reject the necessity to prove or disprove the truthfulness of Scripture through epistemological arguments as a prerequisite to doing theology. For them, the prerequisite is 'divine revelation' as a real personal encounter with God. For Karl Barth's view see his *Evangelical Theology: An Introduction* (Grand Rapids, MI: Eerdmans, 1963), pp 3-59, and George Hunsinger, *How to Read Karl Barth: The Shape of his Theology* (New York, NY: Oxford, 1991).

[36] Students familiar with Karl Barth's doctrine of the Word of God have noticed some important similarities with Gause's 'Theology of the Word'. Barth's doctrine of the Word of God is a threefold Trinitarian understanding. The three distinct but inseparable forms of the Word of God are: revealed, written and proclaimed, see Karl Barth, *Church Dogmatics*, I/1 (Edinburgh: T. & T. Clark, 1936), pp. 98-140. The three-part structure of Word is related, each part to the others, like three concentric circles. The inner most circle is the incarnated Word, Jesus Christ. The second circle is the witness of Scripture, which gives access and clarity to the inner circle, Jesus Christ. The outer circle represents the proclamation of the witness of Scripture by the Christian community – a proclamation that mediates to us the word of God (Daniel L. Migliore, *Faith Seeking Understanding:*

cause it is inscripturated Word. Through the agency of the Holy Spirit, Scripture performs that which God desires of it – to reveal God by God so humanity may know God as the triune community. God redeems those who are repentant and damns those who reject him. Scripture's authority and performance as divine speech, then, is grounded in the Word of God.

The 'proof' of Scripture comes through the personal reception of the Word of God in Jesus Christ through the powerful presence of the Holy Spirit. By letting Christ be formed in an individual personally and by bearing witness to the Word and the life it brings, one demonstrates the validity of Scripture.[37] The 'proof' of Scripture is God's responsibility; however, the Church testifies to the Scripture's authority by receiving the divine Word, living according to divine Word and proclaiming divine Word. The Pentecostal community is marked by the living relationship with God through its worship of the living God and its witness to the world. Divine revelation initiates redemptive worship and propels the community into purposeful mission as cooperative vessels of preaching the Word – a sacramental responsibility.

The Holy Spirit not only inspired Scripture but also continues to inspire the community both in the interpretation of Scripture and in the proclamation of the Word of God (2 Tim. 3.16; 2 Pet. 1.20).[38] The

---

An Introduction to Christian Theology [Grand Rapids, MI: Eerdmans, 2nd ed., 2004], p. 40). Gause, however, has shared with me that he has come to his own understanding without much dependence on Karl Barth. He said that Helmut Thielicke's work was an important source for his own development of revelation. See especially Helmut Thielicke, *The Evangelical Faith, Volume II: The Doctrine of God and of Christ* (trans. Geoffrey Bromiley; Grand Rapids: MI, 1977), pp. 1-60. From my perspective, Gause's theology of 'Word' in particular and his theological orientation overall is closer to the moderate Reformed tradition (L. Berkhof and H. Thielicke) with a distinctive Wesleyan accent concerning both salvation and inspiration.

[37] Gause, *Living the Faith*, p. 58.

[38] It is important to compare John Wesley with Hollis Gause concerning ongoing inspiration of the Holy Spirit. Both men affirm that the Spirit is still inspiring the community. For Wesley, the inspiration of the Spirit is necessary for interpreting Scripture. In Wesley's *Explanatory Notes Upon the New Testament IV* (Salem, OH: Schmul Publishers, reprint) concerning 2 Tim. 3.16 he wrote, 'The Spirit of God not only once inspired those who wrote it, but continually inspires, supernaturally assists those that read it with earnest prayer', p. 554. For Gause, inspiration certainly involves the necessity of inspiring the worshipping community in interpreting Scripture, but inspiration also continues in the ongoing miracles and speech gifts manifesting in the community. Gause is clearly Wesleyan in his view that the Spirit inspires the community to interpret Scripture but, as a Pentecostal, he moves beyond Wesley in his view that the Holy Spirit is still speaking to and through the community. This speech is inspired speech, thus God still speaks! John Calvin's commentary on 2 Tim. 3.16 is interesting for a point of contrast. For Calvin, God 'hath spoken to us' through people of the past as 'organs of the Holy Spirit' but it is 'the elect alone' who have eyes to see the 'majesty of God displayed' in Scripture. The elect 'see' because they alone have been 'enlightened'. See John Calvin (trans. William

Pentecostal worshipping community is the proper context for the interpretation of Scripture.

The action of the Spirit in the Word is a threefold activity. The worshipping community must attempt to recapitulate the threefold process of inspiration of the Spirit. The inspiration of the written word is a threefold activity. First, the Word goes forth by the breath of God (2 Tim. 3.16), which is the out-breathing of God – expiration. Second, the Word flows into the human vessel of inscripturation (2 Pet. 1.21), which is the in-breathing of God – inspiration. Third, the human vessel of speech or writing is the agent of God for oracular utterance, which is the breathing-out of what the Spirit has breathed in. The gifts of the Spirit along with the proclamation of Word through preaching, teaching, hymn writing, etc., are all valid ways in which the Spirit still speaks to the community – hence inspiration is still continuing.[39]

The Holy Spirit is the agent of inspiration which affirms that divine Word is still actively revealing God through Scripture, speech and miraculous activity in and through the contemporary Pentecostal community. God speaks through the preaching of the Gospel and the gifts of the Holy Spirit. The speech gifts (tongues and interpretation, prophecy, word of wisdom and word of knowledge) and miracles in ministry of the Word (Heb. 2.3-4) are ways in which the Spirit continues to speak authoritatively. When the Spirit speaks through miracles and speech gifts, it will always be in continuity with the inscripturated Word, because God will not contradict himself.[40] Scripture as 'canonical prophecy' functions as a means to validate the gifts, whereas 'charismatic prophecy' (one of the gifts of the Spirit) affirms the ongoing inspiration of the Spirit in the contemporary Pentecostal

Pringle), *Commentaries on the Epistles to Timothy, Titus and Philemon* (Grand Rapids, MI: Eerdmans, 1948), p 249. For Calvin, Scripture spoke truthfully about God. For the elect alone, truth as information can be objectively discovered through the subjective internal witness of the Spirit. The Scripture is 'illuminated' through the internal witness of the Spirit in the elect person, thus enabling Scripture to function like spectacles so that the elect can clearly see the truths of God. For Gause, the Scripture spoke and speaks (present tense). Therefore one does not discover truth; rather, one encounters the Truth through the agency of the Spirit. Scripture does help us to understand and clarify the redemptive encounter through the present inspiration of Scripture by the Spirit. For Calvin one needs to see the past through the illumination of the Spirit, but for Gause one needs to see/hear/heed the divine voice speaking presently through Scripture. Gause moves outside of the evangelical Reformed tradition by affirming 'inspiration' as a synergistic relationship of the Spirit with the community. This is different from Calvin's monergistic understanding of 'illumination'.

[39] My summarization of his unpublished lecture notes, 'Pentecostal Hermeneutics' (August 31, 2004).

[40] Gause, *Living the Faith*, pp. 54-55 and 'Pentecostal Hermeneutics.'

community. From this perspective, Scripture is closed functionally.[41] Scripture is the infallible authority, for it flows from the very nature of God and serves to evaluate ongoing gifts to the community. Charismatic prophecy as a continuing gift is fallible testimony even though it is inspired speech.

> This is a safeguard against the tyranny of a rationalistic, historical-grammatical exegetical papacy. Proper exegesis does not assume a kind of "verbal deism" as if God turned silent upon the completion of the canon. The work of the Holy Spirit in the instruction and guidance of the church takes on a timeless and seamless significance in the refrain of Revelation 2:7: "He that hath an ear let him hear what the Spirit saith [present indicative verb; "is saying"] unto the churches.[42]

The preaching of the Word of God provides a sacramental opportunity for those who preach and those who hear.[43] Unless the one preaching (which includes any form of teaching and exhorting) is inspired by the Holy Spirit, she or he cannot declare 'thus saith the Lord'.[44] Gause has stated passionately that ministers of the Gospel should not step into the pulpit unless they know they have a word

---

[41] Gause does not want to close the canon in an absolute sense, because God is still speaking. However, it is clear that he affirms the priority of interpretive authority to 'canonical prophecy' in relation to 'charismatic prophecy'. Canonical prophecy is infallible whereas charismatic prophecy is fallible. For a non-subordinate but equal relationship between canonical word and charismatic word see Rick D. Moore, 'Canon and Charisma in the Book of Deuteronomy', *JPT* 1 (Oct. 1992), pp. 75-92. Working out of Deuteronomy, Moore grounds canon (written word) and charisma (charismatic word) in pneumatology. He affirms 'the place and role of both inscripturated word and prophetic utterance' as a 'dialectical and complementary relationship between canonical word' and what he calls 'charismatic revelation', p. 76. Both canonical writing and/or inscripturated revelation along with prophetic utterance and/or charismatic speech stand on their own side by side with the other as two inter connected revelatory channels. In his, 'A Letter to Frank Macchia', *JPT* 17 (Oct. 2000), pp. 12-14, Moore suggests that Pentecostals should move away from the Protestant formulation of *Sola Scriptura* and develop a more relational understanding of Spirit and Scripture under the rubric of *Solus Spiritus*. Moore states, 'Indeed all the words of Scripture are from the Spirit, even though not *all* of the words of the Spirit are *from* Scripture.' The relationship between Scripture and the Spirit is '*Solus Spiritus with the Scripture*' because 'the Spirit is God and Scripture is not', p.13 (his emphasis). For further reflection on Moore's Wesleyan Pentecostal proposal see Frank D. Macchia, 'A Reply To Rickie Moore', *JPT* 17 (Oct. 2000), pp. 15-19.

[42] An unpublished personal copy of R. Hollis Gause's lecture notes, 'Distinctives of a Pentecostal Theology' (9/11/03), pp. 6-8 (p. 8). See also R. Hollis Gause, *Revelation: God's Stamp of Sovereignty on History* (Cleveland, TN: Pathway, 1983), p. 50.

[43] It is sacramental because one cannot hear God without encountering God and the Word of God is irresistible in its procession to either save or damn, depending on the individual's response.

[44] Gause affirms that women are also called of God to preach, pastor and lead. See Kimberly Ervin Alexander and R. Hollis Gause, *Women in Leadership: A Pentecostal Perspective* (Cleveland, TN: Center for Pentecostal Leadership and Care, 2006).

from God for the people of God.[45] One cannot preach the Gospel unless she or he knows the written Word, and one cannot know the written Word unless one knows the living Word, Jesus Christ. For we, like Paul, are 'not ashamed of the Gospel of Christ: for it is the power of God unto salvation for every one that believeth' (Rom 1.16; KJV). 'At the center of all this [preaching] is the living Word, Jesus Christ.'[46] All Scripture and thus preaching of Scripture ultimately testify of Jesus Christ.

Before summarizing, I think that it is important to recognize that Gause holds to a 'high view' of Scripture, not because he affirms inerrancy but because of the ontological status of Scripture – it is God breathed! The ongoing inspiration of Scripture causes the written Word once again to become spoken Word, which brings the personal encounter with the living Word. Therefore, written Word is always the authoritative Word of God for the Pentecostal community as long as it is inspired by the Spirit and interpreted by a worshipping community.[47]

From my vantage point, Gause's interpretive method of Scripture is an academic theological exegetical approach.[48] He practices a grammatical-historical exegetical method that clearly moves into a more synchronic literary analysis of Scripture.[49] He appreciates the narrative coherence of Scripture as can be attested by his three-part classical narrative understanding of God as creator-redeemer-consummator. Scripture testifies to the progressive unfolding of God's self revelation to humanity and in particular to the remnant community who participates in the 'one salvation'. He reads the OT as promise and the NT as fulfillment, which also contains further promises. Thus Scripture generates real worship that is proleptic in nature and invites the reader/listener to participate in the promises of God that anticipate the complete fulfillment in the eschaton.[50]

---

[45] I have heard him on more than one occasion make such statements concerning the Word proclaimed.

[46] Gause, *Living the Faith*, pp. 57-58.

[47] For further discussion see, Kenneth J. Archer, *A Pentecostal Hermeneutic for the Twenty-First Century: Spirit, Scripture and Community* (London and New York: T&T Clark International, 2004), pp.156-191 and 'The Spirit and Theological Interpretation: A Pentecostal Strategy', *Cyberjournal for Pentecostal/Charismatic Research* 16 (2007), <http://www.pctii.org/cybertab1.html>.

[48] He earned a PhD in New Testament from Emory University, utilizing the historical- critical method of form criticism in his doctoral work on Luke's Gospel.

[49] 'Pentecostal Hermeneutics' (August 31, 2004).

[50] More could be said about his theological hermeneutic, like the significant role the Book of Acts plays in his overall interpretive posture and understanding of Scripture, his promise (OT) and fulfillment (NT) approach to the unity of Scripture, and recently his argument to employ a 'redemptive' hermeneutic when interpreting Scripture, in particu-

In summation, divine revelation is rooted in God's triune character
and orientation to commune with humanity in a personal way through
his Word and Spirit. Through divine speech, God communicates God,
which is an ontological encounter with a personal subject. Divine revelation always involves encountering Word and Spirit, which proclaims judgment and offers redemption. One cannot experience God's
redemption without first standing in God's judgment. One cannot
experience divine revelation unless one has a personal encounter with
the living God – an 'I–thou' encounter. We are saved by God's initial
revelatory activity; it flows out of his graceful character and through
personal faith in Christ Jesus, the living Word. Divine revelation is
irresistible in the sense that it always elicits personal response. Hence
judgment is not the living God overlooking or ignoring human sinfulness; rather, it is God passionately placing upon Jesus the judgment we
deserve. The result is that we are then graciously acquitted. Because
divine revelation is always personal and particular, 'general revelation'
and its corollary 'natural theology' are misguided human quests of
truth.[51] Worship, then, is the only appropriate response to God's gracious revelation of the divine self.

The Holy Spirit is the agent of divine Word, spoken, incarnated, inscripturated and sacramental. God is still speaking today by the agency
of the Holy Spirit but never in contradiction to the inscripturated
Word and always in testimony to the living Word. Therefore, 'any
doctrine of revelation that does not make the Person of the Holy Spirit

---

lar Genesis 3. For helpful clues, I would encourage readers to take a closer look at his two
commentaries (Romans and Revelation; cited earlier), *Women In Leadership* and his theological exposition of soteriology in *Living in the Spirit: The Way of Salvation*. The point I
am making is that the study of Scripture is an aspect of personal and corporate worship
and necessary preparation for the proclamation of 'Thus saith the Lord.'

[51] Concerning his rejection of general revelation, see his *Preaching of Paul*, pp 29-31.
Gause delineates the following reasons for why he rejects the doctrine of general revelation. The following is adapted from, 'Revelation of God', pp. 37-38.

1. It assumes that God can be known by his works.
2. Such knowledge is knowledge of an object not a person.
3. This view of revelation is impersonal and lifeless.
4. The doctrine of general revelation assumes that there is a body of knowledge
    about God that can be gained by human investigation.
5. This division of revelation separates the knowledge of God's judgment from
    the knowledge of God's redemption.
6. This assumption is that knowledge of God may be received without the work
    of the Holy Spirit.
7. The static quality of general revelation is transferred to special revelation.
8. The concept of general revelation leads to a so–called natural theology; that is a
    theology built on the evidences in nature.
9. It is a non-empowering, lifeless revelation.

foundational will be mechanical, rationalistic (humanistic) and static.'[52] And that's the point!

Divine Revelation, Scripture and Epistemology

In the remaining section of this essay, I will address divine revelation in relationship to Scripture and to epistemology.[53] Our Pentecostal response to divine revelation is one of worship and witness. Scripture is the penultimate witness of God's historic disclosures. Most of us would agree with William J. Abraham's testimony that he did not become Christian because he learned a theory of knowledge. He became a Christian first and foremost by coming to love the God proclaimed by the church. 'In bringing people to faith the church articulated a very particular vision of God, creation, and redemption that had to be seen as a whole.'[54] Scripture along with our worship and witness is our strongest epistemological argument.

Revelation is rooted in the scriptural claim that there is a God who has personally communicated.[55] For Pentecostals, God continues to communicate with humanity. I am in agreement with Gause's definition of revelation as God's self disclosure through the event of divine encounter. God reveals Godself as the triune Being – Father, Son and

[52] Gause, 'Revelation of God', p. 42. For one example of a contemporary conservative evangelical view that embraces exactly what Gause is warning us about – verbal deism and the cessation of present speech of God, see Peter Jensen, *The Revelation of God: Contours of Christian Theology* (Downers Grove, IL: InterVarsity Press, 2002). Jensen writes, 'The gospel has been launched, the Scripture has been completed and the church has been founded. We have the [past] prophetic gift in abundance in the *Scriptures*; contemporary prophecy is only a diversion. Prophecy "has passed away"' (p. 273: my italics and parentheses). Jensen is a cessationist and Pentecostals are non-cessationists. This book is a testament to how very different Wesleyan Pentecostalism is from conservative Reformed Evangelicalism, despite the many similarities.

[53] Epistemology is a subdivision of philosophy and is concerned with a rational systematic account of knowledge and its justification. However, Scripture does not identify nor endorse any particular epistemological method. Christianity has not unanimously adopted or developed a particular epistemology. Christian theologians have used various epistemological methods including a Barthian approach of non-method. I believe the truthfulness of our experience of divine revelation can be reasonably communicated without it becoming an object of human investigation or committed to a particular method to validate it.

[54] William J. Abraham, *Crossing the Threshold of Divine Revelation* (Grand Rapids, MI and Cambridge, UK: Eerdmans, 2006), p. xiii. Also see his important work, *Divine Revelation and the Limits of Historical Criticism* (New York, NY: Oxford University Press, 1982).

[55] See the brief but helpful essay by Stephen N. Williams, 'Revelation' in Kevin J. Vanhoozer (gen. ed.), *Dictionary for Theological Interpretation of the Bible* (Grand Rapids, MI: Baker Academic, 2005), pp. 678-680 (p. 678). I encourage those who desire to delve into this important theological topic to begin here and then start working through his selective yet significant bibliography.

Holy Spirit. The Spirit brings us to the Son and through the Son we see the Father. God, through revelation, calls a person into divine fellowship – communion. However, this costly invitation by God on behalf of fallen humanity demands one to bow in worshipful response through confession of sin and expression of gratitude. Furthermore, through the Spirit, the person becomes united to the body of Christ, thus communally formed as a witness of the gracious love and righteous holiness of the living God.

God's activity of communication to humanity is necessary for revelation to occur. Divine speech and divine action are interconnected as a concomitant act when interpreted by the 'word of God'. Divine communication is an inseparable relationship of word and event form the nexus of revelation, with Jesus Christ being the center.[56] The 'incarnation is the definitive disclosure of the personal reality of God; in this respect, incarnation is the heart of revelation' and 'revelation aims not only at intellectual response or cognitive acknowledgement, but also at personal repentance and transformation.'[57] In other words, divine 'revelation, in the distinctive Christian sense, is not merely God's making available information about himself but the personal unveiling of God that transforms and reconciles the believing recipient of revelation.'[58]

Returning to Gause's view of divine revelation, there is an essential relationship between inscripturated Word (Scripture) and living Word (Jesus Christ).[59] Both are 'Word of God' because of the agency of the Holy Spirit.[60] The function of divine speech is to bring one into relationship with God through Jesus Christ by the agency of the Spirit.[61] From this perspective of divine revelation as self disclosure of person, Scripture makes two significant contributions. First, it mediates the speech of God, thus becoming a catalyst for divine encounter as an

---

[56] Williams, 'Revelation', p. 679.

[57] Williams, 'Revelation', p. 680.

[58] James Leo Garrett, Jr., *Systematic Theology: Biblical, Historical, and Evangelical,* volume 1 (Grand Rapids, MI: Eerdmans, 1990), p. 45. For Garrett, the specific Christian understanding of divine revelation always involves special revelation which is the historical disclosure of God to the people of Israel and in Jesus Christ', p. 45. He does, however, affirm a non-salvific understanding of general revelation that incorporates Barth's view of special revelation (that God initiates revelation) and Calvin's view (that general revelation is non-salvific) (p. 53). Garrett's view is the standard more Reformed evangelical view.

[59] Of course, this would also include personally spoken word and sacramental word.

[60] I prefer to use a small 'w' when making reference to Scripture as word of God and capital 'W' when referring to Jesus as Word of God. The point is that first and foremost the Word is a person and not a book.

[61] I see the need further to develop this in a pneumatological way. Rickie Moore's proposal which puts Spirit in relationship with Jesus Christ as source and authority for both charismatic word and canonical word is instructive. See note 40.

opportunity for redemptive communion. Second, Scripture provides the penultimate authoritative communication for understanding our salvific relationship with the social Trinity.[62]

The economy of the social Trinity's doing is rooted in the ontological reality of God as relational Being.[63] The Holy Spirit is coequal, coeternal and exists personally in the perichoretic relationship of the social Trinity. The Person of the Spirit is the powerful presence of God, who proceeds from the Father and is sent by the Son to initiate divine encounter (divine revelation) and draw one into the mysterious divine dance (redemption). The Spirit's initiatory encounter brings about a real transformative moment for the individual. This activity of the Spirit upon a depraved human enables the person to respond to or even reject God's gracious invitation to salvation. Rejection of God's gracious invitation grieves the Spirit and if one persists, he/she will bring damnation upon himself or herself.

Divine revelation is a particular 'narrative reality' and cannot be understood fully apart from the grand metanarrative of Holy Scripture. We make sense of our particular existence through narrative. We interpret reality, including our understanding of God, through narrative. When interpreting, we tell stories.

> The human world, it has been said, is story-shaped. We all instinctively understand the world by telling stories about it. If the Bible offers a metanarrative, a story of all stories, then we should all be able to place our own stories within that grand narrative and find our own perception and experience of the world transformed by the connexion (sic).[64]

The Revelation of God is always a particular moment of divine self-disclosure that is intended to be shared with others. For example, the paradigmatic revelatory activity of the Exodus establishes Israel as God's particular people and affirms that the God of Abraham, Isaac and Jacob is the God of Israel and Jesus Christ. Jesus, who is Emmanuel, is the definitive revelation of God to humanity. These particular acts of salvific revelation are to be proclaimed by the Christian community to the nations.[65] Thus, God's own identity is itself a *narrative* identity. 'It is the particular story of Israel and Jesus.'[66]

---

[62] For this section of the essay, I am focusing on these two 'relational' qualities of Scripture. I also affirm that Scripture is particular, personal, propositional, progressive, penultimate, and pneumatic.

[63] See Gabriel Fackre, *The Doctrine of Revelation: A Narrative Interpretation* (Grand Rapids, MI: Eerdmans, 1997), pp. 26-31, especially pp. 26 and 30.

[64] Richard Bauckham, *Bible and Mission: Christian Witness in a Postmodern World* (Grand Rapids, MI and Carlisle, UK: Baker Book House and Paternoster, 2003), p. 12.

[65] Bauckham, *Bible and Mission*, pp. 27-54, especially p. 37.

[66] Bauckham, *Bible and Mission*, pp. 12-13.

Scripture contains realistic narratives and is a realistic metanarrative.[67] Scripture, then, should be read canonically. A canonical hermeneutic is a way of reading the Bible from Genesis to Revelation as a whole story. We will encounter various stories, humorous and tragic episodes, inviting poems, haunting prophecies and hopeful affirmations within the overarching story.[68] Yet a canonical reading of Scripture places limits upon the possible interpretations generated by the Scriptures by providing necessary literary clues to valid readings and resistance to potential misreadings of the Scripture.[69] In other words, 'the canon constructs and controls the meaning of the Bible'.[70] Furthermore, 'the Bible as a canon is indispensable to Christian faith because it transmits "the word of God"'.[71]

Scripture as narrative tells an overarching theological story, which generates its own world. We recognize the plot of this story as having a beginning, middle and end. The plot moves the action forward and identifies the purpose of God. The beginning starts with creation and identifies God as the creator. The middle is concerned with redemption and identifies God of Israel as the redeemer of all humanity. The middle has 'two primary movements: the liberating work of God in Exodus and the saving work of God in the advent of Jesus Christ (New Exodus).'[72] The end is concerned with the final consummation of God's redemptive purpose for all of creation. The purpose of Scripture is to offer testimony to the 'narrative reality' of the living God as it becomes a catalyst for divine encounter through its ability to communicate Word of God because of the working of the Spirit.

Christian identity is formed by entering narratively into the 'the strange new world of the Bible' (K. Barth) and finding our narrative reality confronted and (re-)shaped by the past memory as we construct the future possibilities of the coming of Christ Jesus. Scripture narrates God's identity and mediates God's presence, which confronts our interpretation of reality. This initial encounter lays bare our true identity as rebellious people and invites us to become a part of God's redeemed

---

[67] Bauckham, *Bible and Mission*, pp. 12-16.

[68] See Joel B. Green, 'The (Re-)turn to Narrative', pp. 11-36, and 'Reading the Gospels and Acts as Narrative', pp. 37-66, in Joel B. Green and Michael Pasquarello III, eds., *Narrative Reading, Narrative Preaching: Reuniting New Testament Interpretation and Proclamation* (Grand Rapids, MI: Baker Academic, 2003), especially, p. 51.

[69] See Kenneth J. Archer, *A Pentecostal Hermeneutic*, pp. 156-91.

[70] George Aichele, *The Control of Biblical Meaning: Canon as Semiotic Mechanism* (Harrisburg, PA: Trinity Press International, 2001), pp. 2 and 222. This work takes seriously the postmodern challenges and yet offers a helpful response without returning to modern academic fundamentalism or liberalism.

[71] Aichele, *Control of Biblical Meaning*, p. 218.

[72] Green, 'Reading the Gospels and Acts as Narrative', p.51.

people.[73] Scripture serves as the penultimate faithful witness of the social Trinity's revelatory and redemptive activity in words, visions, and deeds.

In sum, Scripture as a canonical metanarrative communicates the story of the social Trinity. Scripture is the realistic story of God's self-disclosure in space and time with humanity and for humanity's' redemption. Scripture is a gift of the Spirit working with humanity for humanity.[74] Scripture serves as the penultimate witness of God's particular revelatory redemption for all of creation.

By affirming Scripture as a canonical metanarrative I have embraced the scandal of modernity and have become an affront to postmodernity.[75] Modernity placed 'epistemology' front and center concerning the validation of all truth claims. This in turn led to a quest for universal foundational truth based upon universal epistemological standards. The human quest for the universal undermined the particularity of Scripture and even the uniqueness of Christianity as a 'revealed' religion. The Christians of modernity were grouped into two camps: modernist (also called liberals) and academic fundamentalists.[76] The irony was that both shared the same epistemological foundation.[77] No wonder others like Karl Barth, John Howard Yoder and our own R. Hollis Gause,

---

[73] Bauckham, *Bible and Mission*, p. 110. The Bible as a metanarrative suggests that the whole of reality is interpreted through and by this narrative. This implies that humanity needs to be reshaped through this story, but this does not mean the Bible desires to annihilate all stories. It is hospitable to stories which contribute to its story without competing with it. To compete with or deny the biblical story is idolatry. Hence aspects of storied cultures and ethnic diversity are important appreciations of the biblical narrative that accommodates diversity in a coherent unity of narrative in which people find formational rehabilitation through surrendering to God.

[74] Gabriel Fackre, *The Doctrine of Revelation*, p. 15.

[75] Modernity has always resisted 'particularity' of truth claims. Postmodernity has affirmed particular narratives, while simultaneously resisting metanarratives as an oppressive universal story. See Anthony C. Thiselton, *Interpreting God and the Postmodern Self: On Meaning, Manipulation and Promise* (Grand Rapids, MI: Eerdmans, 1995).

[76] Of course there were other Christian theologians who do not fit neatly into either group.

[77] See Kenneth J. Archer, *A Pentecostal Hermeneutic*, ch. 2. I affirm Scripture as inspired but avoid affirming Scripture as inerrant. In order for inerrancy to make sense, one needs to embrace the epistemological views of modernity, which, to say the least, are hostile to forms of Christianity that affirm the ongoing (miraculous) activity of God beyond biblical times. Furthermore, inerrancy, once defined by pages of what it does not mean, becomes epistemologically irrelevant (only the original autographs along with the message of salvation are inerrant) and often dangerously suspicious as an argument for verbal deism, resulting in reducing revelation to a propositional, cognitive truth to be believed. Inerrancy cannot guarantee doctrinal correctness or agreement. For me, inerrancy is nonsensical and should not be the litmus test for 'orthodox' Pentecostal Christianity. For a brief discussion of a high view of Scripture based upon inspiration that avoids the language of inerrancy, see John Christopher Thomas, *Ministry and Theology: Studies for the Church and Its Leaders* (Cleveland, TN: Pathway, 1996), pp. 13-20.

who were forged in the fires of the demise of modernity yet captivated by the revelation of God, opted for God to be the epistemological ground.[78]

I suggest that we can offer an apologetic which has epistemological ramifications without embracing one particular epistemological method.[79] Our most persuasive apologetic to the world is that of our response of worship and witness to God's intervening revelation.[80] Instead of presenting a 'theory of knowledge' that can substantiate our truth claims about God, we follow Scripture in witnessing to the truthfulness of God through our personal and Christian community testimony. Our *non-coercive* witness to the world is how the Bible itself points the way to truth.[81] 'Witnesses are not expected, like lawyers, to persuade by the rhetorical power of their speeches, but simply to testify to the truth for which they are qualified to give evidence.'[82] Telling the biblical story, especially the story of Jesus, is an essential part of our witness. 'Witness, then, mediates the particularity of biblical story and the universality of its claim.'[83]

Our witness offers its greatest epistemological challenge to the world when the community retrieves from Scripture its narrative identity, lives in solidarity with the victims of society and testifies to the hope it has because God's kingdom is coming. Our personal witness is lived out in Christian community as a contrast society.[84] We, in words and deeds, testify of the living God who rules his kingdom altogether differently from the imperialistic nations of the world. God's remnant community finds her present existence in these nations as she longs for

---

[78] For a thorough introduction to Yoder's works see, Craig A. Carter, *The Politics of the Cross: The Theological and Social Ethics of John Howard Yoder* (Grand Rapids, MI: Brazos, 2001).

[79] For further help with epistemology as it relates to God's intervention through divine revelation and flows out of 'canonical theism', see Abraham, *Crossing the Threshold*, especially pp. 35-42.

[80] For this section on witness I am drawing heavily upon the argument of Bauckham, *Bible and Mission*. See also his *Jesus and the Eyewitnesses: the Gospels as Eyewitness Testimony* (Grand Rapids, MI and Cambridge, UK: Eerdmans, 2006), pp. 505-508.

[81] Bauckham, *Bible and Mission*, p. 100, 'The biblical motif of witness, drawn like so much of the New Testament's missionary conceptuality and vocabulary from the later chapters of Isaiah and developed especially in the Gospel of John and the book of Revelation, images history as a global contest for the truth in which the God of Israel and Jesus will demonstrate his true and sole deity to the nations. God's people are the witnesses to his truth and his great acts of salvation.'

[82] Bauckham, *Bible and Mission*, pp. 99-100.

[83] Bauckham, *Bible and Mission*, p. 112.

[84] I do not want to romanticize our Pentecostal communities. We have problems, but loving, disciplining, and caring communities do exists. Corporate and personal confession of sin is also a necessary part of worship and does not take away from our witness but strengthens it.

the coming of her groom. Witness that lives out the command to love God and love one's neighbor nonviolently in community is the strongest validation of the Gospel of Jesus Christ to a watching hostile postmodern world.[85]

Like our witness, Pentecostal worship has epistemological implications. Worship is our response to God's gracious revelation. From within the arena of creation, our worship is directed to God. Because the church is the body of Christ, she, along with the Spirit, is the redemptive presence of God in and to the world. As we worship God in the beauty of holiness, God manifests his presence in powerful and convicting ways – including signs and wonders. As we worship, our sacramental acts, songs and preaching offer testimony to Jesus, the Savior of the world, and the one who has sanctified and filled us with his Holy Spirit. Our worship is filled with shouts of praise, sighs of grief and times of repentance. Worship not only brings glory to God but mediates God's presence to humanity.

We realize that our Pentecostal community must be shaped and reshaped by the grand metanarrative of Scripture – God's story. We pray for God to sanctify us, to heal us and to make us witnesses. Thus, we surrender to the lordship of Christ and the leadership of the Spirit, and in our brokenness we offer testimony to the One who has ransomed us and will save us – and not only us but all who call on the name of the Lord.[86] Divine revelation is the Spirit of worship and witness.

In conclusion, Pentecostal worship is not a means to an end but an end in itself. The Pentecostal community has a responsibility to minister to the world as witnesses which flows out of our worship of God. We testify of God's activity. We are able to do so because God's story of revelation has made room for our story of personal redemption, transforming us into the people of God. We have been shaped by the strange world of the Bible and the uneasy and yet assuring presence of the Holy Spirit. Witness is not so much a pragmatic activity as an ontological existence in the world as the body of Christ and the temple of the Holy Spirit. Our acts are doxological because they are reciprocal and inseparable 'relational' privileges of the Pentecostal community – responsibilities made possible through divine revelation. We have been

---

[85] I am calling for us to return to the early Pentecostals' practice of peacemaking. For why this is so essential in a postmodern context, see Thiselton, *Interpreting God and the Postmodern Self*. Furthermore, I believe 'peacemaking' is an essential aspect of the 'Gospel' and an implicit aspect of the Pentecostal Fivefold Gospel. For more development, see Kenneth J. Archer and Andrew S. Hamilton, 'Anabaptism-Pietistism and Pentecostalism: Scandalous Partners in Protest', *SJT* (forthcoming).

[86] For a more developed and integrated discussion concerning worship as the way of doing Pentecostal theology see Kenneth J. Archer, 'A Pentecostal Way of Doing Theology: Method and Manner' in *IJST* 9.3 (July 2007).

privileged to be invited as frail human beings to join the social Trinity in the mysterious dance of authentic life, which heals the past and creates positive possibilities for the future. And that's the point!

★★★★★★★★★★★★★★★★★★

Abstract

This essay is an explanation of R. Hollis Gause's theology of divine revelation. This essay is not an attempt to codify his theology but to guide the reader into Gause's theological posture and pattern of thought by means of his accessible primary writings, which develop his understanding of divine revelation. Divine revelation is the key to his theological method, which opens the door of understanding to his theology. Divine revelation is the Word's intrusive revelation to humanity. Revelation and redemption are interwoven and are foundational to his understanding of Pentecostal theology. Pentecostal theology is primarily a theology of worship and witness. At the end of the essay, I further sketch the relational connections of revelation with Scripture and epistemology for a postmodern world.

8

Boundless Love Divine: A Re-evaluation of Early Understandings of the Experience of Spirit Baptism

Kimberly Ervin Alexander[*]

> Oh, boundless love divine!
> How shall this tongue of mine
> To wondering mortals tell the matchless grace divine
> That I a child of hell,
> Should in His image shine!
> The Comforter has come![1]

There has been little argument from the onset of the Pentecostal revival that the experience of Spirit baptism, with its accompanying manifestation of speaking in tongues, has been the most notable of the distinguishing characteristics of the movement. This is not to suggest that Spirit baptism and *glossolalia* are the *only* distinguishing features;[2] neither is it meant to suggest that this experience can or should be isolated from other experiences and doctrines central to the spirituality of the movement. The Pentecostal doctrine of Spirit baptism is not an

---

[*] Kimberly Ervin Alexander (Ph.D., Open University [St. John's College, Nottingham]) is Associate Professor of Historical Theology at the Pentecostal Theological Seminary, Cleveland, TN.

[2] William J. Kirkpatrick, 'The Comforter Has Come', *Hymns of the Spirit* (Cleveland, TN: Pathway, 1969), p. 93.

[2] Don Dayton argues, 'Perhaps even more characteristic of Pentecostalism than the doctrine of the baptism of the Spirit is its celebration of miracles of divine healing as part of God's salvation and as evidence of divine power in the church' (Donald Dayton, *Theological Roots of Pentecostalism* [Peabody, MA: Hendrickson, 1987], p. 115). It might also be argued that Pentecostal churches were known as much for their adherence to the doctrines of sanctification and holiness as a standard of living as they were for Pentecostal manifestations. In fact, holiness and Pentecostal experience were synonymous in the view of both insiders and outsiders. See R. Hollis Gause, 'The Historical Development of the Doctrine of Holiness in the Church of God' (unpublished paper) and 'A Pentecostal Theology: Perils and Prospects' (unpublished paper). See also R. Hollis Gause, 'Issues in Pentecostalism' in *Perspectives on the New Pentecostalism* (ed. Russell Spittler; Grand Rapids, MI: Baker Book House, 1976), pp. 106-16.

'add-on' to Evangelical theology nor is the experience simply an ecstatic episode. Steven J. Land writes, 'Thus, the point of Pentecostal spirituality was not to have an experience or several experiences, though they spoke of discrete experiences. The point was to experience life as part of a biblical drama of participation in God's history'.[3] What it does suggest is that a new understanding of baptism in the Spirit, and the accompanying manifestation, did distinguish these believers from their contemporaries and from the churches from which they came. Although this distinction was viewed by many as divisive and sectarian, for those who had experienced Spirit baptism it served as a marker signaling that they were now a part of a Last-Days move of God. Land writes, 'It was this fifth motif ['The baptism in the Holy Spirit evidenced by speaking in tongues'] that, more than anything else, served as a "sign" that the "evening light" was shining before the darkness when no one could work.'[4]

It has become standard rhetoric in classical Pentecostal circles to describe the purpose of Spirit baptism as 'power for service' or 'power for witness'. The 'Statement of Fundamental Truths' of the Assemblies of God (AG) states that with Spirit baptism 'comes the enduement of power for life and service, the bestowment of the gifts and their uses in the work of the ministry.' The expanded statement explains that 'With the baptism in the Holy Spirit come such experiences as: an overflowing fullness of the Spirit', 'a deepened reverence for God', 'an intensified consecration to God and dedication to His work', 'and a more active love for Christ, for His Word and for the lost'.[5] The AG also delineates 'Four defining truths' which state the following with regard to Spirit baptism:

> With the experience comes the provision of power for victorious Christian living and productive service. It also provides believers with specific spiritual gifts for more effective ministry. The baptism of Christians in the Holy Spirit is accompanied by the initial physical sign of speaking in other tongues (unlearned languages) as the Spirit of God gives them audible expression.[6]

---

[3] Steven J. Land, *Pentecostal Spirituality: A Passion for the Kingdom* (JPTS 1; Sheffield, UK: Sheffield Academic Press, 1993), pp. 74-75. Land argues for an integrated core (the fivefold gospel), which correlates with religious affections (gratitude, compassion and courage). He says, 'My thesis is that the righteousness, holiness and power of God are correlated with distinctive apocalyptic affections which are the integrating core of Pentecostal spirituality. This spirituality is Christocentric precisely because it is pneumatic; its "fivefold gospel" is focused on Christ because of its starting point in the Holy Spirit' (p. 23).

[4] Land, *Pentecostal Spirituality*, p. 18.

[5] http://ag.org/top/Beliefs/Statement_of_Fundamental_Truths/sft_full.cfm#7

[6] http://www.ag.org/top/beliefs/index.cfm

The Church of God (Cleveland, Tennessee) (COG) 'Declaration of Faith' states succinctly: '[We believe] in the baptism with the Holy Ghost subsequent to a clean heart.'[7] However, in explaining the 'The Principal Distinctive' of Pentecostalism, Ray H. Hughes, former General Overseer, writes, 'It can all be summed up by saying that the purpose of Pentecost is to supply equipment for service, adequacy for vocation, and enduement of power for the task of world evangelization.'[8]

The Church of God in Christ (COGIC) 'Affirmation of Faith' states, 'We believe that the baptism in the Holy Ghost, according to Acts 2:4, is given to believers who ask for it.'[9] This statement, like that of the COG says nothing about purpose. However, the more lengthy statement, 'The Doctrines of the Church of God in Christ', explains the position more fully:

> We believe that the Baptism of the Holy Ghost is an experience subsequent to conversion and sanctification and that tongue-speaking is the consequence of the baptism in the Holy Ghost with the manifestations of the fruit of the Spirit (Galatians 5:22-23; Acts 10:46, 19:1-6). We believe that we are not baptized with the Holy Ghost in order to be saved (Acts 19:1-6; John 3:5). When one receives a baptismal Holy Ghost experience, we believe one will speak with a tongue unknown to oneself according to the sovereign will of Christ. To be filled with the Spirit means to be Spirit-controlled as expressed by Paul in Ephesians 5:18-19. Since the charismatic demonstrations were necessary to help the early church to be successful in implementing the command of Christ, we therefore, believe that a Holy Ghost experience is mandatory for all men today.[10]

The International Pentecostal Holiness Church, in the amplification of their doctrinal tenet regarding Spirit baptism, maintains

> We believe that the Pentecostal baptism with the Holy Ghost and fire is obtainable by a definite act of appropriating faith on the part of the fully cleansed believer (Luke 11:13; 24:49; Acts 1:5, 8; 2:38, 39). We believe that this great blessing, which provides the enduement of power to witness for Christ, is available to all believers whose hearts are cleansed from sin by the blood of our Lord Jesus Christ. Since the Bible teaches that our bodies are temples of the Holy Ghost (1 Corinthians 6:19, 20)-and that the temple of God is holy, which temple ye (believers) are (1 Corinthians 3:16, 17)-we do not believe that God will fill an unclean temple or vessel with His Holy Spirit. In other

---

[7] http://churchofgod.cc/about/declaration_of_faith.cfm
[8] Ray H. Hughes, *What is Pentecost* (Cleveland, TN: Pathway, 1963), p. 21 quoted in Ray H. Hughes, *Church of God Distinctives* (Cleveland, TN: Pathway, 1989), p. 26.
[9] http://www.cogic.org/believe.htm
[10] http://www.cogic.org/dctrn.htm

> words, we believe, because the Bible teaches and requires it, that in
> order to receive the baptism with the Holy Ghost, a person must have
> a clean heart and life as a prerequisite for this great blessing. Remem-
> ber, the blood of cleansing must first be applied, then the oil, which is
> a type of the Holy Spirit (Leviticus 14:14, 17).[11]

These statements or explanations all maintain that Spirit baptism is
subsequent to initial salvation and that the purpose is power for witness, evangelism and fulfilling the Great Commission. While all Pentecostals would not agree with theologian J. Rodman Williams' adamant
assertion, many would. He writes, 'This [subsequent experience of
Spirit baptism] is not salvation but implementation; it is not transformation into a new creature but his commissioning for the sake of Christ and the gospel.'[12]

Drawing from Acts 1.8, Pentecostal preachers, leaders and theologians have often limited the function to be a vocational one *only*.[13] The
result of this vocational view is that the experience has been regarded
as utilitarian. In its simplest translation, 'power for witness' has been
translated into boldness as contrasted with intimidation or introversion.
While extroversion may be a perceived result of Spirit baptism, the
verb in Acts 1.8 is a verb of being not doing. As Land says, 'The point
is to walk in and live out of the fullness of God, to exist in radical
openness, meek yieldedness and passionate zeal for the things of God.'
He continues, 'Being filled with the Spirit is being yielded to, directed
and empowered by God to give a witness more consistent with his
Spirit to Jesus Christ.'[14] Spirit-filled believers *bear* witness to Jesus. The
witness that was received on the Day of Pentecost was a witness that
the Resurrected Jesus had ascended and had poured out the Spirit.

This paper will attempt to re-assess the early understanding of Spirit
baptism through the voices of those testifying to the experience. First,
a survey of early doctrinal statements and definitions will be offered.
Secondly, testimonies from early Pentecostalism will be examined. It is
believed that hearing these voices will shed light on how early Pentecostals viewed their transformation. The examination will pay close
attention to manifestations (visions, sensations, prophetic messages) that
accompanied the experience as well as any interpretation offered by the
witness(es). Thirdly, conclusions will be drawn with regard to the con-

---

[11] http://arc.iphc.org/theology/amp4.html

[12] J.R. Williams, 'Baptism in the Holy Spirit' in *IDPCM*, p. 360.

[13] See Peter Hocken, 'The Meaning and Purpose of "Baptism in the Spirit"' *Pneuma*
7.2 (Fall 1985), pp. 125-33. Hocken argues that the *meaning* of Spirit Baptism can be
spoken of differently than one speaks of the *purpose* of the experience. Purpose may be
linked to service but meaning lies in the transformational nature of the experience and in
the believer's new relationship to the persons of the Trinity.

[14] Land, *Pentecostal Spirituality*, p. 170.

tinuity/discontinuity of the testimonies with early apologetic and polemical statements made by the leadership of the movement. Finally, suggestions for how this material might strengthen current discussions will be offered.

A Third Experience: Early Apologetics and Polemics

The Pentecostal movement first identified itself as the 'Apostolic Faith' movement, a term inherited from Charles Fox Parham.[15] The revival in North America, by most accounts, actually began as a 'self-aware' movement in Los Angeles in 1906. That is, those gathered at the home of Richard and Ruth Asberry on Bonnie Brae Street, who later moved to Azusa Street and opened a mission to house the growing revival, were actively seeking the experience of Spirit baptism with the 'Bible evidence' of speaking in tongues.[16]

Though most early Pentecostals considered themselves to be noncreedal, many did adopt 'Statements of Faith', identifying the commonly held doctrinal tenets of the Pentecostal Movement, or their branch of it. Such a statement is found in the inaugural issue of *The Apostolic Faith*, the monthly publication of the Apostolic Faith Mission at 312 Azusa Street. This statement includes a tenet on Spirit baptism, which identifies 'speaking in new tongues' as evidentiary. It reads,

> The Baptism with the Holy Ghost is a gift of power upon the sanctified life; so when we get it we have the same evidence as the Disciples received on the Day of Pentecost (Acts 2:3,4), in speaking in new tongues. [sic] See also Acts 10:45, 46; Acts 19:6; 1 Cor. 14:21. "For I will work a work in your days which ye will not believe though it be told you." – Hab. 1:5[17]

---

[15] This paper will not attempt to rehearse the story of the origins of the movement. For the most recent treatment of the historical account, see Cecil M. Robeck, Jr., *The Azusa Street Mission and Revival: The Birth of the Global Pentecostal Movement* (Nashville, TN: Nelson, 2006). See also Vinson Synan, *The Holiness-Pentecostal Tradition: Charismatic Movements in the Twentieth Century* (Grand Rapids, MI: Eerdmans, 1997) for a history of the movement as it spread beyond Los Angeles.

[16] Clearly, those leading and attending this revival were not the first to have this experience. There had been sporadic outpourings as well as expectations of this type of outpouring for decades in other parts of the world, but those other revivals were not catalytic in the way that Azusa was, nor did they necessarily see the experience as normative. Agnes Ozman had sought for and experienced Spirit baptism with the outward manifestation of tongues in Kansas City on January 1, 1901. Accounts of other revivals, including the Shearer Schoolhouse revival in North Carolina (1896), where around 100 people reportedly spoke in tongues, detail this same type of outpouring. However, there is little evidence that most of these understood tongues as evidentiary in the way that the adherents at Azusa understood it.

[17] *The Apostolic Faith* 1.1 (Sept. 1906), p. 2.

This statement is telling theologically. First, it states that the experience is a baptism 'with the Holy Ghost'. This hallmark experience of the revival has been correlated with the language used by John the Baptist (Mt. 3.11; Mk. 1.8; Lk. 3.16; Jn 1.33), by Jesus (Acts 1.5) and by Peter (Acts 11.16). Secondly, the experience is understood to be a gift consisting of power. There is here neither an explanation of the kind of power received nor one of its purpose. Thirdly, the gift is subsequent to the experience of sanctification. Fourthly, it is evidenced by 'speaking in new tongues' in the same way that it was evidenced in the experience of the disciples on the Day of Pentecost. Scriptures referenced in addition to Acts 2.3-4 reveal that the Azusa leaders understood the accounts in Acts 10 (Cornelius's family) and Acts 19 (Ephesian believers) to be recurring incidents of the experience of the disciples in Acts 2. Finally, the citation of the Habakkuk text reveals that they understood this to be a 'new work' of God.

Although the statement is by itself theologically significant, its real significance is found contextually. An examination of the full doctrinal statement is telling of the movement's polemic. The Holiness churches, from which many of these leaders had come, had identified sanctification with Baptism in the Holy Spirit.[18] It was incumbent upon the leadership of the movement that they both differentiate the two experiences and show the biblical support for the validity of Spirit baptism and speaking in tongues.

The initial sentence states, 'The Apostolic Faith Movement stands for the restoration of the faith once delivered unto the saints---the old time religion, camp meetings, revivals, missions, street and prison work and Christian Unity everywhere.'[19] The claim of this statement is that everything that follows (ten tenets) is consistent with the 'faith once delivered unto the saints'. The first eight tenets deal with aspects of initial conversion: repentance, godly sorrow, confession, 'forsaking sinful ways', restitution and faith. The next statement identifies justification as the 'first work'. The 'second work' is sanctification. The statement reads, 'Sanctification is the second work of grace and the last work of grace.'[20] Following this claim is a lengthy explanation and definition of sanctification followed by scriptural warrant. The point of the explanation is that sanctification 'makes us holy' and is an act of cleansing. The polemic increases with the following:

> The Disciples were sanctified before the Day of Pentecost. By a careful study of Scripture you will find it is so. "Ye are clean through the

---

[18] See Robeck, *Azusa Street Mission and Revival*, pp. 51-58 for a discussion of this schism.

[19] *AF* 1.1 (Sept. 1906), p. 2.

[20] *AF* 1.1 (Sept. 1906), p. 2.

word which I have spoken unto you" (John 15:3; 13:10); and Jesus had breathed on them the Holy Ghost (John 20:21, 22). You know, that they could not receive the Spirit if they were not clean. Jesus cleansed and got all doubt out of His Church before he went back to glory.[21]

What follows is the statement regarding Spirit baptism discussed above. It seems that the extreme position, which implies that Spirit baptism is not a work of grace, is a reaction to those in the Holiness churches and tradition who had previously identified sanctification as Spirit baptism.

A similar argument may be found in the writing of Hattie M. Barth in *The Bridegroom's Messenger*. In an article titled, 'Justification, Sanctification and Baptism of the Holy Ghost', she writes,

> The baptism of the Spirit, or immersion in the Holy Ghost, can hardly be called a work of grace, for by it we are neither saved nor sanctified. It is typified, no doubt by the holy of holies, and there was no altar there, and no earthly light, only the sheckinah [*sic*] glory. We are saved and sanctified by the blood, the Spirit being the agent, who supplies the blood, bearing witness with our spirit, both to our justification and sanctification. Rom. 8:16; Heb. 10:18.[22]

Barth is arguing with those who claim that Spirit baptism is either received in initial conversion or is synonymous with sanctification. She has previously defined both justification (using the language of penal substitution but curiously moving toward the language of regeneration) and sanctification (using the language of crucifixion and surrender). In each of these sections she has illustrated the works with analogies from the tabernacle furnishings and feasts.[23]

Barth goes on to define the experience of Spirit baptism: 'This baptism means the complete filling and possessing of a cleansed temple by the Holy Ghost. It means the sweetest communion, abiding in the holy of holies.' She concludes further that it 'is our equipment for service'.[24]

The explanation of Spirit baptism offered in *The Pentecost* published by J.R. Flower and C.J. Quinn from Indianapolis, Indiana concurs with this differentiation:

---

[21] *AF* 1.1 (Sept. 1906), p. 2

[22] Hattie M. Barth, 'Justification, Sanctification and Baptism of the Holy Ghost', *The Bridegroom's Messenger* 1.6 (January 15, 1908), p. 2.

[23] In discussing justification, Barth uses the brazen altar, as well as the laver, as an analog. When discussing sanctification, she refers to entering the Holy Place where one finds the table of shewbread. She also sees justification as Passover and sanctification as being represented by the Feast of Unleavened Bread (Barth, 'Justification', p. 2)

[24] Barth, 'Justification', p. 2.

> Jesus did not say ye shall receive power after that you are sanctified but that ye shall receive power after that the Holy Ghost is come upon you.

> We are saved and sanctified by faith in the atoning blood of Jesus Christ, but the baptism of the Holy Ghost is a gift of God on the saved and sanctified life.[25]

This same article, however, goes on to discuss the depth of the experience:

> What are the results of a real Pentecostal experience? Are the fruits of the Spirit manifested in the lives of those who receive it as well as the gifts? These are questions that have been puzzling the holiness world for sometime. The fruits of the Spirit peace, [sic] love, joy, long suffering [sic] and patience are manifested in their lives to a greater degree than in the lives of those who have not received the baptism of the Holy Ghost. If the fruits are not manifested, there is something wrong with your experience. When the Holy Ghost comes in, it is only natural that He should manifest Himself and show forth His nature in the baptized individual.[26]

The writer goes on,

> The baptism of the Holy Ghost does not consist in simply speaking in tongues. No. It has a much more grand and deeper meaning than that. It fills our souls with the love of God for lost humanity, and makes us much more than willing to leave home, friends, and all to work in His vineyard, even if it be far away among the heathen.[27]

Noteworthy is this combination of an impartation of the love of God that is understood deontologically: 'the love of God for lost humanity'.

The Spirit and the Bride by George F. Taylor is perhaps the earliest book-length apologetic for Spirit baptism as a distinct work. Written in 1907, the book is subtitled 'A Scriptural Presentation of the Operations, Manifestations, Gifts and Fruit of the Holy Spirit In His Relation to the Bride with special reference to The "Latter Rain" Revival'.[28] In the preface, Taylor states that he intends to answer questions scripturally with regard to the new movement.[29] He states that he has devoted one

---

[25] *The Pentecost* 1.1 (Aug. 1908), p. 4.

[26] *The Pentecost* 1.1 (Aug. 1908), p. 4.

[27] *The Pentecost* 1.1 (Aug. 1908), p. 4.

[28] G.F. Taylor, *The Spirit and the Bride* (Dunn, NC: n.p., 1907).

[29] Because this manuscript was written very early in the Pentecostal revival, it is valuable as a near catalog of the objections raised by those in both holiness and non-holiness traditions. It is also clear that Taylor, at this point, understood tongues to be the tongues of nations, or *xenolalia*. He writes, 'On the day of Pentecost the one hundred and twenty spoke in other languages as the Spirit gave utterance. A person who has only the manifestation of tongues can speak in another language only as the Spirit gives utterance, but a

chapter to the question 'Do all who receive the Baptism of the Spirit speak with other tongues?'[30] Taylor also devotes a chapter to the differentiation between sanctification and Spirit baptism. Probably the most influential section of this work is Taylor's interpretation of the parable of the ten virgins (Mt. 25). His conclusion is,

> Then the difference between the wise and the foolish virgins is the former have received the Baptism of the Holy Spirit, the latter have not. The ten virgins are virgins – sanctified – before the bride is called into her chamber; but they fail to obtain the Baptism of the Spirit, hence are among the "left ones".[31]

Taylor contends that one purpose of Spirit baptism is to establish 'a permanent relationship between the Spirit and the Bride.' For Taylor, the cry, 'The Spirit and the Bride say, "Come"' is 'an unceasing call for the coming of the Bridegroom'.[32]

The earliest statement that may be called a doctrinal statement in the Church of God was published in the August 15, 1910 edition of the *Evangel*. It is a publication of a list of 'the teaching that is made prominent'. A committee had been appointed at the 1909 General Assembly with the purpose of composing a list of beliefs. These 'teachings' were to be used in the qualifying of ministerial candidates. The eighth tenet is 'Baptism with the Holy Ghost subsequent to cleansing. The endue-ment of power for service; Matt. 3;11, Luke 24;49-53; Acts 1;4-8 [*sic*].'[33] This statement is followed by tenet nine: 'The speaking in tongues as the evidence of the baptism with the Holy Ghost – John 15;26, Acts 2;4, Acts 44-46, Acts 19;1-7 [*sic*].'[34] These statements are consistent with those of the Apostolic Faith Mission at Azusa Street.

Similarly, the statement regarding the doctrinal teaching of the Glad Tidings Hall, Apostolic Faith Mission in New York City, published in *The Midnight Cry*, states that they teach 'the Baptism of the Holy Ghost as received on the day of Pentecost with speaking in tongues as evi-

---

person who has the gift of tongues can speak other languages at will, and, no doubt, several different languages' (Taylor, *Spirit and the Bride*, p. 63). He explains further, 'That person who has received the gift of tongues has a bridge from him across Babylon to every creature on earth' (p. 104). A re-evaluation of the shift from seeing tongues as *xenolalia* or 'missionary tongues' to *glossolalia*, as well as an assessment of how widespread was this early view would be a fruitful study in the future. For a helpful introduction to the history of this shift in terminology and understanding, see G.B. McGee, 'Initial Evidence' in *IDPCM*, pp. 784-91.

[30] Taylor, *Spirit and the Bride*, 'Preface', p. 5.

[31] Taylor, *Spirit and the Bride*, p. 115.

[32] Taylor, *Spirit and the Bride*, p. 128.

[33] *The Evening Light and Church of God Evangel*, August 15, 1910, p. 3. See also *General Assembly Minutes 1906-1914: Photographic Reproductions of the First Ten General Assembly Minutes* (Cleveland, TN: White Wing, 1992), p. 245.

[34] *Minutes*, p. 245.

dence (Acts ii, 4; Mark xvi, 17).'[35] The paper, while differentiating the crisis experiences, points to the integration and continuity of the *via salutis*:

> There is no difference in regard to the Purity of the life between the Sanctified and Baptized Saint. Both are Holy. Sanctification is Christ enthroned in the heart. The baptism of the Holy Ghost is His Spirit Poured out. Endued with power from on high. It is Jesus in justification. It is Jesus in Sanctification. It is Jesus who baptizes in the Holy Ghost. If we follow Jesus we will be like Him.[36]

In Church of God General Overseer A.J. Tomlinson's 1913 work, *The Last Great Conflict*, he expounds on the purpose of being baptized in the Holy Spirit. He speaks of the Spirit as 'our Pilot' constantly moving us 'forward toward the goal.'[37] Tomlinson explains,

> The Holy Ghost is given for service not for pleasure. He is to guide into all truth, even into the fellowship of the mystery. The natural man cannot comprehend the things of God, but 'the Spirit searcheth all things, yea, the deep things of God.' Then if you have Him dwelling in your mortal body you may expect to be led deeper and yet deeper until the end is reached.[38]

While Tomlinson uses the standard rhetoric of 'service', he does go on to speak of a deeper relationship. In other words, the Spirit, as 'guide' or 'Pilot' does not simply lead a person geographically but also into a deeper union with God. Tomlinson speaks teleologically and sees this as an ongoing relationship, moving the believer toward the end.

Tomlinson's defense of tongues as evidence is based on the personal nature of the Spirit and on Jesus' teaching on the Spirit in John 14-16. If the Spirit is to 'testify' of Jesus, he must speak.[39] Witnesses must use 'words, signs or writing.' He supports this with accounts from Acts 2, 10 and 19.[40]

One of the most well developed doctrinal statements is found in the 1911 'Constitution and General Rules of the Pentecostal Holiness Church'. The 'Basis of Union' statement includes the following:

> We believe also that the Pentecostal baptism of the Holy Ghost and fire is obtainable by a definite act of appropriating faith on the part of

---

[35] *The Midnight Cry*, vol. I, 2nd ed., no. 1 (Mar.-Apr. 1911), p. 4.

[36] *The Midnight Cry*, p. 3.

[37] A.J. Tomlinson, *The Last Great Conflict* (Cleveland, TN: Walter E. Rodgers, 1913), p. 77.

[38] Tomlinson, *Last Great Conflict,* pp. 76-77.

[39] The term 'witnessing in the Spirit' was often used to refer to speaking in tongues, especially messages in tongues in corporate worship.

[40] Tomlinson, *Last Great Conflict,* pp. 110-12.

the fully cleansed believer, and that the initial evidence of the reception of this experience is speaking with other tongues as the Spirit gives utterance (Luke 11:13; Acts 1:5; 2:14; 8:17; 10:44-46; 19:6).[41]

Though in substance this statement is essentially the same, there are several phrases that have been incorporated that are noteworthy. First, there is an enhancement in the language used to refer to the experience; this statement designates the experience as the 'baptism of the Holy Ghost and fire'. This is significant historically because the union involved here is a merger involving the Pentecostal Holiness Church and the Fire Baptized Holiness Church. Prior to the Pentecostal revival of 1906, the FBHC had advocated an experience of 'fire baptism'.[42] Secondly, the statement describes *how* the experience is obtained: 'by a definite act of appropriating faith on the part of the fully cleansed believer'. Thirdly, this statement refers to speaking with tongues as 'initial evidence'.[43] The implication of the use of the term 'initial' is that there are other evidences. What this statement does not address is the purpose or function of Spirit baptism.

Related to this statement is an extensive doctrinal exposition, *From Passover to Pentecost*, completed by J.H. King of the Pentecostal Holiness Church in 1913.[44] Using the analogies of the Old Testament feasts, like Hattie Barth has done earlier, King offers an apologetic for the experiences of initial salvation, sanctification and Spirit baptism. He defends both subsequence and tongues as a sign. Significantly, King explores the transformational nature of the experience, seeing its significance in relation to salvation. Like the earliest polemics, King too differentiates the experience from sanctification. He writes, 'There is nothing in the feast of Weeks, or Pentecost, that has the remotest idea of cleansing attached to it.'[45] King sees the significance of Spirit baptism in the fact that it is first poured out on the Day of Pentecost, after Jesus' crucifixion, resurrection and ascension. Pentecost was a celebration of the harvest. He writes,

---

[41] 'Constitution and General Rules of the Pentecostal Holiness Church' (1911) http://pctii.org/arc/1911.html

[42] See Synan, *Holiness-Pentecostal Tradition*, pp. 51-53.

[43] The term 'initial evidence', as opposed to 'Bible evidence' or 'Bible sign', may have been coined by J.H. King (so Vinson Synan, in a personal conversation at Regent University, Virginia Beach, Virginia, March 2005). See also G.B. McGee, 'Initial Evidence' in *IDPCM*, p. 784. J.H. King was the General Overseer of the Fire Baptized Holiness Church when it came into the Pentecostal movement in 1908. At the time of the union, King was away on a missionary tour and was made 'Assistant General Superintendent' (H.V. Synan, 'King, Joseph Hillery' in *IDPCM*, p. 823).

[44] Joseph. H. King, *From Passover to Pentecost* (4th ed.; Franklin Springs, GA: Advocate, 1976).

[45] King, *From Passover to Pentecost*, p. 119.

This feast of weeks was at the time of full harvest. The harvest was not fully reaped, but only the beginning of reaping in full. When all was harvested and garnered, then they were to keep the feast of Ingathering, or Tabernacles, according to Deut. 16:13. The baptism of the Holy Ghost is the beginning of the fullness of God imparted to believers. We are filled with God's fullness in Pentecost, but not in all the fullness of God. We are but entering the harvest field of the full gospel, and it is ours to gather in all the grain, as far as it belongs to this age. All that we receive in this time of the Spirit's dispensation is styled 'firstfruits of the Spirit' but this is but a token of the full harvest in the beyond, which will continue through eternal ages.[46]

In this statement, one notes both the soteriological (impartation of the fullness of God) and eschatological ('a token of the full harvest in the beyond, that will continue through eternal ages') dimensions of Spirit baptism.[47]

An extraordinary, but rarely noted theological contribution of King's discussion is his understanding of 'fullness'. For King the 'fullness' received in this experience is an 'inward revelation and indwelling' of the Trinity. He writes, 'God as a Trinity – Father, Son and Holy Ghost – was revealed in those who were baptized in Jerusalem, and this was never known by any one previous to that event.'[48]

With regard to function, King draws from Old Testament 'type and symbol'. He delineates such purposes as 'blessings and power going

---

[46] King, *From Passover to Pentecost*, p. 121.

[47] For a later extensive elaboration of these same dimensions, see R. Hollis Gause, *The Preaching of Paul: A Study of Romans* (Cleveland, TN: Pathway, 1986), p. 101. In his discussion of Romans 8, Gause discusses these same dimensions: 'Life in the Holy Spirit produces the resurrection life in the believer: "And if the Spirit of the One who raised Jesus from the dead, dwells in you, the One who raised Christ from the dead shall also quicken your mortal bodies through His Spirit who dwells in you" (8:11). The Holy Spirit has provided life in the full reversal of sin; this includes spiritual life. The emphasis here contrasts with the death of the body; so Paul assures the believer of the resurrection of the body. The assurance is based on redemption through Christ. First, it is based on the resurrection of Christ; He is "the firstfruits of them that slept" (1 Corinthians 15:20-23). Second, God raised His Son from the dead through the agency of the Holy Spirit (Romans 1:4; Acts 13:33-35). Third, if the personal Spirit whom God used to raise Christ from the dead dwells in us, He will raise us as He did Christ. The presence of the Holy Spirit is the believer's assurance of his own bodily resurrection (cf. 2 Corinthians 5:1-5)' (p. 101).

[48] King, *From Passover to Pentecost*, p. 119. Land comments on this perspective of King's, as well as a similar view held by D. Wesley Myland (Land, *Pentecostal Spirituality*, pp. 198-99). It is likely that King was informed by the former General Overseer of the FBHC (then the Fire Baptized Holiness Association), B.H. Irwin, who saw one of the benefits of the baptism of fire as an experience that 'personally introduces the believer to the different persons of the Trinity' (William T. Puriton, 'Red Hot Holiness: B.H. Irwin and the Fire-Baptized Holiness Tradition', unpublished paper presented at the 27th Annual Meeting of the Society for Pentecostal Studies in special joint session with the Wesleyan Theological Society, March 12-14, 1998, p. 9).

forth from the Holy Trinity within us';[49] illumination,[50] warfare,[51] and witness.[52] Surprisingly, what King does not explore fully is the significance of the giving of the law at Sinai for understanding Pentecost and Spirit baptism.[53]

D. Wesley Myland's sermon 'The Yielded Life' was published in *The Latter Rain Evangel*, January 1909.[54] Myland, pastor of United Tabernacle in Columbus, Ohio, declares,

> Pentecost is not glory alone; nor is it power alone. Pentecost is the glory of God's power and the power of His glory. These two things are always manifest where there is true Pentecost, for when the power strikes you, you begin to shout 'glory' for fear you will die, and many would die if they could not say it. When you cannot say it well enough in your *mother* tongue, God gives you another tongue. Indeed the ordinary tongue never could bring the highest glory to God.[55]

Myland emphasizes the role of Spirit baptism in worship. He asks, 'We have worshipped the Lord in holiness; thought we made a pretty good start at it, but who has worshipped the Lord in the *beauty* of holiness? No soul that has not known his Pentecost.'[56] Pentecostal experience, Spirit baptism, 'brings to the soul, among other blessings, *true worship*.'[57] This worship, which is due to the Lord, must be in Spirit and in truth. In response to those who would put service to the Lord first, Myland asserts that worship must precede service. Alluding to the imagery of the parable of the ten virgins, he states, 'This is an important phase of this Pentecostal Movement, for even if the Bride was perfect, she must have a real spirit of worship before she enters into the marriage feast.'[58] Perhaps more than any other early leader, Myland integrates soteriology, ecclesiology, and eschatology, grounding the experience in worship issuing in service.

This brief survey of doctrinal statements and discourse regarding the purpose and function of Spirit baptism in the early Pentecostal movement reveals that leaders felt a necessity to differentiate the experience from the prerequisite experience of sanctification. This context of ani-

[49] King, *From Passover to Pentecost*, p. 125.

[50] King, *From Passover to Pentecost*, p. 125.

[51] King, *From Passover to Pentecost*, p. 126.

[52] King, *From Passover to Pentecost*, p. 127.

[53] R. Hollis Gause explores this in his exposition of the 'Passover to Pentecost' paradigm (unpublished lecture). He sees the giving of the law at Sinai foreshadowing the writing of the law on our hearts by the Spirit.

[54] D. Wesley Myland, 'The Yielded Life', *The Latter Rain Evangel* 1.4 (January 1909), pp. 3-5.

[55] Myland, 'Yielded Life', p. 3

[56] Myland, 'Yielded Life', p. 4.

[57] Myland, 'Yielded Life', p. 4.

[58] Myland, 'Yielded Life', p. 4.

mosity produced an apologetic which placed Spirit baptism outside of the *via salutis*. However, more thoughtful reflection, even within the earliest period, produced explanations regarding the significance of the experience that identify it as transformational and as a part of the *via salutis*. At least two leaders, Tomlinson and King, speak of the experience as deepening the relationship with God, or of revealing more of God.

Experiences in the Spirit

Walter Hollenweger in identifying the African roots of Pentecostalism, delineated five characteristics common to both black spirituality and Pentecostal spirituality:

(1) 'orality of liturgy'; (2) 'narrativity of theology and witness'; (3) 'maximum participation at the levels of reflection, prayer and decision-making and therefore a form of community that is reconciliatory'; (4) 'inclusions of dreams and visions into personal and public forms of worship'; (5) 'an understanding of the body/mind relationship that is informed by experiences of correspondence between body and mind'.[59] Land has lifted Hollenweger's work to the forefront and views Pentecostal spirituality as a 'confluence' of this black spirituality and Wesleyan spirituality – a confluence that is essentially 'transformationalist'.[60]

There is no better way to view this spirituality than by reading the testimonies recorded in the periodicals and journals produced by the revival. Because of the movement's evangelistic orientation there were many of these publications, which now allow readers a century later to view the revival as it occurred. These periodicals were published with frequency and with a sense of urgency that is reflected in the formatting. *The Apostolic Faith*, published at the Apostolic Faith Mission at 312 Azusa Street is replete with testimonies of those receiving 'their Pentecost', either at the Mission or in some other Pentecostal outpost around the world. Other periodicals, such as *The Bridegroom's Messenger, The Pentecostal Testimony* and *The Church of God Evangel*, give us a similar view.

Another valuable source for this 'inside look' may be found in personal journals and diaries kept by itinerant ministers within the movement. In these journals, one may read the ministers' own testimonies as well as reports of the revival or camp meeting services in which he/she ministered. These primary witnesses, along with the primary witness found in the periodicals, will be utilized as a way of hearing these voices testify of their experiences of being baptized in the Spirit.

---

[59] Land, *Pentecostal Spirituality*, p. 52.
[60] Land, *Pentecostal Spirituality*, p. 51.

The inaugural issue of *The Apostolic Faith* (Sept. 1906) announced that 'Pentecost Has Come'. In order to demonstrate that this was a restoration of what was 'recorded in the book of Acts', the editors printed numerous testimonies, along with their own observations of what had been happening since the movement's beginning in April of the same year. One of the most remarkable of those testimonies, and especially relevant to this study, is found on page one. It reads,

> A Nazarene brother who received the baptism with the Holy Ghost in his own home in family worship, in trying to tell about it said, 'It was a baptism of love. Such abounding love! Such compassion seemed to almost kill me with its sweetness! People do not know what they are doing when they stand against it. The devil never gave me a sweet thing, he was always trying to get me to censuring people. This baptism fills us with divine love'.[61]

Given the context, and especially the opposition by Nazarene leaders and preachers, this testimony is quite telling. Notice the descriptions of his change in disposition: 'abounding love', 'compassion', 'sweetness', 'divine love'. In opposition to what others were doing (standing 'against it', 'censuring people') this man describes being baptized and filled with the love of God.

Similarly, a report in the same issue describes a preacher who was baptized in the Holy Spirit and began speaking 'Zulu and many other tongues more fluently than English and interprets as he speaks.' The account goes on to say that he was used by the Lord to 'stir a whole city'. The writer concludes, 'He is filled with divine love. His family were first afraid to see him speaking in tongues, thinking he had lost his mind, but when his wife and children felt the sympathy and divine love which the Holy Ghost puts in people's hearts, they said, "Papa was never as sane in his life."'[62] Again, there is a juxtaposition of the 'before and after' dispositions and affections in the one experiencing Spirit baptism.

In another observation of Azusa, a participant reports that, while some are 'opposing and arguing', others are 'falling down under the power of God' at the altar, 'feasting on the good things of God.'[63] This description, too, denotes a disposition that is to be contrasted with those who argue and oppose. Those who are at the altar, under the power of God, are 'feasting'. Again, there is an intimacy or union with God experienced in this nourishment.

J.H. King, a leader in the Holiness movement was, at first, one of those who opposed and fought the revival. In 1885 he had experienced

---

[61] *The Apostolic Faith* 1.1 (Sept. 1906), p. 1.
[62] *The Apostolic Faith* 1.1 (Sept. 1906), p. 1.
[63] *The Apostolic Faith* 1.1 (Sept. 1906), p. 1.

sanctification and describes that transformation as a 'marvelous change'. He explains, 'I found my ear was filled with light, love, and glory ... I seemingly was taken out of myself and thought I was within a few feet of the gates of heaven.' To King, however, the Pentecostal message, which had been quickly disseminated to the Southeast by G.B. Cash-well, appeared fanatical.[64] After a careful study of the Acts accounts, King became convinced that those baptized in the Holy Spirit would speak in tongues. He testifies of his own experience of February 15, 1907:

> As I was seeking, the Scripture recorded in John 7:37-39 seemed to be applied to my heart, and I was persuaded to rest unreservedly upon this promise. There was a joy in my heart, and I began uttering praise with my lips. There came into my heart something new, though the manifestation was not great. There was a moving of my tongue, though I cannot say that I was speaking a definite language. I only know that there was some moving of my tongue as I had never experienced before. I had some assurance that the Comforter had come into my heart. There was a peace that permeated my spirit, and I was resting in the Lord in a very blessed manner. Soon the Word began to be opened to me in a new way, and it seemed as if I had a different Bible ... during all the remaining months of that year I preached with such inspiration and power as I had never before experienced.[65]

King's testimony also reveals a transformation, and it is noteworthy that he does not mention a resulting inclination toward foreign missions, though the experience has clearly affected his vocation. His transformation resulted in a new way of seeing Scripture and more Spirit-anointed preaching. It is especially noteworthy that King uses

---

[64] It should be noted that King's caution was undoubtedly conditioned by his previous experiences in the Fire Baptized Holiness Association, under the leadership of B.H. Irwin. Irwin's movement was marked by openness to further works or baptisms in the Spirit beyond sanctification and what often resulted in excess. After Irwin's confession of immorality, King succeeded him as General Overseer. See Synan, *Holiness-Pentecostal Tradition*, p. 59. In the latter years of the 1940s King published a history of the Pentecostal Holiness Church that included a history of the Fire Baptized Holiness Association. He reflects upon the excesses of that movement: 'Where the Holy Ghost is mightily working and multitudes are under His control, or are the subjects of His powerful operations, in convicting, converting, saving, sanctifying and filling souls, of all classes, ages and temperaments, there will be the working of "wicked spirits in high places" producing strange, wild, abnormal manifestations in order to counteract by counterfeiting the work of the Holy Ghost. The Holy Ghost is never the author of insane religious manifestations, but it is the product of satanic demonry, working through man's insane religious nature to offset the influence and effect of the Spirit's glorious work' (Joseph Hillery King, 'History of the Pentecostal Holiness Church', unpublished, pp. 14-15).

[65] J.H. King, quoted in B.E. Underwood, *Christ – God's Love Gift: Selected Writings of Joseph Hillery King*, vol. I (Franklin Springs, GA: Advocate, 1969), p. 13.

the Wesleyan language of 'assurance' with regard to *glossolalia*. This
assurance resulted in peace and 'resting in the Lord'.

The testimony of another prominent leader, Charles Harrison Mason, of the Church of God in Christ, is published in *The Apostolic
Faith*.[66] Mason confesses that he had struggled over the new doctrine
and over the interpretation of Mark 16.17-18. He reveals that he had
been given a vision before coming to Los Angeles. Then, in Los Angeles, he was given a 'parable'. He explains,

> I went to the altar and the Lord put a parable before me. If you were
> going to marry, would you be sad? I said, no, when I was going to be
> married, I was glad. He then showed me this was wedlock to Christ. If
> there was anything imperfect about me, He would make it right and
> marry me anyway. Then my faith was settled and laid firmly hold on
> the promise.[67]

An unsigned exhortation in an earlier edition of *The Apostolic Faith*
emphasizes this union or marriage resulting between Jesus and the one
baptized in the Spirit. Commenting on Mt. 11.29, the author writes,
'The Lord showed me that this yoke was the covenant of the New
Testament in His blood, and we put this yoke on when we are baptized with the Holy Ghost. This covenant is a marriage covenant. We
are married, not for one day or year or life, but eternally married.' The
writer concludes the analogy with praise, 'Hallelujah! Jesus and I are
united. He baptized me with love.'[68] This testimony and interpretation
of the experience describe its result as 'covenant' and 'union', both of
which are biblical metaphors of salvation (see Rom. 6.5; Phil. 2.1).[69]

Four testimonies describing reception of the Spirit are remarkably
similar. These detailed accounts provide valuable insight into how the
recipients interpreted the work of the Spirit at the time of the experience. It has already been noted that C.H. Mason had received a visionary confirmation before going to Azusa. He describes what
occurred at Azusa as he returned to his seat and began to focus on Jesus. At this point,

> the Holy Ghost took charge of me. I surrendered perfectly to Him and
> consented to Him. Then I began singing a song in unknown tongues,
> and it was the sweetest thing to have Him sing that song through me.
> He had complete charge of me. I let Him have my mouth and every-
> thing. After that it seemed I was standing at the cross and heard Him as
> He groaned, the dying groans of Jesus, and I groaned. It was not my
> voice but the voice of my Beloved that I heard in me. When He got

---

[66] *The Apostolic Faith* 1.6 (Feb.–Mar. 1907), p. 7.
[67] *The Apostolic Faith* 1.6 (Feb.–Mar. 1907), p. 7.
[68] *The Apostolic Faith* 1.2 (Oct. 1906), p. 3.
[69] Seymour develops this marriage analogy in *The Apostolic Faith* 2.13 (May 1908), p. 4.

through with that, He started the singing again in unknown tongues. When the singing stopped, I felt that complete death. It was my life going out, but it was a complete death to me. When He had finished this, I let Him hold my hands up, and they rested just as easily up as down. Then He turned on the joy of it. He began to lift me up. I was passive in His hands. I was not going to do a thing. I could hear the people but did not let anything bother me. It came to me, 'I charge thee, O daughters of Jerusalem, that ye stir not up nor awake my Beloved until He please.' S. S. 8. 4. He lifted me to my feet and then the light of heaven fell upon me and burst into me filling me. Then God took charge of my tongue and I went to preaching in tongues. I could not change my tongue. The glory of God filled the temple. The gestures of my hands and movements of my body were His. O it was marvelous and I thank God for giving it to me in His way. Such an indescribable peace and quietness went all through my flesh and into my very brain and has been there ever since.[70]

In September 1908 *The Pentecost* published an extended testimony of Ruth Angstead, composed on November 24, 1907. She begins, 'I have a precious story to tell, for I too plunged into that "fountain opened in the house of David for all sin and uncleanness" and found all the horrible bondage of my spirit, soul and body go like darkness before day.' She continues, 'Our union, so sweetly begun, grew to such preciousness and glory as the months and years sped by, with panting hunger that He should manifest His "never failing" love and almighty power in the vessel He had washed in His own life blood.'[71] Angstead describes a visionary experience in which she not only saw but also felt the pains of the crucifixion and the agony of Gethsemane, much as Mason has described. She narrates the experience,

I tasted of the cup of His suffering. It seemed my very heart would break and the blood oozed from the pores of my body. I then had a glimpse of the Celestial City of Glory. A stream pure as crystal flowed from under the throne, winding about, with trees of life on either side. Oh such wonderful flowers and mansions. No tongue or pen could describe these or the wonderful glory from His radiant countenance which lighted the whole, no, not through the ceaseless ages of eternity. [*sic*] Then I saw the ascension and His glorious return in the clouds with ten thousand of His angels. Beloved of earth He cometh soon.[72]

Her vision transported her to hell and to the judgment of nations. She states, 'A remnant I could not see were ever reached by His love.' After telling of a struggle with Satan, whom she says tried to stop her communion with God, Angstead describes hearing God speak, 'I was

[70] *The Apostolic Faith* 1.6 (Feb.–Mar. 1907), p. 7.
[71] *The Pentecost,* 1.2 (Sept. 1908), p. 1.
[72] *The Pentecost,* 1.2 (Sept. 1908), p. 1.

determined God should accomplish his pleasure in this and He said "Do not leave the room till I sing through you in tongues."[73] She then describes the result of the visionary experience:

> Then I sank out of self in such glorious worship before the Father, far too deep for any utterance. There seemed to be many waters surging through my being, then the Holy Spirit sang through me four songs, such beautiful words and music. I never could sing much. I was a spellbound listener to the songs just bursting forth from the glorified Jesus through His Holy Spirit. The first three, as I sang them each time – often in English – were new to me, but the fourth was that glorious old song "All glory and praise to the Lamb that was slain:" [*sic*] Then I spoke in tongues, each time interpreting, magnifying Father, Son and the precious blood.[74]

This testimony of a mystical vision and journey in the Spirit reveals the depth of the experience for Ruth Angstead. This account is particularly illustrative of R. Hollis Gause's explication of Pentecostal theology as a 'Theology of Worship', in which he delineates three elements: *rapture*, *rapport* and *proleptic*.[75] Angstead is caught up in ecstatic experience or *rapture* in which Gause contends 'the emotions are transported to the level of worshipping in the Holy Spirit, both in song and prayer.'[76] *Rapport* can be noted in her intimate communion with God, going so far as to identify with and share in the sufferings of Jesus. The third element, *proleptic*, or 'anticipation of the worship to be enjoyed when believers will fall before the thrones of the Father and of the Lamb in the consummation of the kingdom of God' is experienced as she participates in heavenly worship through song.[77]

Church of God General Overseer Tomlinson testifies of his own experience of Spirit baptism, which occurred January 12, 1908. He describes his experience in *The Last Great Conflict*:

> He [G.B. Cashwell] preached on Saturday night, and on Sunday morning, January 12, while he was preaching, a peculiar sensation took hold of me, and almost unconsciously I slipped off my chair in a heap on the rostrum at Brother Cashwell's feet. I did not know what such an experience meant. My mind was clear, but a peculiar power so enveloped and thrilled my whole being that I concluded to yield myself up to God and await the results. I was soon lost to my surroundings as I lay there on the floor, occupied only with God and eternal things. Soon one of my feet began to shake and clatter against the wall. I could not hold it still. When it got quiet the other one acted the same way. Then

---

[73] *The Pentecost*, 1.2 (Sept. 1908), p. 1.

[74] *The Pentecost*, 1.2 (Sept. 1908), pp. 1-2.

[75] R. Hollis Gause, 'Distinctives of a Pentecostal Theology', unpublished paper.

[76] R. Hollis Gause, 'Distinctives of a Pentecostal Theology', p. 36.

[77] Gause, 'Distinctives of a Pentecostal Theology', p. 21.

my arms and head were operated. My jaws seemed to be set, my lips were moved and twisted about as if a physician was making a special examination. My tongue and eyes were operated on in like manner. Several examinations seemed to be taken, and every limb and my whole body examined.

My body was rolled and tossed about beyond my control, and finally while lying on my back, my feet were raised up several times, and my tongue would stick out of my mouth in spite of my efforts to keep it inside my mouth.

At one time, while lying flat on my back, I seemed to see a great sheet let down, and as it came to me I felt it as it enveloped me in its folds, and I really felt myself literally lifted up and off the floor several inches, and carried in that sheet several feet in the direction my feet pointed, and then let down on the floor again. As I lay there great joy flooded on my soul. The happiest moments I had ever known up to that time. I never knew what real joy was before. My hands clasped together with no effort on my part. Oh, such floods and billows of glory ran through my whole being for several minutes! There were times that I suffered the most excruciating pain and agony, but my spirit always said "yes" to God.[78]

Curiously, Tomlinson's extensive description at first centers on the physical aspects of this experience and he describes the Spirit's work as that of a doctor performing an examination.[79] From this physical description, Tomlinson moves to describe the visionary aspects of his Spirit-baptism experience. Tomlinson journeys in the Spirit:

In vision I was carried to Central America, and was shown the awful condition of the people there. A paroxysm of suffering came over me as I seemed to be in soul travail for their salvation. Then I spoke in tongues as the Spirit gave utterance, and in the vision I seemed to be speaking the very same language of the Indian tribes with whom I was surrounded.[80]

Tomlinson continues to describe his 'travels' to South America and Africa. When seeing Jerusalem he writes that while he was there, '...I endured the most intense suffering, as if I might have been suffering similar to that of my Savior on Mount Calvary. I never can describe the awful agony that I felt in my body.'[81] From Jerusalem he was transported to Northern Russia, France, Japan and 'North' among the

---

[78] Tomlinson, *Last Great Conflict*, p. 234.

[79] This is especially curious for someone who is adamantly opposed to the use of doctors and medicine! It is consistent, however, with his understanding of Jesus as the Great Physician. Apparently, the other *Paraclete*, the Holy Spirit, is a physician as well.

[80] Tomlinson, *Last Great Conflict*, p. 234.

[81] Tomlinson, *Last Great Conflict*, p. 235.

Eskimos. In each place he speaks the language of the people – an experience that is preceded by a 'paroxysm of suffering'.

In addition Tomlinson describes 'terrible conflict' with the devil. He claims,

> I came into direct contact with him. While in this state came the most awful struggle of all. While talking in an unknown tongue the Spirit seemed to envelope me, and I was taken though a course of casting out devils. A real experience in the vision, and the last verses of Mark sixteen came very vividly before my mind.[82]

His vision concluded with a scene of 'multitudes of people awakened and coming this way. Among them were Mrs. Tomlinson and my children.'[83]

Tomlinson interprets his vision as one in which he is shown his mission: he sees his whole family on mission together; he says that he was able to speak ten different languages in the vision; in each place, 'multitudes' came to the light. He concludes, 'I do not know whether God wants me to go to these places or not, but I am certainly willing to go as He leads.'[84]

One may observe in this description the transformative nature of the experience. Tomlinson apparently saw this experience as a kind of therapeutic change, going so far as to use the language of medical procedure. The result is a new focus and a new way of seeing. The similarities with the experience of Angstead are striking. Both experienced visions involving transport, suffering the agony of the crucifixion and spiritual warfare. These mystical experiences are in keeping with the tradition of mysticism where one identifies with the suffering Christ and communes intimately with him. The difference, for Tomlinson at least, is that the result is a vision for the lost.

The testimony of Marie Burgess Brown, founder of Glad Tidings Hall (later Glad Tidings Tabernacle) in New York City, recorded in *The Midnight Cry,* is similar to that of Tomlinson. In 1906, after a period of tarrying for several days at a Pentecostal mission, Brown is baptized in the Spirit and is transported by the Spirit. She writes,

> In searching the word of God I found I had not what the disciples had when they received their baptism and it created a deeper hunger in my heart for all he had for me. And on the third day of waiting (tarrying) He came just as He came to them in that upper room. He did not make me a Peter or a John, but just a witness, and for five hours He filled and flooded my whole being.

---

[82] Tomlinson, *Last Great Conflict,* pp. 235-36.
[83] Tomlinson, *Last Great Conflict,* p. 236.
[84] Tomlinson, *Last Great Conflict,* p. 236.

> Then He opened my eyes to see the great need of this dark world. It seemed as if I went from one foreign field to another and in each field He would pray through me in the language of that people. I knew it not – but He did. There seemed to be great stone walls about each field and I could hear them cry for Jesus and as the Holy Spirit would begin to pray in the language of each field, I could see the walls begin to crumble and fall.
>
> How this cry touched my heart, as every cry of the Holy Spirit will and I said, 'Lord, send me, send me,' that those who want Jesus may find Him.[85]

This experience allowed Brown to both see and hear the need and cries of those who were lost. She exhorts that the devil wants to 'blind your eyes' so that you do not see the 'Lamb of God'. She warns, 'And while you are looking at other things and what others have done and are doing – Behold He cometh!' For Brown, Tomlinson and others the experience of Spirit baptism is about being given new eyes and ears to hear the cries of the lost and the voice of God.[86]

A Salvific View of Baptism in the Spirit

Without question, early Pentecostals 'officially' viewed Spirit baptism in a category other than a soteriological one. The earliest statements of faith, or creeds, attempted to separate the experience from the realm of a work of grace. There are at least two reasons for this compartmentalization. First, preparatory instruction by proto-Pentecostals like Frank Sandford and Charles Parham had proclaimed that there would be a restoration of apostolic Christianity that would commence with the outpouring of the Spirit as on the day of Pentecost (Acts 2). Those on whom the Spirit was poured out would speak with the tongues of the nations; the Bible evidence or sign was missionary tongues.[87] Secondly, the revival and its accompanying doctrine and practice caused a serious rift in the Holiness churches that, for the most part, had taught that the second experience, sanctification, was an experience of baptism in the Holy Spirit.[88] Early Pentecostals were put on the defensive and were

---

[85] Marie Burgess Brown, 'A Testimony by Mrs. Marie Burgess Brown', *The Midnight Cry*, vol. I, 2nd ed., no. 1 (Mar.–Apr. 1911), pp. 1-2.

[86] Brown, 'Testimony', p. 2.

[87] This background is explored in depth by D. William Faupel in *The Everlasting Gospel* (JPTS 10; Sheffield: Sheffield Academic Press, 1996; repr. Blandford Forum: Deo Publishing, 2009). It has not been within the scope of this paper to explore early understandings of tongues and the shift from *xenolalia* to *glossolalia*. This is, however, a much-needed study.

[88] See Dayton. For more recent and comprehensive scholarship examining this terminology and how it was used by John Wesley and John Fletcher see Lawrence W. Wood,

forced to write apologetically and sometimes polemically. The result was a sharp differentiation between the two experiences. This rigid approach produced definitions and doctrinal tenets that stated unequivocally that 'sanctification was the second and last work of grace' and that Spirit baptism was not a work of grace. The end result of this has been a vocational view that sees Spirit baptism as 'equipment for service'. This has developed into a diminishing of the necessity of the experience. Questions emerge such as 'If Spirit baptism is necessary for evangelism, why is Billy Graham such a successful evangelist?' or 'If I'm not called to be an evangelist, if that is not in my gift mix, then why would I need to speak in tongues?'[89]

In reading the more thoughtful reflections of Pentecostals, and especially in reading the testimonies of those receiving the experience, even in the earliest months of the revival, one is made aware that this experience did more than just 'equip'. These testimonies, and the theological reflection written in light of the experience, reveal that this was a transformative crisis experience. Much of the description utilizes the language of soteriology: union with Christ, marriage, covenant. The typological interpretations presuppose process or progress, either through the Holy Place to the Holy of Holies or through the Hebrew calendar, from one feast to the next. These places, furnishings or feasts were connected, each dependent on the former and anticipating the next. This implies, though not always stated directly, that Spirit baptism is an experience in the *via salutis* or to use the phrase early Pentecostals would have employed, *the way*.

Most recently, Gause's work *Living in the Spirit* has explicitly stated that Spirit baptism 'has a place in the redemptive order and experience because of its relationship to and dependence on the cross, resurrection and ascension of Jesus. As a redemptive experience it is transformational in the cultivation of righteousness and its anointing for the pursuit of holiness.'[90] As a part of the way, it 'is the climax of all preceding experiences in salvation'.[91]

Even those who have a sense of calling at the time of the experience describe the process therapeutically: new vision, being 'operated on' by the Spirit. This language is linked to the idea of becoming a 'new creation' or to healing and restoration, all soteriological language.

The Meaning of Pentecost in Early Methodism: Rediscovering John Fletcher as John Fletcher's Vindicator and Designated Successor (Lanham, MD: Scarecrow, 2002).

[89] This raises again the importance of a re-evaluation of the function of tongues. If Spirit baptism is vocational only, then interpreting tongues as *xenolalic* makes the most sense. But if the meaning of Spirit baptism is more significant, then there is more significance to the act of speaking in tongues when one is filled with the Spirit.

[90] R. Hollis Gause, *Living in the Spirit* (Cleveland, TN: R. Hollis Gause, 2007), p. 13.

[91] Gause, *Living in the Spirit,* p. 13.

What is most striking is the mystical experience described by several in which they are transported through visions by the Spirit. This 'vision quest' gives them solidarity with the suffering Christ, resulting in their pain and groaning. In mystical traditions, these visions are a part of the ladder-like pursuit of holiness, anticipating the beatific vision, when one sees God and is made like him. It seems that this visionary means by which those being baptized in the Spirit see Jesus in his passion gives credence to Blaine Charette's recent offering that sees *glossolalia* as a sign of the recovery of the *imago dei*. Charette writes,

> It is noted in scripture that one cannot see God's face and live. We are not at present prepared for such a face to face encounter. And yet the goal of redemption is that we will one day see his face. In the meantime the Spirit of God is active in our lives transforming us ever more into his likeness. It has been the argument of this paper that, as an essential element in this process of moving us towards our own true face, the Spirit causes us to speak with a genuine voice. It is a voice that gives expression to the truth of God's purpose for his creation and to our actual longings as his people. Glossolalia is the true voice given us today that helps form the true image of tomorrow.[92]

What is common to all of the early testimonies and stated most clearly by Myland, is that Spirit baptism is related to worship. It is received in worship and produces what Myland calls 'true worship'. While none of the earliest doctrinal statements and little of the earliest exposition recognized this fact, outsiders would have made that observation immediately! Pentecostal worship has always been demonstrative, in the sense that it demonstrates the reality of the presence of God. There is always response to the entry of God's Spirit, whether by weeping, shouting, dancing, jerking, singing, clapping or leaping. Gause would concur on this connection to worship, noting, 'We can expect the coming of the Holy Spirit where believers join together in praising and blessing God.'[93] In fact, he explains the 'normalcy' of the manifestation of tongues in Spirit baptism in terms of worship:

> This experience represents a profound rapport between two persons: the divine person, the Holy Spirit, and the human person, the believer. These two persons meet together through kinship and affection in such intimacy that the believer becomes fully responsive to the Holy Spirit. As He acts, wills, and communicates, the responding believer speaks and acts. This act of submission and responsiveness is essential to other acts of submission and responsiveness to the Holy Spirit.[94]

---

[92] Blaine Charette, 'Reflective Speech: Glossolalia and the Image of God', *Pneuma* 28.2 (Sept. 2006), p. 201.

[93] Gause, *Living in the Spirit*, p. 210.

[94] Gause, *Living in the Spirit*, p. 209.

First and foremost, however, this experience transformed the affections. Joy and peace are experienced. Others testify that they are 'baptized in Divine Love': love for God, neighbor and the world. This Wesleyan way of describing the experience clearly indicates that it is a soteriological work, by grace, through faith.

Spirit baptism is an experience along the way of salvation whereby I can worship in Spirit and in truth; where the Spirit of God is imparted into me; where I groan as the Spirit groans; where I sit in heavenly places, both participating in and anticipating the glory to come; where I am baptized in Divine Love; where I receive a new vision of those who are lost and I begin to see them as God the Father sees them, as Jesus who died for them sees them and as the Spirit who is always drawing and wooing sees them. This experience *makes* me a witness, transforming me into one who bears witness of the risen and ascended Christ who has sent this that the world now sees and hears in my life of worship and witness.

The question then becomes, to what theological category does Spirit baptism belong? The problem with theological categories is that they become compartments, where we place various doctrines, experiences, practices and even biblical texts. These compartments are then 'hermetically sealed'[95] and insulated one from the other. There is no integration.

One more early testimony may help us to see that integration more clearly.

'Living in the Presence'

On Thursday, March 30, 1911, while in the Bahamas, Rev. Carl M. Padgett made this entry in his diary:

> Today one year ago I received the baptism of the Holy Ghost. It seems to me such a short year. The year has had its attendant trials, but I believe I can say that it has been the best year of my life. How near the Lord has been to me. All the black deeds of my life, all my mistakes, for I have been so unworthy of his love, are all under the blood of Jesus. And now I want to live for the glory of my Lord, do I think that I will be good, do I think that I will live holy, No, I have tried it and proved a failure, in my nature was vileness, but the Lord took it out and by His grace and power I do live holy, by His power I can over come. [*sic*] May the words of my mouth and the meditations of my heart be acceptable in His sight. Living in the presence of my Lord, in his holy sanctuary, where the cloud of His glory rests, there is where I want to dwell.

[95] I am grateful to R. Hollis Gause for this description.

Preach on the street tonight about the second coming of Jesus.[96]

We come back to the question: Is Spirit baptism soteriological or vocational? And the answer is 'Yes!'[97]

★★★★★★★★★★★★★★★★★

Abstract
This paper's purpose is to re-assess the early understanding of Spirit baptism through the voices of those testifying to the experience. First, a survey of early doctrinal statements and definitions is offered. Second, testimonies from early Pentecostalism are examined to see how early Pentecostals viewed their transformation. Close attention is given to manifestations (visions, sensations, prophetic messages) that accompanied the experience as well as interpretations offered by the witness(es). Third, conclusions are drawn with regard to the continuity/discontinuity of the testimonies in relation to early apologetic and polemical statements made by the leadership of the movement. Finally, suggestions are offered for how this material might strengthen current understandings of the matter.

---

[96] Carl M. Padgett, unpublished diary, March 30, 1911.

[97] Steven J. Land is well known among his students for setting up a seemingly either/or question, which he calls a 'false choice', before answering the question, 'Yes!'

9

Weaving the Courage of God and Human Suffering: Issues and Challenges in the Doctrine of Atonement

Sang-Ehil Han[*]

About a quarter century ago when my journey in theology began at Lee College, I remember being a part of the group of students who had decided one day to wear a badge to class which said: 'we are of Gause'. It was an expression of our collective appreciation for the teaching ministry and theology of R. Hollis Gause. His theological speech was indubitably brilliant, creative, and provocative. But, most significantly, it was readily clear to us that his theological speech arose out of his passionate love affair with God. The words he spoke were a true testimony of his 'heart'. Moreover, with him, theological speech represented a lived reality as well. Words often lose their 'power' because they neither originate out of, nor correspond to, the life of the one who expresses them. This was not true with him. A particular case in point, especially during his recent years, was his theology of suffering germane to the doctrine of atonement. The suffering of the crucified God was not a mere abstract concept to romanticize the suffering condition of the present; it is rather a radical yet living reality that summons us to have courage and hope in the face of suffering as well as to participate in a compassionate embrace of suffering others. In this, we love as God loves. So was (and is) the life and testimony of Dr. Gause. I have witnessed his graceful embrace of suffering in the face of losing his loved ones. But this inward quality time and again finds outward manifestations in his compassionate embrace of others in suffering. It is an outflow of love where heart is conjoined with words expressed and life lived.

[*] Sang-Ehil Han (Ph.D., Emory University) is Associate Professor of Theology at the Pentecostal Theological Seminary in Cleveland, TN, USA and also serves as the Assistant Dean of Academics.

Introduction

The history of humankind does consistently tell the stories of violence and suffering. But what stands at the center of violence and suffering is the morality in human beings. That is, human beings are open to possibilities and hence responsible for their intentions and actions. What is then the ground for this morality in human beings? According to the creation narratives, it is the image of God in us that bears witness to our intimacy with God. This illustrates the fact that God stands as the ultimate 'ground' as well as the 'paragon' for our being and doing in the world. The elemental grammars of life for human beings (i.e. the 'is' and the 'ought' of our creaturely existence) issue out of God and his way of being in the world. Understood in this way, the stories of violence and suffering raise questions that are deeply 'theological' in nature. First and foremost, they raise questions about God. Only then do they also become questions about us as well as our relationship with God through Jesus Christ.

Thinking theologically, then, the starting point for the doctrine of atonement is our rightful acknowledgement of God whose love and holiness are eternal and perfect. It is on this theological ground that we are led to explore the nature and necessity of our union with God whose personal being and moral qualities we, human beings, had come to violate. Theological explorations in the doctrine of atonement thus address multifarious yet critical questions: What exactly has God done in and through the person and work of Jesus Christ? How did the coming of God in Jesus Christ affect the whole creation as well as the nature of our relationship with God? If the 'change' effected in us is spoken in terms of 'reconciliation' of relationship or 'restoration' of the image of God in us, what does this mean in the concrete realities of life wherein we continue to wrestle with the presence of violence and suffering? What does it mean for us to image God in heart and life when, in fact, the 'captain' of our salvation (i.e. Jesus Christ) is made perfect through sufferings (Heb. 2.10)? This study is a modest attempt to unearth some of these issues and challenges inherent in the doctrine of atonement.

In order to deal with these questions, we will consider some clusters of atonement theories along with their familiar metaphors and/or terms, e.g. ransom, sacrifice, substitution (penal and satisfaction), and moral example or influence. This study is not meant to be exhaustive in nature either historically or biblically. By highlighting some features in each cluster of these theories and metaphors, the study aims to open up various theories of atonement toward the direction sensible to a Wesleyan-Pentecostal theology and spirituality. This is intended to address the *depth grammar* of 'atonement', that is, being 'at one place' with God in Jesus Christ.[1] This is then aligned with the question of what it means to be fully human in the suffering condition of humanity. To ascertain the issues at hand from a contextual viewpoint, this study will further examine as a case study the world of *han* (a distinctive cultural pathos among Koreans). The study of *han* will then provide an understanding both to the details and the depth of human entanglement in brokenness and suffering. This is to underscore the theological demand that a viable understanding of the atonement of Jesus Christ should be holistic in nature if it is to be real and efficacious in the complexities of our broken reality.

The study hence proposes to view the atonement work of Jesus Christ in light of the entire life of Jesus Christ with the cross as its culmination. The blood poured out at the cross of Christ represents more than his dying there but the pouring out of his entire life as he had journeyed from Bethlehem to Calvary.[2] The cross is more than a single event in history but is the ultimate embodiment of the way of Jesus Christ in life. Taken in this way, the atonement of Jesus Christ provides more than a mere 'rescue from' death but a 'passion for' life patterned after the way of Jesus Christ in life. Insofar as his atonement is inclusive of his life journey that was missionally anointed of the Spirit, it *re-presents* for us the way of Jesus Christ to follow in the power of the Spirit. The Passion of Christ stands as the master narrative for all human passions and therefore governs all other stories of human life that the Spirit continues to write in us and through us.[3] The atonement

---

[1] Frances F. Hiebert, 'The Atonement in Anabaptist Theology', *Direction* 30.2 (2001), pp. 122-38 (128-9). The term 'atonement' ('at-one-ment') means to be 'at one place' with God. It refers to 'all the ways in which God and humans have been reconciled through the work of Jesus Christ. It points not only to Christ's death, but to all the various phases of his activity on behalf of humanity including his ministry, his death, and his resurrection. It also includes the idea that unless a person responds appropriately to the work of Christ, for that person, atonement is not efficacious. The work of Christ, however, also includes the actualizing power of his Spirit whereby people are able to appropriate Christ's saving work' (128). See also Ian A. McFarland, 'Christ, Spirit and Atonement', *IJST* 3.1 (2001), pp. 83-93 (83-85). McFarland interestingly cites the high-priestly prayer of Jesus in John 17 as a central text calling for our being 'at one' with God in the person of Jesus Christ. In this vein, our being 'at one place' with God in Jesus Christ truly comes into fruition only as we are sanctified in heart and life by the truth of God.

[2] R. Hollis Gause, 'Atonement' (unpublished paper). In his dying, Christ recapitulates all that was lost in humanity by journeying from Calvary back to the Garden of Eden: 'He [Christ] went to the place where we died; he died where Adam and his children died, in the Garden ... he did this as the Prince of life; so, when he had gone to the depths of our death, he came up out of death in the victory of His resurrection'. Hence, Jesus Christ *is* the atonement. His death cannot be understood as an event singled out or separated to the whole of the atonement work that is Jesus Christ.

[3] See Hiebert, 'The Atonement in Anabaptist Theology', *Direction*, p. 128. Hiebert notes that the gospel of Jesus Christ was 'not only the good news of salvation but also a

work of Jesus Christ 'substitutes' the agony of God in Jesus Christ with our agony in sin. But it also directs life to the way of Jesus Christ that was pneumatically mediated. In our confession of the triumph of God's grace in Christ's atonement death that defeats violence and its victimization cycle,[4] we also celebrate the newness of life in the power of the Spirit. Joining with Christ in this manner of dying, suffering becomes redemptive as it serves as the gateway through which the Spirit takes us to the wounded heart of God and allows us to take on the divine courage in Jesus Christ and to hope in the eschatological triumph of God's grace.

1. Theories and Metaphors

As important as the doctrine of atonement is for the Christian faith, it is interesting to note that our Christian understanding of the doctrine did not grow out of a precise system of thought developed by early Christians. Unlike other creedal controversies – e.g. the Trinity, the nature of Christ, the *filioque* debate – no church council was ever held to ascertain an orthodox understanding of the doctrine. This observation is instructive as we approach various theories and metaphors on atonement. On the one hand, it allows some theological freedom to explore helpful ways to interweave some essential features of the atonement highlighted in various theories. On the other hand, it allows us to experiment with new metaphors or theories that might best couch them.[5] After all, the multifarious factors surrounding the doc-

---

series of directives for the Christian on how to live, how to follow Christ … in following Christ, humanity could be brought back into the life of God'.

[4] Rene Girard, *Things Hidden Since the Foundation of the World* (trans. S. Bann and M. Metteer; Stanford: Stanford University Press, 1987). Making a reference to the Biblical narrative of Cain's murder of Abel, Girard points out how history bears a witness to the claim that violence is at the very foundation of human culture. What subverts this violent foundation and its cycle of victimization is the cross of Christ that negates violence and its perpetuation. At the cross, the divine power is exercised to embrace the suffering for the sake of others. With this embrace, violence was redeemed and its vicious cycle of victimization broken.

[5] For example, Hans Boersma explores the 'hospitality' metaphor in his work, *Violence, Hospitality and the Cross: Reappropriating the Atonement Tradition* (Grand Rapids: Baker Academic, 2004). See also Murray Rae, 'The Travail of God', *IJST* 5.1 (2003), pp. 47-61. Murray Rae uses 'travail' as a viable atonement metaphor appealing to a motherly imagery that relates atonement to a birth pang. See also W.J. van Asselt, 'Christ's Atonement: A Multi-Dimensional Approach', *CTJ* 38 (2003), pp. 52-67. Asselt notes various ways that models and metaphors of atonement have been distinguished from one another and concludes that, to a certain extent, some elements of various theories and metaphors are present in each one of them. In conclusion, Asselt argues for the substitution model as the 'higher' model into which the essential elements of other models can be organized (pp. 65-67).

trine of atonement seem to resist being categorized under any single theory or metaphor without it being re-imagined or broadened to accommodate some distinct features about the atonement emphasized in others. We should also keep in view whether a particular theological construction in this regard addresses the concrete realities of life (that is, the fracturing and alienation from the elemental grammars of life) and their demands without being driven by them. Otherwise, the theological speech about the atonement of Jesus Christ becomes a fanciful game played only in a metaphysical realm.[6]

On the other hand, it also reminds us that we can speak of the cross of Christ and his atoning work only as stewards of a mystery. Like those gathered at the cross, one can only stand 'at a distance' realizing that the reality of the crucified God is utterly incomprehensible. Rae thus fittingly articulates: 'Theological speech is not illustration … but interpretation.… No metaphor or analogy or doctrine, therefore, is capable of re-presenting the One who presents himself to us through the power of the Holy Spirit'.[7] Theological speech to bear witness to the reality of the cross of Christ becomes possible only as the Spirit who testifies of Christ enables and guides us into the truth.

2.1. The Ransom-Victory Model

The atonement of Christ in this particular model is explained with the biblical metaphor of 'ransom' in Mk 10.45: 'For even the Son of Man did not come to be served, but to serve, and to give His life a ransom for many'. That is, Jesus had offered up his life as the ransom with a view toward obtaining 'release' for all of humanity placed under the bondage of the devil. Construing this atonement model, Irenaeus in his work, *Adversus Haereses* (Against Heresies), understood that the ransom was paid to the devil. Behind the idea was the awareness to take seriously the reality of evil and its pervading presence throughout the cosmos. Humanity was understood as being held captive by the devil since they have fallen into sin at the devil's temptations. Irenaeus hence explained that the incarnation of the Word whereby the Son of God enters the stream of cause and effect in human history was necessarily foreordained by God from all eternity and recapitulated all that was lost

---

[6] Charles E. Brown, 'The Atonement: Healing in Postmodern Society', *Int* 53.1 (1999), pp. 34-43 (p. 39). Brown rightly addresses the society's loss of powerful deep symbols as well as unhealthy misconstruals of certain symbols, e.g. cross, that perpetuate the victimization of the abused and oppressed. Brown notes, 'as anyone recovering from childhood sexual abuse can attest, powerless is not always a Christian virtue, and neither submission a sign of saintly character' (p. 36).

[7] Rae, 'The Travail of God', p. 49.

in humanity.[8] Although Jesus at the cross was offered up as the ransom to the devil, God reclaimed him and, in doing so, all the ransomed sinners along with him. Gregory of Nyssa then later reformulated this ransom idea describing Christ's crucifixion and resurrection in terms of a trick that God played on the devil. The devil was fooled in the crucifixion as, in his dying, the divinity of Jesus Christ was kept in veil under his humanity. Like a greedy fish, Gregory of Nyssa explained, the devil swallowed the hook of divinity veiled underneath the exterior of Christ's humanity. The immediate upshot of this is the destruction of the devil's domain and the restoration of freedom to humanity.

In conjunction with the ransom-victory model, reference should also be made to Gustav Aulen's seminal work, *Christus Victor*, a publication of his lectures delivered at the University of Uppsala in 1931. In this work, Aulen insists that the atonement of Christ should be viewed in terms of divine struggle and victory. In this cosmic drama of salvation, Christ triumphs over evil and thus provides the ground of victory for the believers as well as their reconciliation with God. Aulen calls for the recovery of the 'classic' atonement motif over against abstract legal theories that began to gain ground since the Middle Ages, pointing out that the Christus Victor model was most dominant in the New Testament and a thousand years of church history thereafter.[9] A central text here is Col. 2.14-15: 'Having wiped out the handwriting of requirements that was against us, which was contrary to us ... having nailed it to the cross. Having disarmed principalities and powers, he made a public spectacle of them, triumphing over them in it.'

The ransom-victory atonement model carries with it some notable weaknesses as well as strengths. First, placing God in a cosmic duel with evil seems to bring into question the sovereignty of God's reign for all times. Second, under no circumstances would the devil ever have had any rightful claim on humanity. Third, what God does in the atonement work of Jesus Christ must also be characteristically consistent with who God is in God's moral perfections. The atonement of Jesus Christ cannot be spoken of in deceptive terms. Fourth, the 'cosmic' nature of divine struggle and victory may be considered as distanced from our present struggle against historical evil. Hence, the issue has to do with the transitioning of the divine struggle and victory in

---

[8] Brown, 'The Atonement: Healing in Postmodern Society', p. 37.

[9] Gustav Aulen, *Christus Victor: An Historical Study of the Three Main Types of the Atonement*, (trans. A.G. Herbert; Eugene, OR: Wipf & Stock, 2003). See also Alister E. McGrath, *Christian Theology: An Introduction* (Oxford, UK; Cambridge, MA: Blackwell, 1994), pp. 347-48. McGrath argues that Aulen's claim of the victory motif as being dominant in the patristic era is an overstatement. It was one of the components comprising patristic soteriology. Aulen's Christus Victor theory has, however, helped to legitimate conversations about 'forces of evil' in the intellectual world.

the cosmic realm into the engagement of the historical evil in the present. Fifth, a sense of finality attached to the cosmic victory may engender a naïve and triumphalistic approach to the depth and profundity of human brokenness furthered by human vulnerabilities and vicissitudes of life. Sixth, it does not seem to address forcefully the necessity of Christ's death as well as the significance of God's judgment on sin and sinners.[10]

Despite several possible weaknesses already pointed out, the ransom-victory model shed light on some critical aspects of the atonement of Jesus Christ. Along with the proponents of the ransom-victory model, it is helpful for us to see the cross of Christ as a powerful reminder, even a source of empowerment, to resist evil with the confidence to triumph over it at the end. The cross of Christ exposes the true nature of evil and deconstructs its unlawful hold on humanity. 'In the murder of Jesus', Darby Kathleen Ray thus states, 'the true face of evil is unmasked for all to see, its claim to authority discredited, and its seductive potential squelched'.[11] The cross of Christ in this particular model also offers humanity glimpses of God who identifies with the suffering other (i.e., the poor and oppressed). For this reason, Irenaeus understands the atonement work at the cross within the context of the mystery of Christ's incarnation by describing it as 'the impassible becoming capable of suffering'.[12] Imagining God in this manner then evokes in us a shared sense of solidarity knowing that the struggles of the suffering other are enveloped in both Christ's suffering and triumph over multifarious forms of unjust violence in the world. In a concrete and real way, this is what it would mean for us to call him Christ. That is, we join with him at the cross, first and foremost, as the suffering other being encouraged and empowered. In joining with him, however, we are equally assured of the fact that the path of resistance and compassion we walk on following the Christ leads not to a destructive end but a liberative one.

2.2 The Sacrifice Model

If the ransom-victory model views the atonement as dynamic in nature, the sacrifice model tends to speak of Christ's atonement as primarily 'objective'. Jesus Christ was a 'sacrifice' offered unto God;

---

[10] Asselt, 'Christ's Atonement: A Multi-Dimensional Approach', p. 57. For Asselt, another strong objection to Aulen's view is to point out the fact that the victory motif both in the Bible and the history of Christian doctrine becomes prominent only in the context of reading the crucifixion in its linkage to the resurrection.

[11] Darby Kathleen Ray, *Deceiving the Devil: Atonement, Abuse, and Ransom* (Cleveland: Pilgrim, 1998), p. 125.

[12] Irenaeus, *Against Heresies*, 3.16.6.

hence, the atonement work here is characteristically 'God-directed'. But the term 'sacrifice' is quite difficult to grasp in precise terms since there are numerous references to denote a variety of sacrifices in the Old Testament. Moreover, the terminology has been historically evolved and converged with practices of similar kinds from multifarious backgrounds. Notwithstanding the difficulty noted, various Old Testament terms for sacrifice and its practices can perhaps be clustered in terms of some elemental features they share. R. de Vaux in this regard speaks of three basic elements: gift, communion, and reconciliation.[13] In other words, sacrifice involves giving and receiving by God, affects the establishment of communion with God, and addresses the sin problem of humanity. These elements of sacrifice reappear when the sacrifice metaphor is used in the New Testament to describe the atoning death of Jesus Christ.[14] Jesus 'tastes death for everyone' (Heb. 2.10), is made 'propitiation for the sins of the people' (Heb. 2.17), affects us to 'become partakers of Christ', and establishes a new covenant between God and humanity (Heb. 8.6-9).

The sacrifice metaphor can also be traced to other New Testament keywords such as ἱλασμός (*hilasmos*), ἱλαστήριον (*hilasterion*), and κα-ταλλαγή (*katallage*).[15] The word ἱλασμός (*hilasmos*) appears in 1 Jn 2.2: 'He himself is the propitiation for our sins, and not for ours only but also for the whole world'. The idea conveyed here is that Jesus Christ himself constitutes the sacrificial covering by which humanity is forgiven and cleansed of their sins. In so doing, the blood of Jesus (that is, the pouring out of his life) functions as the basis for believer's experience of forgiveness and cleansing.[16] Herein, Christ's sacrifice by shedding of blood is not primarily purposed to bring appeasement to an angry God. In general, the Johannine literature as a whole portrays

---

[13] R. de Vaux, *Ancient Israel: Its Life and Institutions*, vol. 2 (trans. John McHugh; New York: McGraw-Hill, 1961), pp. 451-56.

[14] The sharing of the elements should not imply any downplay of the contrast between the Old Testament provision of sacrifice and that of Christ. The sacrifice in the Old Testament is involuntary, absent of morality, temporal, symbolic, and promissory in nature. It involves a flawed (that is, sinful) priesthood and altar whereas the sacrifice of Christ is voluntary, godly and righteous, actual, fulfilling and involves a perfect and eternal priesthood and altar. Moreover, Christ's sacrifice conjoins sacrifice and judge in one person (Rom. 8.34) and represents the perfect harmony of triune God. Hebrews 9.14 hence speaks of this in the language of trinitarian worship, 'who [Christ] through the eternal Spirit offered Himself without spot unto God'.

[15] See Asselt, 'Christ's Atonement: A Multi-Dimentional Approach', pp. 58-59.

[16] Gause ('Atonement', unpublished paper) notes: 'Christ's entire manifestation in the flesh in His first advent (birth, life, death, resurrection and ascension) is a sacrifice offered to God. The pinnacle of that sacrifice is the cross in which he manifested both death and life. His manifestation of life and death is under the anointing that the Father gave Him; the oil of that anointing is the Holy Spirit. The purpose of the atonement is that believers should be drawn into this community of fellowship and anointing'.

God as a loving Father who even sends his Son into the world of sinners for the sake of their salvation (Jn 3.16-17).[17] This is further evidenced in the use of the word ἱλασμός (*hilasmos*) in 1 Jn 4.10: 'In this is love, not that we loved God, but that He loved us and sent His Son to be propitiation for our sins'. The text here makes it clear that the ground for Christ to become our 'propitiation' is none other than the love of God.

Second, Paul uses the word ἱλαστήριον (*hilasterion*) to denote the atonement death of Jesus (Rom. 3.25). ἱλαστήριον (*Hilasterion*) is used in the Septuagint to translate כפרת (*kapporeth*), the golden plate on the ark of covenant. It was on this plate that the blood of sacrifice was sprinkled on the Day of Atonement in keeping with the covenantal relationship between God and the people of Israel. Jesus Christ and his atoning blood are now set forth to substitute the ancient כפרת (*kapporeth*) and the sacrificial blood sprinkled on it. What holds the covenant between God and humanity is then neither an inanimate object nor the blood of a lesser being. It is now the living person of God whose very life his blood represents is being poured out for the lesser.[18]

Third, Paul also uses the word καταλλαγή (*katallage*) (and the verb καταλλάσσω [*katallassein*]), a term that can be traced to the verb ἀλλάσσω (*allassein*), meaning 'to change', to exchange', or 'to replace'. A central text where these words appear is Rom. 5.10-11. Here a reference to the atoning death of Christ is made with a 'change' in relationship in view. The text makes it clear that Christ's death as the atoning sacrifice terminates the enmity and estrangement between God and humanity. Insofar as sin is a violation of the personal God, not just violation of a law or failure to observe it, what is required to remedy the situation is no less than a restoration of the broken relationship with God.

A 'slippery slope' with the sacrifice model is keeping together the unmeritorious (i.e. 'outside of us') nature of the atonement with the 'integrity' of human beings as meaningful participants in it. Insofar as God is the sole ground of being and existence, the fracturing of relationship with God irrevocably damages the elemental grammars of life for human beings. We have rejected being at one place with God and henceforth alienated ourselves from both the 'origin' and the *telos* (τέλος) for our creaturely existence. The possibility to restore this fractured relationship cannot be, however, traced in ourselves since we are

---

[17] John Christopher Thomas, *The Pentecostal Commentary on 1 John, 2 John, 3 John* (Cleveland: Pilgrim, 2004), pp. 89-90.

[18] Gause, in 'Atonement', notes: 'The greatest treasure of heaven and of the heart of the Creator is sacrificed for the creature – creatures who are the enemies of God'. See also Hiebert, 'The Atonement in Anabaptist Theology', p. 122. The uniqueness of Christ's sacrifice is, Hiebert notes, that 'God, not humanity, atones for sin'.

no longer capable of coming to God. Hence, the sole option is for God to come toward us. In the coming of God, however, what is in the nature of God and in all of God's divine perfections must be fulfilled. The sacrifice model helps us see the necessity of God's coming toward us in Jesus Christ as well as the necessity of his dying for our atonement. The enormity of our offense (i.e. an offense against God) demands the sacrificial means to be of equal or greater value. Moreover, the sacrificial 'covering' must actively fulfill the righteousness of God. For this reason, as observed earlier, it is helpful to understand the 'sacrifice' metaphor in Christ's atoning death as being inclusive of Christ's whole existence – i.e., birth, life, death, resurrection and ascension. In this, the newness of life that Christ's atonement provides and our incorporation into it already have in view our living in the way of Jesus under the anointing of the Holy Spirit. Our identification with the sacrificial death of Christ is not so much about death itself but rather our conformity to the manner and character of his dying that transforms lives as living *unto* God, that is, resisting evil and walking in righteousness. Speaking of our dying with Christ, Paul thus admonishes: 'But present yourselves as being alive from the dead, and your members as instrument of righteousness to God' (Rom. 6.13). 'Claimed by Christ', McFarland asserts, 'death now becomes the gateway to life with God'.[19]

2.3 The Substitution Model

The substitution model is understood as constituted with two major components: punishment and satisfaction. With regard to the idea of 'punishment', Christ's death represents a punishment meted out to Christ in his becoming the sinner's substitute and taking on the sins of humanity. It is apparent that the idea of punishment carries with it a heavy juridical overtone. Making a reference to Deut. 21.23, Paul thus states in Gal. 3.13 that 'Christ has redeemed us from the curse of the law, having become a curse for us'. However, Anselm favored another juridical notion, 'satisfaction', with regard to Christ's death. Here he has taken an either-or approach and severed the notion of punishment from his view of atonement. He preferred to speak of Christ's death in terms of satisfaction. Moreover, he placed Christ's satisfaction within the framework of Christ's merit, which is of infinite worth. For Anselm, Jesus Christ alone is able (as God) and obligated (as a human being) to offer the satisfaction required to remedy the fallen state of humanity. In his willing obedience, Christ as the God-man restored 'the order and beauty of the universe (God's honor) through his satis-

---

[19] McFarland, 'Christ, Spirit and Atonement', p. 89.

faction'.[20] The Reformed tradition, however, held the ideas of punishment and satisfaction together and went on to view Christ's atonement death as satisfaction paid *through* punishment. A further distinction was made between Christ's passive and active obedience. Christ's 'passive' obedience relates to his vicarious suffering over the punishment rendered, whereas his 'active' obedience refers to his active fulfillment of the entire law of God. On the one hand, the penal substitution model underscores the 'costliness' of the cross along with the vicarious nature of Christ's suffering; but, on the other hand, it underscores God as both sovereign and holy seeking to bring about a fulfillment of His law and justice in a fallen world.

The idea of 'punishment' in the atoning death of Christ has been known to be problematic for some who view it as valorizing unjust violence.[21] For them, linking the idea of punishment with the death of Christ portrays the cross as a symbol of violence. That is, at the cross, the victimization of the innocent was executed with a divine sanction as fulfilling the justice of God. In a similar train of thought, the penal characteristic of substitution in the atonement is also viewed as fracturing God's justice from His mercy. Punishment as the necessary means to 'satisfy' the wrath of God can certainly be read, for some, as lacking, if not obscuring, the inexhaustible love presupposed of God. Without questioning the legitimacy of some of these critical concerns, a more constructive reading on the substitution model is perhaps possible. For instance, Hans Boersma helps us see how the idea of 'punishment' here presupposes the distinction between law and justice. Borrowing insights from Jacques Derrida,[22] Boersma argues that punishment in the atonement death of Jesus Christ targets the fulfillment of God's eschatological justice rather than a blind enforcement of law(s). That the atoning death of Christ has in view the fulfillment of God's eschatolog-

---

[20] Asselt, 'Christ's Atonement: A Multi-Dimensional Approach', p. 60. Asselt notes how some recent studies on Anselm's doctrine of satisfaction unveils the fact that the idea of 'satisfaction' originates not in 'Germanic law but rather in private penitential and confessional practice of medieval churches and monasteries'. Apart from the caricature of a jealous tyrant or bloodthirsty Germanic potentate, the Anselmian God should be re-imaged in terms of the feudal image which 'stood for rationality prevailing against the inroads of self-will and chaos … Anselm uses feudal imagery because the feudal hierarchy provided an illustration of the order which he found in the universe'.

[21] Joel Green and Mark Baker, *Recovering the Scandal of the Cross: Atonement in the New Testament and Contemporary Contexts* (Downers Grove: InterVarsity, 2000); see also Timothy Gorringe, *God's Just Vengeance: Crime, Violence, and the Rhetoric of Salvation* (Cambridge: Cambridge University Press, 1996).

[22] Hans Boersma, 'Eschatological Justice and the Cross: Violence and Penal Substitution', *ThT* 60 (2003), pp. 186-99. Boersma quotes from Derrida: 'law (*droit*) is essentially deconstructable …. Justice itself, if such a thing exists, outside or beyond law, is not deconstructable. No more than deconstruction itself, if such a thing exists. Deconstruction is justice' (p. 189).

ical justice then allows us to see the cross as a powerful symbol in the present deconstructing any and all unjust enforcement of law(s) that fail to carry out a true justice God's holiness demands. Punishment is not merely retributive either. It also serves other goals such as prevention, rehabilitation, and deterrence. Moving toward the goal of eschatologi-cal justice, the idea of punishment carries with it then the notion of restoration. Boersma here helpfully locates the idea of punishment within the framework of the concept of judgment in the Old Testa-ment that accords with covenant faithfulness. Read in this way, pu-nishment paves the inroads to healing and hope by subverting the constant pattern that has proven to be destructive for the people of Israel. Constructively re-introducing the idea of punishment in the atonement death of Christ, Boersma then images God as the One who yearns for the return of His people and the restoration of covenant relationship (Isa. 65; Ps. 81.8; Deut. 5.29).[23]

Perhaps, we can think further and broaden the base for the 'substitu-tion' metaphor. Generally, in the Reformed tradition, the atonement death of Christ is understood as representing a substitution that is both Godward and juridical in nature. But it seems that the idea of substitu-tion in the atonement can be considered as humanward and affectional as well. If Christ's atonement represents a substitution that is restorative in kind, the 'change' effected here seems to demand a 'real' change (that is, beyond the juridical) in human beings as they pursue to be 'at one place' (i.e. atonement) with God. That is, the atonement suffering of Christ should affect the restoration of the image of God in a real and meaningful way. Moreover, this becomes possible if the substitution that Christ's atonement represents is understood within the trinitarian framework.[24] How exactly should we to understand the cry of the Son's heartbreak in Mt. 27.46: 'My God, My God, why have you forsaken Me?' Does it represent a fracture in the community of God? Is it not theologically feasible to view it as a vivid demonstration of the wounded heart of God over the suffering other (i.e. humanity)? In other words, the cry of the Son (i.e., the suffering Other) is echoed with a silent weeping of the Father as this reciprocity is mediated by the Spirit. The upshot of this is a theological construction that the suf-

---

[23] Boersma, 'Eschatological Justice and the Cross: Violence and Penal Substitution', pp. 191-94. Thinking in this way, Boersma observes how exile (Deut. 30.1-10; Jer. 31.31-34; Ezek. 36.26-27) as a divine punishment served the goal of restoring the justice of God and the covenant relationship between God and the people of Israel.

[24] Asselt, 'Christ's Atonement: A Multi-Dimensional Approach', pp. 61-62. Asselt ar-gues that the Reformed tradition traces the idea of penal substitution all the way to the trinitarian relationship in God. Especially in the doctrine of *pactum salutis*, Asselt argues, 'substitution, which took place historically when Christ died on the cross, is a reflection or analogy of the "inner-workings" of God in his intra-trinitarian life'.

fering of God in Christ is indeed the outworking of the intra-trinitarian drama. The cross of Christ as a trinitarian event then issues forth the shared wound of God that longs to restore the broken humanity. Moreover, in effecting a substitution (i.e. restoring our union with God), the Spirit of Christ even now communicates in groanings and sighs the selfsame compassion of God that we are to image for the suffering other.

2.4 The Exemplarist Model

This particular atonement model interprets the cross of Christ as representing a persuasive demonstration of the love of God. Developed most notably in the writings of Peter Abelard, this atonement model helped reverse the direction of Anselmian thinking by placing its emphasis upon the subjective impact of the cross of Christ.[25] That is to say, the love of God demonstrated at the cross sets forth God's intense and persuasive love toward us and serves as a divine catalyst to instigate a reciprocal love toward God. The death of Christ, and the love of God it demonstrates, binds us to God in Jesus Christ through love. Though subjective in nature, this particular view of the atonement should not be misconstrued as taking a reductionist approach to Christ's death. That is, Christ's death provides more than a mere example of love although it is exemplary in nature. The love of God shown in Christ's death is an unwavering proof about how far God would go to inspire us to reciprocate the love of God.[26] It is the culmination of all that went before in the life and teaching of Jesus Christ both by word and example. It stands as the pinnacle bearing forth a witness to all of his life's teachings. The forgiveness of sins that the cross of Christ bears a witness then becomes effectual only as we respond favorably to the love of God.

A central strength of this particular model turns out to also be its weakness as well, that is, its 'subjective' reading of the atonement death of Christ. The model presupposes that human beings already possess certain spiritual and moral qualities with which they are expected to respond to the love of God demonstrated at the cross. Lacking any and all objective aspects of atonement, however, even the death of Christ remains exemplary at the end. Even at the cross of Christ, the love of God is primarily understood as taught and demonstrated. Here the death of Christ is not thought of in terms of the fulfillment of God's

[25] McGrath, *Christian Theology: An Introduction*, p. 355.

[26] For a comparison with Wesley's view on the atonement, see Randy L. Maddox, *Responsible Grace: John Wesley's Practical Theology* (Nashville: Kingswood, 1994), pp. 106-109. Wesley understood the sacrificial death of Jesus 'to be much more than the Representative of humanity; he was most fundamentally the Representative of *God*' (p. 109).

justice and righteousness. Devoid of any aspects of substitution whether initially or finally, it seems unclear if 'grace' functions in the manner we generally understand it does. That is, grace precedes any human activities in order to enable and/or empower us to move toward God. Without God's grace preceding us, humanity stands as depraved and deprived of innate capacity to acknowledge God. Even if the death of Jesus demonstrates the love of God perfectly and concretely, the question still remains whether humanity is able to or empowered to receive it as such?

3. A Synopsis

We have observed various atonement models and their metaphors with a modest vision to construct a Wesleyan-Pentecostal reading on the subject matter. In and through the process, it became evident that essential features of the atonement are spread among these models and metaphors. A viable Wesleyan-Pentecostal reading on the atonement should have these features interwoven. In keeping with this, the study has raised several significant points to bear in mind. First, the atonement of Jesus Christ provides the ground and assurance of our *present empowerment* to resist and triumph over struggles against evil, whether systemic or personal. Second, the atonement of Jesus Christ is transformational in nature effecting a *change in relationship*, that is, establishing a dynamic relationship with the living Christ. Third, the atonement of Jesus Christ is not tenable apart from the necessity of *God's initial coming* toward us as well as his *sacrificial dying* on our behalf. The justice and the righteousness of God are thus vicariously fulfilled. Fourth, the atonement of Jesus Christ calls for our conformity to the manner and character of his dying which, in turn, represents our *living unto God* (i.e., walking in holiness and righteousness). By being baptized into the death of Christ, we are to walk in the newness of life; herein the death and resurrection of Jesus Christ are held together in his atonement. Fifth, the atonement of Christ has in view the eschatological vision, i.e. the *eschatological fulfillment of God's justice*. This is brought about by God's divine courage to place his hope upon us to return, restoring the covenantal faithfulness with him. The manner of God's divine courage is here twofold: judgment and longsuffering. Sixth, the atonement of Christ has in view the *restoration of the image of God* in us restoring and sustaining the covenant of life at creation. In this, creation and redemption are held together. Seventh, the atonement of Christ is the outworking of the intra-trinitarian drama *inviting us to participate* and mirror the wounded heart of God. In the process, human life finds the inroad to partake the life in the community of

God. Eighth, the atonement of God sets forth *the reciprocal relationship* between God and humanity in which we are led to love as God loves. Finally, the atonement of Christ cannot be adequately grasped unless it is understood as inclusive of his whole existence (i.e. his birth, life and teaching, death, resurrection, ascension and his promised return). To become beneficiaries of Christ's atoning death is to have ourselves placed in the *way* of Jesus Christ, *journeying* with him *in the power and anointing* of the selfsame Spirit of God. With these critical points on the atonement in view, we now turn to a case study that would allow us to test the viability of our theological findings in light of questions emerging from a particular cultural context.

4. The World of Han and the Christian Doctrine of Atonement

Han is a culture-specific emotion that defies a precise definition; hence, it cannot be naively equated with general human emotions.[27] Situated in the narrative particularities of Korean culture, *han* represents a complex web of intense emotions interwoven over a long period of accumulated painful experiences and suffering.[28] Some aspect of this accumulation comes in a form of historical inheritance that predates an individual whose life suffers from the presence of *han*. Hence, Un Koh, a celebrated Buddhist poet, describes the Korean *Sitz im Leben* in this way: 'they (Koreans) are born of the womb of *han*, grow up in the bosom of *han*, live out *han*, and die leaving *han* behind'.[29] *Han* can be either personal or collective. *Han* as personal is often responded to by

---

[27] See Amelie Oksenberg Rorty, 'Introduction', in *Explaining Emotions* (Amelie Oksenberg Rorty, ed.; Berkeley: University of California Press, 1980), pp. 1-7. For that matter, as Rorty helpfully explains, all human emotions exist in a complex web of relationality. For instance, when one discharges her anger at a loved one, the elements of love and hate are often interwoven in a single manifestation of one's angry emotion. The particularities of narrative context then become critical in determining the nature of the emotion expressed.

[28] Suk-Mo Ahn, 'Toward a Local Pastoral Care and Pastoral Theology: The Basis, Model, and Case of *Han* in Light of Charles Gerkin's Pastoral Hermeneutics' (unpublished Ph.D. dissertation, Emory University, 1991). Ahn writes: '*Han* is not so much a feeling and temporal emotion ... it is more like a complex of emotions, or a core of a group of feelings, which is engraved on the heart or takes place in it, after a long duration of painful experiences and sufferings' (p. 305). See also Hyun Kyung Chung, '"Han-pu-ri": Doing Theology from Korean Women's Perspective', *The Ecumenical Review*, 40 (Jan. 1988), pp. 27-36 (p. 30). Explaining the complexities involved in *han*, Chung describes *han* as a kind of 'lump' or 'knot' at the core of one's being that carries with it 'a sense of unresolved resentment against injustice suffered, a sense of helplessness because of the overwhelming odds against, a feeling of total abandonment ... a feeling of acute pain of sorrow in one's guts and bowels making the whole body writhe and wiggle' (p. 30).

[29] Un Koh, 'Overcoming *Han*', *Han-Guk-Sa-Whe-Yeon-Gu* [Korean Society Review], 2 (1984), pp. 132-46 (p. 138).

active retaliation of anger or hate against the victimizer. There are occasions whereby the victimized, out of fear or fright, passively suppresses the pains of *han* into the depth of her psyche only to have it
resurface later in vengeful actions. Personal *han* can also be expressed in
a form of self-resignation. Being overwhelmed by a profound sense of
helplessness and despair, a victim directs anger against her own self. As
Andrew Sung Park notes, this is 'the sad *han* of many victims … victims negate the self already negated by offenders even to the point of
self-extermination.… It lets go of everything, including the self'.[30]

The collective *han*, conversely, represents a shared national psyche
amongst Koreans grounded in the repeated national crises over the
nation's five thousand year history. The *han* of this kind becomes a
collective memory deeply buried in various aspects of life in society.
The collective *han* associated with the stories of Korean women adds
yet another distinctive dimension. The strong patriarchal structure of
Korean society has long yielded a corporate despair shared by Korean
women. Being born as the female gender has been customarily understood as being born into the life of *han*.[31] The corporate despair of this
kind is not to be readily identified with a sense of absolute despair as
the corporate despair of this particular kind has often led to a mature
embrace of the life given with a view toward a profound sense of
openness that awaits a possible future transformation of circumstances
refusing to succumb to the power of violence and its victimization
cycle.[32]

Han also has two distinctive levels: the original and the secondary.
The secondary *han* refers to the suppressed web of emotions caused by
intense life experiences of unprovoked injustice. The *han* of this kind
remains at the level of consciousness wanting to arrive at its satisfactory
resolution in the present.[33] In this, *han* can be driven by either *won*
(intense emotion of grudge or hate) or *jeong* (deep emotion of affection
or love). Driven negatively, it becomes *won-han* that finds its resolution
in a retaliatory action; driven positively, *jeong* governs one's *han* and
becomes *jeong-han*.[34] In the case of the latter, *han* is sublimated and

[30] Andrew Sung Park, *The Wounded Heart of God: The Asian Concept of* Han *and the Christian Doctrine of Sin* (Nashville: Abingdon Press, 1993), p. 34.

[31] Hyo-Jae Lee, *Yeo-Sung-Kui-Sa-Hoe* [*Womanhood and Society*] (Seoul: Jung-Woo, 1979), pp. 54-57. The *han* of this kind represents the loss of elemental human integrity and freedom. See also Hyun-Kyung Chung, *Struggle to be the Sun Again: Introducing Asian Women's Theology* (Maryknoll, NY: Orbis, 1990), pp. 32-35. Chung argues for a genuine repentance to recover the elemental integrity of full humanity for Asian women.

[32] For a fuller discussion on the mature-natured *han*, see Jae-Hun Lee, *The Exploration of the Inner Wounds – Han* (Atlanta: Scholars Press, 1994), pp. 37-38.

[33] Yul-Kyu Kim, *The Ore of* Han *and the Stream of* Won (Seoul: Joowoo, 1981), pp. 21-28.

[34] Jae-Hun Lee, *The Exploration of the Inner Wounds – Han*, pp. 35-37.

even becomes resources of raw and intense passions that drive a person to construct a moral consciousness to negate actively the vicious circles of the violence-structure of personal or societal injustice. Yet moving deeper beyond the level of secondary *han* exists a more archetypal kind of *han*, i.e. the original *han*. The *han* of this kind exists at the level of unconsciousness and resides beyond the scope of conscious modification.[35] As unmodified and archetypal in nature, the original *han* constitutes a kind of 'ontological depth'[36] that functions as the primordial cause prompting external manifestations of unreleased emotions of secondary *han*. An effective resolution of *han* at the secondary level hence necessitates an individual to address the issues and challenges of original *han*.

The multifarious features associated with the notion of *han* represent concrete forms in which the reality of violence and human suffering takes place in a given culture. Our theological construction of the atonement needs not be driven by the demands emerging from a particular cultural context. But, at the same time, it should provide a fitting response to address them. Otherwise, the theological answers we provide in this regard become confined to the metaphysical, lacking power to be translated into the historical. For this reason, we can perhaps juxtapose our previous findings on Christ's atonement in various models and metaphors with the detailed 'demands' emerging from the culture of *han*. Herein, it seems possible and helpful to construe the doctrine of the atonement in four different sets of dialectical correlation.

1. In order for the doctrine of atonement to be efficacious in the culture of *han*, the dialectic between personal and communal (or collective) has to be maintained. The world of *han* unveils the fact that *han* is transferable from personal to communal and also, at times, from communal to personal. Hence, a viable resolution of *han* should not take an either-or but a both-and approach. Thinking in this way, the atonement of Jesus Christ should entail a divine courage that responds both to the personal and the systemic evil in the world. To speak of this in the language of *han*, one sees at the cross of Christ *han* (i.e. human suffering) being positively conjoined with the embrace of *jeong* (i.e. love and affection) and stirs up a collective moral consciousness to

---

[35] Jong-Chun Park, 'Paul Tillich's Categories for the Interpretation of History: An Application to the Encounter of Eastern and Western Churches' (unpublished Ph.D. diss., Emory University, 1986), p. 229.

[36] Whether *han* at the original level can be described as ontological or not is debatable. That it is beyond conscious modification gives some credence to the possibility of it being defined as ontological. But, it should also be noted that the accumulation (or deepening) of *han* is associated with the life events in the historical. Here *han* is distanced from similar Western metaphysical notions, e.g. Augustine's original sin or Kierkegaard's *Angst*.

resist evil and effect a change in the world of human brokenness. Atonement hence functions as the substructure for refashioning human life through the work of sanctification that is both personal and social.

2. The dialectic between the original (archetypal) and actual (secondary) must also be maintained. While it is needful to resolve *han* at its secondary (i.e. conscious) level, it is to no avail if *han* at the original (i.e. unconscious) level is not addressed. In the Christian doctrine of atonement, we also note how it is directed at the removal of both the original and the actual sin. As for the original sin, the power to bring this about is not inherently in us; likewise, the original *han* cannot be resolved by our conscious modification. For this reason, the Christian doctrine of atonement has to underscore the 'external' (i.e. *outside of us*) element of grace while demanding our conscious cooperation enabled and empowered by it. Herein, what God does for us should effect an affectional change in us that manifests externally in our conscious participation in the covenantal life with God.

3. The dialectic between promise and fulfillment must also be kept in tension. The Christian doctrine of atonement speaks of this in terms of God's longing to bring about the eschatological fulfillment of justice. God in Jesus Christ enters into the stream of cause and effect and, together with us, yearns for the final restoration of the covenant of life established at creation. Herein, the courage of God is interwoven with human suffering. This is also reflected in the 'mature' *han* where the courage to embrace present suffering is directed at the *telos* of the journey. The *telos* (i.e. the hope of future transformation) guides and nourishes the journey in the present. The atonement of Jesus Christ is then the culmination of divine courage that foreshadows the eschatological fulfillment of the promise (i.e. the covenant of life) established at creation.

4. Creation and redemption should also be understood in a dialectical correlation. The atonement of Jesus Christ does not merely represent a 'rescue' from damnation; it also entails a passion for 'life' in God and with God. For this reason, we have observed that atonement restores the image of God that has to do with our active remembering of the past mediated by the Spirit. Herein, the covenant of life established at creation is being restored at redemption. Christ's atonement becomes the means by which human life again becomes interwoven with our Creator. Human life recovers the forgotten stories of its origin and is henceforth positioned to journey toward its ultimate *telos*, acknowledging that God is both the 'origin' and '*telos*' of human life. What Christ's atonement brings has to do with much more than our liberation in the present. We are liberated 'for' God and called to dwell in him as he dwells in us. In the culture of *han*, however, a resolution often tends to

focus on the issues and challenges in the present (i.e. historical evil, whether personal or systemic) without necessarily relating them to the questions about the 'foundation' and 'purpose' of human life.[37] In other words, while providing episodic release from hardships and suffering, the resolution of this sort fails to provide the 'depth grammar' for life. For this reason, the Christian doctrine of atonement provides a corrective to the ways in which resolution of *han* is understood.

Conclusion

The mystery of the cross escapes theological categories provided by various atonement traditions in the history of Christian Church. Models and metaphors constructed therefore help us see diverse yet crucial facets contained in the atonement of Jesus Christ. What the doctrine of atonement should include as essential elements become even more clear when it is viewed in light of concrete realities of human brokenness, e.g. violence and suffering in the culture of *han*. At the end, the atonement of Jesus Christ stands as divine courage interwoven with human suffering. At the cross of Christ, a sense of shared solidarity between God and humanity finds its ultimate expression (i.e. death). But, what is entailed in his death is really the life in the community of God. It is the love that is in the community of God being manifested to the fullest extent. As such, it issues forth the 'depth grammars' for life encouraging and empowering us to participate in the way of life in God. In order to partake of it, we are to love as God in Jesus Christ loved us. We are to walk in the anointed way of Jesus where love is perfected in living by the power and presence of the Holy Spirit.

★★★★★★★★★★★★★★★★★★

Abstract
Discussions about the doctrine of atonement have often been focused on the single event in history, the death of Jesus Christ at the cross, without taking into consideration the fact that it encapsulates the entire life journey of Jesus Christ that was missionally anointed of the Spirit. Atonement represents not only a mere 'rescue from' damnation but also provides the 'depth grammar for' living unto God. The study first explores various atonement models and metaphors to discover some essential features associated with the atonement of Jesus Christ. This then allows us to see how a viable Wesleyan-Pentecostal reading on atonement necessarily interweaves multifarious components of

---

[37] That *han* at the original level is beyond conscious modification and hence resolution directs resolution to be entirely about the secondary manifestations of *han*. The enduring presence of original *han* then makes it impossible to speak of a holistic or ultimate resolution of *han*. Human life is a journey from one form of *han* to another, experiencing release that is only episodic or temporary in nature.

atonement spread in various models and metaphors. Moreover, when pitted against the issues and challenges emerging from a particular culture of *han*, what seems apparent is the need for a holistic understanding of atonement that addresses the suffering condition of humanity at various levels and dimensions. Herein, the cross of Christ represents the courage of God interwoven with human suffering effecting us to become partakers of the journey into the wounded heart of God and, in so doing, the life in the community of God.

10

Dancing with the Spirit: Story, Theology, and Ethics

Terry L. Johns[*]

Introduction[1]

In the newly published revision of his most important work, *Living in the Spirit: The Way of Salvation*, Hollis Gause calls for 'Pentecostal theology [that unifies] its doctrines of salvation and baptism with the Holy Spirit.'[2] *Living in the Spirit* makes significant advancement toward this goal and provides an important contribution to the larger discussion concerning the form and content of constructive Pentecostal theology. Inherent also is a profound challenge to give critical/reflective attention to the experience that is central to the Pentecostal ethos. This is crucial not only for faithful development and articulation of theological and ethical frameworks, but also for fidelity to God. As a Spirit-filled community of believers, we are responsible to exemplify lived relationships that truthfully reflect the presence of the Holy Spirit in our lives. The Pentecostal ethos, by virtue of its identity with empowered Holy living, identifies the necessity for integration of theology and ethics.[3]

[*] Terry L. Johns (D.Min., Columbia Theological Seminary) is Associate Professor of Social Ethics at the Pentecostal Theological Seminary, Cleveland, TN.

[1] It is an honor to be included in this celebration of the life, ministry and scholarship of Dr. R. Hollis Gause. It is a special honor to be a colleague of my former teacher. Few students have the honor of continuing to learn from their seminary mentors. His commitment to biblical Pentecostal theology has significantly informed and blessed my life. I only hope that my efforts faithfully represent his influence.

[2] R. Hollis Gause, *Living in the Spirit: The Way of Salvation* (Cleveland, TN: R. Hollis Gause, 2005), p. 15.

[3] Stanley Hauerwas argues that 'theology's inherently practical character, its unmistakable status as a pastoral discipline, simply defies strong systematization. Christian ethics is a mode of theology. Indeed, to begin by asking what is the relation between theology and ethics is to have already made a mistake. Christian convictions are by nature meant to form and illumine lives. Christian ethics is at the heart of the theological enterprise' in *The Peaceable Kingdom: A Primer in Christian Ethics* (Notre Dame: University of Notre Dame Press, 1983), pp. xvi–xvii.

This in turn requires theological formulation that no longer 'separates the cognitive from the affective, reason from passion',[4] but recognizes that Spirit filled life in Christ is radically transformational.[5]

For Gause, the unification of salvation and Spirit baptism is specifically concerned with the place of Spirit baptism within 'the way of salvation'.

> This experience is the climax of all preceding experiences in salvation, and is provided in the atoning work of our Lord Jesus Christ. There is a strong emphasis on vocational/missional purposes of this baptism, but its purpose is not vocational alone.
>
> This experience has a place in redemptive order and experience because of its relationship to and dependence on the Cross, resurrection and ascension of Jesus. As a redemptive experience, it is transformational in the cultivation of righteousness and its anointing for the pursuit of holiness.[6]

In other words, baptism with the Holy Spirit is 'a quality of being and a manner of life'.[7] With this claim the discussion is expanded beyond the issue of redemptive order to include concern for personal and social ethics. My focus will be on this latter emphasis. Two elements of the Pentecostal ethos are of particular interest to this discussion: Pentecostal story and theological reflection on this story. More specifically: does Pentecostal story and theological reflection lend support to interpretation of Spirit baptism as 'a quality of being and a manner of life'?

Narrative: The Place of Story

Contextualization is critical to the discussion because the 'socio-cultural context of a group plays a vital role in the formation of theology' (contextualization of interpretation). That is, 'the context of the community (in)forms the interpretation'.[8] In this sense, it is a text to be read and

---

[4] Samuel Solivan, *The Spirit Pathos and Liberation: Toward an Hispanic Pentecostal Theology* (JPTS 14; Sheffield: Sheffield Academic Press), p. 37. Solivan calls for a 'third pole as an interlocutor between orthodoxy and orthopraxis' which he refers to as *orthopathos*. '*Orthopathos* links us in community with those who suffer. It shapes and informs the epistemological perspective of those who speak and act prophetically'. This allows the theologian 'to bridge the gap between critical reflection and interpersonal engagement' and affirms 'the important contribution that personal experience can have on critical theological formation and dialogue' (p. 37).

[5] Thus avoiding the 'dangers of an emotion and experience centered theology'. R. Hollis Gause, 'Issues in Pentecostalism', in *Perspectives on the New Pentecostalism* (ed. Russell P. Spittler; Grand Rapids: Baker Book House, 1976), pp. 106-16 (114).

[6] Gause, *Living in the Spirit*, p. 13.

[7] Gause, *Living in the Spirit*, p. 8.

[8] Robby Waddell, *The Spirit of the Book of Revelation* (JPTS 30; Blandford Forum: Deo Publishing, 2006), pp. 92, 97-98.

interpreted:[9] 'the meaningful action of a faith community as a social text which is subject to hermeneutical investigation'.[10] Reading a social text is a narrative-theological move 'allowing the ethos and experience of the tradition to inform the interpretation theologically'.[11] This is possible because:

> the Pentecostal community is bound together by 'shared charismatic experiences' and 'shared story'. The Pentecostal narrative tradition provides the Pentecostals with an experiential, conceptual hermeneutical narrative that enables them to interpret Scripture and their experience of reality.[12]

The Pentecostal community is by no means homogeneous.[13] It is a diverse community that includes multi-varied experiences and stories. The challenge is to identify experiences and stories that may be described as commonly 'shared'. A way of addressing this is by identifying experiences and stories that serve as 'symbols' for the basic ethological core. Symbols are relevant to ethological identification because they:

> function to synthesize a people's ethos – the tone, character, and quality of their life, its moral and aesthetic style and mood – and their world view – the picture they have of the way things in sheer actuality are, their most comprehensive ideas of order.[14]

There is little debate that Spirit baptism is the most identifiable experience associated with Pentecostalism. The centrality of Spirit baptism to Pentecostal core identity has led to an elevation of the importance of Luke-Acts as the key biblical text to bring meaning to the experience. Historically, the Lukan corpus has maintained such a centrality within the Pentecostal ethos that the interpretive lens has been described as one that 'reads the rest of the New Testament [and life] through Lukan eyes, especially with the lenses provided by the

---

[9] For additional discussion on 'experience in community' as a text to be read see *Pneuma* 15.2 (1993), pp. 129-222.

[10] Murray Dempster, 'Paradigm Shifts and Hermeneutics: Confronting Issues Old and New', *Pneuma* 15.2 (1993), pp. 129-35 (p. 129).

[11] Waddell, *The Spirit of the Book of Revelation*, p. 101. Since Wesleyan Pentecostals are committed to a quadrilateral construction for theological authority – Scripture, reason, tradition and experience – the claim that the story of this community (tradition) is a text to be interpreted does not seem so unusual.

[12] Kenneth J. Archer, *A Pentecostal Hermeneutic for the Twenty-First Century: Spirit, Scripture and Community* (JPTS 28; London: T & T Clark International, 2004), pp. 97-98.

[13] The variance in experience is self-evident to most Pentecostals. Challenges to the identity of the guiding narrative (central story) and early theology of Pentecostalism as homogeneous are increasing as more recent historical studies on the tradition have been published. For example, Joe Creech, 'Visions of Glory: The Place of the Azusa Street Revival in Pentecostal History', *Church History* 6 (Sept. 1996), pp. 405-24.

[14] Clifford Geertz, *Interpretation of Cultures* (New York: Basic Books, 1973), p. 89.

Book of Acts'.[15] This is an important hermeneutical shift toward biblical narrative material: not only for descriptive purposes, but also for
theological understanding. This attention to the narrative of Acts (in
particular texts concerned with Spirit baptism) has been a primary influence in establishing the predominant status that the Azusa Street
Revival maintains within the diversity of Pentecostalism. Azusa Street
is depicted as the most influential location for 'the second Pentecost' or
'latter rain' outpouring of the Holy Spirit baptism. Whether it is the
source for a homogeneous Pentecostal ethos and theology is certainly
debatable. However, it is likely that it serves as a homogeneous symbol.

> Azusa was the sign for which emerging Pentecostals had hoped; it was
> the symbolic moment that provided the impetus to believe. Azusa has
> shaped academic literature because it so indelibly shaped the way early
> Pentecostals understood themselves and their movement. They were
> participants in a worldwide revival – an eschatological act of God. If, in
> their minds, Azusa represented both the initial outpouring and the blu-
> eprint for interpreting similar stirrings, it is no wonder it would ulti-
> mately shape the way we tell the Pentecostal story.[16]

This shared Pentecostal ethos implies that there is narrative quality
to life. To have an identity requires a story. This story is not only personal: it is a story within a community of like travelers who share the
essential ethos. The community story also participates in the larger
story of God. Thus, it is both transformational and formational. It is
transformational because it requires relationship with God. It is formational because it is an eschatological journey with God, in the Holy
Spirit, through participation in a Spirit-filled community of faith (charismatic community), where character formation takes place within the
dialectic[17] of holy worship and holy witness.[18]

---

[15] Donald Dayton, *Theological Roots of Pentecostalism* (Grand Rapids: Zondervan, 1987),
p. 23. Cf. Robert W. Wall, 'Purity and Power According to the Acts of the Apostles',
Pneuma 21.2 (1999), pp. 215-31.

[16] Creech, 'Visions of Glory', p. 424.

[17] By dialectic I mean a process of dialogue and synthesis. It does not imply an anti-
thetical relationship.

[18] For detailed discussions on the issue of character formation, cf.; Cheryl Bridges
Johns, *Pentecostal Formation: A Pedagogy Among the Oppressed* (JPTS 2; Sheffield: Sheffield
Academic Press, 1993); Steven J. Land, *Pentecostal Spirituality: A Passion for the Kingdom*
(JPTS 1; Sheffield: Sheffield Academic Press, 1993); Stanley Hauerwas, *A Community of
Character: Toward a Constructive Christian Social Ethic* (Notre Dame: University of Notre
Dame Press, 1981), and *The Peaceable Kingdom: A Primer on Christian Ethics*; Glenn Stassen
& David Gushee, *Kingdom Ethics: Following Jesus in Contemporary Context* (Downers
Grove: InterVarsity Press, 2003). Alasdair MacIntyre, *After Virtue, Second Edition* (Notre
Dame: University of Notre Dame Press, 1984); John Howard Yoder, *The Politics of Jesus*
(Grand Rapids: Eerdmans, 1972).

The identification of Spirit baptism and narrative connection to Luke-Acts and Azusa Street as shared elements of Pentecostal ethos is the initial consideration. In order to discern their meaning and significance for this ethos, theological reflection is necessary. Since identification of ethos is approached by reflection on key narratives, theological reflection will follow a similar pattern.

Narrative: The Interpretation of Story

As noted, the orientation toward a narrative understanding predisposed Pentecostals to read life and Scripture through a particular lens. The shifting to narrative understanding through focus on Luke-Acts represents a move toward a more subjective hermeneutic, a more practical experiential bent,[19] while maintaining commitment to the discerned truth of Scripture.[20] This Luke-Acts hermeneutical lens is similar to the narrative theological focus called for by Kenneth Archer and Robby Waddell.

Archer posits a critical narrative approach 'that embraces a *tridactic* negotiation for meaning between the biblical text, the Holy Spirit and the Pentecostal community. Meaning then is arrived at through a dialectical process based upon an interdependent dialogical relationship

---

[19] While remaining committed to the work of Christ as central to soteriology, the Pentecostal *full gospel* is uniquely pneumatic due to its Lukan-Spirit hermeneutic (Donald Dayton, *Theological Roots of Pentecostalism* (Grand Rapids: Zondervan, 1987), p. 23. I agree that the experience of the Spirit is central to Pentecostal understanding of God, life, theology and Scripture. However, the discussion on Pentecostal hermeneutics is more complex than the current discussion implies (which is limited by the focus of the essay). For more developed discussions, cf.: Kenneth Archer, *A Pentecostal Hermeneutic for the Twenty-first Century Spirit, Scripture and Community*; Jamie K. A. Smith, *The Fall of Interpretation: Philosophical Foundations for a Creational Hermeneutic* (Downers Grove: InterVarsity Press, 2000); John Christopher Thomas, 'Reading the Bible from Within our Traditions: A Pentecostal Hermeneutic as Test Case,' in Joel Green & Max Turner (eds.), *Between Two Horizons: Spanning New Testament Studies and Systematic Theology* (Grand Rapids: Eerdmans, 2000). A plethora of articles on the issue may also be found in two primary Pentecostal scholarly journals: *Journal of Pentecostal Theology* and *Pneuma*.

[20] For an informative review of hermeneutical approaches by Pentecostalism's first generation, see Kenneth Archer, 'Early Pentecostal Biblical Interpretation', *JPT* 18 (2001), pp. 32-70. Archer notes the diversity of interpretive approaches but concludes that central to any Pentecostal hermeneutic is the illuminating work of the Holy Spirit. Archer also argues that 'subjective hermeneutic' is not inferior to a perceived more objective/rational model: 'The Modernist attempt to be a neutral interpreter by setting aside one's "experience" and/or presuppositions is a false illusion ... [because] there is a pietistic, experiential, heart-felt approach to interpretation among Pentecostals. However, I strongly disagree that this is a "subjective hermeneutic" that may contaminate the objective truth' (p. 41). (In a footnote, Archer states that he is making this point in argument against a Modernist perspective of 'subjective.') Cf. note 16.

between Scripture, Spirit and community'.[21] Such an approach understands theology as being more than academic/rational. Theology is a
'discerning reflection upon the living reality' of the divine-human relations actualized through the experience of the Holy Spirit.[22] This discerning reflection takes seriously the significance of worship, the place
of community, the authority of Scripture, the centrality of prayer and
commitment to the *missio Dei* as integral to this living reality.[23] Commitment to this reflective/active, active/reflective, encounter offers
Pentecostals the possibility of a theological process that holds in healthy
tension the spiritual/experiential dimension of life with the criti-
cal/reflective dimension necessary for understanding. It also guards
against the pitfalls of domination by emotionalism on the one hand and
rationalism on the other. This more holistic approach is consistent with
the ethos of Pentecostalism: one that is committed to the *fullness of truth*
so that 'being, behavior and beliefs conform fully to the truth intended
for us'.[24]

Waddell proposes that a theological hermeneutic is the most appropriate for a Pentecostal reading of texts. Waddell, following Rickie
Moore, views Scripture as 'an event' so that 'a theological reading is
not merely a deduction but rather a revelation'. Therefore, a Pentecostal theological hermeneutic is 'a divine encounter, an experience with
the living God'.[25] Experience of the Spirit of God is essential if meaning is to be derived.[26] For Waddell, as for Archer, discernment of
meaning, through hearing the voice of the Spirit is only possible
through participation in the community of faith. More specifically, 'the
hermeneutical model encourages a *tridactic* dialectical and dialogical
interdependent relationship between Scripture, Spirit and Community
for the negotiation of meaning.[27] Thus, the Pentecostal story for meaning should be found in the interrelatedness of its narrative experiences:
Spirit-baptism, Scripture and community story.

---

[21] Archer, *A Pentecostal Hermeneutic for the Twenty-First Century*, p. 157. Archer's hermeneutic builds on John Christopher Thomas' discussion of the interpretive process of
the interrelated process between Spirit, community and Scripture described in Acts 15
(Cf. John Christopher Thomas, 'Women, Pentecostals and the Bible: An Experiment in
Pentecostal Hermeneutics', *JPT* 5 (1994), pp. 41-56.

[22] Land, *Pentecostal Spirituality*, p. 34.

[23] Land, *Pentecostal Spirituality*, pp. 32-42. In this context, prayer refers to an openness
that faithfully hears and responds to the Spirit of Truth (p. 36).

[24] Jackie David Johns, 'Pentecostalism and the Postmodern Worldview', *JPT* 7 (1995),
pp. 73-96 (93).

[25] Waddell, *The Spirit of Revelation*, p. 111. See also Rickie D. Moore, 'Canon and
Charisma in the Book of Deuteronomy', *JPT* 1 (1992), pp.75-92.

[26] Experience of the Spirit/spiritual experience includes the full dimension of initial
Spirit baptism and the life in the Spirit that follows.

[27] Archer, *A Pentecostal Hermeneutic for the Twenty-First Century*, p. 185.

Story: Searching for Meaning

The story of context begins with the outpouring of the Holy Spirit on an ethnically, culturally, socio-economically diverse group of faithful believers. Most within this community were disenfranchised from the larger culture – and even the Church – due to one or a combination of these demographic factors. Yet it was on this diverse marginal group that God chose to 'pour himself out'.

The birth of the modern Pentecostal movement took place in this revival of the Spirit that crossed ethnic and cultural barriers. The outpouring of the Holy Spirit baptism brought a spiritual power and fervor that resulted in an energized commitment to the great commission (Mt. 28.19), the ethics of the Sermon on the Mount (Mt. 5-7) and the great commandment (Mt. 22.37-40). Pentecostal pioneers took seriously the charge to 'go into all the world and make disciples'. This missionary zeal was accompanied by a deep commitment to love others and seek justice evidenced by the establishment of orphanages and soup kitchens, solidarity with the poor and disenfranchised, empowerment of women for ministry, ethical commitment to biblical truth, resistance to contamination by the dominant culture (in the world but not of it), and commitment to the Prince of Peace that resulted in a non-violent, pacifist stance in the face of world turmoil.[28] 'Azusa's leaders were ethical restorationists; they abandoned the conventional means by which society ordered reality (education, social status, race and gender categories) and [by] doing so, they assaulted the status quo'.[29]

The call and commitment to witness and mission was understood in relationship to the radical transformation that was experienced. There was not a rigid bifurcation of holy living and witness. If not arrived at

[28] Unfortunately, many of these early commitments have begun to fade in North American Pentecostalism. Solidarity with the poor and disenfranchised has too often been replaced by secular success models and the prosperity gospel (which seems to be a devaluing of the word *gospel*). Women have been disallowed to participate in the higher levels of decision-making through denial of the highest level of ordination for ministry and exclusion from top leadership positions. If care is not taken, commitment to biblical truth may become contaminated by our newly found fascination with the dominant culture. Sadly, an integral aspect of Pentecostal spirituality – commitment to peace and justice – has fallen by the way side for too many. Our hope for maintaining the heart of the Pentecostal ethos may rest with our brothers and sisters in the majority world. For a provocative discussion along these lines see Cheryl Bridges Johns, 'Presidential Address: The Adolescence of Pentecostalism: In Search of a Legitimate Sectarian Identity', *Pneuma* 17.1 (1995), pp. 3-17. Regarding pacifism, see: Jay Beaman, *Pentecostal Pacifism* (Hillsboro: Center for Mennonite Brethren Studies, 1989). For an annotated listing of early Pentecostal statements regarding the pacifist stance go to www.thirdway.cc hosted by Thirdway Peace and Justice Fellowship, San Francisco, CA.

[29] Creech, 'Visions of Glory', p. 412. This narrative reading of the social text also indicates that early Pentecostals were not only committed to evangelism and worship, but also to social justice.

by careful reflection, at the very least it seemed intuitive to these early Pentecostals that separating the character of the witness from the message of the witness was not plausible. Thus, these messengers, empowered by the Holy Spirit, went forth in holy prophetic witness.[30]

The development of doctrine faithfully represented this Holy Spirit empowered lifestyle. Pentecostals were faithful in their commitment to take the message of Pentecost to the whole world. But this was not a message developed and delivered with myopic vision. These Pentecostals entered a new dance of life. Everything changed for them: the old passed away and all things were new. The music changed and the world was encountered to a new melody; they were now members of a holy community of faith and children of the King. Most importantly the dance partner changed – for they were now dancing with the Holy Spirit. They committed their hearts, minds and will – their very being – to move in step with this newly found partner. Commitment to the gospel message reflected this harmony.

The primary expression of doctrine came through the preaching of the gospel message (though tracts, newsletters and periodicals were also common methods of expression). Preaching was characterized by a 'spiritual anointing' often expressed in exuberant and passionate delivery styles. Preachers spoke 'as the oracles of God' while the Spirit directed their speech. The outcome was a doctrinal pattern that emphasized a profound Christology. There is little evidence to suggest that this Christology (maybe even pneumatic Christology) resulted from a formalized theological process.[31] It arose, rather, from this Spirit anointed preaching in various locations across the world. Its content was focused on Jesus and thus has been categorized as the five-fold gospel: Jesus is (1) saviour; (2) sanctifier; (3) healer; (4) Holy Spirit baptizer and (5) soon coming king.[32] This *full gospel*,[33] represented by

---

[30] Reading the narrative 'story' of Pentecostalism may offer a legitimate response to the ethical concerns of Walter Hollenweger, who in 'The Critical Tradition of Pentecostalism', *JPT* 1 (1992), pp. 7-17 (9) notes that we live in 'a world which is at its wits' end over the problems of racial division, war, individual and social ethics and needs more than ever the ministry of Christian thought'. This narrative reading indicates that early Pentecostals had a sense of social concern that addressed these issues. Hopefully, Pentecostals will find a way to embrace this heritage, live it and preserve it for future generations.

[31] Douglas Jacobsen does note that even though 'experience was a crucial dimension' of these early Pentecostals, 'it was experience guided by theological truth that really mattered. Experiences needed to be examined and evaluated. As a result, first-generation Pentecostals were constantly arguing with each other about how best to describe their faith and fellowship with God. The early movement was literally awash in a sea of theological debate' (*Thinking in the Spirit: Theologies of the Early Pentecostal Movement* [Bloomington: Indiana University Press, 2003], p. 3).

[32] Donald Dayton, *Theological Roots of Pentecostalism*, pp. 19-23. Dayton eventually argues for a four-fold pattern as more representative of the entire Pentecostal movement (dropping sanctification), but admits that the five-fold pattern is more representative of

the five motifs, provided a 'soteriological foundation for the [Pentecostal] message.'[34] The baptism with the Holy Spirit not only energized missionary efforts, but also redirected hearts and minds toward Jesus Christ.

It is difficult to determine which came first for early Pentecostals: theology or spiritual experience. It may be that they developed together in a dynamic dialectic such as action/reflection, reflection/action. It could be that early Pentecostals took a more experiential approach. One thing is clear: this new found Pentecostal experience had a profound transformational impact on those who were receptive.

Theological Reflection

Baptism with the Holy Spirit is central to the Pentecostal ethos and must be considered as integral to theological formulation. Theology claiming to be Pentecostal must not only be faithful to this ethos, but must be born of it. Theology *masked* as Pentecostal that is simply

---

the Holiness wing. For others who identify this motif, cf.: John Christopher Thomas, '1998 Presidential Address: Pentecostal Theology in the Twenty-first Century', *Pneuma* 20.1 (1998), pp. 3-19; Steven J. Land, *Pentecostal Spirituality: A Passion for the Kingdom* (JPTS 1; Sheffield: Sheffield Academic Press, 1993), p. 18. It is important to note that Land views these motifs as being primary to the preaching and teaching during the first ten years of the movement. He argues that the 'full gospel', in Pentecostal understanding, is the 'whole Bible rightly divided' (p. 126). William Faupel agrees that the five-fold gospel is a particular distinctive, but argues that 'the second coming of Jesus was the central concern of the initial Pentecostal message.' *The Everlasting Gospel: The Significance of Eschatology in the Development of Pentecostal Thought* (JPTS 10; Sheffield: Sheffield Academic Press, 1996; repr. Blandford Forum: Deo Publishing, 2009), p. 20. Robert M. Anderson, *Vision of the Disinherited: The Making of American Pentecostalism* (New York: Oxford University Press, 1979), pp. 79-92, agrees with Faupel. N. Bloch-Hoell, *The Pentecostal Movement: Its Origin, Development and Distinctive Character* (Oslo: Universitetsforlaget, 1964), pp. 22-151, identifies the Pentecostal order of salvation as conversion, justification by faith, instantaneous and successive sanctification and baptism with the Holy Spirit. He adds supernatural healing as a gift of grace.

[33] 'Full gospel, then, means the full experiencing of all the possible ways in which Christ can minister to us on the basis of His earthly mission and heavenly session. The objective gospel must be clarified subjectively as a package of God's provisions "for us." What happened to Jesus in His mediatorial activities forms the objective basis of the gospel, but one does not really hear the gospel as "good news" until the results of His objective acts are certified to us as to their meaning for us. This good news as subjective gospel explains to us that the purpose of His passion-glorification is to regenerate us, heal us, fill us with holy love and Spirit, and finally to return for us to share His glory. It is not a question of either/or, objective gospel or subjective gospel, for all evangelicals would agree that there is a subjective dimension in the gospel' (William G. MacDonald, 'Pentecostal Theology: A Classical Viewpoint' in *Perspectives on the New Pentecostalism* [ed. Russell P. Spittler; Grand Rapids: Baker Book House, 1976], pp. 58-74 [63]). These elements of the full gospel continue to be expressed by Wesleyan Pentecostals.

[34] Faupel, *The Everlasting Gospel*, p. 42.

drawn from other traditions with 'Spirit' added is not sufficient expression of an ethos that is born of an encounter with the divine Spirit of God.[35] As Terry Cross has aptly stated:

> While Pentecostals share many theological tenets in common with other Christians, we have experienced God in ways others do not confess. Rather than viewing theology as a description of our distinctives, we need to understand the all-encompassing difference which our experience of God makes in every area of our lives – especially those that are theological. For Pentecostals, the beginning and end of theological reflection will be infused with our experience of God through his Spirit. We are a people invaded by the Spirit; therefore, we cannot think, live or write as if this experience of the living God were peripheral. Pentecostal theology will reflect the reality of God's encounter with humans.[36]

To claim the experience of Spirit baptism is not experience as normally understood is an important qualifier. As an encounter with the Divine 'in ways others do not confess':

> It is an experiential or experimental sense of the presence of God of such strength that one knows with the deepest sense of certainty that one not only believes in God but 'knows' Him – in the Hebrew sense of the word, 'know' as experience. In Catholic traditional spirituality this is known as the 'presence of God felt' and it is deemed to be a pure gift from God, a gift for which one can dispose oneself but only God Himself, as Sovereign, can dispense. It is not acquired by merely human effort.[37]

Knowing God through experience (Hebrew ידע) is knowledge that is an integration of the heart and mind and results from 'active and intentional engagement in lived experience.'[38] It moves beyond objective concepts to relational encounter: God, 'the one who lives in the midst of history and who initiates covenant relationships', encountering the knower.[39] Therefore, the baptism of the Spirit, as understood along

---

[35] This is not intended to imply that doctrines of historic Christian faith are alien to the Pentecostal ethos. Land clearly lays out the relationship of Pentecostalism to historic Christian faith in *Pentecostal Spirituality*, pp. 15-57. It does, however, imply that the particular ethos requires a theology birthed from this *peculiar* encounter with God and resultant community passion to effectively express the relationships.

[36] Terry L. Cross, 'The Rich Feast of Theology: Can Pentecostals Bring the Main Course or Only the Relish?', *JPT* 16 (2000), pp. 27-47 (33-34).

[37] J. Massyngberde Ford, 'The New Pentecostalism: Personal Reflections of a Participating Roman Catholic Scholar', in *Perspectives on the New Pentecostalism* (ed. R.P. Spittler; Grand Rapids: Baker Book House, 1976), pp. 208-29 (211).

[38] Thomas H. Groome, *Christian Religious Education* (San Francisco: Harper & Row, 1980), p. 141.

[39] Cheryl Bridges Johns, *Pentecostal Formation*, p. 35.

Pentecostal lines, is 'a personal disclosure of God particularly as to His immediacy'.[40] Knowing God through experience of the Spirit connects the heart and mind. Those who share this experience within the community of faith 'reflect on the meaning of God's presence but cannot divorce experience of God from the reflection'.[41] 'Knowledge of God, therefore, is measured not by the information one possesses but by how one is living in response to God'.[42] Clark Pinnock describes this dynamic:

> The Pentecostal community [consists of] a people baptized in the Holy Spirit [who are] continually interacting with God. They are a people caught up in the story of God and in the momentum of the Spirit of the last days and are engaged in a mission which is itself a sign of the last days. They deal with a God who is free and personal and who responds to them in surprising and unpredictable ways. They are blessed to be simple Biblicists, relatively uncorrupted by traditions foreign to Scripture. They are, therefore, free to experience the dynamic presence of God. To them, God is not a metaphysical iceberg but a living person.[43]

The self-understanding that God is near is an altering reality that results in a right ordering of life.[44] God is near refocuses the approach to life and the place God maintains in it. 'There is a deep awareness of the nearness of God and a holy familiarity. Along with it, the extraordinary *charisms* (glossolalia, gifts of the Spirit and miracles) are manifested. The *charisms*, therefore, must always be interpreted in the context of the presence of God'.[45] Yet, even with this deep awareness of the presence of God, the realization of the tension between experience of God and reality of God remains present. God is always more than a given experience and, likewise, the Spirit is not identical to experience of the Spirit.[46] Thus, the sense of holy awe is maintained and reducing experience of the Spirit to existentialism is avoided.

The Christian life lived in the Spirit is 'essentially the interplay of the extraordinary and the ordinary'.[47] The dialectic of interplay provides 'a standpoint' from which to survey all Christian truth: 'the lens through which we look at everything else rather than the direct object

---

[40] David A. Dorman, 'The Purpose of Empowerment in the Christian Life', *Pneuma* 7 (1985), pp. 147-165 (147-48).

[41] Cross, 'The Rich Feast of Theology', p. 35.

[42] Cheryl Bridges Johns, *Pentecostal Formation*, p. 35.

[43] Clark Pinnock, 'Divine Relationality: A Pentecostal Contribution to the Doctrine of God', *JPT* 16 (2000), pp. 3-26 (10).

[44] Cheryl Bridges Johns, *Pentecostal Formation*, pp. 95-96.

[45] Simon Chan, *Pentecostal Theology and the Christian Spiritual Tradition* (JPTS 21; Sheffield: Sheffield Academic Press, 2000), p. 55.

[46] Hollenweger, 'The Critical Tradition of Pentecostalism', p. 9.

[47] Chan, *Pentecostal Theology and the Christian Spiritual Tradition*, p. 55.

of our intense gaze. There is a kind of holy boldness or empowered holiness when we look at the world with a receptive attitude towards God's empowering presence'.[48] 'We (Pentecostals) are not just evangelicals who speak in tongues! We are a people invaded by the Spirit, therefore, *we cannot think, live or write as if this experience were peripheral*'.[49] Since spiritual experience is central, there is an epistemological shift from a more Enlightenment-rationalistic model to a Spirit-faith model.[50]

The presence of the Spirit within the community of faith 'insures that what it says and does are in continuity with its risen Lord'.[51] The implication is that *baptism with the Spirit* as encounter with the presence of God permeates all of life for the Pentecostal and cannot be ignored in the quest for theological meaning (or construction). There is an intimate relationship between spiritual experience (spirituality) and theology that cannot be denied. The two are not identical, but there is an integration of the two that renders them inseparable. Karl Barth corroborates this unavoidable integration:

> Only in the realm of the power of the Spirit can theology be realized as a humble, free, critical, and happy science of the God of the Gospel. Only in the courageous confidence that the Spirit is the truth does theology simultaneously pose and answer the question about truth. Unspiritual theology would be one of the most terrible of all terrible occurrences on this earthly vale.[52]

Cross correctly states that 'Pentecostal theology will reflect the reality of God's encounter with humans'.[53] There are certain identifiable aspects of this divine encounter that are reflected in existing Pentecostal theology.

---

[48] Pinnock, *Flame of Love*, p. 10. Simon Chan adds: 'the Pentecostal experience is the lens through which we look at everything else rather than the direct object of our intense gaze. There is a kind of holy boldness or empowered holiness when we look at the world with a receptive attitude towards God's empowering presence' (*Pentecostal Theology and the Christian Spiritual Tradition*, p. 71).

[49] Cross, 'The Rich Feast of Theology', p. 34 (emphasis mine)

[50] This takes seriously the Wesleyan-Pentecostal commitments to John Wesley's emphasis on the various stages of faith (convincing grace, saving grace and sanctifying grace) and Pentecostal life in the Spirit.

[51] Robert W. Wall, 'Purity and Power According to the Acts of the Apostles', *Pneuma* 21.2 (1999), pp. 215-31 (229). 'Without the Holy Spirit, Christianity degenerates into a futile humanistic striving after goodness, the 'bootstrap' religion about which there has been justified complaint'. Lycurgus Starkey, *The Work of the Holy Spirit: A Study in Wesleyan Theology* (Nashville: Abingdon, 1962), p. 8.

[52] Karl Barth, *Evangelical Theology: An Introduction* (Grand Rapids: Eerdmans, 1963), pp. 55-56

[53] Cross, 'The Rich Feast of Theology', p. 34.

It is important that the pneumatic emphasis of Pentecostal theology does not foster the misconception that other significant aspects are missing. As has been argued earlier, the presence of the Spirit within the Pentecostal community of faith 'insures that what it says and does are in continuity with its risen Lord'.[54] This is evidenced by the primary theological themes of the first ten years of the movement[55] which are consistent with the christocentric focus of historic Christian faith: Jesus is (1) saviour; (2) sanctifier; (3) healer; (4) Holy Spirit baptizer; and (5) soon coming king. This *full gospel*, represented by the five motifs, provided a 'soteriological foundation for the [Pentecostal] message',[56] and established an ethical core for its theology. Implied is an integration of holiness and power: an ethical/moral dimension to baptism with the Spirit 'so that our being, behaviour and beliefs conform fully to the truth intended for us'.[57] An ethical dimension implies transformative/formative empowerment for 'sanctifying intensification drawing the believer more consciously into ever deeper intimacy with Christ'[58] that in turn inspires a formative creativity in tune with the Holy Spirit for theological understanding and construction.

If baptism with the Holy Spirit is empowerment for 'sanctifying intensification' then a utilitarian or vocational purpose cannot be the predominant motif for meaning. Certainly, the vocational element of witness is an important and necessary component.[59] However, to reduce Spirit baptism to utility alone fails to take seriously the nature and character of the Holy Spirit as divine person.

The experience of baptism with the Holy Spirit is an intimate relational encounter with the holy God who exists in eternal '*perichoretic interrelatedness*'. God is a personal, relational, social God and each person of the trinity fully participates in the life of the others.[60] According to Catherine Mowry LaCugna, *perichoresis* is:

> being-in-one-another, permeation without confusion. No person exists by him/herself or is referred to him/herself; this would produce number and therefore division within God. Rather, to be a divine person is *by nature* in relation to other persons. Each divine person is irresistibly drawn to the other, taking his/her existence from the other,

---

[54] Wall, 'Purity and Power According to the Acts of the Apostles', p. 229.

[55] The first ten years are identified by a number of scholars as representing the heart of Pentecostal theology. Cf. Hollenweger, *The Pentecostals*; Land, *Pentecostal Spirituality*.

[56] Faupel, *The Everlasting Gospel*, p. 42.

[57] Jackie David Johns, 'Pentecostalism and the Postmodern Worldview', p. 93.

[58] Amos Yong, *The Spirit Poured Out on All Flesh: Pentecostalism and the Possibility of Global Theology*, p. 99.

[59] It is not my intention to devalue or undervalue the vocational element, but rather to highlight the soteriological elements.

[60] Land, *Pentecostal Spirituality*, p. 197.

containing the other in him/herself, while at the same time pouring self out into the other. While there is no blurring of the individuality of each person, there is also no separation. There is only the communion of love in which each person comes to be what he/she is, entirely with reference to the other.[61]

This is consistent with the witness of Scripture in that God is revealed to us as self-communicating love. This self-communication is not due to necessity or duty (which would place limitations on an eternal and limitless God). Rather, it is the result of the very nature and character of God. It is who God is – his very being. God is love (1 Jn 4.8). Because this love is the self-expression of God's very character and is not due to necessity or duty: God loves the world with this same love that defines his being.[62]

It is also important to note that this self-giving love is expressed within social community. The persons of the social trinity are in loving relationship with one another: each fully giving of themselves to the other. Implied by this social relationality is an identity of person that is also socially defined. That is, person is more than self-awareness and is only identifiable within a community of mutual relationships and responsibility. This *perichoretic* relationality of the immanent trinity suggests that person is defined as 'from one another, for one another'.[63] This should be the central understanding of the church in fellowship (*koinonia*): for to be baptized in the Spirit is to participate in this divine life. Through this participation 'a new divine presence is experienced. In the Spirit, God dwells in humanity. The experience of the Spirit is therefore the experience of the Shekinah, the divine indwelling'.[64] The context for this experience is holy community.

God has entered human history through his own self-disclosure in creation, divine encounters, the incarnation of Jesus Christ, and the outpouring and continuing presence of the Holy Spirit.[65] God is not contained in or by human history, but this 'human history' is in God who created all things. So, history moves with God on an eschatologi-

---

[61] Catherine Mowry LaCugna, *God for Us: The Trinity & Christian Life* (San Francisco: HarperSanFrancisco, 1991), p. 271.

[62] For further development of this idea see: Jürgen Moltmann, *The Trinity & the Kingdom* (Minneapolis: Fortress, 1993), pp. 51-54.

[63] Stanley J. Grenz, *The Social God and the Relational Self: A Trinitarian Theology of the Imago Dei* (Louisville: Westminster John Knox, 2001), p. 55.

[64] Jürgen Moltmann, *The Trinity and the Kingdom*, p. 104. It is not evident that Moltmann has in mind the Pentecostal baptism with the Holy Spirit in this statement. However, the truth expressed is consistent with Pentecostal teaching.

[65] Not only is God the 'wholly other' in contradistinction to humankind, but he is also the ever present one who entered human history and 'emptied himself, taking the form of a slave, being born in human likeness' (Phil. 2.8).

cal journey.[66] We enter into the history of God at initial salvation, continue along the way as the Holy Spirit conforms us to the image of God, and reach destination at the consummation of all things when God becomes all in all and we are perfected in him. This is an integrative process, in and by the Holy Spirit, which forms us day by day finally to be received by God in the eschaton for the fulfilment of his eternal purposes. God provides us with his salvation to prepare us for this destined fullness and purpose in him. Every aspect of salvation serves this purpose including Spirit baptism.

At every point in this eschatological journey the holy God who is 'other' is also 'near' engaging us by the presence of his Holy Spirit.[67] There is a mutuality of relationship in which God offers himself to us, calls us to response and then responds to us. God is personal and relational. Our relational experience with God is *true* spiritual relationship: not just a *mystical* one. It 'is not [just] mystical because the reality of the spirituality is in a concrete context of love and passion, pain and pleasure, happiness and sorrow'.[68] Our spirituality no more removes our humanness than Christ's divinity removed his. Moreover, Christ suffered for us and with us, therefore, this spirituality 'does not only mean our experience of God; it also means God's experience with us'.[69] It is a *real* encounter that cuts to the very core of our being, transforming our affections, so that we are truly participants in the divine life as well as the life of the community of faith. There are concrete realities that result from this experience that witness to both dimensions of 'quality of being and manner of life'. This includes, but is not limited to, holy worship/living and holy witness so that there is 'integration of belief, affections and practice'.[70]

Final Reflection and Implications

The preceding discussion has attempted to identify key components within the Pentecostal ethos that provide hermeneutical keys through which theological reflection may be processed. Due to the narrative focus of Pentecostal story and dependence on the narrative text of

---

[66] Land, *Pentecostal Spirituality*, p. 198.

[67] Clark Pinnock in *Flame of Love* notes: 'God is not a Being who dwells at a distance from the world, nor is God a tyrant exercising all-controlling power. Of course God is not the world and the world is not God, yet God is in the world and the world is in him. Because he is at the heart of things, it is possible to encounter God in, with and beneath life's experiences. By the Spirit, power of creation, God is closer to us than we are to ourselves' (p. 61).

[68] Waddell, *The Spirit of the Book of Revelation*, p. 111.

[69] Moltmann, *The Trinity and the Kingdom of God*, p. 4.

[70] Land, *Pentecostal Spirituality*, p. 41.

Luke-Acts to discern meaning from this story, a narrative hermeneutical approach was identified as an appropriate lens with which to view this interpretive process. A truthful narrative reading has been attempted. Hopefully, fidelity to God, to Scripture, to the Pentecostal experience of Spirit baptism, and to the Pentecostal story has been evidenced. If so, the following reflections have some merit:

1. Early Pentecostals lived a life that exemplified a commitment to holy living and empowered mission. Their lifestyle did not represent any bifurcation between baptism with the Spirit and holy living. As a matter of fact, they understood holy living to be a requirement of God for his people. The implication is that limiting the purpose of Spirit baptism to vocational only was not indicative of this early ethos.[71]

2. A narrative approach to theological reflection offers opportunities for a more holistic understanding. Narrative takes seriously the full range of God's communication with us: through Scripture, in relationship through the Spirit, through community and story.

3. Our commitment to theological reflection and construction is first a spiritual exercise. It by necessity is also intellectual, but as members of a community of faith in relationship with God there is an integration of knowing, being and doing that allows the Spirit to form within us a relational understanding of life, Scripture and theology.

4. God is a loving God whose very identity is defined by self-communicating love. As participants in the divine dance, baptism with the Spirit is a baptism into this love. This means that Spirit baptism is indeed 'a quality of being and a manner of life'.

5. If love is central to God's identity, then it is also central to ours. Salvation involves God's efforts through the work of the Holy Spirit to conform us to this image of love. Thus, the community of faith becomes an egalitarian community of love ('from one another, for one another') in *perichoretic* relationship where divisions 'between men and women, rich and poor, [racial and ethnic identity], and religious differences' are broken down.[72] This is social justice. This is holy and ethical living. This is living in and establishing the peaceable kingdom of God.

---

[71] This is deduced from the narrative reading. The majority of early Pentecostal published material leans toward the vocational understanding. However, the lived and expressed witness of the people indicates an understanding that includes the soteriological dimensions of Spirit baptism.

[72] Murray Dempster, 'Pentecostal Social Concern and the Biblical Mandate of Social Justice' *Pneuma* (Fall 1997), pp. 129-53 (148).

Postscript

An attempt has been made to reflect on a process for theological construction that is faithful to the ethos of the Pentecostal faith community. Hopefully, this reflection on theology, ethics and story is helpful to those who seek ways to remain true to this ethos. The ultimate goal is an earnest desire to discern the best way to 'hear what the Spirit is saying to the churches' and at the same time avoid distractions that distort or even mute the Spirit's voice. To do this, Pentecostals must avoid becoming 'masters of accommodation' and once again embrace an identity of 'resident aliens' and the marginalization such a move requires.[73] Cheryl Bridges Johns eloquently articulates these sentiments:

> The same fire which birthed the movement and which has the capacity to devour it, is the only hope of a mature Pentecostalism. In this fire there would emerge a new form of Pentecostal scholarship. It would not be a scholarship based on shame, assuming that scholarly work has to fit the categories of others. Pentecostal scholars would not feel obligated to relate to the tyranny of Evangelical rationalism nor would they acritically jump on a postmodern bandwagon. Pentecostal scholarship would be work filled with wonder and passion as well as work which employs critical reflection. It would be a scholarship based on humility, knowing that it has no claim other than the singular holiness of God. Behind the wall of Pentecostal tradition, there are powerful epistemological, hermeneutical systems, models and worldviews yet to be articulated.[74]

This essay has been an attempt to look 'behind the wall of Pentecostal tradition' to discover some of these valuable resources. The task is not complete. More work is needed on this important discussion concerning the relationship between Spirit baptism, life in the Spirit, and soteriology. While we seek for more truth: may we continue to dance.

It has been said that 'dinosaurs died because they couldn't dance'. For Pentecostals, the issue is not to dance or not dance, but:

'With whom shall we dance?'

★★★★★★★★★★★★★★★★★

---

[73] Cheryl Bridges Johns observes that 'Pentecostals are no longer resident aliens. Rather, Pentecostals have become masters of accommodation' ('The Adolescence of Pentecostalism: In Search of a Legitimate Sectarian Identity', *Pneuma* 17.1 [1995], p. 8). For additional discussion on the church as Resident Aliens see Stanley Hauerwas & William Willimon, *Resident Aliens: Life in the Christian Colony* (Nashville: Abingdon, 1989).

[74] Cheryl Bridges Johns, 'The Adolescence of Pentecostalism: In Search of a Legitimate Sectarian Identity', p. 17

Abstract

Central to the Pentecostal ethos is the experience of baptism with the Holy Spirit. The predominant understanding of the purpose of Spirit baptism within Pentecostalism is vocational empowerment for witness and mission. A narrative approach to Pentecostal history, theological reflection, and reading of the Lukan corpus, reveals that Pentecostals have also understood Spirit baptism to function soteriologically as transformational empowerment for righteousness and holy living.

11

The Development and Significance of Centralized Government in the Church of God

David G. Roebuck*

Introduction

The cool January air was filled with anticipation as delegates gathered for the eighth General Assembly of the Church of God in 1913. The 164 delegates believed they were participating in the restoration of the New Testament church, and the record of that Assembly reveals the seriousness with which the young Church of God understood its mission and emerging government.

On the opening morning of the Assembly, delegates from each state stood and greeted the congregation with a testimonial song. The seven delegates from Florida sang 'Where He Leads Me I Will Follow', and the four from New Mexico rendered, 'I Would Not Be Denied'. Tennessee had the largest number of delegates represented. Approximately 125 strong, they offered 'The Home of the Soul'. No delegates were present from churches in Virginia or the Bahamas, but eight members of a band that had recently ministered in the Bahamas sang 'The Fields Away' in honor of the work there. State Overseer R.M. Singleton was the only representative of Colorado. Whether he was not inclined to present a solo or simply not encouraged to do so, he did not sing for the Assembly.

Later that day, several of the state overseers briefly reported their work during the previous year. The overseers noted the great need for evangelism, the opposition they had encountered, and the necessity of additional laborers in the harvest. T.L. McLain described a tent meeting in Benton, Tennessee. According to Overseer McLain, '14 were

* David G. Roebuck (Ph.D., Vanderbilt University) is director of the Hal Bernard Dixon Jr. Pentecostal Research Center and an Assistant Professor of Religion at Lee University, Cleveland, TN.

baptized in water, the jailor's wife got sanctified at home and after-
wards came to the meeting and received the Holy Ghost'. The reports
indicated that the Church of God was already ministering to multiple
ethnic groups in at least Colorado, New Mexico and Florida.

Also on that first full day of activities, General Overseer A.J. Tomlinson presented his annual address in which he reviewed the work of
the Church the previous year and introduced topics of business for the
Assembly. The general overseer reported 3,056 members in 104
churches in ten states and the Bahamas.

The restoration of the New Testament form of church government
was particularly important to General Overseer Tomlinson. He challenged the delegates,

> At this Assembly we should earnestly seek to reinstate and reestablish
> the government under which banner the brave Apostles and their con-
> temporaries fought, bled and died to sustain. If His government was of
> such importance as to call forth the blood of its supporters to sustain it,
> is its importance any less today? If they gave their lives to sustain it,
> isn't there a just cause for us to give our lives, if need be, to reestablish
> it before His return? Bring it back without causing any offence to any-
> one if possible, but bring it back at any cost![1]

A Primer on Church Government

What was this form of church government that Tomlinson suggested
had cost the Apostles their lives and for which those Church of God
members in 1913 should be willing to shed their blood as well? Tomlinson was not the first church leader to use hyperbole to discuss
church government, and differences related to church government
have caused deep divisions among Christians through the centuries.
There are of course many reasons for the multitude of Christian denominations and independent congregations that exist in the world
today. Differing views on church government take their place alongside doctrine, ethnicity, personality conflicts, and power struggles as
areas of continuing disagreement and conflict between Christians.

Those who write about church government usually talk about three
distinct models: episcopalianism, presbyterianism and congregationalism. Broadly speaking episcopalianism emphasizes the role of the bishop (*episcopos*) who ordains and governs regional and congregational
leaders. Often there is an archbishop who serves over other bishops
and one or more synods of bishops that have jurisdiction at a general

---

[1] Church of God, *Echoes from the Eighth General Assembly of the Churches of God* (Cleveland, TN: Church of God, 1913), p. 15. This introduction was first published as 'Church
of God Chronicles: Bring it Back at Any Cost', *Church of God Evangel* 91.2 (February
2001), p. 13.

level. Episcopalianism, especially as the Roman Catholic and Orthodox traditions practice it, has been the dominant model of church government throughout much of Christian history.

Presbyterianism developed during the Reformation as a reaction to the rule of bishops. It is a representative rather than hierarchical form of church government. A plurality of elders (presbyters, from *presbuteros*) govern at the local (session), regional (presbytery) and general (synod and assembly) levels. Distinctions are often made between ruling elders (laity) and teaching elders (pastors).

Congregationalism emphasizes the autonomy of the local church. Each local church operates independently of any authority other than Christ. Local churches often voluntarily join with other congregations to sponsor ministries and to form associations and conventions to which they send messengers, but these larger bodies only have authority to recommend to the local churches. Government within the local church varies widely in the congregational model. Some congregations select a single elder or senior pastor who works with a board of deacons, while other congregations adopt a plurality of elders.[2]

Although these were the dominant models being practiced at the beginning of the twentieth century, Tomlinson was not looking to restore any of these three models, and today the Church of God does not explicitly lay claim on any of these three specific models. What type of church government was Tomlinson trying to restore? And what does the Church of God mean when it claims to have a 'centralized government'?

---

[2] In this section I have depended on an excellent introduction to church government: Steven B. Cowan, ed., *Who Runs the Church?: 4 Views on Church Government* (Grand Rapids: Zondervan, 2004). See also Chad Owen Brand and R. Stanton Norman, eds., *Perspectives on Church Government: Five Views on Church Polity* (Nashville: Broadman & Holman, 2002). Regarding the history of views on church government, Richard N. Longenecker has suggested that, until the middle of the nineteenth century, the prevailing view regarding church government was that there was a divine order in Scripture that must be correctly interpreted and followed. Following J.B. Lightfoot's commentary on Philippians, published in 1868, a shift was made toward the idea that 'the organization of the church is to be seen not as a divine ordinance but as a social necessity.' According to Longenecker, Lightfoot argued that the orders of ministry were based on circumstances and modeled after existing social structure. Subsequent Protestant scholars began to see nascent forms of each of the three prominent systems of church government in the New Testament. By the middle of the twentieth century, the emphasis was shifting again, this time away from the significance of the form of church government toward discussions of the mission of the church and community formation. See Richard N. Longenecker, ed., *Community Formation in the Early Church and in the Church Today* (Peabody, MA: Hendrickson, 2002), pp. xi–xix (p. xii).

The Meaning of Centralized Government

Church government has been an important theme in the Church of God from our founding. I frequently tell Church of God History and Polity students that the Church of God was birth out of differences related to the question 'Who is in the Church?' Although some have suggested that Pentecostals have not been traditionally interested in ecclesiology, Dale Coulter has clearly shown that ecclesiology was central to early Church of God leaders.[3]

But the Church of God did not begin with what we call 'centralized government,' and we did not label our government as such until well after centralized government was already substantially developed. A computer search reveals that the use of the phase 'centralized government' does not appear in the *Minutes of the General Assemblies of the Church of God* until the general overseer's address to the 44th General Assembly in 1952. During that address General Overseer H.L. Chesser noted that the Great Commission was the main objective of the Church of God and called for adoption of the slogan 'A Church of God in Every Town.' Chesser went on to describe how such a vision might become reality. Along with a call to depend on the power of the Holy Spirit, church planting, evangelism, missions, Bible Schools, and a strong ministry, Chesser included the importance of 'church organization and government'.[4] According to Chesser, 'Time and space would not permit to tell the advantages and blessings of the government of the Church.' He went on to highlight the Church's unique governmental identity by suggesting that, although the Church of God was involved with other denominations in the Pentecostal Fellowship of North America, the National Association of Evangelicals, and local evangelistic campaigns, it 'is entrenched in centralized government' and should be careful not to lose its identity through these cooperative relationships. Chesser further stated that while the Church of God had withstood many storms, its government had 'done much to protect the name and influence of Pentecost against fanaticism, immorality, deadbeats, bums and general crookedness. It is our firm opinion that the Bible generally substantiates the organization and government of the Church'. Chesser concluded by calling on every minister licensed by

---

[3] Dale A. Coulter, 'The Development of Ecclesiology in the Church of God (Cleveland, TN): A Forgotten Contribution?', *Pneuma* 29.1 (2007), pp. 59-85.

[4] H.L. Chesser, 'General Overseer Address' in Church of God, *Minutes of the Forty-fourth General Assembly of the Church of God* (Cleveland, TN: Church of God, 1952), pp. 8-17.

the Church of God to 'feel no embarrassment by talking about its organization and government'.[5]

For General Overseer Chesser, the centralized government of the Church of God was biblical, had protected the church, and was something for which Church of God ministers should be proud. Yet although Chesser was defending the system of government which he called 'centralized', he did not actually define what he or the Church of God meant by the term centralized.

Six years after General Overseer Chesser used the phrase 'centralized government', in his General Assembly address, R. Hollis Gause Jr. published the first edition of his *Church of God Polity*. Gause had been teaching at Lee College since 1947, and among other classes he taught a course on parliamentary law. Gause's views are important here, because not only did Gause's book become a standard in Church of God History and Polity courses at denominational educational institutions, but Gause himself also served as parliamentarian at Church of God General Assemblies for four decades.

In his Forward to *Church of God Polity*, Gause specifically focused on the Church's centralized government. He wrote,

> Basically the Church of God has a centralized government. This we believe to be Scriptural since the Jerusalem Council took the authority to render a decision affecting all the many local congregations (Acts 15). This was accepted by the apostles and was circulated among the churches.
>
> This centralization, however, is not of such intense character as to render local government weak and powerless. In order to preserve the values of both factors in government and to adhere to the principles of Scriptural government, the Church has several courts. These courts are as follows: local, district, state and territorial, and general.[6]

In his superbly subtle style, Gause established the role and meaning of centralized government in the Church of God. For Gause several facts had to be initially stipulated. First, centralized government is based on the Scripture, specifically the account of the Jerusalem Council

---

[5] Chesser, *Minutes of the Forty-fourth Assembly*, pp. 15-16. The suggestion that centralized government offers both protection and benefits is a frequent argument in the Church of God for our form of government. See H.D. Williams, *Benefits of Centralized Church Government* (Cleveland, TN: Church of God General Headquarters, n.d.).

[6] R.H. Gause, *Church of God Polity* (Cleveland, TN: Pathway, 1958), p. 11. Although Gause noted that his book contained the 'flavor of its author' despite the fact that much of it was a selection of quotations from General Assembly minutes, he acknowledged that 'the value and accuracy of this work has been helped greatly by the committee appointed by the Supreme Council'. Charles W. Conn, author of the official history of the Church of God, *Like a Mighty Army* (Cleveland, TN: Pathway, 1955), chaired the committee, which also included James A. Cross and Earl P. Paulk. See Gause, *Church of God Polity*, pp. 7-8.

described in Act 15. Second, the Jerusalem Council, and by implication the General Assembly, has authority to make decisions affecting local churches. Third, the apostles, and by implication the clergy at all levels, accept and propagate the decisions of the General Assembly. Fourth, the General Assembly does not 'lord over' or overpower local churches. Fifth, as a means of protecting the values and needs of both the General Assembly and local churches, the Church of God had developed specific polity for local, district, territorial and general levels.

Gause did not explain what he meant with his statement that the Church 'basically' has centralized government. Whatever he meant, centralized government is not easily defined; like other models of church government it is based on a narrow range of Scripture, and the Church of God must diligently strive in every generation to protect the balance between the local and general that centralized government attempts to maintain.

Gause began his discussion of polity with the local church and its relationship with the General Assembly. The General Assembly governs local churches, which choose to become members of the Assembly. Local property is owned by the General Assembly, and is managed under the auspices of the state overseer. Although the state overseer appoints pastors, local churches may express their preference for their pastor.[7] It was in terms of the relationship between the local church and the General Assembly regarding property that Gause noted the 'central government' of the Church of God.[8]

Although Gause began his discussion of local church polity by describing the relationship between the local church and the General Assembly, when he turned to levels of government beyond the local church, he was careful to preserve the integrity of the local church. In his discussion of district polity he again used cautious language to note that 'a degree of centralization' is supported by the example of the Acts 15 Jerusalem Council. Gause further argued that the Jerusalem Council was made up of two groups: apostles, who held offices that can never be replicated, and representative elders, who were local officers meeting together as the council. With this argument Gause made two critical points. First he rejected an episcopal order of bishops outside the local church. The ministry of bishop has its origins in the local church. Second he affirmed an 'extension of government beyond the local level … [through the] gathering of all elders of the Church, or as in the case

---

[7] Gause, *Church of God Polity*, pp. 15-18.
[8] Gause, *Church of God Polity*, pp. 29-30. The issue of property ownership was also discussed in the chapter related to standing boards and committees in that when necessary all properties revert to the control of the General Board of Trustees. See pp. 118-21.

of the Jerusalem Council a representative group of elders.'[9] Consequently it is clear that, for Gause, centralization refers to the relationship between the General Assembly and local representatives. These representatives serve at different levels from local to general, but they do not form a hierarchy of bishops. Centralization is in the General Assembly not in an episcopal form of government.

The final reference to centralized government in *Church of God Polity* occurred in the chapter regarding clergy where Gause quoted an action of the General Assembly in 1956. As a rationale for prohibiting Church of God ministers from establishing or assisting independent congregations, the General Assembly recognized its polity to be centralized and ruled, 'Believing a centralized form of government to be the Biblical standard for our churches, the Church of God early adopted such a form of government and has consistently practiced a centralized form of government.'[10] Again the relationship here is between the minister and the General Assembly in that the General Assembly requires that Church of God ministers only serve congregations that are in relationship to the General Assembly.

In his revised edition of *Church of God Polity* published in 1973, Gause highlighted the fact that essential to understanding centralized government is the principle that the General Assembly has 'full power and authority to designate the teaching, government, principles and practices of all the local churches composing said Assembly.'[11] However, this authority of the Assembly is founded in the reality that the General Assembly is composed of members of local churches. Finally, it is important to note that, while these members represent local churches, they are empowered to vote according to their own personal interpretation of Scripture.[12]

Based on this understanding of centralized government as propagated by R. Hollis Gause,[13] the remainder of this chapter will explore

[9] Gause, *Church of God Polity*, p. 42.

[10] Gause, *Church of God Polity*, p. 141. See also Church of God, *Minutes of the Forty-sixth General Assembly* (Cleveland, TN: Church of God, 1956), p. 27.

[11] R. Hollis Gause, *Church of God Polity*, rev. ed. (Cleveland, TN: Pathway, 1973), p. 89.

[12] Gause, *Church of God Polity*, rev. ed., p. 90.

[13] It must be admitted that this is my interpretation of Gause's position and that everyone may not agree with Gause or my interpretation of Gause. There are some who have equated centralized government with episcopal government. This chapter demonstrates that the two are not historically the same, but that it is possible for centralized government to evolve into episcopal government. For an example see William Pospisil, *Scriptural Church Government* (Mulakusha, India: C.G.I. Press, 1960). One widely distributed tract came close to this position when its discussion of church government focused on the authority of the general overseer. See Earl P. Paulk, *Church Government* (Cleveland, TN: Church of God General Headquarters, n.d.). Michael L. Baker acknowledged the Gener-

how centralized government developed and is practiced in the Church of God. An historical review reveals that many of the early ministers, such as the Spurlings and W.F. Bryant, were Baptists. Not surprisingly, the earliest General Assemblies functioned similarly to an association of Baptist churches. How then did centralized government development?

Early Church of God Government

The Church of God dates its origins to the work of Richard and R.G. Spurling and their founding of the Christian Union on August 19, 1886. The only extant document we have from that time is the ordination credentials of R.G. Spurling signed by his father Richard Spurling. Later documents of significance include *The Lost Link*, a booklet written by R.G. Spurling and published in 1920[14] and A.J. Tomlinson's *The Last Great Conflict.*[15] Tomlinson's book is our best source for information about the Church of God from 1886 to 1910 when Tomlinson began publishing *The Evening Light and Church of God Evangel.*[16]

A survey of *The Lost Link* reveals that R.G. Spurling was keenly interested in church government. He believed that Christ had established

al Assembly as the highest governing authority in the Church of God, but described a 'concentric approach' at each level in which the pastor is the center of church management at the local level, the state/regional overseer is the center at the state/regional level, and the general overseer and International Executive Committee is the center at the international level. See Michael L. Baker, *You and Your Church: An In-depth Look at the Church of God Cleveland, Tennessee* (Cleveland, TN: Pathway, rev. ed., 2003), pp. 56-57. Ray H. Hughes Sr. suggested, and I agree, that centralized government is a combination of both congregational and episcopal forms of government. He went on to suggest that centralized government includes 'facets' of congregational, presbyterian, and episcopal forms. See Ray H. Hughes, *Church of God Distinctives* (Cleveland, TN: Pathway, 1968), p. 90.

[14] R.G. Spurling, *The Lost Link* (Turtletown, TN: By the author, 1920).

[15] A.J. Tomlinson, *The Last Great Conflict* (Cleveland, TN: Walter E. Rodgers, 1913).

[16] Tomlinson recorded the history of the foundation of the Church of God in a chapter entitled, 'Brief History of the Church That Is Now Recognized as the Church of God.' This history was repeated without attribution to Tomlinson in Church of God, *Book of Minutes* (Cleveland, TN: Church of God, 1923). It is *Book of Minutes* that became the primary source for those writing about Church of God history though Charles W. Conn's *Like a Mighty Army* in 1955. But we must note that Tomlinson was not present at three seminal events in the life of the Church of God: the forming of the Christian Union in 1886, the Shearer Schoolhouse revival in 1896, and the organization of the Holiness Church at Camp Creek in 1902. He knew participants in those events well and wrote while in good relationship with them. But he wrote about those events through his own eyes, and although discrepancies are minor, not every detail of his account was accurate. For example, he stated that R.G. Spurling was ordained on September 26, 1886, while the ordination document was dated September 2, 1886. It is possible that this was simply a typographical error. Tomlinson also states that Richard Spurling died at age 74, but other evidence suggests he was 81 at the time of his death. See Tomlinson, *Last Great Conflict*, pp. 184-98 and especially p. 187.

the Church and church government, that the Church had apostatized in AD 325, and that it was necessary for the Church of God to restore the original government practiced in the New Testament. Spurling wrote, 'So Christ spoke all the law, precepts and government of His Church. To add anything is a step in apostasy.'[17] He went on, 'It is God's law and government we want to restore – the law of Christ. We want to honor God and not man. We do not want to be a Luther or a Calvin or a Wesley, but we want a more God honoring reformation.'[18]

As part of their apostasy, the Christian Church, according to Spurling, had replaced God's law with creeds, and he rejected any church organization that judged its members based on a creed. According to Spurling, at their best creeds are human creations and despite whatever truth is found in them they cannot claim infallibility. Additionally, creeds have not merely divided Christians; they have often led Christians to persecute one another.[19]

Spurling was Baptist and as such strongly supported a congregational model of church government. He rejected any kind of apostolic succession or church union that denied the freedom of the local congregation. He wrote,

> Well, what about church identity, apostolic succession and ministerial authority? All such claims are a failure. Apostolic succession was alright as long as God's law was obeyed, but when the church began to make laws and depart from God's law succession became a delusion. When man began to ordain men to preach certain doctrines and not upon Testament authority and qualifications, apostolic authority came to naught. We need not question anything about succession or apostolic lines of ministry since God's law and government has been forsaken for 1500 years.[20]

Spurling specifically affirmed Baptist historian G.H. Orchard's understanding of the independence of early Christian congregations. Referring to Orchard's *History of Foreign Baptists,* Spurling wrote,

> He says during the greater part of three centuries the churches remained about as they were established and were independent of each other, neither were they joined together by association, confederacy or any other bond but that of charity.... Christian societies instituted in the cities of the Roman empire were united only by the ties of faith and charity. Independence and equality formed the basis of their internal constitution.[21]

---

[17] Spurling, *The Lost Link*, p. 10.
[18] Spurling, *The Lost Link*, p. 34.
[19] Spurling, *The Lost Link*, p. 35.
[20] Spurling, *The Lost Link*, p. 32.
[21] Spurling, *The Lost Link*, p. 34.

Spurling had a deep sense of individual liberty and individual conscience being led by the Holy Spirit, but this was not meant to preclude individuals being in fellowship with one another. He reasoned,

> Some think Christians ought not to be united in any bond of fellow-
> ship while others are not satisfied with the law and government of
> Christ and the Holy Spirit but must have a great many more laws and
> governments. So between the two extremes there is a wise and reason-
> able middle ground of truth which unprejudiced and honest Spirit led
> Christians can surely find in the words and acts of the Savior and His
> followers under the leadership of the Holy Ghost.[22]

For Spurling, love binds Christians together even when they disagree. Christians must remain in a local church, formed by covenant, but
there must be freedom within that church for individuals to read and
interpret the Bible for themselves. The local church should exclude
only if a person teaches something that is clearly contrary to the New
Testament.

Spurling's ideas shaped the formation of the Christian Union in
1886, the organization of the Holiness Church at Camp Creek in
1902, and the earliest General Assemblies. The call to join the Christian Union in 1886 incorporated his insistence that church government
be based on God's law, the individual's right and responsibility to interpret Scriptures, and the commitment to do this in the context of
Christian community. His proposition as recorded in our earliest history
was,

> As many Christians as are here present that are desirous to be free from
> all man made creeds and traditions, and are willing to take the New
> Testament, or law of Christ, for your only rule of faith and practice;
> giving each other equal rights and privilege to read and interpret for
> yourselves as your conscience may dictate, and are willing to set to-
> gether as the Church of God to transact business [as] the same, come
> forward.[23]

We know very little about events between 1886 and 1903. We
know that, following Baptist polity, the Christian Union called R.G.
Spurling to be their pastor, and his father Richard ordained him on
September 2, 1886. We know that R.G. Spurling established several
other congregations and that in 1902 he organized the Holiness
Church at Camp Creek out of the remnant of the earlier revival at
Shearer Schoolhouse. We know that, following Baptist polity, the
Camp Creek congregation called Spurling to be their pastor and that a
year later on June 13, 1903, the congregation called A.J. Tomlinson as

---

[22] Spurling, *The Lost Link*, p. 42.
[23] Tomlinson, *Last Great Conflict*, pp. 185–86.

pastor. We have no reason to believe that these congregations acted in any way other than according to congregational polity.

Such an assumption seems particularly justified when one observes that the first General Assembly acted in a manner similar to a Baptist associational meeting. According to Tomlinson's account, in 1905 the churches faced some problems that demanded an answer. They concluded that a meeting of the congregations would be in order, based on Israel's annual meetings and based on the Jerusalem Council recorded in Acts 15.[24] Twenty-one delegates gathered together in a private home January 26-27, 1906. Their first item of business was to declare that the Assembly itself was judicial rather than legislative or executive. By this they meant that, as an Assembly, their intent was to search the Scriptures and interpret their findings for the benefit of the local churches. The Assembly could not make God's law because God's law was recorded in the New Testament. Further, they would not execute God's law, as that action was the responsibility of the local church.[25] The language of their minutes consistently affirmed that they recommended items to the local churches, who were encouraged to ratify those recommendations. They did request that the local churches demonstrate some responsibility to the Assembly, however, by asking deacons to report back to the next Assembly regarding church members who participated in family worship and who had or had not quit using tobacco. The Assembly concluded,

> It seemeth good to the Holy Ghost and us, being assembled with one accord, with the Spirit of Christ in the midst, and after much prayer, discussion, searching the Scriptures and counsel, to recommend these necessary things and that they be ratified and observed by all the local churches. It is the duty of the Church to execute the laws given us by Christ through His Holy Apostles.[26]

The earliest Assemblies continued to function much like Baptist associational meetings with a high degree of freedom and responsibility given to the congregations that met together each year. Examples are numerous: The second Assembly in 1907 continued to 'advise and recommend' to the local churches.[27] Their conclusion regarding choosing helpers and assistants in the ministry was that one should 'be led by the Spirit rather than ecclesiastical bodies or rulers'.[28] As late as the

---

[24] *General Assembly Minutes, 1906-1914*, p. 124.

[25] This belief was acknowledged again by the third Assembly in 1908 and by the fourth Assembly in 1909. *General Assembly Minutes, 1906-1914: Photographic Reproductions of the First Ten General Assembly Minutes* (Cleveland, TN: White Wing, 1992), pp. 41 and 59.

[26] *General Assembly Minutes, 1906-1914*, p. 19.

[27] *General Assembly Minutes, 1906-1914*, p. 23.

[28] *General Assembly Minutes, 1906-1914*, p. 25.

seventh Assembly in 1912, the Assembly received 'messengers' – a term for delegates widely used among Baptists – from a sister organization known as the Church of God Mountain Assembly.[29] And the Assembly regularly affirmed that it was judicial only and not legislative or executive. The conclusion of the minutes of the third Assembly is further evidence that they continued to practice congregational polity: 'The above minutes are not laws made by the Assembly, but only the laws given to us by Christ and His disciples searched out by that body and brought to light that the Churches might take action upon the same as they see fit.'[30]

One of the best examples of the reluctance of the Assembly to assert its will over the will of the local churches came during the discussion of what became know as the 'Church Teachings' in 1911. As a means of assisting candidates for the ministry, the previous Assembly had appointed a committee to prepare examination questions and Scriptural references as a tool for ministerial preparation. The work of that committee was published in the August 15, 1910, edition of *The Evening Light and Church of God Evangel* with the explanation that 'The Church of God stands for the whole Bible rightly divided. The New Testament is the only rule for government and discipline. Below is given some of the teaching that is made prominent.'[31] This brief introduction was followed with a list of doctrines and scriptural references rather than creedal statements asserting the correct position on any particular doctrine. For example, the first item read simply, 'Repentance: Mark 1:15, Luke 13:3, Acts 8:19'. It might be assumed that the absence of an explanatory statement on the meaning of repentance was because there was little disagreement among the churches on the doctrine of repentance. But more importantly, with their anti-creedal stance, they were very careful not to wield their doctrinal views on others. The list intended to be what it said it was – a list of teachings and related scriptural references. It was not meant to tell the ministerial candidate what to believe regarding those doctrines.

Further support for this conclusion lies in their discussion of the issue of tithing when the sixth Assembly considered the list of Teachings. The list included the simple words, 'Tithing and Giving' with several scriptural references. The record of their discussion is telling of both the fact that they did not all agree on the subject and their charitable commitment to allow for differences to exist among them. The minutes read,

[29] *General Assembly Minutes, 1906-1914*, pp. 140–41.

[30] *General Assembly Minutes, 1906-1914*, p. 55.

[31] 'The Church of God', *The Evening Light and Church of God Evangel* 1.12 (Aug. 15, 1910), p. 3.

> The point on Tithing and giving was discussed at length.... There was quite a good deal of discussion by brethren who looked at it from their standpoint. Some favoring the tithing system and offerings or giving besides. Some favoring giving and disregarding the tithing. All favored giving and all admitted there was no compulsion but all should walk in the light as God is in the light.[32]

Despite the liberty they granted to each other, there must have been a desire by some to reach a decision, and they came back to the topic following their noon break.

A conclusion was finally reached when the General Overseer read and expounded Hebrews 7, bringing in other Scriptures bearing on the subject. The following minute was then read and approved.

> It is advised that liberty be granted to teach tithing and giving with the understanding that the church is not to enforce tithing on the members, but teach the members the blessedness of tithing and to exhort them to seek for the abundance of grace that will evidently lead them or enable them to practice it from choice. No one objects to tithing or teaching that people ought to tithe, provided the churches do not undertake to enforce it. The teaching is, therefore, recommended to remain as it appears in the above named issue of the paper.[33]

These examples show that the Church of God took questions of doctrine and Christian practice seriously; the General Assembly was both careful not to violate personal liberty in interpreting Scripture and to allow for items to be further reviewed as new light and understanding became available. In time, however, the Church of God moved away from congregational government and the General Assembly increasingly took a more authoritative role in the life of the denomination.

The Shift to Centralized Government

If a 'centralized government' is defined as the congregations granting full authority to the General Assembly, how then did the Church of God shift to a centralized government from its earlier baptistic and congregational form of government? This shift in the importance of the General Assembly can be attributed in large part to three factors: the influence of A.J. Tomlinson, the expansion of ministries beyond the congregation, and the need to provide adequate ministers for the congregations.

A.J. Tomlinson had come to the Holiness Church at Camp Creek after having grown up in a nominal Quaker family and practiced his

---

[32] *General Assembly Minutes 1906-1914*, p. 87.
[33] *General Assembly Minutes 1906*-1914, p. 89.

early ministry among the radical holiness branch of American evangelicalism.[34] Although he frequently attributed his ecclesiology to R.G.
Spurling, he was not steeped in the Baptist model of church polity as
Spurling had been. Further, although Spurling was significant to the
early development of the Church of God, it is likely that, had he remained the most influential leader, the Church of God might never
have been more than a few mountain congregations. Having come
into the mountains from somewhere else, Tomlinson was able to develop a more expansive vision for the Church, and he fulfilled this
vision through serving as moderator of the Assemblies and later as general overseer, as well as through fostering an increased role for the
General Assembly in the life of the denomination.[35]

Like Spurling, Tomlinson had a deep conviction that they were restoring the Church of God and thus church government as revealed in
the New Testament. For Tomlinson this was a process that would take
time and could best be done through the corporate wisdom of the
Assembly representing all the churches rather than through a single
congregation. Recommendations of previous Assemblies were often
revisited in a search for a better understanding of church government
as additional light was available to the Assembly.[36]

At first the changes were subtle. For example, although the Assembly continued to 'advise' local congregations, the meaning of 'advise'
took on a different significance. This can be seen in the changing attitude toward tobacco. Living in a culture in which the use of tobacco
was common, the Assembly struggled for several years regarding the
degree to which tobacco users should participate in the life of the
Church. The first Assembly had delineated the evils of tobacco and had
recommended that the deacons encourage members to give up its

[34] For the best treatment of Tomlinson see R.G. Robins, *A.J. Tomlinson: Plainfolk Modernist* (Oxford: Oxford University Press, 2004).

[35] This is not to suggest that Tomlinson did not have an early appreciation for the congregational model of Church government. Robins suggests, 'Sandford's theocratic authoritarianism, the radical congregationalism of independent holiness, and the moderate congregationalism of the Society of Friends could each lay claim to A.J. by the time he joined the Holiness Church at Camp Creek.' See Robins, *A.J. Tomlinson*, p. 171. Wade H. Phillips has argued that Tomlinson's shift toward an autocratic understanding of the role of general overseer and centralized government was due to the influence of Frank W. Sandford, leader of the Shiloh ministry near Durham, Maine, which Tomlinson visited on two occasions. See Wade H. Phillips, 'The Corruption of the Noble Vine: An Analysis of the Influence of Frank W. Sandford and Richard G. Spurling, Jr. on the Life and Ministry of A.J. Tomlinson and the Church of God (Cleveland, Tennessee)' (Un-published manuscript in Hal Bernard Dixon Jr. Pentecostal Research Center, Cleveland, TN).

[36] Examples include discussions of the selection of pastors and the care of churches in 1908, divorce and remarriage in 1909, and tithing in 1911. See *General Assembly Minutes 1906-1914*, pp. 49, 51, 65, 87.

use.[37] When reporting the discussion of the subject yet again, the minutes of the sixth Assembly in 1911 recorded,

> [Advice] was finally given by the General Overseer that ministers who are receiving persons as members into the Lord's Church should humbly, tenderly, and lovingly advise those who might be eligible to membership not to present themselves for membership if they use tobacco in any form unless they in that selfsame moment decide to renounce the habit and by the grace of God declare themselves total abstainers hereafter.[38]

Here it is clear that Tomlinson is wielding the most influence in the discussion and that the local churches are being directed rather than merely encouraged. Further when candidates for membership are being advised, the real meaning clearly carries the weight of insisting rather than that of suggesting.

The sixth Assembly in 1911 discussed the question of what is the Church of God and its highest tribunal. Tomlinson had already begun to focus on this issue in *The Evening Light and Church of God Evangel.*[39] At the Assembly Tomlinson stressed the importance of getting the church in 'perfect order' suggesting that the salvation of the lost depended on the church being in perfect order.[40] Then in his Prefatory Notes to the minutes of the seventh Assembly in 1912, Tomlinson wrote, 'The General Assembly meets once a year for the purpose of searching the Scriptures and obtaining light and information concerning the Bible Church and its government. This body of Christians is not legislative, nor executive, but judicial only.'[41] He went on,

> It is also for the purpose of more closely uniting those who attend in fellowship and love. This latter feature should not be despised, and every one who possibly can do so should make preparations to attend the annual feast.
>
> It is quite different from a camp meeting, in that there is important business to attend to, and questions to consider and settle, and Bible plans to search out and put in operation that will lead to a more rapid

---

[37] *General Assembly Minutes 1906-1914*, pp. 11-12.

[38] *General Assembly Minutes, 1906-1914*, p. 91.

[39] See for example A.J. Tomlinson, 'Christ Our Lawgiver and King', *The Evening Light and Church of God Evangel* 1.17 (November 1, 1910), pp. 1-3. Dale Coulter rightly suggests that Tomlinson seems to be obsessed with the idea of the Church. Coulter notes that the topic was discussed at almost every Assembly, was a significant part of many of Tomlinson's Annual Addresses, was the subject of over 30 of Tomlinson's articles in the *Church of God Evangel* over a seven-year period of time, and was the topic taking the most space in *The Last Great Conflict*. See Coulter, 'Development of Ecclesiology in the Church of God', pp. 60-61.

[40] *General Assembly Minutes, 1906-1914*, p. 99.

[41] *General Assembly Minutes, 1906-1914*, p. 122.

rate of evangelizing the world, and thus prepare the way for the return of our Lord.

We commend these pages to the honest, sincere searcher after truth, and to those who are, or may become interested in the re-establishment of the Bible Church with all of its former graces, gifts and glory.[42]

Tomlinson declared to the eighth Assembly in 1913,

The Church of God is the greatest, wisest and most glorious govern-ment that has ever been inaugurated on this earth. To be called upon, as is this honorable body and sacred Assembly, to search out and apply the laws of the greatest and most glorious government that has ever made its appearance on this earth, should certainly be considered the highest honor conferred upon man.[43]

At the tenth Assembly in 1914 he continued his emphasis, 'Before me and around me is gathered a body of noble men and women who do not expect to rest until the very deepest mystery is solved and the Church of God is revealed in her completeness as she appeared in the days of the apostles.'[44]

Included in restoring this 'glorious government' was the restoration of offices beyond the local church – particularly the office of general overseer. By 1907 the Assembly recognized the possibility of an au-thority figure outside the local church that might have some influence in the selection of a pastor for the local church.[45] This was further de-veloped as the number of churches grew until by 1909 a general mod-erator, later called general overseer, was selected. The duties of the general moderator primarily related to matters that might arise between Assemblies such as helping to fill pastoral vacancies and issuing minis-terial credentials.[46] The Assembly also approved state overseers in 1911.

Justifying those offices during the eighth Assembly in 1913, F.J. Lee specifically tied the office of general overseer to James at the Jerusalem Council, a connection that Tomlinson had already made as early as 1910 in the pages of *The Evening Light and Church of God Evangel*.[47] Then in 1914 Tomlinson spoke at length about the role of James in the Church. According to Tomlinson, although James was not an

---

[42] *General Assembly Minutes, 1906-1914*, p. 122.

[43] *General Assembly Minutes, 1906-1914*, pp. 169-70.

[44] *General Assembly Minutes, 1906-1914*, p. 300.

[45] *General Assembly Minutes, 1906-1914*, p. 29.

[46] *General Assembly Minutes, 1906-1914*, p. 69.

[47] F.J. Lee, 'Confirmation of Actions of Past Assemblies', in *General Assembly Minutes 1906-1914*, pp. 180-89 [p. 185]; Tomlinson, 'Christ Our Law-Giver and King,' pp. 2-3. I am indebted to Dale Coulter for reminding me of this connection in *The Evening Light and Church of God Evangel*. See Coulter, 'Development of Ecclesiology in the Church of God,' p. 78.

apostle, James followed in the tradition of Moses and clearly had the last word in interpreting Scripture. Reflecting the language of James, Tomlinson had not only begun to speak more forcefully for his views on items being discussed, he had already begun to conclude those discussions with the King James language of James in Acts 15, 'my sentence therefore is this'.[48]

It is critical to note here that, although the general overseer, after the order of James, occupied the chief executive office of the General Assembly and in that role declared the final decisions, Tomlinson did not see himself as acting *ex cathedra*. For Tomlinson, Christ was the head of the Church, and the General Assembly searched the Scriptures to find Christ's laws. It was in that context that the word central may have been used to describe Church of God government for the first time. Tomlinson wrote, 'If the Bible teaches anything it certainly teaches centralization with Jesus as the great head of the Church and all the members in their respective places in the body.'[49]

Additionally, Tomlinson insisted that this was not an episcopal form of government. Rather he used the word 'theocracy' to describe what he believed was the form of church government that the apostles practiced. Theocracy existed when representatives of the churches met together in council, led by a general overseer, and searched the Scriptures for Christ's laws until they reached a conclusion that had approval of the Holy Spirit.[50] According to Tomlinson, the episcopal government that developed after the first century was a poor imitation and departure from that of the apostles. Particularly onerous, in his view, was the divisive and creed-making council of bishops that met at Nicea in AD 325 in stark contrast to the representative Jerusalem Council comprised of apostles and elders.[51]

This attempt to restore apostolic government led to both an increased role of the general overseer and an expansion of ministries. Congregational government naturally faces the dilemma of how suc-

---

[48] *General Assembly Minutes, 1906-1914*, pp. 270, 296-300, 319.

[49] A.J. Tomlinson, 'Holding Together with True Love and Humble Devotion', *Church of God Evangel* 6.11 (Mar. 13, 1915), p. 1. I am indebted to Dale Coulter for discovering this reference. Tomlinson's insistence that this was not an episcopal government did not preclude the role of bishops in the Church but centered the authority of the Church in the General Assembly rather than the bishops. Nor did it preclude a hierarchy among the bishops. Wade H. Phillips used the term 'episcopal hierarchy' to discuss the growing role of bishops and particularly the general and state overseers in church government. See Wade H. Phillips, 'Concise History of the Church of God of Prophecy' (unpublished manuscript in Hal Bernard Dixon Jr. Pentecostal Research Center, Cleveland, TN, 1997), pp. 11-12.

[50] For an excellent discussion of this process see Coulter, 'Development of Ecclesiology in the Church of God', pp. 78-81.

[51] *General Assembly Minutes, 1906-1914*, pp. 300-303.

cessfully to accomplish ministry that requires the resources of more than one congregation. Tomlinson's vision led to the development of ministries such as a denominational publishing house and periodical, a Bible Training School, and an orphanage. These required cooperative efforts, such as the appointment of boards and the purchase of property. These actions were the outgrowth of biblical government and could best be accomplished by the Assembly rather than by individuals or local churches. Desiring the results of ministry that they saw in the New Testament, the Assembly members eagerly followed Tomlinson in the development of these ministries and even in the adoption of a monetary plan that sent monies to state and general treasuries in order to pay for these ministries.[52]

Two of the most significant issues related to the move toward centralized government were ministerial credentialing and the appointment of pastors. A key value of congregational government is the selection of a pastor by the local congregation. Yet as early as 1907, there were differing opinions in the Church of God between the choices of local churches calling pastors, on the one hand, and leaders appointing pastors, on the other. Spurling insisted that it was best for churches to call their pastors, but he recognized that Paul had sent some ministers. The Assembly concluded that either the local church calling the pastor or pastors being sent was acceptable, provided the Holy Spirit directed the decision.[53]

Probably as a result of the lack of suitable ministers, this tension continued to dominate subsequent Assemblies, however. The selection of pastors and the credentialing of ministers was discussed at the third, fourth, fifth, sixth and seventh Assemblies.[54] Finally at the ninth Assembly in 1913, Tomlinson ruled with 'my sentence therefore is this' that stronger churches could select their own pastors but the selection was subject to the approval of the state overseer. The rightness of this decision was then approved by a manifestation of the Spirit in the form of a message in tongues and an interpretation.[55]

---

[52] *General Assembly Minutes, 1906-1914*, pp. 47, 81-82, 97 and 266. The Church of God frequently states that one of the advantages of centralized government is its superior ability to create and enhance the ministries of the Church. For an example, albeit with a focus on a 'central headquarters' rather than the General Assembly see G.W. Lane, *Program and Purpose: What We Do and Why We Do It* (n.p.: n.p., n.d.), p. 15.

[53] *General Assembly Minutes, 1906-1914*, p. 29.

[54] *General Assembly Minutes, 1906-1914*, pp. 49, 61-62, 81, 105, 137.

[55] *General Assembly Minutes, 1906-1914*, p. 270.

Later Emphases on Centralized Government

With the primacy of the General Assembly firmly established by the tenth Assembly in 1914, the course was set for this form of Church polity to continue to shape the development of the Church of God. Over the decades the denomination expanded its structure to accommodate growth and the development of new ministries. I have already noted General Overseer Chesser's reference to centralized government in 1952 as a means of protecting the Church of God and giving the movement a unique identity. The next occurrence of the term 'centralized government' occurred four years later in 1956 when the forty-sixth Assembly prohibited Church of God ministers from serving as pastors of independent congregations. The prohibition was prefaced with the words, 'Believing a centralized form of government to be the Biblical standard for our churches, the Church of God early adopted such a form of government and has consistently practiced a centralized form of government.' The prohibition further stated, 'ministers who persist in doing so are out of harmony with our declared policy of centralized government; and appropriate action should be initiated by proper authorities against offending ministers.'[56] Rather than defining the meaning of 'centralized government,' the statement assumes that the readers know the meaning and that the principles of centralized government clearly prohibit a Church of God minister from participating in an independent congregation. It appears that the primary purpose of the prohibition was to maintain the doctrine and structure of the Church of God by insuring that all ministries led by Church of God ministers be in right relationship with the General Assembly. This prohibition became part of the 'General Instructions' found in the section on 'Ministry' in the 'Supplement to the Minutes' and continues there with the modification of a reference to Acts 15:13-29 added in 1994.[57]

The statement regarding clergy and independent churches remained the only reference to centralized government recorded in the 'Supplement to the Minutes' until 1980. At that time a recommendation came to the General Assembly with the stated intention of clarifying the relationship between local churches and the Assembly. As a way of explanation, the minutes record,

> WHEREAS, the government of the Church of God is centralized by and through the General Assembly, and

---

[56] Church of God, *Minutes of the Forty-sixth General Assembly*, p. 27.
[57] Church of God, *Minutes of the 65th General Assembly of the Church of God* (Cleveland, TN: Pathway, 1994), p. 231.

> WHEREAS, various resolutions have been passed by the General As-
> sembly regarding the rights and duties of the local church and its trus-
> tees in such a government, and
> WHEREAS, it is important that persons unfamiliar with the church
> understand fully the role of the local church and its local trustees
> WE, THEREFORE, RECOMMEND:
> That a section entitled, 'Relationship of the Local Church to the Gen-
> eral Assembly' be added to the supplement to the Minutes of the Gen-
> eral Assembly presenting the proper role of the local church in our
> church government.[58]

The section included seven specific statements regarding the relationship between the local church and the General Assembly. In summary these included: (1) the Church of God has a centralized form of
government; (2) local churches are the result of the ministry of the
General Assembly, become constituents of the General Assembly, and
cannot withdraw from the General Assembly; (3) the General Assembly has the 'full power and authority to designate the teachings, principles, and practices' of local churches; (4) the General Assembly
governs the Church of God at all levels from international to local; (5)
the General Assembly has vested the office of State Overseer with full
authority over local churches including the pastor, the Board of Trustees, and property; (6) the local Board of Trustees can act on behalf of
the local church as long as it is in keeping with the Church of God and
can be replaced if it is not in keeping with the Church of God; (7)
local churches are 'bound by the decisions of the General Assembly in
matters of doctrine, teaching, and polity'.[59]

This new addition became part of the 'Supplement' under 'Church
– Local' and remains there. What is especially significant here is that
'centralized government' is the affirmation that the highest authority of
the Church of God lies with the General Assembly and that local
churches are subject to the General Assembly in matters related to pastoral appointment, control of properties, doctrine, teaching, principles,
practices and polity.

A 1994 action by the General Assembly led to the invoking of 'centralized government' in several places in the minutes. The action related to the ownership of property and likely was motivated by court
cases in which the Church of God was challenged regarding local
property. The recommendation that was passed by the sixty-fifth Assembly read:

---

[58] Church of God, *Minutes of the Fifty-eighth General Assembly of the Church of God*
(Cleveland, TN: Pathway, 1980), pp. 38-39.
[59] Church of God, *Minutes of the Fifty-eighth Assembly*, p. 39.

> That the Executive Council be authorized to reorganize, amplify, and
> clarify as necessary all information in the General Assembly Minutes
> pertaining to property ownership and the various boards of trustees. It
> is understood that no changes will be made in the intent of the meas-
> ures, only rearrangement and updating. Further, the Executive Council
> shall make this material in its reorganized form available to every pastor
> and ordained minister as soon as possible following the General Assem-
> bly.[60]

As a result of this action, a number of changes were made in the
'Supplement to the Minutes' that invoked the principle of centralized
government. For example, additional language that further defined the
meaning of centralized government was added at the beginning of the
section identifying the relationship of local churches to the General
Assembly. The new text read,

> The Church of God (Cleveland, Tennessee) has a centralized (by legal
> definition 'hierarchical') form of church government. The General As-
> sembly, the highest authority of the Church of God, governs the own-
> ership of all church property, both real and personal. All property is
> held in trust for members composing said General Assembly.[61]

The final use of the idea of centralized government to date came in
2000 when various offices were given the right to use the title bishop.
For example, the general overseer was given the right to use the title
presiding bishop and state and territorial overseers were given the right
to use the title administrative bishop. As an explanation for this action,
the General Assembly was reminded that the term bishop had once
been used in the Church of God. Further, the Assembly concluded, 'as
a Biblically centralized body, the church has positions of responsibility
which may be more accurately designated by the title bishop.'[62]

Conclusion and Implications

It is clear from the historical evidence presented here that church polity
has continually evolved over the history of the Church of God. With
our beginning among Baptists, our earliest form of church government
was congregational. But in time with the emergence of the General
Assembly, the development of offices, such as the general overseership,
and the expansion of ministries, the Church of God began to practice
what it called centralized government. Eschewing both congregational
and episcopal modes, centralized government defined the relationship

---

[60] Church of God, *Minutes of the 65th Assembly*, p. 89.

[61] Church of God, *Minutes of the 65th Assembly*, p. 192. See also 208-209 and 215-16.

[62] Church of God, *Minutes of the 68th General Assembly of the Church of God* (Cleveland,
TN: Pathway, 2000), p. 81.

between local congregations and the entire Church as best manifested in the General Assembly. It attempted to balance the values of both the local and general church but gave primacy to the General Assembly, because the Assembly was comprised of representatives of the local churches.

In conclusion let me offer the following comments for further reflection:

First, centralized government is an attempt to be both pragmatic and true to Scripture. Its scriptural foundation lies primarily in the single example of the Jerusalem Council in Acts 15. The interpretation and extension of the Acts 15 model continued to develop as the Church searched the Scriptures for solutions to problems it was facing.

Second, at its best, centralized government seems to utilize the best of the typical textbook models of church government – congregational, presbyterian and episcopal. It honors the local congregation, the General Assembly is comprised of the local churches, and bishops set forth by local churches are given places of leadership in the denomination at all levels.

Third, because church polity is always developing, the Church of God continually faces the possibility of shifting away from a balance between the local church and the general church and toward either congregationalism or episcopalianism. We began with a congregational model of church government but came to realize the biblical and practical necessity of centralized government. Yet because our polity allows for modifications with a majority vote at the General Assembly, there is no guarantee that forces of change will not push the Church of God toward one side or the other.

Fourth, centralized government demands that local congregations believe that church government at every level is receptive to the gifts the local church has to offer. If the General Assembly only uses the idea of centralized government in ways that seem to protect the bureaucracy of the Church of God, then the Church faces the danger that the actions of the General Assembly may appear to be irrelevant and or condescending to the local church. Although some actions strengthening the General Assembly may be necessary, they must also be seen to serve the local church rather than simply those who are in general leadership.

Finally, centralized government depends on the participation of local churches in the General Assembly. Yet, with increased costs of attending and with some questioning the relevance of the General Assembly to local church life, the Church of God faces the possibility of insufficient input from local churches – a prospect that could lead to the transformation of centralized government into the episcopal model.[63] In what some scholars are calling a post-denominational age, the Church of God should actively seek ways to cultivate the participation of local churches in the General Assembly. In 2007, as with the Christian Union in 1886, there must be an ongoing sense that we are sitting together as the Church of God.

★★★★★★★★★★★★★★★★★★

Abstract

The paper traces the development of what the Church of God identifies as its form of government, namely, 'centralized government'. We thereby mean that we practice a form of church government centered in the General Assembly, which is comprised of local churches. This is not language typically used in textbook discussions of church government, nor is it the original form of government practiced by the denomination. The Church of God originally practiced a congregational form of church government, but with the increased significance of General Assemblies, the development of denominational ministries, and the increasing role of the office of general overseer, a central government gradually evolved. By 1913, General Overseer A.J. Tomlinson called the Assembly to acknowledge not only the role of the Jerusalem Council in Acts 15 but also the importance of James as general overseer at that meeting. With Tomlinson's influence, the government of the Church of God began to change radically toward that which we practice today. A few concluding reflections on future prospects are offered.

---

[63] Harold Bare has suggested that the lack of participation of both laity and clergy along with other factors has led to the concentration of power and authority in the International Executive Committee and the increasing irrelevance of the General Assembly. If he is correct, then the case can be made that the Church of God now practices episcopal government rather than centralized government. See Harold L. Bare Sr., 'The Evolution of Leadership in a Sacred Bureaucracy: A Socio-historical Study of the Church of God' (University of Virginia, Ph.D. dissertation, 1996), pp. 92, 152-53; and Harold L. Bare, Sr., *Power and Authority in the Church of God* (Charlottesville, VA: H & L Enterprises, 1996).

12

Practices in the Spirit:
A Pentecostal Model of Pastoral Formation

James P. Bowers[*]

Introduction

One of the more influential reflections in my pastoral formation came from R. Hollis Gause in a theology class while I was a student at the (then) Church of God School of Theology. Hollis Gause observed, 'One must not only speak the Word, one must speak the Word in the *spirit* of the Word or the *character* of the Word is violated.' Those words reinforced the mentoring I was experiencing as I dialogued with a seminary colleague and read after others who were wrestling with the question of the relationship between Scripture, theology, and the ministry practice of the Church.[1] In a real sense, Hollis Gause's articulation of the theology-laden and value loaded nature of the manner and methods of ministry has challenged and shaped my faith journey and ministry practice for nearly 30 years.

This study, then, is a continuation of a pilgrimage begun under Hollis Gause's tutelage; but, of course, he is not responsible for what I have

[*] James P. Bowers (Ph.D., Southern Baptist Theological Seminary) is Vice-President for Academics at the Pentecostal Theological Seminary in Cleveland, TN.
[1] Jackie D. Johns and I carried on a conversation for many years about these issues that began during time we shared at the Church of God Theological Seminary in 1979-1980. Cheryl Bridges Johns, Craig Dykstra, Hollis Gause and Steve Land were also key dialogue partners. Some of the works influencing my thinking at that time included Craig R. Dykstra, *Vision and Character: A Christian Educator's Alternative to Kohlberg* (New York: Paulist, 1981); Findley B. Edge, *The Greening of the Church* (Waco, TX: Word, 1971); Lois E. Le Bar, *Education That Is Christian* (Old Tappan, NJ: Fleming H. Revell, 1958); Lawrence O. Richards, *A Theology of Christian Education* (Grand Rapids: Zondervan, 1975); James D. Smart, *The Teaching Ministry of the Church* (Philadelphia: Westminster, 1954); Howard A. Snyder, *The Problem of Wineskins: Church Structure in a Technological Age* (Downers Grover, IL: InterVarsity, 1975); Robert C. Worley, *Change In The Church: A Source Of Hope* (Philadelphia: Westminster, 1971); Mildred Bangs Wynkoop, *Foundations of Wesleyan-Arminian Theology* (Kansas City, MO: Beacon Hill Press, 1967).

written. My hope is this essay honors his lifelong contribution to theologically reflective and faithful practice exhibited by so many graduates and faculty of the Pentecostal Theological Seminary he helped birth. The thesis of this study is that the practices of the seminary's pastoral excellence project, based largely on the seminary's Wesleyan-Pentecostal Community of Faith approach, represent a distinctively Pentecostal model of pastoral formation. Through reflection on the actual experience of seminary students and practicing pastors, the dimensions of this Pentecostal model of pastoral formation will be proposed.[2]

Emergence of a Wesleyan Pentecostal Model of Theological Education

Early perspectives on Pentecostalism viewed the movement as little more than fundamentalist Christianity plus speaking in tongues. It was not uncommon, as most observers know, for Pentecostalism to be referred to as simply 'the tongues movement'. Later analyses, however, affirmed the reality of distinctive *theological* formulations and spiritualities.[3] This development has been followed by many 'Pentecostal' projects in biblical studies, hermeneutics, homiletics, missiology, theology, historiography, counseling, leadership, and formation.[4]

Paralleling the emergence of distinctive scholarship has been the birth and development of indigenous theological education. Pentecostals have demonstrated an increased inclination to provide graduate ministerial training grounded in their particular spiritual and theological vision.[5] Movement of the Church of God (Cleveland, Tennessee) into this arena occasioned the development of a distinctive model of theological education at its seminary and, eventually, a revisioning and extension of core aspects of the model in its Lilly Endowment funded 'Sustaining Pastoral Excellence' and 'Making Connections' projects with practicing field pastors.

---

[2] I intend the conclusions to be provisional proposals open to dialogue, clarification, and modification. They represent a beginning for talking about a distinctive Pentecostal approach to pastoral formation.

[3] Donald Dayton was one of the first to posit a theological gestalt of themes as representing the heart of the movement and its spirituality. See Donald Dayton, *Theological Roots of Pentecostalism* (Grand Rapids: Zondervan, 1987). See also Steven J. Land, *Pentecostal Spirituality: A Passion for the Kingdom* (JPTS 1; Sheffield, UK: Sheffield Academic Press, 1993), p. 18.

[4] Walter Hollenweger comments on this development in Walter J. Hollenweger, 'The Critical Tradition of Pentecostalism', *JPT* 1 (Oct. 1992), pp. 7-9. Accounting for this kind of work at the Pentecostal Theological Seminary would require reciting the bibliographies of the entire faculty.

[5] According to the Association of Theological Schools, American Pentecostal seminaries include Assemblies of God Theological Seminary, Pentecostal Theological Seminary (Cleveland, TN); and Urshan Graduate School of Theology (United Pentecostal Church International).

A Church of God Seminary

In the mid 1970's, consideration for the development of a denominational seminary dating back a decade resulted in the founding of the 'Church of God Graduate School of Christian Ministries', later to be named, 'Church of God School of Theology', then 'Church of God Theological Seminary' and eventually the Pentecostal Theological Seminary.[6] Concern for the impact of study in non-Pentecostal schools on Church of God ministers and teacher-scholars figured prominently in the desire to have such a seminary.[7] R. Hollis Gause became the first dean and director of the school that would come to be accredited by the Southern Association of Colleges and Schools (SACS) and the Association of Theological Schools (ATS) and offer four masters' and the doctor of ministry degrees.[8] With no other graduate schools in the Church of God, the founding of the seminary represented the first opportunity for advanced educational training within the denomination. Despite historically rooted misgivings and resistance to graduate level ministerial education, the 'Church of God Graduate School of Christian Ministries' was entrusted with training leaders for its denomination when it became only the third Pentecostal seminary in the United States.

A Wesleyan-Pentecostal Model

Development of the Pentecostal Theological Seminary's model of theological education can be understood as proceeding through four stages over the last three decades. In the first stage, the seminary began as a Church of God graduate school for ministry training with an explicit commitment to indoctrinating students in Church of God denominational distinctives – specifically, the Declaration of Faith – and the Holiness-Pentecostal interpretation of the Christian faith.[9] The curriculum of the school consisted of 'Biblical Theology, Systematic Theology,

---

[6] The shift from 'Church of God Graduate School of Christian Ministries' to 'Church of God School of Theology' was motivated by a desire to identify more clearly the school as a professional school (seminary) rather than as a traditional university style graduate school. Interview with James M. Beaty, Cleveland, TN, 15 March 2007.

[7] A fellowship for Church of God ministers attending seminary was organized at the 1974 General Assembly. A newsletter for 'The Seminarian Fellowship' in 1975 claimed a membership list of 52.

[8] James M. Beaty, H.D. Williams, and R. Hollis Gause served on a General Education Board subcommittee that made site visits at other seminaries, consulted with the Association of Theological Schools, and conducted feasibility studies for the founding of a seminary. R. Hollis Gause was named the first dean and director of the school in 1974.

[9] *Church of God Graduate School of Christian Ministries Catalog, 1975-1976* (Cleveland, TN), p. 3.

Historical Theology, Practical Theology, and denominational distinctives'.[10] All the major areas were referred to as 'Theology' to emphasize the unity of the curriculum and the centrality of theological confession in their work.[11] Other notable curricular features included an internship requirement – reflecting an emphasis on apprentice and practice-based learning – and the 'Seminar On Ministry'. The 'Seminar On Ministry' connected the school to various denominational departments in an annual campus hosted conference.[12] Beyond these curricular components, areas of study for students looked similar to other seminaries.[13]

With commitment to denominational distinctives and the Holiness-Pentecostal theological perspective, the seminary's early practice of requiring ministerial students to participate in faculty or staff led community of faith groups and in community worship chapels further laid the groundwork for its model of training. Students and faculty participated in such groups for experiences of '(1) Christian koinonia – genuine sharing, caring, and support and (2) reflection on questions of ministry and ministerial identity'.[14] Chapels were specifically intended to 'cultivate the spiritual graces and maturity necessary to a Holy Spirit-filled life and the conduct of the ministry of the gospel'.[15] Hollis Gause, as first dean of the seminary, considered 'the center of the campus to be the chapel'.[16] While not unique in seminary life, these practices reveal an implicit community of faith vision with a holistic orientation to ministerial formation 'where the students and faculty interact as a body, grow as a body, and thereby minister to the physical, spiritual and material needs of each other'.[17]

Following this stage of beginnings, newly arriving next-generation faculty members in the 1980s ushered in the formative second stage of

[10] *Church of God School of Theology, 1979-1980* (Cleveland, Tennessee), pp. 22-23. This was the curriculum projected in the seminary Catalog. Development in some curricular areas – historical and practical theology among them – was gradual and uneven.

[11] Interview with R. Hollis Gause, Cleveland, TN, 8 March 2007.

[12] R. Hollis Gause was instrumental in starting these seminars with this purpose.

[13] The original program was only one year in duration. The denominational context of study at the seminary was heightened by location of the school in Cleveland, Tennessee, the denominational headquarters for the Church of God. Later, most seminary presidents would be denominational executives coming from other leadership positions but chiefly from the Executive Committee of the Church of God. The school was located in Cleveland, Tennessee, to keep the denomination close to the school and the school close to the denomination. Interview with Beaty.

[14] See *Church of God School of Theology Catalog, 1981-1983* (Cleveland, TN), p. 30.

[15] See *Church of God School of Theology Catalog, 1980-1981* (Cleveland, TN), p. 22.

[16] Gause observed in interview that the chapel at the center makes all other activities in the seminary 'exercises in worship' (Interview with R. Hollis Gause, Cleveland, TN, 8 March 2007).

[17] *Church of God School of Theology Catalog, 1980-1981* (Cleveland, TN), pp. 22-23.

the seminary's development. The seminary began with the help of many well-established Church of God teacher-scholars who had been trained largely in schools less than receptive to their Pentecostal spirituality. Most had extensive previous teaching ministries at other Church of God sponsored schools.[18] With this new generation of younger faculty who were beginning constructively and intentionally to engage their disciplines, teaching, and ministry practice from within their Pentecostal identity, an unmistakably distinct and overtly confessional ethos began to shape the seminary.[19] Faculty members began to publish dissertations, theses and other works that provided leadership for other young teacher-scholars in the Society for Pentecostal Studies while also reflecting and shaping their own internal dialogue, development, and teaching at the seminary. The seminary quickly gained a reputation for having some of the most creative scholars and engaged faculty in Pentecostalism.[20]

With this new group of faculty members came also new seminary curricular developments. Having begun with a traditional seminary curriculum with additional requirements in Church of God denominational distinctives, now, courses appeared specifically reflecting the Holiness and Pentecostal identity and experience of the Church of God. Courses were developed on holiness, healing, Holiness-Pentecostal history, John Wesley's theology, church growth, pneumatology, and 'Pentecostal' foundations for ministry.[21] There was also a more explicit affirmation and articulation of the place of the community of faith groups in the curriculum as the seminary moved toward embracing a more intentional community of faith model of theological education. It was becoming clear that a Holiness or Wesleyan-Pentecostal theological vision was greatly influencing the development of the seminary curriculum and its training model.

---

[18] Among those faculty in this category would be Delton L. Alford, French L. Arrington, J. Martin Baldree, Raymond Barrick, James M. Beaty, Esdras Betancourt, R. Jerome Boone, Don N. Bowdle, Raymond R. Brown, Hector Camacho, Edward E. Call, Winston Elliott, Wilfredo Estrada-Adorno, Robert E. Fisher, Ollie J. Lee, Hubert L. Seals, John A. Sims, Laud O. Vaught, Herbert J. Walker, Paul L. Walker, Horace S. Ward, and Edward L. Williams.

[19] This new generation of Pentecostal faculty and scholars included Robert D. Crick, Lloyd David Franklin, Harold D. Hunter, Cheryl Bridges Johns, Jackie D. Johns, Steven J. Land, F.J. May (a founding member of the faculty), Oliver C. McMahan, L. Grant McClung, Rickie D. Moore, and John Christopher Thomas.

[20] The location of the editorial leadership of the *Journal of Pentecostal Theology* at the seminary did much to reinforce this perception.

[21] Compare seminary catalogs from 1979 through 1990 to note this shift. One of the more interesting changes was the deletion of a course on the 'Theology of Berkouwer' (1983-1985 Catalog), a reformed theologian, for a course on the 'Theology of Wesley' (1985-1987 Catalog).

Fuller integration of Pentecostal perspectives in the teaching, scholarship, and seminary curriculum advanced by the faculty was evident in what could be considered the third stage of the school's development. Beginning in the late 1980s, formative impulses behind the seminary's birth converged into an emerging identity and model. More distinctively Pentecostal-oriented courses developed with the addition of offerings such as 'Church Leadership: A Pentecostal Perspective', 'Pentecostal Ministry Supervision', 'Pentecostal Strategies of Missions', 'Spiritual Gifts in the Third Century', 'The Pedagogy of the Holy Spirit', 'Footwashing', 'Pentecostal Spirituality', 'Pentecostal Explorations of the New Testament', and 'Pentecostal Explorations of the Old Testament'.[22] These courses reflected the spiritual and intellectual journeys of the seminary faculty and their deepening apprehension of the implications of their shared confession for their work as teachers of future ministers and as scholars in their respective disciplines.

Evidencing a matured vision of its approach, the seminary came to affirm explicitly a Wesleyan-Pentecostal Community of Faith model. Earlier reference to the functional value of community of faith groups gave way to an articulated expectation that student ministers would be formed in the context of covenant relationships as part of 'a community of faith, worship and study'.[23] Co-curricular experiences, seminary community dynamics, and guided ministry internships were all intentionally embraced as integral to student development.[24] Commitment to a Wesleyan-Pentecostal Community of Faith approach was accompanied by efforts to affirm and embody a more holistic vision of formation leading students to 'integrate being and doing'.[25]

---

[22] These courses are listed in roughly the chronological order in which they were added to the published curriculum of the seminary spanning a period of about 12 years. Some senior faculty credit Ray H. Hughes, Sr., a former seminary president, with influencing the Pentecostal course language.

[23] The first reference to covenant relationships and school commitment to being a community of faith appears in the 1990-1992 *Catalog*. See *Church of God School of Theology Bulletin, 1990-1992*, vol. 12 (Cleveland, TN), p. 6. The seminary's 1989 self-study for the Southern Association of Colleges and Schools and the Association of Theological Schools documented the school's decision to revise its purpose statement to reflect the reference to being 'a community of faith, worship and study, which nurtures covenant relationships and creates awareness of the world mission and global diversity of the church'. See James M. Beaty, ed., *Self-Study of Church of God School of Theology* (Cleveland, TN). Submitted to The Southern Association of Colleges and Schools and The Association of Theological Schools in the United States and Canada, 1989, p. 4.

[24] Beaty, *Self-Study of Church of God School of Theology*, p. 9.

[25] Beaty, *Self-Study of Church of God School of Theology*, p. 8. It should be noted that earlier published descriptions of the seminary curriculum described the relationship between the different areas or disciplines as that of 'Foundation', 'Interpretation', and 'Application', language that reflects a theory to practice approach. See *Church of God School of Theology Catalog, 1983-1985* (Cleveland, TN), p. 6.

Educational Vision and Practice

Due in part, perhaps, to an extended period of discernment for the shape of the seminary model, the curricular intentionality of Pentecostal Theological Seminary faculty and administration has not led to written explanations of the seminary vision. Some faculty members have commented on aspects of their personal educational assumptions.[26] A full accounting of the seminary's story and curricular vision, however, has not been given. Students do receive an orientation to the seminary's model through lectures given in the required 'Pentecostal Foundations for Theological Study and Ministry' course. Current practices of student formation at the seminary, however, reveal four central curricular assumptions.

Wesleyan–Pentecostal Theological and Interpretive Framework

Reflecting its early commitment to a Holiness-Pentecostal perspective on the Christian faith, a theological and interpretive framework based on that perspective informs seminary course content, theological reflection and construction, contextual considerations, ministry development, and formational experience. Whether the discipline is biblical studies, spirituality-theology, historical theology, or life and ministry of the church, the backdrop for the educational process usually involves attention to the implications of Wesleyan-Pentecostalism. In light of the 'five-fold gospel' gestalt, a dynamic Christological emphasis shapes the curricular experience.[27] This confessional orientation is evident in various course descriptions and syllabi reflecting a focus on a constructive 'Wesleyan-Pentecostal' approach to the respective area of study.

Various courses specifically engage students in consideration of the implications of their context within Wesleyan-Pentecostalism as part of teaching and learning. While faculty members encourage a critically reflective appropriation of the tradition, students know they will be confronted with a passionate commitment to its particular claims. All

---

[26] See, for examples, James P. Bowers, 'A Wesleyan-Pentecostal Approach to Christian Formation', *JPT* 6 (1995), pp. 55-86; Cheryl Bridges Johns, 'Athens, Berlin, and Azusa: A Pentecostal Reflection on Scholarship and Christian Faith', *Pneuma: The Journal of the Society for Pentecostal Studies* 27.1 (Spring 2005), pp. 136-47; Jackie David Johns, 'Yielding to the Spirit: The Dynamics of a Pentecostal Model of Praxis', in *The Globalization of Pentecostalism: A Religion Made To Travel* (ed. Murray W. Dempster, Bryon D. Klaus, and Douglas Petersen; Carlisle, CA: Regnum, 1999), pp. 70-84; Rickie D. Moore, 'A Pentecostal Approach to Teaching Old Testament Introduction' (Paper presented to the Society for Pentecostal Studies, Cleveland, TN, March 10, 2007); and John Christopher Thomas, 'Pentecostal Explorations Of The New Testament: Teaching New Testament In A Pentecostal Seminary', *JPT* 11 (2002), pp. 120-29.

[27] On the role of this gestalt in Pentecostal spirituality, see Bowers, '*A Wesleyan-Pentecostal* Approach', pp. 74-78; Dayton, *Theological Roots*, pp. 15-23; Land, *Pentecostal Spirituality*, *p. 403*; and Thomas, 'Pentecostal Explorations', p. 122.

students, whatever their personal confession or theological tradition, are expected to integrate their story, call, theology, discipleship, and ministry in their seminary training. Students are specifically required to demonstrate such integration in practicum reflections, senior papers, and doctoral projects. Entering and graduating student questionnaires administered by the seminary continue to indicate this distinctive emphasis is a primary reason many students come to the seminary and is greatly valued by all students.[28] Students consistently rate the preparation received for integration of their faith – mostly Wesleyan-Pentecostal - with ministry practice and scholarship at the Pentecostal Theological Seminary to be very effective.[29]

Community of Faith Context
Developing from within the Wesleyan-Pentecostal vision and specifically supportive of its spirituality is an emphasis on a community of faith context for theological formation. This curricular assumption is evidenced in seminary self-descriptions as 'the church of God gathered for theological education'.[30] The seminary, therefore, practices an ecclesiological commitment as essential to ministerial formation. That is, the theological education model of the Pentecostal Theological Seminary is based on the conviction that students can only be faithfully and effectively prepared for *Pentecostal* ministry from *within* a distinctively *Pentecostal* fellowship or community of faith.

Upon entering the seminary, therefore, students are integrated into communal practices of worship, small group fellowship and accountability, study, and ministry development as part of ongoing *Pentecostal* faith development. Formation for life and ministry is contingent on participation in a Spirit-filled community of discipleship, worship, fellowship, and service. Other considerations certainly shape the educational practices of the school and the experiences of the students, but the fundamental principle of the curriculum and, indeed, of the life of the school must be that the seminary is 'the church of God gathered for theological education'.

In covenantal relationships with peers and faculty in a 'community of faith and ministry development group', all degree-seeking students practice sharing their testimony, discerning their capacities and call for ministry, praying for one another, sharing communal meals, and being accountable for spiritual development and moral life. Student and fa-

---

[28] Church of God Theological Seminary, *Entering Student Questionnaire 2006-2007*, report prepared by the Association of Theological Schools, Table 21.

[29] Church of God Theological Seminary, *Graduating Student Questionnaire 2006-2007*, report prepared by the Association of Theological Schools, Table 19.

[30] *Church of God Theological Seminary Academic Catalog 2006-2008,* vol. XV (Cleveland, TN), p. 9.

culty testimonies, prayer vigils, and group meetings provide specific opportunities and accountability for Pentecostal spiritual experiences and development. In fact, many gatherings are characterized by manifestations of charismatic gifts, participation in sacraments of Footwashing and Lord's Supper, and responses of care and service to those in need inside and outside the group.

These experiences and relationships express an egalitarianism and mutuality in the shared journey of faith and formation being taken by faculty and students in the process of theological education. All students process their ministry development portfolio and internship proposals with their community of faith group members as part of the assessment of their gifts and capacities for ministry. Practices and experiences of these groups together with other communal functions and processes are, thus, a primary and non-negotiable spiritual and educational resource for student formation for Christian life and ministry within an embodied Wesleyan-Pentecostal ecclesiological context.[31]

Know-Be-Do Paradigm

Integrating student life and ministry through an experiential union of heart, head, and hands is the third major curricular assumption of the seminary.[32] The 'Know-Be-Do' paradigm, as students come to see, is an expression of the deepest conviction of faculty about the life of ministry. Course content, pedagogical process, internships, community of faith and ministry development group experience, seminary community life, senior integrative papers, and much more are intended to cultivate the unity of life represented by a holistic formation of persons for ministry. Worship or orthodoxy (knowing), ethics or orthopathy (being), and mission or orthopraxy (doing) are considered inseparable in life and ministry.[33] Although reflections of the traditional seminary theory-practice dichotomy remain in the fourfold seminary curriculum structure, students know from the orientation course for new students, 'Pentecostal Foundations for Theological Study and Ministry', through the stated outcomes for other courses and experiences the goal of their

---

[31] For a discussion of the importance of 'communal pedagogies' in seminary curriculum, see Charles R. Foster, Lisa E. Dahill, Lawrence A. Golemon, and Barbara Wang Tolentino, *Educating Clergy: Teaching Practices and Pastoral Imagination* (San Francisco: Jossey-Bass, 2006), pp. 187-325.

[32] For commentary on this point, see James P. Bowers, 'A Wesleyan-Pentecostal Approach', pp. 78-79; Cheryl Bridges Johns, *Pentecostal Formation: A Pedagogy among the Oppressed* (JPTS 2; Sheffield, UK: Sheffield Academic Press, 1993), p. 122; Steven J. Land, 'A Pentecostal Pastoral Profile for the 21st Century: A Personal Essay' (Paper presented at the State Overseers Inservice, Church of God Theological Seminary, January 2000), p. 5. Land gives an elaborative list of his view of the dimensions of know-be-do formation.

[33] See Land, *Pentecostal Spirituality*, p. 184.

training at the seminary is a full integration of faith and learning, life and ministry, character and calling

Practice–Based Assessment

The early commitment of the seminary to field testing the course preparation of students merits specific mention. Four aspects of the practice-based approach to curriculum can be identified. First, students were initially required to complete an internship practicum in order to receive their degree. This kept the seminary's model not only 'practical', but also compatible with the sponsoring denomination's commitment to demonstration of ministry call and gifts by practice. Second, students apprenticed in the internship with a mentor-pastor trained by the seminary. Faculty, students, and mentor-pastors participated in the orientation, training, and discernment process for these relationships.[34] Third, the seminary's development of the 'Seminar On Ministry' also affirmed the importance of practice. As the seminary collaborated with various church departments to host these events – which brought many clergy and laity to the campus -- opportunities for a flow of influence in both directions became a reality. Fourth, the seminary's vertical scheduling of courses (1992) made it possible for practicing pastors to access the seminary program.[35] In these ways, the seminary cultivated practice-based assessment of its educational work.

The Pastoral Excellence Project:
Revisioning the Wesleyan-Pentecostal Model

From within this educational vision and occasioned by the award of Lilly Endowment 'Sustaining Pastoral Excellence' and 'Making Connections' grants, the Pentecostal Theological Seminary had the opportunity in 2003 to export revisioned core elements of its Wesleyan-Pentecostal Community of Faith model to practicing pastors (many without seminary education) in the interest of pastoral excellence. The project undertaken now involves hundreds of USA pastors and has been the partial impetus for a curriculum revision initiative that may be thought of as the fourth stage in the seminary's curriculum development. The exported model implemented with Church of God pastors is organized around formational practices with parallels to the experiences of seminary students.

---

[34] Interview with R. Hollis Gause, Cleveland, TN, 8 March 2007. Internship requirements are still present for master of divinity degree students, but attention to development of mentors and strategic pairing of students with them is less intentional.

[35] Of course, the seminary had offered a 'Thursday Only' program of courses for practicing pastors from its beginning. All courses moved to the vertical scheduling format in 1992.

Formational Practices

Church of God pastors involved in the seminary's pastoral excellence project participate in ten formational practices intended to sustain pastoral excellence. These experiences take place within a peer group of other Church of God pastors living and ministering in the same geographical area. Groups are led by a facilitator trained in the formational model and coached through the process by the seminary. Project leadership focuses specifically on communicating and sustaining the theological-formational vision and health of the practices associated with the process. While implementation of the project is influenced by contextual and cultural considerations, all pastoral participants share a formational journey reflecting the same pattern of experiences.

Even though the model of practices is consistent across the pastoral peer groups, there is yet a dynamic and spiritually spontaneous dimension to group experience. Within the context of a shared Pentecostal and Church of God faith, groups are immediately responsive to directions, needs, or pastoral issues emerging through their sensitivity to the leadership of the Holy Spirit. Various shared activities of the groups provide the opportunity and encourage members to participate in the formational process in submission to the presence of the Spirit.[36] In a very real sense, then, the context of group practice is charged with an expectation of the experience of the Holy Spirit. The formational practices thus become the means by which the participants respond to the presence and ministry of the Spirit within their group.

Spiritual Retreat and Christian Conferencing

The first and most basic practice in which pastors engage is also the context for several other practices. Pastoral groups begin with a three day 'Covenant Making Retreat'. Withdrawing from their ministry responsibilities and personal and family activities, pastors usually leave their immediate geographical locale to meet together in retreat in order to form their group and launch a formational journey with one another. Through practices of table fellowship, shared prayer and worship, testimony, making covenant, discerning missional context, and personal assessment and planning, pastors lay the foundation for a shared, continuing process of renewal

Spiritual retreat can be seen as having biblical roots in the Old Testament 'Sabbath' practices, Jesus' habit of seeking seclusion with his

---

[36] For a discussion of the significance of attention to the leadership of the Holy Spirit in group Bible study, see Cheryl Bridges Johns and Jackie David Johns, 'Yielding to the Spirit: A Pentecostal Model of Group Bible Study', *JPT* 1 (1992), pp. 109-34; and Bowers, 'A Wesleyan-Pentecostal Approach', p. 80. See also Jackie D. Johns, 'Pedagogy of the Holy Spirit' (Dissertation, Southern Baptist Theological Seminary, 1987).

disciples, and the New Testament 'Christian Day of Worship'.[37] Historically, Christian groups of various types – including Monastics, Pietists, Moravians, and Wesleyans – have utilized practices of seclusion for purposes of spiritual experience, formation, and deepening fellowship. Of course, Holiness and Pentecostal adherents turned to retreat-like 'camp meetings' and 'prayer conferences' for similar reasons. Many contemporary expressions of the practice can readily be found among Christian groups. Seminary project pastors consider their 'Covenant Making Retreat' indispensable to the successful formation and process of their pastoral groups.

Relational and formational dynamics begun in the spiritual retreat continue as pastors 'conference' with one another in monthly meetings.[38] In the biblical tradition of the Acts 15 Jerusalem Council and John Wesley's 'Christian Conferencing', pastors gather to consult and care for one another.[39] Following a model with movements reflecting key practices of the retreat, pastors extend that initiatory experience into the process and context of their lives and expand its scope to address issues and concerns emerging in their practice. Their engagement in this process under the leadership of the Spirit allows for immediate responsiveness to pastoral challenges and enables the appropriation of gifts and graces resident in the group for the mutual benefit of members. Within the boundaries of covenantal and developmental practices and with the assistance of a pastoral facilitator, members discern their group's direction and process toward pastoral excellence while overcoming the destructive effects of alienation, loneliness, and isolation.[40]

Table Fellowship

One of the earliest and continuing practices experienced by project pastors involves sharing fellowship meals with members of their group.

---

[37] See Dorothy C. Bass, 'Keeping Sabbath', in *Practicing Our Faith*: A Way of Life for a Searching People (ed. Dorothy C. Bass; San Francisco: Jossey-Bass, 1997), pp. 75-89.

[38] John Wesley instituted the practice of conferencing with the preachers of the Methodist movement for consultations on 'the best method of carrying on the work of God'. See John Wesley, 'Minutes of Several Conversations', *The Works of John Wesley*, vol. VIII (ed. Thomas Jackson; 1831; repr. Grand Rapids: Baker Book House, 1984), p. 312.

[39] See Kenneth H. Carter, Jr., *A Way of Life in the World: Spiritual Practices for United Methodists* (Nashville, TN: Abingdon, 2004), pp. 85-86; Larry Rasmussen, 'Shaping Communities', in *Practicing Our Faith*, pp. 119-32.

[40] One of the primary benefits of pastoral participation in the pastoral covenant groups has been emotional and relational healing. Given the findings of the administration of the U.S. Congregational Life Survey to Church of God pastors, this represents a significant positive impact. For a profile of the relational and emotional needs of Church of God pastors, see James P. Bowers, 'How Pastors Feel', in *Portrait and Prospect: Church of God Pastors Face the 21st Century* (ed. James P. Bowers; Cleveland, TN: Center for Pentecostal Leadership and Care, 2004), pp. 61-71.

Often, the first encounter group members have as a group is a common meal. During the group forming retreat, pastors are required to share all meals with each other. As the group takes its annual journey together, most continue this practice as part of their monthly meetings.

Such fellowship meals have traditionally functioned as formative community celebrations in Pentecostal congregations much as they did in early church 'love feasts'.[41] Pentecostal worship services and other congregational observances are often accompanied by shared meals. These community meal rituals express and cultivate the relational 'knowing' essential to other aspects of congregational life. Theologically, such meals serve a sacramental function revealing the redemptive nature of the fellowship and the character of relationships in the church. Fellowship with Christ brings the people to the table and into the practice of graced fellowship with one another.

In this light, relationships formed and experienced in the pastoral groups reflect a shared spiritual fellowship and evidence the grace and presence of Christ. The relational hospitality, unity, and transparency practiced in common meals express the reality of this fellowship among pastors. As pastors break bread, they also begin to overcome barriers of isolation and loneliness, mistrust and cynicism, misunderstanding and alienation that often exist among them.[42] This practice reveals and celebrates the deeper spiritual bonds transcending differences between pastors while preparing the relational space for new experiences of grace in their interactions with each other in the group.

Communal Prayer and Worship

Experiences of Spirit-led worship and prayer are also prominent in the pastoral groups. Practices of group formation and processes of peer learning occur within a context of shared prayer and worship. Groups celebrate sacraments of Footwashing and Lord's Supper, participate in spirited praise and worship, and many commit to group-developed prayer covenants. Pastors report personally transforming experiences of spiritual, relational, and emotional healing during such practices. Opportunities to personally receive and offer prayer for pastoral needs and concerns support the establishment of practical relationships of care and prepare a spiritual climate for group interaction.

Nothing is more central to Pentecostal spirituality and congregational life than prayer and worship.[43] Corporate worship is the fundamental vocation and defining practice of congregations. Pentecostal communities, in particular, encounter God, experience transformation, and ex-

---

[41] See 1 Cor. 11.17-22; 2 Pet. 2.13; Jude 12.
[42] See Bowers, 'How Pastors Feel', pp. 61-71.
[43] See Land, *Pentecostal Spirituality*, pp. 71-81.

ercise formation through the corporate ministry of the Word, operation of charismatic gifts, and acts and drama of worship. Congregational life is centered in God and God's presence through worship. Through congregational prayer, the people attend to God's will, appropriate God's grace for their needs, and actualize deeper communion with God.

Pastors center their group journey, with its attendant commitments, in the presence of God through practices of shared prayer and worship. As they worship together, pastors discern the spiritual and covenantal nature of their relationships and, among other things, experience divine approbation of their fellowship. As one pastor noted, 'We have experienced a profound sense of God's presence in our group'. These Spirit-led practices of prayer and worship serve to establish a focal spiritual formation agenda and process for the group. Exercise of charismatic gifts, prayers of concern and intercession, and acts of Spirit-led care bring the group into an immediate and dynamic awareness of the presence of the Holy Spirit. Such a sense of the Spirit's presence initiates the group into a shared spiritual journey of worship and formation and is essential to the group's effectiveness and health.[44]

Sharing Testimony

Along with worship and prayer, the sharing of personal testimonies is a formative practice of the pastoral groups. In similar fashion to the practice of seminary students in campus-based community of faith and ministry development groups, pastors are invited to begin their work on pastoral excellence by 'telling their story'. Most pastors have no other setting where they can tell such stories and reflect on them.[45] In small triads within the pastoral group, pastors recount formative family and spiritual beginnings and prayerfully reflect on their experiences and sense of call for ministry. From shared meals and communal experiences of prayer and worship, pastors move deeper relationally and spiritually with one another through testimony. Affirmation for gifts and calling, responses of care for needs, sharing of pastoral wisdom for challenging situations, and practices of intercessory prayer accompany such times of testimony.

Pastors participating in the sharing of testimonies are doing much more than 'getting acquainted'. As God is the God of history, they are attending to the work of God in their stories in the same way as did

[44] The name chosen for the pilot project, 'Walking in the Spirit: A Program of Spiritual Formation and Pastoral Renewal', reflected the emphasis on the Spirit context of group journeys.

[45] For the significance of this practice for pastoral longevity and health, see Dean R. Hoge and Jacqueline E. Wenger, *Pastors in Transition: Why Clergy Leave Local Church Ministry* (Grand Rapids: Eerdmans, 2005), pp. 207-209.

the people of Israel.[46] They come to know one another as 'subjects' in
God's drama of redemption and begin to discern their communal connection and call. Given prayerfully, these testimonies become the
means by which the Spirit brings transformation to pastoral relationships and opens up new visions for their future arising from shared
reflection on their past experience of God's grace.[47] Individual stories
are woven together through the shared Story of God's presence among
them and a renewed story, experience, and covenant with God becomes possible in the group.

Making and Keeping Covenant

Spiritual retreat, shared meals, communal worship and prayer, and
personal testimony are part of an initial process of making covenant.
Pastors collaborate in their groups to develop a covenant within the
framework provided by the seminary project model.[48] This covenant
reflects the commitments and practices embraced by pastors in order to
take their journey of care, peer resourcing, accountability, and development. Practicing pastors intentionally 'make covenant' in a process
of dialogue, confession, prayer, and worship. The 'covenant making
service' during the 'pastoral covenant group' retreat often involves
sacraments of Footwashing and Lord's Supper and is a powerfully
transformative experience for pastors. As one pastoral facilitator noted,
'The covenant making *process* may be more important than the group
covenant'.[49]

Making covenant as pastors is an enactment of a core reality of
Christian life and ministry. Faith and ministry is essentially communal
and covenantal. Christ called and commissioned a community of disciples.[50] For Pentecostals, in particular, the experience of the charisms
of the Spirit is rooted in community. As pastors make covenant, they
testify to their spiritual and missional interdependence, rediscover the
power and resources of a corporate faith, and renew their shared cove-

---

[46] See Eugene H. Peterson, *Eat This Book: A Conversation in the Art of Spiritual Reading*
(Grand Rapids: Eerdmans, 2006). Steve Land speaks of Pentecostal testimonies in relation
to the experience of believers having 'walked with the children of Israel, the prophets,
the apostles and early church believers'. See Land, *Pentecostal Spirituality*, p. 73.

[47] On the connection of memory, interpretation, reflection, and the future in testimony, see Jackie David Johns and Cheryl Bridges Johns, 'Yielding to the Spirit', pp. 126-27.

[48] The project model reflects expectations for pastors to commit to (1) enter into covenant with each other, congregations, state/denominational leadership, and the seminary
for the pursuit of pastoral excellence; (2) be inclusive of the diversity of Church of God
pastoral ministry; (3) participate in the prescribed practices and process of formation.

[49] Observation made by Pastor Ronnie Reid in the Florida Facilitators' Consultation
in Tampa, Florida, 27 February 2007.

[50] See Gerhard Lohfink, *Jesus and Community: The Social Dimension of Christian Faith*
(trans. John P. Galvin; Philadelphia: Fortress, 1984).

nant to God and one another. In these renewed covenant relationships, the practical integrity of their ecclesial spirituality and theology is restored.

That said, keeping the covenant made is the *essential* and *continuing* precondition to the formational process within the group. Covenant is a *process* not an *event* for the groups. Not only is the experience of 'kept covenant' an antidote to the cynicism and mistrust of competitive pastoral and denominational life, accomplishing significant development goals requires transparency and vulnerability which cannot exist outside assured relationships of trust, care, and accountability. Focus group consultations and evaluative survey responses indicate 'keeping covenant' establishes the 'safe space' needed for pastoral change.[51] One pastoral participant observed, 'Covenant is what makes real growth and change happen'.[52]

Discerning Missional Context

Pastors move into the more developmental side of the formational practices by giving attention to discerning their missional context. As seminary students are led to reflect on context through course pedagogies, community of faith and ministry development groups, integrative courses, and theses, project pastors are also engaged in an intentional process of interpreting their larger ministry environment. Typically, broader cultural profiles are juxtaposed to regional or community demographic data to enable pastors to work together to better understand ministry challenges and opportunities. The initial stage of this process in the covenant making retreat surfaces missional needs and goals for group focus, but discerning context is an ongoing practice as pastors conference together monthly in their pastoral covenant group.

Important affirmations are reflected in this process of discerning missional context. Pastors are practicing and simultaneously reinforcing a communal, even covenantal, approach to ministry which enables them to transcend individualism – the lone ranger syndrome – and find again the passion of being part of a missional movement. Collectively, they discern what the particular call of the Spirit is in their context. Thus, they are practicing 'contextual theology' in a process of Spirit-led discernment. Given the dearth of effectively vision-based congregational ministry in the Church of God (and in America), these pastors are

---

[51] Project leadership conducts quarterly consultations with pastoral facilitators of all pastoral covenant groups and receives direct feedback on the effect of various dynamics of the project process. In addition, pastors participate in annual surveys developed to evaluate the process. Qualitative comments and scaled responses affirm the importance of covenantal relationships and commitments for a healthy, trustworthy process.

[52] Comment from pastoral participant in the Florida Facilitators' Consultation in Tampa, Florida, 27 February 2007.

'practicing in the Spirit' an important contextually, interpretive process
that can be integrated into their parish work as well as inform their
personal development.[53]

Personal Assessment and Development Planning

The developmental dimension of the pastoral covenant group experience does become much more personal when pastors participate in
assessment exercises to determine their formational needs. Within the
context of their 'Covenant Making Retreat,' group members are invited to respond to pastoral excellence assessment instruments allowing
for self-directed evaluation of spiritual, emotional, relational, physical,
financial, ministerial, and familial health and wellness.[54] Individual pastoral assessments are processed within the covenant group with a triad
of peers under the supervision of a trained facilitator. Utilizing dialogical processes of reflection, discernment, and accountability with pastoral peers, pastors set covenantal goals to address areas of need through a
personally crafted development plan.

Such processes of personal assessment and development are giving
expression to basic commitments of Christian discipleship and ministry.
Pastors are participating in scripturally-based practices of self-
examination, confession, spiritual and moral accountability, mutual
exhortation, and prayer in the interest of faithful and healthy pastoral
life.[55] Given the holistic concern for all areas of life, these ministers are
doing more than learning the latest 'leadership techniques'. They are
attending to the state of their souls and lives with an intentionality not
experienced by most anywhere else in their lives.[56] Earlier practices of
spiritual, moral, and theological accountability – rooted in the Wesleyan heritage of Pentecostals – have been weakened in most Pentecostal communities. Consequently, many pastors involved in this project

[53] Survey data from various sources confirms the lack of vision-driven ministry in
many American congregations. Research on Church of God (Cleveland, TN) congregations found nearly three-fourths not successful in the implementation of a clear vision.
See Ron Cason, 'How Pastors Lead', in *Portrait and Prospect*, p. 46.

[54] For further information about the criteria for the process, see the Pentecostal
Theological Seminary Center for Pentecostal Leadership and Care website at
www.pentecostalleadership.org.

[55] On the basis of exploration of the themes of sin and holiness in the Johannine
community, New Testament scholar Chris Thomas argues 'we must devise ways to make
accountability a regular and meaningful part of our lives as Christian leaders'. See John
Christopher Thomas, *Ministry & Theology: Studies for the Church and Its Leaders* (Cleveland,
TN: Pathway, 1996), pp. 156-57.

[56] Such practices of spiritual nourishment have been identified as contributing to pas-
toral longevity in national studies conducted by Pulpit and Pew at Duke Divinity School.
See Jackson W. Carroll, *God's Potters: Pastoral Leadership and the Shaping of Congregations*
(Grand Rapids: Eerdmans, 2006), pp. 206-207.

rarely participate in any form of personal evaluation or development.[57] Within the spiritually formational and collegially accountable pastoral covenant group process, pastors are experiencing and taking personal responsibility for a positive and constructive assessment and development practice that produces results.[58]

Collaborative Learning, Mentoring, and Resourcing

Building on the personal assessment and development planning process, practices of collaborative learning, mentoring, and resourcing experienced in the pastoral groups are instrumental to achievement of personal development goals. As pastors conference monthly and connect outside their group meetings, they stimulate one another to growth and learning, share guidance and support, and become strategic resources for their mutual development. Strong bonds of support and care develop between pastors as they become an intentional 'community of practice'. Pastors are able to deal more successfully with the dynamic nature of contemporary knowledge while using the social resources of a community of learners to enlarge their perspective, increase their understanding, and, ultimately, renew their pastoral practice.[59]

Beyond the strictly developmental benefits of such collaboration, and more importantly from an ecclesial perspective, pastors are expressing and providing opportunity for the actualization of core aspects of their spirituality. They are moving from competitive alienation with one another to relationships of mutual respect, interdependence, and affirmation through experiences of shared learning, emotional support, and empathetic resourcing. The egalitarian and mutual nature of their collaboration creates opportunities for mentoring and discipling inexperienced pastors, exercise and affirmation of spiritual gifts, 'sanctification' of destructive or dysfunctional relationships, and deeper levels of personal discipleship for all participants. A formational polity process is at work among the pastors helping to birth a new vision and paradigm for mission.

---

[57] Survey results from the administration of the U.S. Congregational Life Survey of Church of God pastors found nearly 90% without any opportunities for such evaluation. See Cason, 'How Pastors Lead', p. 43.

[58] Impact on pastoral life and functioning has been chronicled and documented in a series of five program reports submitted to Lilly Endowment's Religion Division.

[59] Evaluative survey and qualitative data collected by the Pentecostal Theological Seminary's Center for Pentecostal Leadership and Care suggests the positive impact on attainment of pastoral development goals. On the benefits of participation in a 'community of practice', see Etienne Wenger, *Communities of Practice: Learning, Meaning, and Identity* (Cambridge, UK: Cambridge University Press, 1998), pp. 275-77; Etienne Wenger, Richard McDermott, and William M. Snyder, *Cultivating Communities of Practice* (Boston, MA: Harvard Business School Press, 2002), pp. 1-21.

Shared Theological Praxis

Within this collaborative process, significant contributions are also made to the formational journey of pastors through structured opportunities for theological reflection on ministry. Pastors devote substantial amounts of time in their monthly pastoral covenant group meetings to conversations about various issues and concerns of pastoral practice. Group facilitators have been trained to use case studies provided either by the seminary's Center for Pentecostal Leadership and Care or by participant pastors to engage the group in an intentional process of shared theological reflection.

These lively theological discussions of pastoral issues connect with vital needs in ministerial formation and congregational life and, again, reflect biblically and historically rooted practices of pastoral consultation.[60] Survey responses from Church of God pastors indicate less than half (43%) give priority to biblical or theological considerations in making ministry decisions or developing programs.[61] The collegial process of theologizing occurring in the pastoral groups, therefore, is an important resource for pastoral and congregational renewal. Most pastors have no other 'safe space' where they can engage in such dialogue. Their group process specifically involves shared reflection on interpreting pastoral and congregational issues, identifying good, biblical, and faithful Pentecostal pastoral practice, and choosing appropriate responses for their context.

Congregational and Missional Collaboration

The practices and dynamics of group life and pastoral formation described ultimately culminate in congregational and missional collaboration between participating pastors and their congregations. Within their pastoral covenant group meetings and in their shared contexts of ministry, pastors move into expressions of care, resourcing, and ministry partnership which impact their congregations and their mission. Pastoral covenant group discussions of congregational needs and missional challenges in their geographical context inevitably lead to collaborative activities. From sharing financial, material, and personnel resources to strategizing for new church development, pastors are engaged in practices of congregational and missional collaboration birthed

---

[60] From the Old Testament 'schools of the prophets' and the New Testament 'Jerusalem Council' to the great church councils and various later forms of conferencing, communal theological reflection on issues of import has characterized pastoral leadership. Project pastors are experiencing this process in the grassroots context of their ministries.
[61] See Ron Cason, 'How Pastors Lead', p. 42.

not by a programmatic mandate but by responsiveness to the immediate leading of the Holy Spirit![62]

The larger significance of such collaboration relates to the lack of effective support and collaborative structures at the grassroots level of
ministry. Most districts – the local denominational polity -- have dete-
riorated and no longer function as a means for congregational or missional collaboration. From within the pastoral covenant groups,
however, fresh expressions of care, accountability, resourcing, and
ministry development are emerging with the potential to reform and
reestablish a lost connectional polity. The pastoral covenant group and
its practices are culminating in congregational and missional collaboration representing a post-denominational, grassroots, and covenant-
based polity with a focus on pastoral renewal, congregational development, and missional revitalization.

Practices in the Spirit

With this description of the four central curricular convictions informing the Pentecostal Theological Seminary's model of theological education and its revision and exportation in the ten major practices of the
pastoral excellence project, it is possible to identify the formational
sources guiding the institution's pastoral leadership development. From
this perspective, the dimensions of a Pentecostal model of pastoral formation and its implications for seminary curriculum development and
pastoral leadership development programs can be suggested.

Formational Sources

Various sources of authority and influence can be identified as functioning in the seminary's process of pastoral leadership development.
Several of these are overtly acknowledged; others are important but
operate more or less at an unconscious level. Evident among the
sources are (1) the Wesleyan-Pentecostal tradition; (2) Church of God
faith and ethos; (3) Scripture; (4) the social sciences; (5) a seminary
education tradition; (6) the Holy Spirit; (7) student experience and
ministry practice; and (8) various faculty pedagogies.

A dialectical interplay exists between these influences in the seminary
pastoral development process. Commitment to a Wesleyan-Pentecostal
theological and interpretive framework and to indoctrination of
Church of God ministers in denominational spiritual, moral, and doc-

---

[62] Numerous examples of such congregational and missional collaboration are emerging and have been shared in structured consultations and evaluative responses collected by
the Center for Pentecostal Leadership and Care at the Pentecostal Theological Seminary.

trinal standards are guiding norms. From these perspectives, Scripture emerges as well as a 'foundational' authority in arbitrating competing claims between authorities and providing the meta-narrative and epistemology for the formational process. Study and interpretation of Scripture, therefore, has historically been at the 'core' of the curriculum.

Other authorities have a secondary but significant role in curricular decisions and ministerial formation. Student assessments make use, among other things, of psychological profiles that inform ministry development journeys. Project pastors follow a 'pastor-centered, pastor-directed' *andragogically* shaped process grounded in a social science understanding of adult development. Pastoral survey results informing curriculum revision and project based training arise from an *empirically-based* study. Teaching-learning experiences reflect a particular *seminary tradition* of education, student life experience and ministry practice, and various faculty pedagogies. Faithful and effective pastoral formation is, therefore, dependent on discerning integration of these authorities within a Spirit-led hermeneutical process grounded in Scripture, Wesleyan-Pentecostal faith, communal reflection, and disciplined description of faith experience and ministry practice.[63]

A Pentecostal Model of Pastoral Formation

Within the context of these authorities and the proposed process of discernment, the following dimensions of a distinctively Pentecostal model of pastoral formation are suggested for consideration. Features of this model are based on the authorities posited and on reflections on seminary practices with students and project pastors. While the project process expands certain elements, there is still an essential continuity in the approaches to both seminary constituencies. The grounding of this model in core affirmations and marks of Pentecostal spirituality establishes its relevance for other pastoral development programs initiated by Pentecostal denominations and schools.

---

[63] My colleagues, Ken Archer and Jackie Johns, have spoken to the nature of a Pentecostal hermeneutical process as have I in previous writing. See Ken Archer, *A Pentecostal Hermeneutic for the Twenty-First Century: Spirit, Scripture, and Community* (JPT 28; London: T & T Clark, 2004). Bowers, 'A Wesleyan-Pentecostal Approach', pp. 80-81; Jackie D. Johns, 'Yielding to the Spirit: The Dynamics of a Pentecostal Model of Praxis', pp. 79-80. In this regard, Don Browning also proposed the need for 'descriptive theology' within practical theology. See Don S. Browning, 'Toward a Fundamental and Strategic Practical Theology', in *Contextual Approaches to the Structure of Theological Education* (ed. Barbara G. Wheeler and Edward Farley; Louisville, KY: Westminster/John Knox Press, 1991), pp. 295-328.

Biblical Authority and Epistemology

From the perspective of the seminary's practice in its work with students and project pastors and given the centrality of the Scriptures for Pentecostals, biblical authority and epistemology is foundational to Pentecostal pastoral formation. Commitment to the 'absolute authority of Scripture' means the Scripture (1) becomes arbiter of conflicts of authority, (2) functions as 'The Story' or meta-narrative interpreting human story/stories, and (3) is means of experience with the Living Word – Christ.[64] All dimensions of pastoral formation – purpose, context, process, content, and relationships – should reflect a dynamic and real scriptural authority.

Adherence to a biblical epistemology is similarly a criterion for educational or formational practice grounded in scriptural authority. Such an epistemology is experiential, testimonial, relational, communal, spiritual, practical, affective, holistic, and integrative in nature. The 'know-be-do' paradigm embraced at the Pentecostal Theological Seminary expresses a commitment to such a biblical and Pentecostal epistemology.[65] Pedagogical strategies, teaching-learning processes, and curricular structure must reflect this epistemology for Scripture to actually be authoritative in pastoral formation. As a holistic and integrative Pentecostal spirituality requires such an epistemology, pastoral training programs based merely on transferring information or knowledge, modifying behavior, or developing skill are inadequate for Pentecostal leadership development.

Pentecostal Confession

Given the narrative nature of Pentecostal spirituality, pastoral identity and leadership requires a personally and communally confessional approach to formation. This is reflected in the Wesleyan-Pentecostal theological and interpretive framework at the Pentecostal Theological Seminary. Particularity is endemic to personal faith, congregational life,

---

[64] The Pentecostal Theological Seminary's catalog refers to the 'absolute authority of Scripture'. Such phraseology is consistent with the views of most Pentecostals. Steve Land speaks of the relation to the Word for Pentecostals as being 'to experience life as part of the biblical drama of participation in God's history'. He further notes, 'For those early Pentecostals to abide in the Word was simultaneously to abide in Jesus and the written Word'. See Land, *Pentecostal Spirituality*, pp. 74-75. Mark Cartledge observes, 'Therefore the testimony of Scripture as the supreme witness to the purposes of God in Christ functions in a *critical* way even as the testimony of the church as community functions in a cohering sense'. See Mark J. Cartledge, *Practical Theology: Charismatic and Empirical Perspectives* (Carlisle, UK: Paternoster, 2003), p. 61.

[65] For a discussion of the features of a distinctively Pentecostal epistemology, see Cheryl Bridges Johns, *Pentecostal Formation*, pp. 35-36; Jackie D. Johns, 'Pentecostalism and the Postmodern Worldview', *JPT* 7 (1995), pp. 73-96; also Bowers, 'A Wesleyan-Pentecostal Approach', pp. 78-80.

and ministry functioning. As Mark Cartledge concludes, 'While tradition may have a negative connotation, it is now widely accepted that we all do our theology from some kind of position or tradition, that is a linguistic-cultural context'.[66] Historically, culturally, religiously, and socially shaped experience, interpretation, and practice in matters of faith is inescapable and, thus, 'traditioning' is inevitable.[67]

Generically 'Christian' theological education cannot provide the formation needed for pastoral functioning within the Pentecostal tradition, or, for that matter, within any tradition. Against the backdrop of the broader Christian tradition, effective Pentecostal pastoral formation must provide a critically constructive appropriation of and indoctrination in Pentecostal faith (fourfold or fivefold) in order to sustain personal and communal identity, form spirituality, and strategically serve mission. Anything less, in the guise of a more 'inclusive' education, ultimately undermines the spirituality, faith, practice, and mission of the Pentecostal movement.[68]

Ecclesial Context

Formation for congregational leadership within the Pentecostal movement – especially in light of a biblical epistemology and Wesleyan /Holiness nuanced spirituality – presumes discipleship experience within a community of faith.[69] This priority is biblically, theologically, and practically indicated. Unfortunately, formation-in-community cannot be assumed, thus, pastoral development should proceed in a communal even covenantal context of relationships.[70]

This ecclesiological emphasis mandates participation in the various practices and relationships of a *Pentecostal* community of faith. Pente-

---

[66] Cartledge, *Practical Theology*, p. 54.

[67] According to the Carnegie Foundation study of seminary education, the 'internal goods' sought by seminary educators for students are 'first, a deepening sense of identification with their religious tradition, and second, their confident and competent participation in the leadership of its religious communities'. Of course, these 'goods' are intimately related. See *Educating Clergy*, p. 373.

[68] It seems to me that Allan Bloom long ago exposed the myth behind the supposed increased tolerance and understanding conventionally associated with non-convictional learning. See Allan Bloom, *The Closing of the American Mind: How Higher Education Has Failed Democracy and Impoverished the Souls of Today's Students* (New York: Simon and Schuster, 1987), esp. pp. 25-43.

[69] Cheryl Bridges Johns, among others, concurs with this point. See Johns, *Pentecostal Formation*, p. 36. See also J. Johns, 'Pentecostal Worldview', pp. 92-94.

[70] See Robert Banks, *Reenvisioning Theological Education: Exploring a Missional Alternative to Current Models* (Grand Rapids: Eerdmans, 1999), pp. 204-207; and Carnegie Samuel Calian, *The Ideal Seminary: Pursuing Excellence in Theological Education* (Louisville, KY: Westminster/John Knox, 2002), pp. 24-25. Calian identifies healthy community relationships as the 'most outstanding factor' in whether students consider a school to be excellent.

costal experience, rather than simply being an individual matter, is 'embedded in the narratives, symbols, and practices of our Christian communities'.[71] This also anticipates the need for pastoral leadership development for shepherding congregations in core ecclesial practices (worship, witness, community, discipleship, and care). An ecclesial context for pastoral formation suggests the priority of *church* in relation to *academy* in their integration in seminary life.

Holistic Development

Formation for pastoral ministry, especially in light of a Wesleyan emphasis, is integrative and holistic. Persons preparing for ministry are viewed in their wholeness with holiness of head, heart, and hand as the goal. Orthodoxy, orthopathy, and orthopraxy become the agenda for leadership development.[72] Thus, story, call, character, and gifts must be integrated in formation.[73]

Biblical epistemology, Holiness theology, and 'Pentecostal' spirituality support the necessity of holistic pedagogies sufficiently formational, communal, and integrative to address the full dimensions of pastoral development. A narrative 'know-be-do' spirituality needs a narrative 'know-be-do' pedagogy and educational experience. Formation of the person over against informational agendas must be the goal for pastoral development.

Pneumatologically Oriented

Lack of reflection on the formational role of the Holy Spirit is a major deficiency in recent debate about theological education.[74] Within a Pentecostal formational context, responsiveness to the leading of the Spirit is fundamental. As pedagogy becomes hermeneutic, educational practice must reflect the dynamic role of the Spirit. All practices of development are exercised within the Spirit-filled community with gifts and graces dispersed to all participants and through all persons for one another. In this pedagogical process, the Spirit searches, guides, teaches, and reveals God's will and purpose as participants respond to the immediacy of the Spirit's presence.[75]

---

[71] Cartledge, *Practical Theology*, p. 49.

[72] Steve Land has proposed this agenda for Pentecostal discipleship. See Land, *Pentecostal Spirituality*, p. 184.

[73] Banks cites evidence that 'personal formation continues to have a lower priority than academic excellence and professional development'. See Banks, *Reenvisioning Theological Education*, p. 200.

[74] Robert Banks sees this deficiency as expressive of a larger lack of focus on the place of God and evidence of an inadequate theological approach to theological education. See Banks, *Reenvisioning Theological Education*, p. 63.

[75] See Jn 14.26; 16.5-15; 1 Cor. 2.10-14.

Reflecting continuity with an andragogical model, a Spirit-oriented teaching-learning process democratizes formation. Collaborative learning, mentoring, and resourcing by means of Spirit-gifts creates a dynamic, open-ended process. Life in the Spirit becomes the standard for pedagogical process and outcome.

Contextually Shaped

Discerning the connections between call, gifts, and context is also strategic to Pentecostal pastoral formation. Integrity and relevance in mission is contingent on capacities for contextual interpretation and discernment. Formational experience must take seriously matters of ministry context.[76] Real life contemporary issues of ministry must shape the teaching-learning process for pastoral leaders to develop the hermeneutical capacities for effective practice. This explains the Pentecostal Theological Seminary's use of the U.S. Congregational Life Survey to assess contextually the pastoral situation in the Church of God. This empirically-based data brings disciplined analysis of ministry practice concerns into the formational process.[77]

Use of andragogical teaching-learning strategies can support this contextual emphasis. When participants are provided opportunities for self-direction, sharing of experience, interactive learning, and problem-solving, contextual concerns immediately come to the forefront. An andragogical approach is congruent with practices of Spirit-filled community and ministry where all participants contribute from their giftedness.[78]

Missionally Driven

Pentecostal spirituality has God's mission at center. Passion for the Kingdom is passion for mission. Formation for pastoral leadership must engage the immediate (local) and distant (global) mission. A mission driven process engages participants in discerning how God is at work or desires to work in particular settings of ministry. Outcomes chosen

---

[76]Banks, *Reenvisioning Theological Education*, pp. 226-27. It seems to me Craig Dykstra's call for a focus on participation in constitutive 'practices' in theological education is close akin to Banks' missional proposal. See Craig R. Dykstra, 'Reconceiving Practice', in *Shifting Boundaries,* pp. 35-66. See also the emphasis on formation of pastoral leadership 'in their particular context' in Victor J. Klimoski, Kevin J. O'Neil, and Katarina M. Schuth, *Educating Leaders for Ministry: Issues and Responses* (Collegeville, MN: Liturgical Press, 2005), pp. 42-43. Mark Cartledge's argument for the value of empirical assessment of contextual issues also relates to this emphasis. See Cartledge, *Practical Theology*, pp. 61-62.

[77] See Bowers, *Portrait and Prospect.*

[78] *Ibid.*, p. 194. Banks argues for 'more participatory approaches to learning, in which students become more like junior partners in the learning-doing enterprise, rather than just pupils'.

for pastoral formation courses, experiences, or practices should serve this missional concern of the movement.[79]

Central to this emphasis is cultivating collaborative approaches to ministry issues in context. Through community experiences, community of faith groups, teamwork ministry, collaborative learning strategies, and mentoring relationships, students and pastors develop the abilities and inclination to be partners rather than competitors in mission. Seminary experiences, pastoral development programs, and other ministry training venues need to foster capacities for collaborating with others in support of contextually and communally discerned priorities of missional practice.[80]

Practice Centered

The various dimensions of pastoral formation identified must have pastoral *practice* as their goal and standard.[81] Persons are being trained to 'know-be-do' ministry – to lead Pentecostal congregations in the biblically, historically, and theologically shaped activities and experiences of faith and mission. Effective congregational leadership, therefore, must be the 'practice' trajectory of pastoral formation and the final bar of assessment. Theological education, in particular, should perhaps be a form of ministry 'in-service' training.[82] This priority has been reflected in the seminary's ministry practice requirements for students and development focus for project pastors.

While the Pentecostal tradition's emphasis on 'ministry that works' in the interest of prosecuting the Pentecostal mission informs this priority, the deeper concern is the integrity and viability of the Pentecostal movement.[83] Mark Cartledge comments in this regard:

Embedded in these practices are beliefs and values which doctrine seeks to

[79] See Anderson's 'memo' on the need for 'mission outcomes' in theological education in Ray S. Anderson, *The Shape of Practical Theology: Empowering Ministry with Theological Praxis* (Downers Grove, IL: InterVarsity, 2001), pp. 325-26.

[80] Anderson, *The Shape of Practical Theology*, pp. 127-86. See Banks discussion of the implications of a missional model of theological education.

[81] Various assessments of theological education have called for emphasis on cultivating needed 'practices', understood holistically. See for examples, Banks, *Reenvisioning Theological Education,* p. 226; and Ray S. Anderson, *The Shape*, p. 324-26.

[82] Banks, *Reenvisioning Theological Education*, p. 61. Banks does not see any proposal or seminary program that sufficiently places practice at the center. Recent findings by the Auburn Center for the Study of Theological Education concerning the inadequacy of 'practical skills' courses seem to confirm this need (Barbara Wheeler, 'Implications for ATS Deans from Auburn's Graduate Student Research', Presentation to the ATS Chief Academic Officers Society, 23 March 2007).

[83] Grant Wacker noted the dual emphasis on primitivism and pragmatism in Pentecostalism. See Grant Wacker, *Heaven Below: Early Pentecostals and American Culture* (Cambridge, MA: Harvard University Press, 2001).

articulate and defend against contesting claims. When communities do this they affirm their own identity over and against others. The Bible, often used in this context, is the 'property' of the Christian community that offers interpretations not in abstract but based upon practice. This scriptural world creates an interpretive framework and a basis from which and upon which believers can understand reality. In that sense it absorbs and recreates the world in which believers live. Believers therefore make the story of the Bible to be their story.[84]

'Practice' more broadly understood as a communally shaped and shared pattern of activity reflecting and cultivating the core aspects of spirituality is the visible ecclesial expression of the movement.[85] Thus, Pentecostal Theological Seminary faculty have recently identified 'Pentecostal worship, holy witness, and covenant community' as overarching practices of faith and mission. Leadership for such 'practice' is the heart of the pastoral vocation and, thus, should be the center of any model of Pentecostal pastoral formation.

As was discerned and experienced at the Pentecostal Theological Seminary from its earliest days – and as has been discovered by many other schools – forming pastoral leaders for this practice requires resources beyond those present in the seminary community. Maintaining an effective practice-centered pastoral formation process depends on a close practical and theological relationship between the seminary and the church. Certainly, the seminary must provide a practice-attentive curriculum with opportunities for personal formation, mentoring, and reflective experiences of leadership in 'practices'. Ultimately, this agenda can only be realized with an ecology of congregations, mentoring pastors, and denominational leaders committed and invested in a distinctively Pentecostal model and process of pastoral formation.

Conclusion

The goal of this paper has been to demonstrate how the formational practices of the Pentecostal Theological Seminary's pastoral excellence project represent a distinctive model of Pentecostal pastoral formation. With the seminary's core curricular commitments as theological and educational backdrop, reflection on actual practice led to the identification of the theological-formational dimensions of such a model. These dimensions were judged to be particularly supportive of Pentecostal spirituality and mission and, therefore, necessary to any pastoral formation model that would be truly Pentecostal.

---

[84] Cartledge, *Practical Theology*, p. 49.
[85] See Dykstra, 'Reconceiving Practice', pp. 35-66.

Questions for Discussion

1. How important to Pentecostal mission is a distinctive pastoral formation process?
2. How adequate are the proposed 'dimensions' set forth in this paper? What needs further attention or elaboration?
3. How might the Pentecostal Theological Seminary collaborate with other Church of God and Pentecostal institutions to advance a missionally strategic model and ecology for pastoral formation?

★★★★★★★★★★★★★★★★★★

Abstract

Earlier perspectives on Pentecostalism viewed the movement as little more than fundamentalist Christianity 'plus' speaking in tongues. More recent analyses, however, have affirmed particular and distinctive Pentecostal *theological* formulations and spiritualities. This development has given rise to many distinctive 'Pentecostal' projects in biblical studies, hermeneutics, homiletics, missiology, theology, counseling, leadership, and formation. Paralleling the emergence of distinctive Pentecostal scholarship has been the birth and development of indigenous Pentecostal theological education. Increasingly, Pentecostals are concerned to provide graduate ministerial training grounded in their particular spiritual and theological vision.

In the mid 1970's, the Church of God Theological Seminary (Cleveland, TN) developed a community of faith model of theological education around relationships, experiences, and practices integral to Pentecostal spirituality. Formation of distinctively (Wesleyan) Pentecostal ministry and scholarship was the goal of that effort. With the award of Lilly Endowment 'Sustaining Pastoral Excellence' and 'Making Connections' grants, the Seminary has had the opportunity to export revisioned core elements of its model to practicing pastors (many without seminary education) in the interest of Pentecostal pastoral excellence. This refined model is organized around formational practices of spiritual retreat and conferencing, table fellowship, communal prayer and worship, sharing testimony, making and keeping covenant, discerning missional context, personal assessment and development planning, collaborative learning, mentoring, and resourcing, shared theological praxis, and congregational and missional collaboration. This study describes how these practices represent the heart of a Pentecostal model of pastoral formation.

13

Spirited Vestments:
Why the Anointing is Not Enough

Cheryl Bridges Johns[*]

In many ways Pentecostalism is not a culture that overtly suppresses women's abilities and gifts. Women have been affirmed along with men as recipients of the same Spirit who distributes to them gifts and callings. But because of the lack of clear theological reflection and the movement's own assimilation into the larger culture and into the conservative Evangelical ethos, the environment for women is often characterized by ambiguity. As women try to make sense of their identity they become confused.

In regards to women, Pentecostalism is a culture of both exclusion and embrace.[1] Within this tradition, women experience the acceptance of God and a deep sense of his calling, but when it comes to implications of this knowledge, there is little external validation in the life of the church. Pentecostal women are embraced by God but excluded from the priestly centers of ecclesial power. Hence the dilemma; for how does one serve God apart from the church?

It is my contention that at the dawn of the twenty-first century we can no longer rely upon proof texts such as Joel 2.28 for support of women's calling into ministry. This passage represents the embrace, namely that God pours his Spirit out on all flesh. However, heavy reliance upon this text has done little to change the ontological status of women.

The paradox of exclusion and embrace is backed by a strong tradition that was woven into the fabric of twentieth-century Pentecostal-

[*] Cheryl Bridges Johns (Ph.D., Southern Baptist Theological Seminary) is Professor of Discipleship and Christian Formation at the Pentecostal Theological Seminary, Cleveland, TN, USA.
[1] I am using the terms 'exclusion and embrace' from Miroslav Volf, *Exclusion and Embrace* (Nashville: Abingdon, 1996).

ism. It is now time to examine closely how it came to be and to move forward into a new era. Moving forward will mean going beyond the prophetic model for women in ministry with its proof texts. It will mean re-constructing the meaning of being human based upon a Trinitarian reflection of the *imago Dei*. The work ahead will call for a robust re-visioning of God as feminine/masculine. In addition, we must face squarely the issues of personhood, asking the question, 'What does it mean to be human – male and female?'

It is not my intention to belittle the strong historical precedent of the prophethood of believers within Pentecostalism. However, it is my intention to show that women are ghettoized into the prophetic while men are free to be both prophetic and priestly.

Pentecostal women can no longer bear the prophetic burden. It is the heavy mantle that is weighing us down and causing us to drown in self destruction. Prophetic mantles are such colorful and lively attire, but they kill the human spirit when women are denied the right to be vested with priestly garments of authority. Personhood cannot be denied in favor of prophethood.

Before she drowns, weighed down by the trappings of exclusion and embrace, Ophelia needs to be rescued and provided safe space for the reconstruction of life and recapitulation of the *imago Dei*. This endeavor calls for us to adopt, in the ensuing months and years, a 'preferential option for women', and to develop a comprehensive Pentecostal relational theology of life in which women and men can live together in holy communion. Catherine Keller's assertion that 'perichoresis begins at home',[2] serves as the foundation of this paper.

The Prophetic Ghetto

> Let the good sisters feel at perfect liberty to preach the gospel, pray for the sick or well, testify, exhort, etc., but humbly hold themselves aloof from taking charge of the governmental affairs.
>
> A.J. Tomlinson[3]

During its early days the Pentecostal movement provided free spaces for those who were marginalized by traditional culture constraints. In particular, African Americans and women experienced the baptism of the Holy Spirit as liberation. The Azusa Street Revival serves as the paradigmatic heart of this great awakening.

---

[2] Catherine Keller, 'Pneumatic Nudges: The Theology of Moltmann, Feminism and the Future', in the *Future of Theology* (ed. Miroslav Volf; Grand Rapids: Eerdmans, 1996), p. 147.

[3] A.J. Tomlinson, 'Paul's Statements Considered', *Church of God Evangel* 6 (18 Sept. 1915), p. 4.

Boundaries that were long established by society, namely that blacks and whites should be separate, women should be silent and the poor and the rich should remain apart were broken down at Azusa and within the movement as a whole. Clearly, God was doing a new thing.

This new thing, however, was difficult to actualize in a world that did not affirm the radical values of the fledging movement. The tension between the ideal and the pragmatic, what Grant Wacker calls the 'primitive and the pragmatic',[4] has remained within the movement. This is especially true in regards to the status of women.

Prophetic vs. Priestly Ministry

Charles Barfoot and Gerald Sheppard's insightful article 'Prophetic vs. Priestly Religion',[5] is helpful in understanding how women became ghettoized within the prophetic realm. Barfoot and Sheppard utilize Max Weber's premise that religion among the disprivileged classes often exhibits equality to women, but that as these movements institutionalize they emphasize the male monopolized priestly functions.

Barfoot and Sheppard identify two distinct stages of Pentecostalism: prophetic and priestly. The prophetic period (1907-1930) was characterized by a strong belief in the 'Last Days' and the calling of both women and men to fulfill the Great Commission. The emphasis during this time was on personal callings that were known through manifestations of the charismata. Yet, while women were given freedom to preach the gospel they were often forbidden from fulfilling priestly/governmental functions.

As the second phase of the movement took effect, more formal actions were taken to prevent women from full ordination. For example, in 1931 The Assemblies of God passed a resolution to ordain women only as 'evangelists' and to prohibit them from administering the ordinances of the church. A clear example of the emerging distinctions between the prophetic and the priestly can be seen in the joint ministry of Robert and Marie Brown, who served as co-pastors during the 1930's. In 1931 at the meeting of the General Council of the Assemblies of God, Robert Brown expressed the prevailing view regarding prophetic and priestly functions:

> (He) could not help noticing that in the scriptures there was no woman in the priesthood and none in the apostolic ministry. God chose men. He stated that his wife always refrained from 'acts of priesthood.'

---

[4] Grant Wacker, *Heaven Below* (Cambridge, MA: Harvard University Press, 2003).

[5] Charles H. Barfoot and Gerald T. Sheppard, 'Prophetic vs. Priestly Religion: The Changing Role of Women Clergy in Classical Pentecostal Churches', *RevRR* 22.1 (Sept. 1980), pp. 2-17.

> He said he hated to see women put on a white garment and try to look like angels, and go into the baptismal pool to baptize converts.[6]

Agreeing with Brown, the General Council passed resolutions that banned women from priestly functions.[7] Although the Assemblies of God removed these restrictions in 1935, the distain of women 'who put on a white garment' remained deep.

The research of David Roebuck is also helpful in understanding the development of the culture of exclusion and embrace within Pentecostalism. Roebuck points out that within the Church of God there was never a 'golden age' for women in ministry. Rather, from the very beginning of the denomination women's roles were limited to the prophetic realm.[8]

The Angel in the House[9]

Women clergy were further ghettoized due to the domestication of womanhood that took place in American culture following World War II. During this time, the prevailing images of women, both religious and secular, were predominately domestic. For instance, from 1952 to 1956 the *Church of God Evangel* had a regular section entitled 'The Homemaker's Chapel'. In this column, women were encouraged to be good keepers of their homes and loving wives and mothers. The irony of the name of the column should not escape us. Home is linked to chapel and in doing so sacred space and vocation within that sacred space is domesticated.

Within Pentecostalism woman as home-maker soon overshadowed the prophetic calling to the harvest fields in evangelism. Roebuck paints an interesting picture of what occurred during this era:

> because the very fabric of American society was threatened by communism from without and the Church of God proclaimed the importance of God's order as established in creation, particularly the submission of women in this order. By elevating certain roles of women, particularly those related to home and family, women were constricted into a safe, ordered existence. Women in ministry were casualties of that war.[10]

---

[6] *Pentecostal Evangel* (1931), p. 5. Quoted in Barfoot and Sheppard, 'Prophetic vs. Priestly Religion', p. 12.

[7] Under the leadership of A.J. Tomlinson the Church of God made rapid movement to restrict the role of women in priestly/governmental affairs of the Church. As early as 1908 the decision was made to exclude women from being ordained as deaconesses.

[8] David G. Roebuck, 'Limiting Liberty: The Church of God and Women Ministers, 1886-1996', Ph.D. dissertation, Vanderbilt University, May 1997.

[9] I am using the title of Virginia Woolf's essay 'Professions for Women', in *Death of the Mother and Other Essays* (New York: Harcourt, Brace and Jovanovich, 1942), pp. 236-38.

[10] Roebuck, 'Limiting Liberty', pp. 171-72.

These two images, prophetic and domestic prevailed during the 20th century, with the domestic gradually overshadowing the prophetic in the latter half of the century.

It should be noted that many Pentecostal women were among the working poor, which created dissonance between the official images and reality. In the early days of the movement women called into ministry longed to be set free from the restraints of work in order to enter the harvest fields of evangelism. For instance, in 1910, Mollie Bates, in her letter published in *The Evening Light and Church of God Evangel,* revealed her struggles:

> I work in the mill every day, and have been for a number of years, but I feel that the Lord is calling me out to work for him. But it seems so much for me to step out on the promises of God, trusting Him for everything.... If the Lord wants me to go out into His vineyard and work for Him, instead of working in the mills, His will be done; I will go.[11]

By the 1940's women were encouraged to leave the workplace, not because they were needed for the Last Days Harvest, but to be keepers at home. Roebuck points out that during World War II, when women were being encouraged to enter the factories, 'Church of God rhetoric promoting mothers in the home rang loud and clear, so much so that previous recognition that some women might be forced to work was almost inaudible.'[12]

Following World War II the call for women to stay in the home was intensified. Pentecostal periodicals regularly ran articles that blamed the changes taking place in society on working women. In the latter part of the 20th century, Pentecostal leaders and their wives lauded the virtues of the home, criticizing the women's liberation movement and lifting up the submission of women to their husbands. As one woman wrote in the *Church of God Evangel,* 'Why try to be something God never intended you to be? Be a wife, be a housekeeper, be a mother and be glad and rejoice because God has seen fit to bless you with a good husband and living children.'[13] By this time the voices of women like Mollie Bates who longed to leave the workforce for God's army in the kingdom, had all but disappeared.

During this era the evangelist/prophet was further ghettoized and became, in some middle class environments, a strange relic of the past.

---

[11] Mollie Bates, *The Evening Light and Church of God Evangel* 1.18 (Nov. 1, 1910), p. 56 as quoted in Roebuck, 'Limiting Liberty', p. 186.

[12] Roebuck, 'Limiting Liberty', p. 225.

[13] Quoted in Mrs. James Franklin, 'The Women's Page: The Position of Wives', *Church of God Evangel* 53.12 (May 20, 1963), p. 11.

It was now possible to grow up in a Pentecostal church never hearing a woman preach.

Today women desiring to enter ministry have few role models. The evangelists-prophets are almost extinct, and likewise, priestly images for women are largely limited to mainline Protestant churches. In addition, there is another wave of traditionalism and feminist backlash within American culture. The domestic image is still powerful, fueled by organizations such as Focus on the Family. Conservative Evangelicals continue to promote 'biblical roles of men and women' that restrict the ministry of women. Herein is the current dilemma of identity diffusion. The journey to selfhood is considered unbiblical and unfeminine.

In spite of the obstacles toward full humanization and full ministerial authorization, there is still hope for a future wherein our daughters will live 'both magnificently and scripturally.'[14] This hope is contained in the Triune life, revealed in Scripture and made possible by the power of the Holy Spirit.

The Imago Dei: An Evangelical Debate

It is interesting to note that the current debate within Evangelicalism over women's roles interfaces with issues of the identity of the Trinity and with the meaning of the *imago Dei*. In recent decades there has been a turn by Evangelical theologians, such as Wayne Gudrum, John Piper, Andreas Köstenberger,[15] toward grounding women's identity not just in scriptural passages of submission, but also within the nature of God. This turn requires re-visioning the doctrine of God away from the historically orthodox understanding of three co-equal persons toward a view of 'functional subordinationism,' in which the temporal role of subordination of the Son seen in the incarnation is read back into the immanent Trinity.[16]

Kenneth Giles points out that these 'complementarian-hierarchical' Evangelicals have attempted to create a stark separation in the opera-

---

[14] These terms are those which Hollis Gause uses to describe the biblical status of women. They convey the possibility of an authentic selfhood that is grounded in creation. See Kimberly Ervin Alexander and R. Hollis Gause, *Women in Leadership: A Pentecostal Perspective* (Cleveland, TN: Center for Pentecostal Leadership and Care, 2006), p. 45.

[15] John Piper & Wayne Grudem, eds., *Recovering Biblical Manhood and Womanhood: A Response to Evangelical Feminism* (Wheaton, IL: Crossway, 1991); Andreas J. Köstenberger, Thomas R. Schreiner and H. Scott Baldwin, eds., *Women in the Church: A Fresh Analysis of 1 Timothy 2:9-15* (Grand Rapids: Baker, 1995).

[16] Kevin Giles, *The Trinity and Subordinationism: The Doctrine of God & the Contemporary Gender Debate* (Downers Grove, IL: InterVarsity, 2002). Giles offers the best treatment of contemporary Evangelical views on subordinationism.

tions, works and functions of the three divine persons. In doing so, they resort to the ancient Arian controversy, which attempted to subordinate eternally the Son in his being/essence/nature to the Father and therefore in his work or role with the Father.

Complementarian-hierarchical Evangelicals would argue that they are making a distinction between form and function, however, as Giles notes, 'the unity of being and action among the Father, Son and Spirit is a constant theme in the development of the orthodox doctrine of the Trinity ... Who the triune God is (his being) and what the triune God does (his acts) are one'.[17]

It seems that Evangelicals who speak of 'ontological subordination' are more honest than those who attempt to separate role and being. Foremost among the 'ontological subordinationists' is George Knight, who speaks of a 'chain of subordination' within the Godhead.[18] Robert Letham calls for 'subordination in subsistence', making a case for the eternal subordination of the Son within the immanent Trinity because of the subordination of the Son in the incarnation. He writes, 'the revelation of the economic Trinity truly indicates the ontological Trinity'.[19]

Giles makes the point that the driving motivation for Letham's case for the eternal subordination of the Son is his concern to uphold the permanent 'headship' of men.[20] The title of Letham's article should be a clue as to his main concern: 'The Man-Woman Debate'.

Contemporary Evangelicals who appeal to the doctrine of the Trinity to support their belief in the headship of man are making great efforts to keep viable a patriarchal worldview. Knowing that to ground woman's subordination in her inferior nature, as has often been the case in history, would be problematic in contemporary culture that emphasizes equality, they have emphasized 'role' distinctions over nature distinctions. Giles makes clear the real intentions of the hierarchical-complementarian viewpoint:

> for the hierarchical-complementarian, the word *difference* is a code word. It means something that the hierarchical-complementarian cannot ever say or ever admit. In the truly historic position, exegetes and theologians said God made women inferior; the contemporary hierarchical-complementarian emphatically denies this. In our age this an unacceptable idea for anyone to promulgate. The women's revolution has forced men to give up using the word *inferior* or even suggesting

[17] Giles, *'Trinity and Subordinationism,* p. 14.

[18] George Knight, *New Testament Teaching on the Role Relationship of Men and Women* (Grand Rapids: Baker, 1977), p. 56.

[19] Robert Letham, 'The Man-Woman Debate: Theological Comment', *WTJ* 52 (1990), pp. 65-78.

[20] Giles, *Trinity and Subordinationism,* p. 77.

the idea. What hierarchical-complementarians say instead is that God made women 'different' from men. But when we ask how they are different, they mention only one matter: men have been given the ruling role and women the subordinate role in the home and the church.[21]

The move toward the language of 'roles' first appeared in the 1970's. During this time there was the push for the Equal Rights Amendment and a flourishing of Evangelical feminist literature such as Letha Scanzoni and Nancy Hardesty's *All We're Meant to Be.*[22] In the 1980's, Evangelicals such as Aida Besconson Spencer attempted to ground the equality of women in creation, noting that the subordination of woman came only as a result of the Fall and the curse. Spencer makes a case for redemption in Christ as reversing the curse.[23]

In response to 'Evangelical feminists', those advocating the complementarian-hierarchical view of humankind attempt to make their case that the distinction between the sexes is grounded in creation and not the Fall. They move from a hierarchical view of the Trinity, with the Father at the top to a hierarchical view of humankind with the man at the top. Just as God commands and the Son obeys, so too men are to command and women to obey. This chain of command is often referred to as 'the divine order'. There is a 'divine order' in the Trinity, 'divine order' in creation, 'divine order' in the home, and 'divine order' in the church.

As has already been noted, what drives the complementarian-hierarchical view is 'an all-consuming concern to maintain the "headship" of men'.[24] It is a passion that has led, as Giles aptly observes, 'to the most dangerous of all errors – the corruption of the primary doctrine of Christianity, the doctrine of God'.[25]

Historically, the subordination of woman has focused more on her inferior nature. Augustine viewed subordination as intrinsic to original creation, while proposing that sin and death were not. For him the image of God refers to the soul in its rational nature and its representation of God's domination over the natural world. Men possess the capacity for dominion, but women, representing nature or the body, are to be under dominion. Women, therefore, lack the image of God

[21] Giles, *Trinity and Subordinationism*, p. 185.

[22] Letha Scanzoni and Nancy Hardesty, *All We're Meant to Be* (Waco, TX: Word Books, 1974).

[23] Aida Besconson Spencer, *Beyond the Curse: Women Called to Ministry* (Nashville: Thomas Nelson, 1985).

[24] Giles, *Trinity and Subordinationism*, p. 115.

[25] Giles, *Trinity and Subordinationism*, p. 115.

and are related to God's image only by their inclusion under male headship.[26]

This understanding of the *imago Dei,* which has dominated the Western Church, is related to a view of God heavily influenced by neo-Platonic thought. In this world-view God is ontologically static, endowed with timeless characteristics of immutability, omnipotence and omniscience. God is 'pure being'. Humans are messy, material, and full of passion.

Along with the understanding that God is ontologically static is the elevation of reason as the defining element of the *imago Dei.* Commenting on Genesis 1, Martin Luther writes, 'Although Eve was a most extraordinary creature, similar to Adam with respect to the image of God ... still she is a woman ... She does not equal the glory and worthiness of the male.'[27]

The view of women as ontologically inferior is based upon a belief that women are less rational, more emotive, more sensual (material). Maleness equals rationality and maleness conveys most fully the *imago Dei.* Implications of this stereotyping are abundant in Christian literature, even well into the 20th century. In his essay in *Women in the Church,* Thomas Schreiner asserts that women should not teach because they are 'less prone than men to see the importance of doctrinal formulations, especially when it comes to the issue of identifying heresy and making a stand for the truth'. Daniel Doriani echoes the same sentiment in his analysis of Paul's comment that 'Adam was not deceived but the woman was deceived'. According to Doriani, Paul is teaching that 'God created women with an orientation towards relationships more than analysis'.[28]

The view of women as more relational and less rational has created severe limitations on women's roles in society and the church. Government is to be run by rational agents (men) whose emotions do not get in the way of their abilities to govern. Likewise, in the church, governing is to be in the hands of men.

Today, the argument gets more nuanced with the insertion of the language of 'roles'. However, as pointed out above, this language is

---

[26] Augustine, *De Trinitate* 7.7.10. See Rosemary Radford Ruether, 'Christian Anthropology and Gender', in *The Future of Theology* (ed. Miroslav Volf; Grand Rapids: Eerdmans, 1996). See also Kari Borresen, *Subordination and Equivalence: The Nature and Role of Women in Augustine and Thomas Aquinas* (Washington, DC: University Press of America, 1981).

[27] Martin Luther, *Lectures on Genesis Chapter 1–5,* pp. 51-52, quoted in Giles, *Trinity and Subordinationism,* p. 151.

[28] Thomas Doriani, 'History of Interpretation of 1 Timothy 2', in *Recovering Biblical Manhood and Womanhood,* p. 266.

only a cloak for the deep and long held belief in the inherent inferiority of women.

It is my assertion that Pentecostals did not fully address the issue of ontological identity during the early days of the movement. Instead, they took the prevailing view of the inferior ontological status of women and over-laid it with a pneumatology of power. God was pouring his Spirit out upon all flesh, including women. But this out-pouring was intended for functional, not ontological status. Women could prophesy. After all, it was not the agency of the woman involved in prophetic ministry. It was the agency of the Holy Spirit. Under the anointing of the Holy Spirit women could overcome their inferior status and thereby be effective in preaching the gospel.

Pentecostal leaders such as A.J. Tomlinson held firmly to the under-standing of the governing nature of men. While he acknowledged that women were fit to preach the gospel (under the anointing of the Holy Spirit), Tomlinson believed they were to be excluded from positions of administration and voice in the business of the church.

By focusing on Joel 2.28, Pentecostals failed adequately to ground women's empowerment in creation. This failure led them to look to Evangelical theologians for their theology of the ontological status of women. The result was that, during the 20th century, Pentecostals perpetuated an ideology of the ontological inferiority of women while at the same time advocating their liberty to preach. Few have ques-tioned this bi-polar situation.

Only recently have Pentecostal theologians begun to address the on-tological status of women. Hollis Gause, in a recent book co-edited with Kimberly Alexander, grounds his view of women's role in leader-ship in creation:

> Rather than argue that woman is equal to man, we argue that in their humanity (i.e., being in the divine image), they are the same. We will also argue that while the fall defaced and obscured the divine, it did not destroy it because of God's grace. The aim of grace is the restora-tion of this image for humankind through Jesus Christ. The image of God is restored in His life, death and resurrection. Since this image *is* restored in Christ, no human hierarchal systems apply to the place and privilege of the redeemed in Christ.[29]

Gause bases his view that leadership in the church should not be an issue of gender, but of vocation. All offices of the church should be open to women. He grounds this belief in restored creation in Christ and in the nature of the Trinity. Asserting that 'the church is a com-

---

[29] Gause in Kimberly Ervin Alexander and R. Hollis Gause, *Women in Leadership: A Pentecostal Perspective* (Cleveland, TN: Center for Pentecostal Leadership and Care, 2006), p. 25.

munity of love patterned after the community of the Holy Trinity',
Gause notes that 'the relationship between the Father, Son and Holy
Spirit is a relationship of equal divine Persons (the same in substance
and equal in power and glory) who commit Themselves to each other
for the fulfillment of divine work in relationship with creation'.[30]

Furthermore, in regards to submission, Gause makes the following
observation:

> Christ came to do the will of the Father (Hebrews 10:7-9). In the ful-
> fillment of that mission, Jesus said, 'My Father is greater than I' (John
> 14:28). In this pattern of operation, 'the head of Christ is God' (1 Co-
> rinthians 11:3). The Holy Spirit comes into the world as the Comfor-
> ter in Christ's place, because He has been sent by both the Father
> (John 14:16,17) and the Son (John 15:26). He declares the things of
> the Father and the Son (John 16:12-16). The Father fulfills the desires
> of the Son. There is no greater example of this than the sending of the
> Holy Spirit: I will pray the Father, and He will send you another Pa-
> raclete/Comforter' (John 14:16,26). The point of these observations is
> that the submission of the members of the Trinity to the will of the
> others is a submission among equal divine Persons.[31]

Toward a Viable Future

As has been previously stated, the prophetic-evangelistic model for
women is dying out within North American Pentecostalism. The future of women within the movement does not necessarily lie in re-
capturing Joel 2.28. The direction that Gause took in his research is
indicative of where we need to go.

What follows is a brief overview of some of the issues that I believe
need addressing.

First, in light of the resurgence of a hierarchical view of Trinity
within Evangelicalism, Pentecostals need to offer their own counter
responses. The hierarchical view has been popularized in Christian
media, books and seminars.

In regards to Trinitarian reflection, images of God as relational and
dynamic, existing in both co-inherence and unity but also otherness
and distinctiveness, are important for Pentecostal theological reflection.

For women, who traditionally define themselves in terms of a relational web or a matrix of relationships, it is liberating to image God as
constituted and defined relationally. In this way the *imago Dei* becomes
a mirror to see themselves reflected in the light of the Divine light.
God is love, so much so that he emptied himself of the glory that was

---

[30] Gause, *Women in Leadership*, p. 67.
[31] Gause, *Women in Leadership*, p. 67.

rightfully his and took upon himself the form of a suffering human. It is this God, the one who loves to the point of self-denial and suffering, whose image shines forth in the creation of women and men.

It should be noted, however, that the alternative to envisioning God as Transcendent Rational Substance is not 'radical relationalism'. In this paradigm there is the danger of God fusing with the creation in 'pure immanence'. In such a model relationalism threatens 'difference'. There is the need to maintain a sense of divine immutability and sovereignty on the part of God, while at the same time imaging God as the one who opens himself to the mysterious and messy dynamics of relationships.

For women's development it is crucial to understand 'difference' within the *imago Dei,* just as it is important to understand the dimensions of personal relationality. I concur with Catherine Keller on the matter when she states that

> the ongoing formation of selves as either insulated from relation ('masculine' and 'rational') or lost in relation ('feminine' and 'mystical') – emulating merely transcendent or merely immanent God-forms – has hypnotic, stereotypic, force. If indulged, it will continuously sabotage the solidarities and coalitions by which we might work out our differences in responsible relation.[32]

There is the need in imaging humankind and in imaging God to maintain the dialectic of otherness-transcendence and relatedness-immanence. Moltmann calls this dialectic 'immanent transcendence' and uses it as the lynchpin of his pneumatology.

Miroslav Volf observes that this notion of pure relationality eliminates the soteriological dialectic between 'I' and 'not-I.' As a consequence the 'I' dissolves in its relations and becomes the 'not-I'.[33] To express the 'I'-'not I' dialectic, Volf proposes the category of personal interiority. It is his assessment that 'this category is originally at home in the doctrine of Trinity, where it describes the mutual indwelling of divine persons. The one person is internal to the other persons without suspending their personhood.'[34]

Volf's assessment of the notion of pure relationality is of particular importance in regards to issues of female identity. Historically women have been enculturated into an existence of pure relationality, dissolving the 'I' into the 'not I,' often negating their personhood for the sake of relationships. It is important that women develop and retain the 'I'. Only then can they be in the joyful but painful dialectic of true relationality.

[32] Catherine Keller, 'The Theology of Moltmann, Feminism and the Future', p. 148.
[33] Volf, *After Our Likeness,* p. 187.
[34] Volf, *After Our Likeness,* p. 187.

It can be concluded that a relational Trinitarian theology is a fruitful place for Pentecostals in assessing the identity of women and men as created in the image of God. Questions remain about the relational character of women and the rational character of men. However, these questions are best put into a full spectrum of the *imago Dei* rather than in a dichotomizing and subordinating system. When differences are placed on a continuum rather than in a bi-polar scheme, women are freed to move toward the rational side and men are free to move into the relational domain. This imagery is reflected in the Trinitarian life, where there is freedom to direct, freedom to submit, freedom to love and freedom to judge. No one person of the Trinity bears the burden of judging and no one Person bears the burden of love. No one person of the Trinity bears the burden of directing and no one Person bears the burden of submitting. Mutual life is reflected in the freedom to be both the 'I' and the 'not I'.

Male/Female Elements of Being in the Image of God

Just as we cannot create a stark separation in the operations, works and functions of the three Divine Persons, we cannot separate God with masculine vs. feminine imagery.

The tradition found in Syriac Christianity offers rich imagery of the Holy Spirit as creator/nurturer of life. Pentecostals may be tempted to take up the Holy Spirit as feminine, but I do not believe that in the long run such imagery is helpful. It may lead to another 'subordinating' paradigm, locating the work of the Holy Spirit as being sent by the Father and Son as indicative of the subordinate role of women. Feminizing the Holy Spirit also leaves us open to image the Father in rational terms and the Holy Spirit in emotive imagery. This split has been part of the problem within Pentecostalism. The prophetic image available to women retained the emotive side of Pentecostal faith, while the rational, judicial side was made available only to males. In a very real sense, when women were ghettoized into the prophetic realm, the Holy Spirit was also ghettoized away from the governmental and administrative functions of the church.

The other possibility in imaging God is to neuter the Godhead. While it is true that God is Spirit and above any anthropomorphic images, neutering God leaves us without a full-blown image of being human – male and female – created in the image of God.

The alternative is to image God as masculine, God as feminine and to locate masculine/feminine within the fullness of the Godhead. In doing so, we avoid the God image being split and can speak of 'the female element of being' and 'the masculine element of being'.

Object relations theory is helpful toward understanding the mysterious depth of our subjective-objective God images. Object relations theory assists us in understanding how God is both public and private, transcendent and immanent. We see how God images function both positively and negatively. God can be imaged through culture, family, church and tradition. These images of God are necessary and provide the basic 'stuff' of our theology. What is important for us is to see is the power of construction held within human hands.

Acknowledging the power of human construction in the God image does not take away from the God who is, just as our children imaging us and constructing us as mother and father does not take away from our own identity. We are apart from their construction. But for them, we cannot exist apart from their creative and ongoing imaging of us. We are at the same time constructed and apart from construction. God is also at the same time constructed and apart from construction.

The research of D.W. Winnicott, the originator of the British tradition of 'object relation theory' of psychoanalysis, is of particular service in understanding how our imaging God is a dynamic process involving both objective and subjective dimensions. Implicit in Winnicott's theory is a vision of how the feminine mode of being is primal to constructing viable images of self and of God.

Ann Belford Ulanov's research into the theological implications of Winnicott elaborates and continues exploration into not only the female element of being but also the male element of being. Ulanov shows how both elements are critically important in developing personhood and in developing an adequate God image.[35]

Ulanov points out that Winnicott finds the female element of being in all of us, male and female alike. 'It establishes being. Without it, we do not cohere around a central core to unfurl in relation to others in the world. Instead, we split into a true but hidden self and a false self that protects the core but also seals it up.'[36]

The female element of being comes from our earliest experiences with the maternal care-giver (although this person may be a male). The mother's preoccupation with the infant and her body-to-body care allows us to 'dwell with unity with our subjective-object, not yet differentiated as a separate self but in a state of identity with the other... Here "we exist". The "I" is yet to come.'[37]

Women have long been associated with the body, giving care of infants at birth, caring for bodies of their children, loving the bodies of

---

[35] Ann Belford Ulanov, *Finding Space: Winnicott, God, and Psychic Reality* (Louisville: Westminster John Knox, 2001).
[36] Ulanov, *Finding Space*, p. 68.
[37] Ulanov, *Finding Space*, p. 68.

their husbands, caring for the aging bodies of parents and preparing the dead for burial. It is interesting to see the integration of the female element of being in the life of Jesus. His mother gave him the primal sense of unity and care, body-to-body love, 'wrapping him in swaddling clothes'. Later, it was Nicodemus, who first came to Jesus for 'academic discussion' (John 3), who entered the female element of being when he came forward claiming the body of Jesus, touching him, body-to-body, wrapping his body for burial. The women who later came to the tomb could not fulfill the 'womanly duties' because of the resurrection. Instead they were commissioned to witness, a male function in their society. Jesus displayed the female element of being in the institution of the Eucharist, observes Ulanov, 'There connection between God and humanity occurs in a body-to-body communication.... Thus he equates himself with basic food on which we depend to survive.'[38]

Augustine helped turn the feminine body-to-body role over to the church. For Augustine, it was the arms of mother church that received the baptized infant, nurturing the infant into the faith and life. Further development of the doctrine of Mary located the feminine in her role as mediator and intercessor. Both of these developments, feminizing the church and highlighting the role of Mary as mother, further separated the feminine from the image of God.

If we retain the female element of being within the life of God we highlight the state of unity and co-inherence of the Trinity. Furthermore, the female element of being is seen in God as source of life and the ground of all being. 'God's thriving, self-communicating gift of life'[39] is seen in the feminine element of being.

The male element of being accents the separateness of I and other. We may identify with the other, but we do not become the other. Our ability 'to stand back from relationships, explore potentialities and limits' and to 'abstract from our experience of the other, generalize, compare, contrast our experiences,' are part of the male element of being.[40]

For Winnicott, the male element integrates into the presence and symbol of the father. Here a blueprint of the self is offered to the child.[41] Both males and females are in need of this blueprint of the self. Males do not offer the self only to male children. The self is a gift for all of humanity. The male element of being is therefore part of being a whole person, male and female. Females are in need of agency of the

---

[38] Ulanov, *Finding Space,* p. 79.
[39] Ulanov, *Finding Space,* p. 74.
[40] Ulanov, *Finding Space,* p. 70.
[41] Ulanov, *Finding Space,* p. 71.

ability to push through with instinctual energy toward the fulfillment
of goals. When the male element of being is off limits to daughters,
they fuse into the 'not I' of the feminine, never separating and indivi-
duating into a separate entity.

The male element of being is found in the human construction of
monotheism. I would agree with Ulanov in her assessment that
'(R)eligion does not spring from repression of the father, whom we
relocate in the heavens through projection, as Freud contends. Instead,
both ideas, of father and monotheism, represent the world's first attempts to recognize the individuality of man, of woman, of every individual.'[42]

Furthermore, the male element of being is found in the Trinitarian
life as otherness and distinctiveness. It is found in the divine immutability and sovereignty of God.

Both the female and male elements of being are crucial in understanding the meaning of being made in the image of God. God is large
enough and mysterious enough to contain both masculine and feminine identities without having to ascribe these identities too tightly.
The language of 'Father' and 'Son', while helpful in reading the text
written in a patriarchal world, does not define our limit for expressing
the fullness of God. These images reveal an aspect of God that is helpful and necessary for salvation. Yet in order for women to know that
they are created in God's image, a fuller picture has to be developed.
The Scriptures witness to this fuller picture, and by the power of the
Holy Spirit we are able to receive it into our lives.

Giles makes the point that a 'contextual evangelical hermeneutic' is
necessary for a proper reading of Scripture. He observes:

> A contextual evangelical hermeneutic is not a hermeneutic *determined*
> by culture. It is a theology which acknowledges that God places his
> people in an ever-changing world, which is continually throwing up
> new questions. Change and disputation always drive us back to Scrip-
> ture to re-read what it says. Finding ourselves in a new cultural con-
> text – and possibly challenged by other Christians who disagree with us
> – we invariably discover things we had hitherto not seen in Scripture.
> This reminds us that, as we've seen in church history, the Scriptures,
> inspired and illuminated by the Holy Spirit, can speak afresh in every
> age. The Bible can give answers to questions it does not directly ad-
> dress, and it can give new answers to old questions.[43]

Giles's point correlates with what many of us refer to in developing
a 'Pentecostal hermeneutic'. This hermeneutic understands the text as
Spirit-Word, thereby making the agency of the Holy Spirit critical in

---

[42] Ulanov, *Finding Space*, p. 71.
[43] Giles, *Trinity and Subordinationism*, p. 249.

interpretation. The agency of the Holy Spirit is manifest not only in individual interpretation, but in the life of the church as it discerns the will of God in light of the biblical text. Such agency gives the Word power to remake and reform the church, while giving the community of faith the opportunity of coming together around the Word. The issues of slavery and women, in particular, have been re-dressed by the church, allowing the Bible to speak with authority and to critique culture.

The Next Steps

The anointing does make the difference! However, women need the anointing of spirited vestments, an anointing that clothes them with dignity and authority as well as power for service. In order to move Pentecostals toward this vision of Spirit-anointed ministry we have some theological tasks ahead.

First, Pentecostals need to develop an anthropology that images the Triune life as paradigmatic for human life. This means looking carefully at the doctrine of God and the meaning of *imago Dei*. Furthermore, it means that we examine our life together in light of this reflection.

Second, we need more reflection on the meaning of the priesthood of believers in relation to the prophethood of believers. How are Pentecostals to make both vocations available to all people, both male and female? How do these vocations relate to the nature of ordained ministry?

Third, we have work ahead of us in understanding God as masculine/feminine. There are many cultural images that fight against this task, but it is a task that is necessary in developing healthy identities for both women and men. Dialogue with depth psychology as well as Scripture and tradition (some of which has been overlooked) will be helpful in this endeavor. Trinitarian reflection that includes a fuller understanding of God's life as both rational and relational should be part of the work ahead.

★★★★★★★★★★★★★★★★★★

Abstract

In regards to the ministry of women, Pentecostalism is a movement of both exclusion and embrace. During the twentieth century, Pentecostals perpetuated an ideology of the ontological inferiority of women, while at the same time advocating their liberty to preach. At the dawn of the twenty-first century, the Pentecostal movement is in need of moving beyond quoting proof texts, such as Joel 2.28, for the support of women in ministry. We face the challenge of defining the meaning of being female created in the image of God. Women are in need of full humanization, clothing them in an identity that is grounded in the Triune life. In order to move ahead we must reject the trend among some Evangelicals toward a 'functional subordinationism' in regards to the Trinity and to the roles of men and women. Instead, a relational Trinitarian theology serves as the foundation for imaging the meaning of being human – male and female. In addition, our image of God should contain both male and female elements of being.

14

On the Redemption of Shame

Ron Cason[*]

A look at American society in general shows that we as a culture have largely ignored shame and tended to over emphasize guilt. Shame has usually been regarded as little more than a superficial reaction on the level of embarrassment, whereas guilt has been thought to be a profoundly significant internalized action. In other words, guilt has generally been considered a deeper emotion than shame. Shame, for example, has been described as more external to the self and guilt more internal, when actually it seems the opposite is the case. Some believe this may reflect a western bias. That is, most cultures are not as guilt oriented as our own. In fact, western cultures seem to be the exception to the rule. Anthropologists formerly categorized cultures as either shame or guilt oriented. This dichotomy was overdone, but most certainly, cross culturally, shame is more common than guilt. We will look at the distinction between guilt and shame later in this paper. For now, where at times the contrast between guilt and shame cultures may break down, the emphasis and focus of western society has nevertheless been placed upon guilt.

It is further important to see that the Christian faith in western cultures tends to think of sin and atonement primarily in terms of guilt rather than shame. Until recently, this fact was reflected in most of biblical scholarship. In doing research on the subject, one will discover that it is nearly impossible to find any extensive scriptural study of shame before 1985. It is even more difficult finding any theological treatment of this subject.[1] In spite of a plethora of secular articles, both

[*] Ron Cason (D.Min., Columbia Theological Seminary) is the James Hamilton Assistant Professor for Teaching Lay Involvement at the Pentecostal Theological Seminary, Cleveland, TN.
[1] Carl D. Schneider's work, *Shame, Exposure and Privacy* (New York: W.W. Norton, 1977) is still the definitive work on a theology of shame. There has been little written since this work that adds to the subject. James W. Fowler's article, 'Shame: Toward a

psychological and sociological, on the subject of shame, it is still the case that little has been written from the perspective of developing an adequate and appropriate theology dealing with shame. The Church has followed suit with American society in emphasizing guilt over shame. Our theology of atonement speaks of Christ's triumph over guilt. Our assurances of pardon bring up images of a court's verdict and a governor's reprieve. Our training in pastoral care seldom speaks about shame at all. Seldom in either confession or assurance have we dealt with shame as sin. Guilt is certainly redeemed in the atonement, but the relationship between atonement and shame is avoided or over-looked by the American church and biblical and theological scholars in western culture in particular.

Certainly this is not the case in Scripture. While definitive conclusions cannot be drawn simply on the basis of a word count, if the word shame is commonly found in a sin context, then there must be a biblical and theological basis for suggesting a sin–shame paradigm in the atonement and for ministry, in addition to the more common sin–guilt framework. The least we can affirm is when we look at the occurrence and variety of terms in the Old and New Testaments which are translated by some form of shame, it becomes obvious this word carries greater weight and significance in Scripture than we have afforded it in our sermons, theology and liturgy.

In the King James Version, guilty and guiltiness are found 23 times in the entire Bible and only six times in the New Testament. In sharp contrast, shame, ashamed and derivatives occur 235 times: 178 times in the Old Testament and 57 times in the New Testament. The New International Version translators use shame or one of its derivatives 149 times in the Old Testament and 54 times in the New Testament.

There are several different Hebrew terms used to describe shame, including *buwsh* and *bosheth*, *chaper*, *kalam* and *kelimmah*, and *qalown*. New Testament Greek offers the various meanings of αἰσχύνη (*aischyne*), ἐντροπή (*entrope*), and αἰδώς (*aidos*). The primary Hebrew and Greek words found in the Scriptures are *bosh* and αἰσχύνη (*aischyne*). The Septuagint uses αἰσχύνω (*aischyno*) most frequently (96 times) for the Hebrew word *bosh* and its derivatives, translating it to mean 'to put to shame' and 'shame'. It also uses αἰσχύνω (*aischyno*) or 'shame' in eight cases to render the Hebrew term for the Latin *pudenda, erwah*.[2] It is important to note there are different groupings of words in Scripture that are translated 'shame'. One grouping relates to shame felt before, and warning against, a sinful action. This is a discretionary shame that

Practical Theological Understanding', *CC* (Aug. 25–Sept. 1, 1993), pp. 816-19 is one of the few journal articles to address the topic.

[2] H.G. Link, '*aischyno*', *DNTT*, III, p. 562.

speaks of boundaries not to be crossed and limitations upon the self. Shame as discretion often relates to holiness and awe in the presence of a holy God. This is the shame Moses felt at the burning bush. He removes his sandals, for the place where he stands is holy ground. He also wishes to see God's glory, but is permitted to see Yahweh only after he has passed by; no one can see God's face and live. Moses covers his face, afraid to look at God. Holy things and holy places call for a proper sense of deference and awe before their transcendent mystery: the unutterable name of Yahweh, the indescribable appearance of Yahweh, the untouchable Ark of the Covenant. All these reflect the reticence and reverence that characterizes godly shame. Zephaniah 3.5 affirms 'the unjust knoweth no shame.'

There is another word grouping that refers to shame as disgrace. As noted above, the most frequent terms in Scripture for shame are *bosh* and αἰσχύνη (*aischyne*) and their derivatives. Both refer to shame as disgrace. This is shame after a sinful action that hurts, harms, or soils, a disgrace shame that burns in our conscience and memory. Ezra cries out to God on behalf of his people, 'O my God, I am ashamed and blush to lift up my face to thee, my God; for our iniquities are increased over our head, and our trespass is grown up unto the heavens' (Ezra 9.6).[3] The emphasis of this study is on disgrace shame, shame that is often reinterpreted as guilt. Both discretionary and disgrace shame relate to self-attention. Shame interrupts any unquestioning, unaware sense of oneself. All of this manifests the relational character of the shame experience. This relational nature of shame contains a revelatory capacity. A part of the self is revealed to the self. It is the relational aspect of shame which makes self-confrontation inescapable. Normally, the self refuses to see itself; it looks away; it hides from itself. To know oneself as a sinner is painful. There is much that, if left to ourselves, we would rather overlook. We are willing to participate in much self-deception to avoid the pain of self-revelation. But in the exposure of shame before a holy God whom we cannot control or deny, we come into a confrontation with ourselves we otherwise avoid.

'The Scriptures use the term guilt in an objective theological sense – a legal state of guilt rather than a feeling of guilt.'[4] There is little emphasis on a psychological feeling of guilt, although 'it is possible that when a person commits an act of sin and becomes theologically guilty, he usually feels psychologically guilty'.[5] In relation to shame, Scripture clearly has both subjective and objective meanings in mind.

---

[3] See also Judg. 3.25; 2 Kgs 2.17; 8.11; Ezra 8.22; Isa. 29.22; Jer. 6.15.
[4] Lowell L. Noble, *Naked and Not Ashamed* (Jackson, MI: Jackson Printing, 1975), p. 26.
[5] Noble, *Naked and Not Ashamed*, p. 26.

Subjectively, a sense of shame may act in a good sense as a deterrent from wrongdoing (1 Tim. 2.9). On the other hand, some may shrink back from right conduct for fear of what may be said or thought about them, such as those who are 'ashamed of the Son of Man' (Mk. 8.38). More commonly, however, a sense of shame follows shameful action. Occasionally, this is shame for a wrong suffered, as those men were ashamed who had been misused by Hanun the Ammonite (2 Sam. 10.5). But usually it is shame for a wrong done, and where this is a first step towards contrition and repentance, it is frequently praised (and its absence is blamed) in Scripture. Repentance (or failure to repent) is involved in such passages as Ezra 9.6; Jer. 6.15; 8.12; Zeph. 2.1; 3.5; and Rom. 6.21.[6]

We have already seen the predominance of shame language over guilt in the Scriptures, and will see in the following evidence that it is more than a superficial reaction on the level of embarrassment and just as profound an internalized action as guilt, if not more so. In observing that little is heard from our pulpits and theological formulations of the atonement and sin regarding shame, the question arises, why is this the case? It seems obvious part of the answer is found in the fact that western culture tends to cover shame experiences over with guilt. That is, the guilt concept has been extended to cover part of what the Bible and other cultures label as shame. This is partially due to the fact that there is a tendency for the person who has experienced shame to withdraw and hide (Adam and Eve). He or she is less willing to reveal shame than guilt because guilt can be defended and rationalized. Shame is difficult to express because one relives the pain each time they bring it back to memory. It is difficult to confess, to tell other people about. The shame experience is also a threat to the very core of the self, the center of our being. We can externalize guilt and withdraw from the transgression or wrong, but in a shame experience, there is no way we can distance ourselves. There is no way of projecting ourselves out of it because it is totally self-involving. Shame has to do with failure to live up to our own self-ideals, while with guilt we disappoint others or let them down. Shame is about the self – its adequacy and its worth, its defectiveness and its unworthiness. Guilt has to do with self-judgment and remorse about violating rules and principles, or about consciously injuring others. Guilt is about something we have done or contemplated doing; shame is about something we are or are not.

> In my experience of shame, the other sees all of me and all through me, even if the occasion of the shame is on the surface – for instance, in my appearance; and the expression of shame, in general, as well as in

---

[6] Alan Richardson, *A Theological Word Book of the Bible* (New York: Macmillan, 1962), p. 225.

the particular form of it that is embarrassment, is not just the desire to hide, or to hide my face, but the desire to disappear, not to be there. It is not even the wish to sink through the floor, but rather the wish that the space occupied by me should be instantaneously empty. With guilt it is not like this; I am more dominated by the thought that even if I disappeared, it would come with me. What arouses guilt in an agent is an act of omission of a sort that typically elicits from other people anger, resentment, or indignation. What the agent may offer in order to turn this away is reparation; he may also fear punishment or may inflict it on himself. What arouses shame, on the other hand, is something that typically elicits from others contempt or derision or avoidance. It will lower the agent's self-respect and diminish him in his own eyes.[7]

It helps us in our theological work and ministry to contemporary society to clarify our definition of shame and to delineate it from guilt. Guilt and shame are closely related and can become a jumble of painful emotions. When guilt and shame become intertwined, the accumulation of pain, the desire to escape oneself, and the weight of burdens can threaten to overwhelm the individual. Also, by identifying and resolving guilt, shame is more clearly focused so that one can begin to deal with it appropriately. Guilt and shame are similar in that both can cause one to hide, distance oneself from God and others, and try to make amends to feel better. Both can evoke deep feelings of sadness, fear, self-loathing and remorse. The difference between guilt and shame is that guilt is related to behavior, while shame is related to being. 'The association of the word shame with loss of honor and of self-respect suggests why shame may be felt as something different from the guilt involved in a failure to pay a debt, in violation of a prohibition, or in transgression of a boundary.'[8]

True guilt is experienced when we do something that is wrong or fail to do what we know to be right when it is in our power to do it. Guilt also occurs when we break a commitment that we entered into willingly. The solution for guilt is to accept responsibility for having violated moral boundaries, confess the exact nature of wrongs to God, oneself and others, and seek forgiveness. However, forgiveness, especially of oneself, is also closely associated with the shame experience.

One can also reduce the burden of guilt when persons are identified who have been harmed by our wrongs and make amends to them, except when to do so would injure them or others. One may try to rid oneself of guilt by throwing out all the rules, choosing to deny allegiance to previously held moral values. However, choosing to ignore

---

[7] Bernard Williams, *Shame and Necessity* (Berkeley, CA: University of California Press, 1993), pp. 89-90.

[8] Helen M. Lynd, *On Shame and the Search for Identity* (New York: Harcourt, Brace & World, 1958), p. 26. This volume was the ground-breaking work on shame.

rules does not eliminate the guilt. It just requires more energy to suppress the feelings of guilt we are left to deal with on our own because shame has cut us off from the one who has the ability to forgive and cleanse.

We will now look briefly at the Scriptures to see how they define shame as sin. Perhaps the most frequent examined pericope by biblical scholarship in relation to shame is the Genesis account of the fall. We are told the man and woman 'were both naked, and were not ashamed' (Gen. 2.25). The question arises could they know that they were not ashamed without some sense of what shame is, particularly in relation to sin? It seems we can conclude that they must have been created with a capacity for shame. The pericope makes clear that in the security of the intimacy of their relationship, they could be open and exposed to each other without shame being actually felt. At the point where they breached their limits and attempted to 'be like God' (3.5), they 'knew that they were naked; and they sewed fig leaves together and made loincloths for themselves' (3.7). One of the visible results of the fall was that the man and woman actually felt shame in the presence of each other and in the eyes of God, for they hid themselves from his presence in the garden. Also, we are told Adam blamed God for giving him the woman, and Eve blamed the serpent for beguiling her.

The presence of blame in the story of the fall verifies that the experience of shame can occur not just as a possible consequence of an action. That is part of what happens in Eden. But we also see in the story shame felt because Adam and Eve have been shamed. There were no other human beings around to see their state of nakedness, so Adam and Eve did not cover themselves because of what others would think. They had not yet confronted God in the garden. They had not covered themselves because God would see them. Shame, in its profoundest sense, exposes oneself to oneself. For Adam and Eve, the immediate result of their act of sin was an exposure of themselves to themselves. 'Being ashamed is a violation of the self which occurs with human interaction. Wherever there is blame, there is shame. One continually feeds on the other.'[9] In the case of Adam and Eve, we see self-blame. They realize they are less than God intended them to be, less than they were created to be. It is this revelation of the self to the self that is unbearable to face. This self-exposure is at the heart of shame. When we undergo an especially painful shame experience, we often say that we were unable to look at ourselves in the mirror; the self-recognition would be too difficult to bear. Thus, to experience shame is to expe-

---

[9] Ray S. Anderson, *Self Care: A Theology of Personal Empowerment and Spiritual Healing* (Wheaton, IL: Victor Books, 1995), p. 148.

rience, in an unusually deep and painful way, a sense of self-estrangement, a wave of self-rejection, even self-revulsion. We have disappointed and betrayed not only God, but ourselves.

This need to conceal causes us to bury shame as a secret within the self. Fear of exposure of the self to the self only drives us deeper into hiding and we resort to 'fig leaves' in order to maintain a sense of acceptability and decorum. However, it is only outward adornment, for within our being there is an ongoing struggle. The fall distorted and separated the true self and the results were the creation of a false self. One of the characteristics of the existence of this false self is blaming others.

The loving and trusting relationship Adam and Eve had with their creator was broken. But also, they could no longer reveal themselves. 'A person who is unable to love cannot reveal himself.'[10] Therefore, you cover yourself. Blaming is an attempt to cover.[11] This leads to a process of continually covering ourselves which becomes a way of life. Only at brief intervals do we see ourselves as we really are. Then the pain is so great, we immediately resort to our fig leaves again. We also see God brings shame to Israel to make them aware of their need for relationship and the overwhelming shame that occurs when we feel abandoned.[12]

Although the words 'shame' and 'ashamed' are found more frequently in the Old Testament by a ratio of almost four to one, this does not mean shame is less important in the New Testament. *Aischyno* is the Greek word used most often for shame. It denotes the idea of 'disgrace,' though sometimes with an emphasis on the fact that this also

---

[10] Lynd, *On Shame and the Search for Identity*, p. 160.

[11] It is God who makes Adam and Eve aware of the futility of blaming. He allows himself to become the object and focus of their blaming so they can see the destructive nature of hiding and covering up. Only then will they perhaps cry out for reconciliation.

[12] Several scholars have focused on shame and abandonment in the Old Testament. Margaret S, Odell, 'The Inversion of Shame and Forgiveness in Ezekiel 16:59-63', *JSOT* 56 (1992), pp. 101-12, shows a number of Old Testament passages speak of the person not feeling shame because of something they have done, but because their relationship to God has failed (Judg. 18.7; 1 Sam. 25.7, 15, and in the complaint psalms, 25.2, 20; 31.2). She suggests that the command in the Old Testament to be ashamed 'is best understood within the context of complaint rituals that remove shame by examining and addressing the reasons for the failure of the divine-human relationship' (p. 111). Likewise, Lyn M. Bechtel, 'Shame as a Sanction of Social Control in Biblical Israel: Judicial, Political and Social Shaming', *JSOT* 49 (1991), pp. 47-76, speaking of Israel, notes that 'It was not unusual for them to experience God as shaming them. One of the ways in which people felt shamed by God was through divine abandonment' (p. 82). She uses as an example Psalm 89, where 'The shame of which the king complained was not interpreted as punishment for guilt. No lack of obedience, guilty conscience, or shameful behavior on the part of the king was acknowledged. It was simply a matter of divine abandonment' (p. 83).

means being ashamed. Its primary reference is to the shame brought by divine judgment.[13] Both *aischyne* and *entrope* are concerned with the actual experience of shame and its negative or painful results. *Entrope* emphasizes the confusion or disorientation that the experience of shame brings upon a person and often carries the meaning of humiliation or modesty. The fear of *aischyne* might restrain a person from committing sin. *Elencheie* is usually rendered reproach or disgrace and *aeikes* refers to that which is unseemly or shameful.[14]

In judgment, God is the subject, the one who shames. 'The shame he brings is his judgment.'[15] The primary idea when αἰσχύνω (*aischyno*) is used is not a feeling of shame but an act of divine judgment. Mark 8.38 reads, 'Whosoever therefore shall be ashamed of me and of my words in this adulterous and sinful generation, of him also shall the Son of Man be ashamed, when he cometh in the glory of his Father with the holy angels.' There are other themes in the New Testament that speak more powerfully to humanity's experience of shame, but it is important to note here there is a relational aspect to the word shame. People who are in a trusting relationship with God experience vindication, while those who are not, experience shame. Though there is a link between shame and judgment, it is people who are not in a right relationship with the creator and the rest of creation who, because of misplaced trust, experience shame.

Shame as sin is more evident in the writings of Paul than anywhere else in the New Testament. His personal testimony speaks of a transformation that took place in his self-identity because of his encounter with Christ. As he reviewed his life, he related how transformation began on the Damascus Road, which is the event of his conversion. Having been stopped in the road by this encounter, he heard the voice of Jesus ask him why he was hurting himself. 'Saul, Saul, why persecutest thou me? It is hard for thee to kick against the pricks' (Acts 26.14). Thus began his transformation, followed by his uncovering through the work of the Holy Spirit and exposure before a holy God. In this revelatory encounter, Paul sees himself as he really is. Acts 9.6 says Paul arose trembling and ready to change, and he testifies in 1 Tim. 1.13, he was 'before a blasphemer, and a persecutor, and injurious: but I obtained mercy.'

Paul was well aware of the terrible consequences of attempting to fulfill his own need for righteousness. He confessed that he became a 'wretched man', captive to his desperate desires so the 'law of sin' was working within him. Yet, in the midst of this confession he cries out,

---

[13] Rudolf Bultmann, 'αἰσχύνω', *TDNT*, I, pp. 189-91.

[14] Schneider, *Shame, Exposure and Privacy*, p. 145.

[15] Bultmann, 'αἰσχύνω', *TDNT*, I, p. 190.

'I delight in the laws of God after the inward man' (Rom. 7.22). The NRSV says, 'I delight in the law of God in my inmost self.' Paul seems to be saying at the very core of his being, he does not deny or devalue himself. He knows God loves him and has called him into relationship. 'We rejoice in hope of the glory of God…. And hope maketh not ashamed, because the love of God is shed abroad in our hearts by the Holy Ghost which is given unto us' (Rom. 5.2, 5). Redemption of shame involves restoration to a right relationship with God, the relationship intended in creation. The grace of God through the atonement of Jesus Christ brought Paul more than pardon from sin. Paul was also redeemed from shame's disgrace through the blessings of restored personal communion and fellowship with God and others.

Hebrews speaks of the crucified Christ, who 'endured the cross, despising the shame, and sat down at the right hand of God' (12.2). God in human flesh endured the worst shaming humanity can inflict; desertion by his followers, public ridicule, condemnation by civic and religious leaders, and capital punishment by the most shaming means ever devised. Isaiah writes, 'I gave my back to the smiters, and my cheek to them that plucked off the hair; I hid not my face from shame and spitting' (Isa. 50.6). As the old hymn says, the cross is 'the emblem of suffering and shame.' It epitomizes human concepts of defilement and exclusion. The one executed was 'accursed' (Gal. 3.13). Jesus died outside the city wall, shamed as a deceiver of the people whose cause he had espoused. His crucifixion was an act of human shaming. His accusers understood it as exposure before God and the people – a judgment upon sins. Jesus accepted the shame and suffered death to expose the extremity of sin's shameful consequences. Thus he 'despised' or 'disregarded' the shame. In the same act, Jesus also revealed the true nature of God's holiness as the holiness of love. From the cross he forgave his executioners who in ignorance ostracised and shamed him. In his acceptance of such a contemptuous death, his true glory as the undefiled Son of God was revealed. Jesus both shared our shame and bore the shame for all who through this disclosure of God's love find freedom from its dread and power. Shame was exposed, uncovered and redeemed at Calvary.

Having seen the revelatory component in shame, and the pain associated with confronting the false self and exposure of oneself to oneself, note how such revelation is essential in the redemption of shame. Helen Merrill Lynd states from a therapeutic perspective:

> It is no accident that experiences of shame are called self-consciousness. Such experiences are characteristically painful. They are usually taken as something to be hidden, dodged, covered up – even, or especially, from oneself. Shame interrupts any unquestioning, unaware sense of

oneself. But it is possible that experiences of shame, if confronted full in the face, may throw an unexpected light on who one is and point the way toward who one may become. Faced fully, shame may become not primarily something to be covered, but a positive experience of revelation.[16]

As Christians, we would want to eliminate the 'may' language in the above statement. Shame has the power to move one to positive action, to see oneself in the light of God's righteousness and holiness, and therefore, seek forgiveness and restoration to relationship with him that was lost as a result of the fall in the Garden of Eden. The root meaning of shame is 'to uncover, to expose, and even to wound. It is always exposure to one's own eyes.'[17] In the deepest sense, shame is a profound internal revelation of one's basic nature and values. Yes, that one is a sinner in need of redemption, but also estranged from God and in need of reconciliation. In the atonement, the believer is restored to a right relationship with God, a relationship intended in creation that causes us to stand with awe and reverence, completely revealed, in the presence of a holy God. It is the individual's response to the work of the Holy Spirit in self-revelation and exposure that determines whether or not their shame is redeemed or continues to be covered and results in a life embracing a false self. If it is correct that guilt can be expiated but shame, short of a transformation of the self through the redemptive work of Christ on the cross, is retained, then we must opt for the transformation which only God offers. Certainly there are less satisfactory solutions which may partially resolve the feelings of shame, such as relocation, self-improvement, group therapy or psychoanalysis, but transformation is the only whole, redemptive and positive solution.

The conclusion from a study of both Old and New Testaments is that while shame and guilt have objective and subjective characteristics, in the Scriptures guilt is primarily objective in nature, whereas shame is more subjective, although not entirely so. 'Even when shame is objective in nature, it gets its meaning and impact from the profound subjective feeling involved in an experience of shame.'[18] Certainly Scripture bears out the fallacy of perceiving shame as more external to the self and guilt more internal.

Dietrich Bonhoeffer, one of the few theologians to deal with shame, speaks profoundly of it as the symbol of our separation from God. He states, 'Shame is man's ineffaceable recollection of his estrangement from the origin; it is grief for this estrangement, and the powerlessness

---

[16] Lynd, *On Shame and the Search for Identity*, pp. 19-20.
[17] Lynd, *On Shame and the Search for Identity*, pp. 27-28.
[18] Noble, *Naked and Not Ashamed*, p. 27.

of longing to return to unity with the origin.'[19] This disruption manifests itself in a sense of confusion. We see in the Old Testament that confusion so characteristically accompanies shame that the two form a biblical cliché. Shame is at the heart of Israel's response as she again and again is confronted by her own betrayal of the covenant relationship with Yahweh, and by her idolatrous neighbors' defilement of the holy law of Yahweh (Jer. 3.24-25, Ezra 9.6-7, Hos. 4.6-7). So for Bonhoeffer, humanity's predicament is disunion with God, with others, with things and with ourselves. Shame and confusion arise as this disunion comes to consciousness.

The fall pericope in Genesis 3 is dealt with by Bonhoeffer from a theological perspective. Adam sees himself, not God. This is the revelation that comes with sin. He 'perceives himself in his disunion with God. He perceives that he is naked. Lacking the protection, the covering which God and his fellow-man afforded him, he finds himself laid bare. Hence there arises shame.'[20]

> Shame, for Bonhoeffer, at its most profound level, is humankind's grief over its estrangement from God. This is theological affirmation more than biblical interpretation. When he talks about what this feels like, however, Bonhoeffer gets into the psychological dimension of this theologically described state. Shame is primarily related not to being at fault or to guilt but to lacking something.
>
> Being seen by another is a reminder of the lost wholeness of life. Shame is more original than remorse. It may arise whenever there is experience of man's disunion, and the condition of humankind is such that it longs for the restoration of the lost unity.[21]

Bonhoeffer, seeing the solution for shame estrangement in reunion and fellowship with God and others, maintains:

> Shame can be overcome only when the original unity is restored, when man is once again clothed by God in the other Man.... Shame is overcome only in the enduring of an act of final shaming, namely the becoming manifest of knowledge before God.... Shame is overcome only in the shaming through the forgiveness of sin, that is to say through the restoration of fellowship with God and men.[22]

As Bonhoeffer writes in his *Ethics*, shame can be overcome by the restoration of our relationship to God. It is the symbol of our separation and a proper sense of shame involves respect for the space there is

---

[19] Dietrich Bonhoeffer, *Ethics* (ed. Eberhard Bethge; trans. Neville H. Smith; New York: Macmillan, 1955), p. 23.

[20] Bonhoeffer, *Ethics*, p. 145.

[21] John Patton, *Is Human Forgiveness Possible?* (Nashville: Abingdon, 1985), p. 43.

[22] Bonhoeffer, *Ethics*, pp. 145-48.

between us, the boundaries that are not to be crossed. Yet more is necessary than merely acknowledging the distance between us. Distance alone only causes one to experience alienation and threat. 'There must also be a meeting, but one which allows each person to participate in shaping the context in which they meet, and to speak in such a way that the dialectic of covering and uncovering is safeguarded.'[23]

Sin for Tillich is universal, tragic estrangement, based on freedom and destiny in all human beings. Sin, which brings estrangement, is 'our act of turning away from participation in the divine Ground from which we come and to which we go.'[24] Estrangement is the disruption of an essential unity and reflects alienation not only from God and others, but also from oneself. Tillich's concept of estrangement seems to relate to what psychologists call the divided self, the split which occurs between the grandiose and the shameful or idealized self in childhood. He likely was influenced by the depth psychology of his time, including the work of Freud, Jung and Fromm. In dialogue with depth psychology, he maintains, 'The self-estranged self is split into two or more selves which, however, remain within the one self.'[25] Yet we can see that Tillich never develops an adequate theology of shame because he approaches the problem of self-estrangement from the perspective of guilt. One scholar has noted that within the context of a theology of shame, self-estrangement is strikingly nonmoralistic. Speaking of Tillich, it is noted:

> Talk about the best and worst parts of the self is avoided; the grandiose and the idealizing selves are not evaluated as best or worst, but are merely different. Also, and more importantly, a theology of shame finds Tillich's solution – acceptance – inadequate, for it basically commends the suspension of negative judgment, whereas a theology of shame, following Kohut,[26] emphasizes the reconciling effects of positive mirroring between the two inner selves that have been at enmity with one another.

> Self-mirroring is a more powerful and dynamic expression of self-love than is acceptance because it involves a positive regard for the other self, one that eschews any note or form of superiority or condescension. Whereas 'acceptance' implies a tolerant attitude toward the weaker self,

---

[23] Schneider, *Shame, Exposure and Privacy,* p. 39.

[24] Paul Tillich, *Systematic Theology,* II (Chicago: University of Chicago Press, 1951–1963), p. 46.

[25] Paul Tillich, 'Estrangement and Reconciliation in Modern Thought', in *The Meaning of Health: Essays in Existentialism, Psychoanalysis, and Religion* (ed. Perry LeFevre; Chicago: Exploration, 1984), p. 12.

[26] Heinz Kohut, *The Restoration of the Self* (New York: International Universities Press, 1977). See his work on self-splitting when mirroring does not occur, usually from the mother, resulting in narcissistic shame.

mirroring says that I cannot live without my other self, that I am lost
without the other. Thus, whereas a hierarchy of inner selves seems to
be the inevitable corollary of a theology of guilt, a theology of shame
views the inner selves as equals.[27]

It seems obvious the acceptance of the weaker self by the self is not
an adequate basis for a theology of shame. Nor do we want to eliminate either the grandiose or shameful idealized self. These two must
continue to live in tension or balance and be at times frustrated and
gratified. But in relation to redemption that is total,[28] inner reconciliation of these two selves brings healing of narcissistic injury and accompanying shame. Here Bonhoeffer is more helpful in that he sees a
redemptive purpose in overcoming shame, the healing of estrangement
from God that is the human condition. The very notions of estrangement and disunion elicit the idea and image of a tear that must be
mended. Shame reflects an order to things. In fact, discretionary shame
reflects and sustains our personal and social ordering of the world. Disgrace shame is a painful experience of the disintegration of one's
world. A break occurs, because of sin, in our relationship with God,
others and ourselves. We realize we are less than we want to be, less
than we were created by God to be. This realization helps lead to repentance and reconciliation. An important function of shame following
an act of sin is to make us aware of our estrangement from God.

The image of sin as estrangement speaks powerfully to our existence
because it correlates so well with the reconciliation we receive in salvation. The word 'salvation' itself comes from the Latin root *salvus*,
meaning 'health' and 'wholeness'. Shame can be overcome only when
the original unity is restored, when our inner divided selves are reconciled and become whole, when we are once again in right relationship
with our creator, others and ourselves. This restoration is possible because Jesus is not ashamed to be our brother; God is not ashamed to be
our God (Heb. 2.11; 11.16). Reconciliation with God allows us to
grow free of the false values which have been imposed on us by society.
Romans 10.11 states, 'He who believes in me will not be put to
shame.' When a father commits a crime and is sent to prison, the
whole family experiences shame because they are so closely identified
with the father. This is the significance of the Scripture, for Paul is

---

[27] Donald Capps, *The Depleted Self: Sin in a Narcissistic Age* (Philadelphia: Fortress,
1993), pp. 91-92. Capps' work is one of the few that links shame with sin.

[28] R. Hollis Gause, *Living in the Spirit: The Way of Salvation* (Cleveland, TN: R. Hollis
Gause, 2005), p. 39, states 'Repentance is a work of God's grace in the whole person:
mind, emotions and will.... Since man is a sinner in a commitment of his entire self to
sin, the route of repentance must involve the entire self'.

saying we can come into close relationship with God. Complete trust in God will never leave one exposed to shame. Shame will be covered.

In the development of the various theories of the atonement, theologians have desired to emphasize different texts and doctrinal views. A central question of Scripture is, 'How can sinful people ever be accepted by a holy God?' To answer this question and in attempting to understand redemption, three overall perspectives have been developed: '(1) The essence of the atonement is the effect of the cross on the believer. (2) Atonement is a victory of some sort. (3) Christ satisfied God's holiness and justice.'[29] Most scholars recognize the complexity and vastness of the atonement makes it impossible for any one theory alone to explain it fully. 'Even together they only represent a beginning comprehension of the vastness of salvation.'[30] Also, there are positive aspects of each theory, although some are less capable of explaining the atonement based upon scriptural substantiation than others. The final section of this essay will look briefly at the adequacy or inadequacy of these theories of atonement in relation to shame.

The ransom theory of the atonement, sometimes referred to as recapitulation or victory, states Jesus became what we are so that we could become what he is. Rooted in the incarnation, it speaks to how Christ entered human misery and wickedness to redeem it. The work of Christ is first and foremost a victory over the powers which hold humanity in bondage, sin, death and the devil. The atonement is a ransom paid, a rescue or liberation from the slavery of sin. An important truth in this theory is evil and sin were defeated by Christ's atoning work at Calvary.[31] There is in this theory the emphasis upon our separation from God because of slavery to sin and the willingness of Christ to pay a ransom to reclaim or buy back the sinner out of estrangement and back

---

[29] Leon Morris, 'Theories of the Atonement', in *The Concise Evangelical Dictionary of Theology* (ed. Walter A. Elwell; Grand Rapids, MI: Baker Book House, 1991), pp. 46-48 (p. 47). Morris categorizes these as the subjective view or moral influence, the victory theory, the satisfaction theory, penal substitution, and the government theory. This study will refer to what Morris calls the victory theory as ransom and include penal substitution with satisfaction.

[30] Morris, 'Theories of the Atonement', *The Concise Evangelical Dictionary of Theology*, p. 48. Also see Millard J. Erickson, *Introducing Christian Doctrine* (Grand Rapids: Baker Book House, 1992), p. 242, who notes we 'come to see the incompleteness and inadequacy of each one of them by itself.'

[31] Daniel B. Pecota, 'The Saving Work of Christ', in *Systematic Theology* (ed. Stanley M. Horton; Springfield, MO: Logion, 1995), pp. 325-73, (p. 339). 'The death of Christ did defeat the devil (Heb. 2.4; Col. 2.15; Rev. 5.5). Death and hell have been conquered (1 Cor. 15.54-57; Rev. 1.18). The seed of the woman has crushed the serpent's head (Gen. 3.15). Seeing the Atonement as the victory over all the forces of evil must always be a vital part of our victorious proclamation of the gospel.' Pecota goes on to note the need to reject in this theory the idea God was the author of deception in leading Satan to defeat.

into relationship with God. It is also true there is less an emphasis upon guilt in this theory than satisfaction and penal substitution. However, the overwhelming emphasis in this theory is Christ's victory or triumph over guilt. We are in a bondage of our own making and design. Satan took us captive of our own free will. We allowed ourselves to be enslaved. All of these things are true, but relate much more to behavior than being. The load of sin's guilt is what we are ransomed from. Virtually nothing is mentioned concerning the disgrace of sin and how Christ's victory over evil and Satan liberates us from shame. It is often mentioned by theologians that God's love outweighed his anger and this is a powerful motive for his freeing us from captivity. But freedom is never connected with shame as sin. Even liberal theologians speak of ransom in terms of anxiety as the awareness of our alienation from the ground of being, with little reference to shame.

The satisfaction theory of the atonement, sometimes called the Latin view, has carried great weight in both Catholic and Protestant thought. Here the atonement is compensation to the Father, not Satan. 'Christ died to satisfy a principle in the very nature of God the Father.'[32] God's honor has been violated and recompense can only be made either by punishment of sinners or satisfaction being made to God in our behalf. To resolve this conflict, since we are sinners and justly deserve punishment, only Christ, the sinless One, could render the satisfaction price to restore God's honor and purchase forgiveness for humanity's sins.[33]

Penal substitution is also included under satisfaction, since the Protestant Reformers saw sin in light of this to satisfy the breaking of God's law rather than as an insult to God's honor.[34] This is the most popular view by Evangelicals of the atonement, as well as many Pentecostals. Focus is upon the vicarious death of Christ on the cross in our place. He bore the full penalty for sin that we deserved (Mark 10.45; 2 Cor. 5.14). Substitution theory, including penal–substitution, is full of language concerning God's judicial wrath, a court's verdict and a governor's reprieve. Paradoxically, although advocated by most theologians, of all the theories of atonement it has the strongest emphasis upon guilt.[35] As noted earlier, the individual living in the shameful disgrace

[32] Erickson, *Introducing Christian Doctrine*, p. 244.

[33] Pecota, 'The Saving Work of Christ', p. 340. He states this theory 'has much to commend it. It focuses on what God required in the atonement and not on Satan. It takes a much more profound view of the seriousness of sin than do the moral influence and ransom theories. It proposes a theory of satisfaction, an idea that is a more adequate explanation of the biblical materials.'

[34] Morris, 'Theories of the Atonement', p. 47.

[35] Charles Hodge, *Systematic Theology*, 3 vols. (Peabody, MA: Hendrickson, 1999), vol. II, pp. 571-72. 'This expiation of guilt is absolutely necessary before the souls of the

of sin does not respond to a guilt-based message or theory on the atonement. With guilt, they feel cut back, but shame speaks more to being cut off. Because of the relational nature of shame, unlike guilt which calls for restitution, shame cries out for reconciliation.

Finally, the moral influence theory of the atonement talks about Christ's death as a demonstration of God's love. The emphasis is upon God's reconciling love. 'Christ's death was an example for believers to follow, a radical expression of love that influences sinners morally and gives them a pattern to follow.'[36] Criticism of this theory has been harsh, especially by Evangelicals.[37] I agree there are problems with those proponents of moral influence who minimize the fear of God's judgment and the need for sin's punishment. However, very few scholars in our tradition see any benefit at all in moral influence. This should not be the case, for we must agree God's love was never on greater display than in Christ's death for our sins. Scripture says 'For God so loved the world, that he gave his only begotten Son, that whosoever believeth in him should not perish, but have everlasting life,' (John 3.16). 'But God commendeth his love toward us, in that, while we were yet sinners, Christ died for us,' (Rom. 5.8). As noted earlier, shame is sin and all sin needs redemption. The significance of this theory for disgrace shame from sin is its emphasis upon separation from the love of God and the need for reconciliation. The challenge facing us in our various views of the atonement is to remedy the almost total lack of seeing shame dealt with in the atoning work of Christ.

The doctrine of total depravity has four meanings, all of which are valid. First, it refers to the corruption at the very core of one's being, the heart. Second, it signifies the infection of sin in every part of one's being. Third, it denotes the total inability of sinful humanity to please God or come to him unless moved by grace. Fourth, it includes the idea of the universal corruption by sin of the human race. Total depravity was given strong emphasis in the Reformation.

This doctrine is problematic for those in America's narcissistic culture who already lack any sense of worth because of shame. Because they see themselves as less than human, less than the rest of humanity, a message that further reiterates their unworthiness only causes them to

guilty can be made the subjects of renewing and sanctifying grace. We are sinners, guilty, polluted.' Hodge contends the purpose of the atonement is 'to provide for the removal of guilt in a way which satisfies the reason and conscience.'

[36] Phil Johnson, 'The Nature of the Atonement', *Grace to You* (2003) at www.biblebb.com.

[37] Charles Hodge, *Systematic Theology*, vol. II, p. 567. He says the theory 'rejects all ideas of expiation or the satisfaction of justice by vicarious atonement, and attributes all the efficacy of his work to the moral effect produced on the hearts of men by his character, teachings and acts.'

believe they are correct in their belief they can never be accepted by God or others in the body of Christ. Their worse suspicions are confirmed. They only go deeper into hopelessness and isolation.

Although we cannot negate the sin and depravity of humanity, that 'There is none righteous, no, not one' (Rom. 3.10), and 'All have sinned, and come short of the glory of God' (Rom. 3.23), we must emphasize the sinner, when redeemed, becomes reconciled with God and restoration occurs. The sin they have covered, is uncovered before the righteousness of God in Christ. There is no need to hide or project any longer a false self based in disgrace shame. Also, propitiation has been made, 'a covering provided by God to protect the sinner from the judgment of God. Jesus is the propitiation – the atonement cover over the believer.'[38] Here we see the motif of covering and uncovering. Our sin is exposed in the light of God's righteousness and judgment as the Holy Spirit convicts and convinces us of our depravity. We respond by substituting for God's covering one of our own making, but see this is not suitable, that our righteousness is as filthy rags. Then in coming to Christ for salvation, we are covered by him from the wrath to come.

Finally, we must affirm sinners are of worth to God, even though still in sin, which is evident from his love in sending his son to die for them even though they are estranged from him. Then the origins of their shame and isolation and their defensive maneuvers to hide the true self will be abandoned, and they will become able to encounter the true God.

People withdraw from life to avoid the pain of shame. This is a mistake, for the essence of life consists in meaningful relationships. The holy life is constituted by its relation to God. It has its existence in this relationship, one that is necessarily personal. We live and move and have our being not in ourselves, but in relationship to God and others in the body of Christ. Shame reminds us of the deep mutual involvement we have with one another. The recovery and acknowledgment of such interrelatedness will lead us back from our pursuit of an autonomous individualism, and into a life of holiness based in reconciliation with God and others. We must help people overcome their feelings of shame which arise out of failure to meet false societal expectations. But the shame which comes from turning away from God requires something else; reconciliation and the renewal of our relationship with God.

★★★★★★★★★★★★★★★★★★

[38] R.H. Gause, *Living in the Spirit: The Way of Salvation,* p. 86. He emphasizes two words to describe the grounds of justification in the atonement: redemption and propitiation. See his footnotes on this page on this subject and also a warning about 'an extreme application of the penal substitution theory of the atonement.'

Abstract

This essay looks at the problem of sin in relation to shame, desiring to answer the question, does shame need redemption, or does it simply help lead to redemption? Passages from the Old and New Testaments are examined in relation to shame as sin. The problem of shame in contemporary society is also examined, as well as how it is experienced as discretion or disgrace. Distinctions between guilt and shame are drawn through appropriate definitions.

The author is particularly concerned about the lack of emphasis upon shame in the atonement. He briefly looks at three theories of the atonement: the ransom theory, the satisfaction theory, and the moral influence theory, noting the omission of shame in the first two, and what he sees in both as an excessive guilt orientation. The author sees potential in aspects of moral influence that can relate to the redemption of shame. He also speaks to problems the doctrine of total depravity can bring in the redemption of the shame-based individual. Finally, the author reflects on the implications of the redemption of shame for biblical scholars, theologians and ministry practitioners in the Pentecostal context.

15

Grief Observed:
Surprised by the Suffering of the Spirit

Oliver McMahan[*]

Introduction

This paper is written in honor of R. Hollis Gause, Professor of New Testament and Theology at the Pentecostal Theological Seminary. A preeminent Pentecostal scholar, Gause exhibits and gives witness to a very personal dynamic of his Christian faith. In a genuine way, Gause has been able to share his journey into loss and grief during and after the long and eventually terminal illnesses of his wife, Beulah, and his son, Val. His wife suffered for a number of years beginning in 1995, dying in 2002 of hardening of the arteries. His son suffered terminal cancer, beginning in January of 2006, dying in July of that year. Beulah remained at home under Gause's care for many of those years. Val moved to be with his father, under his care for the last several months of his life. During these long periods of grief, Gause would request prayer from the community of the Seminary, update students and colleagues about their condition, and open himself and his family to the care of believers around him.

Moving from Writing to Testimony, Grief Observed

Gause's openness during his grief can be compared to the occasion of C.S. Lewis's grief during the months immediately following the death of his wife, Joy Davidman Lewis. Lewis penned *A Grief Observed*[1] as

[*] Oliver McMahan (Ph.D., Georgia State University; D.Min., Texas Christian University) is Vice-President for Ministry Formation and Professor of Pastoral Care and Counseling at the Pentecostal Theological Seminary, Cleveland, TN.
[1] C.S. Lewis, *A Grief Observed* (San Francisco: Harper Collins, 1961).

'notes'[2] chronicling his thoughts and feelings during the first few weeks after her death. Long before the experience of her death, Lewis had written in his book, *The Problem of Pain,*[3] about the pains of life and death in relation to Christianity, describing the dilemma in his 'Introductory' chapter:

> Christianity is not the conclusion of a philosophical debate on the origins of the universe: it is a catastrophic historical event following on the long spiritual preparation of humanity.... In a sense, it creates, rather than solves, the problem of pain, for pain would be no problem unless, side by side with our daily experience of this painful world, we had received what we think a good assurance that ultimate reality is righteous and loving.[4]

Written in 1940, *The Problem of Pain,* laid out Lewis's thoughts about suffering, but *A Grief Observed,* written in 1961, was his personal testimony on the subject. Lewis was indeed a person of great thought, writing profoundly about many issues related to Christianity.[5] Yet *A Grief*

---

[2] Lewis, *A Grief Observed*, p. 17.

[3] C.S. Lewis, *The Problem of Pain* (San Francisco: Harper Collins, 1940).

[4] Lewis, *The Problem of Pain,* p. 14.

[5] Some of Lewis's works included *The Case for Christianity* (a layman's explanation and defense of the belief that has been common to nearly all Christians at all times, published in 1947), see C.S. Lewis, *The Case for Christianity* (New York: Macmillan, 1952; New York: Iversen-Norman, 1969), *Christian Behaviour* (New York: Macmillan, 1952) (a treatment of the essential elements of Christianity), *The Great Divorce* (New York: Macmillan, 1945; New York: Iversen-Horman, 1969) (a volume dealing with Heaven and Hell), *The Joyful Christian, 127 Readings from C.S. Lewis* (New York: Macmillan, 1977) (excerpts of Lewis's writings from 1942 until his death, ranging from topics including 'Right and Wrong' to 'The Tao'), *Miracles, A Preliminary Study* (New York: Macmillan, 1946; New York: Iversen-Norman, 1969) (a study in the proving and disproving of the miraculous), *The Pilgrim's Regress* (Grand Rapids, MI: Eerdmans, 1943) (a Christian apologia patterned after Bunyan's *Pilgrim's Progress*), *A Preface to Paradise Lost* (New York: Oxford University Press, 1942) (a defense of epic as a literary form in which Lewis argues that ritual, splendor and joy have a right to exist), *The Screwtape Letters* (New York: Macmillan, 1943; New York: Iversen-Norman, 1969) (fictional correspondence between demons, an elder and a novice, pondering questions of temptation and evil), *Surprised by Joy: The Shape of My Early Life* (New York: Harcourt, Brace & World, 1955) (an autobiography of his early life in which Lewis chronicles his conversion), *Till We Have Faces: A Myth Retold* (Grand Rapids, MI: Eerdmans, 1956) (a novel, dedicated to Joy Davidman Lewis, Lewis's wife, describing the love musings of Orual with Psyche of Greek mythology), and other collections, such as W. Hooper, ed., *C.S. Lewis, The Dark Tower and Other Stories* (New York: Harcourt, Brace and Jovanovich, 1977), *Letter to an American Lady* (Grand Rapids, MI: Eerdmans, 1967) (Lewis's supportive correspondence to an ill, impoverished woman in the USA), *The Weight of Glory, and Other Addresses* (San Francisco: Harper Collins, 1949) (a sermon on immortality and other writings during and immediately after World War II), *That Hideous Strength, A Modern Fairy Tale for Grown-Ups; Out of the Silent Planet;* and *Perelandra* (New York: Macmillan, 1946) (a space trilogy). In

Observed represents his journey from the world of analysis into the whirlwind of experience. In *A Grief Observed*, he conveyed the fear of grief by saying, 'No one ever told me that grief felt so like fear.'[6] He confessed his nearness to God by saying, 'But by praising I can still, in some degree, enjoy her [his wife], and already, in some degree, enjoy Him [God]. Better than nothing.'[7] He concluded by reflecting on the nature of the spiritual existence between God and humanity, 'Some-times, Lord, one is tempted to say that if you wanted us to behave like the lilies of the field, you might have given us an organization more like theirs ... [but You, God] make an organism which is also a spirit; to make that terrible oxymoron, a "spiritual animal".'[8]

Lewis's account (or testimony, we could say) of his grief, written in the days that followed the death of Joy Davidman Lewis, was a thesis of sorts for all his writings. Rather than talking *abstractly* about pain, death and the eternal, in *A Grief Observed,* Lewis chronicled his own pain *experientially*. The issues that he had analyzed were now his own. Out of his own chronicles would emerge the underscoring of his con-clusions. As a validation, it was also a scripting and posing with new depth of the same theses he had been communicating throughout his previous writings.

Seeing the Signpost on the Way of One's Journey

Oddly enough, this process of penning his thesis with the life that Lewis had confessed in thought but then lived in tragedy, was a me-thod he had exercised in the early autobiography of his life and con-version, *Surprised by Joy, The Shape of My Early Life and Conversion*.[9] In that account he notes the 'joy' that brought him to salvation and then the perspective of that joy as facilitating something greater.

> As I drew near the conclusion [of conversion], I felt a resistance.... When we set out [to a zoo at Whipsnade in England] I did not believe that Jesus Christ is the Son of God, and when we reached the zoo I did. Yet I had not exactly spent the journey in thought.... It was more like when a man, after long sleep, still lying motionless in bed, be-comes aware that he is now awake.... As for what we commonly call

his writings, Lewis ventured into territory not unrelated to the topics addressed by many Christian thinkers, including Pentecostal and Charismatic scholars.
   [6] Lewis, *A Grief Observed*, p. 3.
   [7] Lewis, *A Grief Observed*, p. 63.
   [8] Lewis, *A Grief Observed*, p. 72.
   [9] C.S. Lewis, *Surprised by Joy, The Shape of My Early Life and Conversion* (New York: Harcourt, Brace & World, 1955).

Will, and what we commonly call Emotion, I fancy these usually talk too loud, protest too much, to be quite believed....[10]

The conclusion Lewis reached was that it was what he called 'joy', not the emotion but something deeper, something spiritual that led to Jesus, the Son of God, that drew him to confession of Christ as Savior. And yet, the reality of this 'joy' was to point to a greater destination. As Lewis continued to write in *Surprised by Joy*:

> But what, in conclusion of Joy? for that, after all, is what the story has mainly been about.... It was valuable as a pointer to something other and outer. While that other was in doubt, the pointer loomed large in my thoughts. When we are lost in the woods the sight of a signpost is a great matter.... But when we have found the road and are passing signposts every few miles, we shall not stop and stare ... not on this road, though their pillars are of silver and their lettering of gold. 'We would be at Jerusalem.'[11]

In Hollis Gause's days, months and years of confessing his journey, testifying of his experience, and being open to the faith community around him while his wife and son endured illness and passing from this life; he underscored the theses of his thought and writing. He allowed the Seminary and Church to observe his grief, dialoging with them, thereby validating the witness of his writing and ultimately his Lord, just as Lewis scripted the authenticity of his work by confessing the experience of his faith in the midst of tragedy.

Further, for Lewis there was a 'signpost' *he* called 'joy', that pointed to the ultimate goal of the New Jerusalem. For Gause, his theological writings and eventual confession of experience identified the 'signpost' of the suffering of the Spirit which pointed to the reality that we will all be transformed into a new body for a New Heaven and New Earth.

Gause had written about the Spirit's work in the midst of the believer's suffering relatively early and continued to write and teach concerning this doctrine.[12] Yet, just as one wakes in life to a reality beyond this

---

[10] Lewis, *Surprised by Joy,* p. 237.

[11] Lewis, *Surprised by Joy,* p. 238.

[12] See R. Hollis Gause, 'The Fellowship of His Sufferings', *Evangel* 59.32 (Oct. 20, 1969), pp. 9-14; *Living in the Spirit: The Way of Salvation* (Cleveland, TN: Pathway, 1980 and later revised and reissued by R. Hollis Gause, 2007); 'Doctrine of Eschatology', in *Living the Faith* (ed. Homer G. Rhea; Cleveland, TN: Church of God School of Ministry, 2001), pp. 337-51; 'Doctrine of the Holy Spirit: Part 2', in *Living the Faith* (ed. Homer G. Rhea, Cleveland, TN: Church of God School of Ministry, 2001), pp. 179-91; 'Doctrine of Salvation: Part 5, Baptism in the Holy Spirit' in *Living the Faith* (ed. Homer G. Rhea; Cleveland, TN: Church of God School of Ministry, 2001), pp. 247-59; R. Hollis Gause, 'The Concept of Suffering in Paul' (unpublished manuscript); 'Treasures in Earthen Vessels, Evidences of Glory, 2 Corinthians 4:7-5:10' (unpublished manuscript,

life, Gause testified of the Spirit's transformation in our bodies by way of death, as he penned his confession of the grief of his wife's and son's own transformation through death.

The Public Witness of Pentecostals and Charismatics Observed

Unfortunately, Pentecostals and Charismatics in the United States have not historically allowed the world to observe their grief, nor seen the signposts of the groaning and suffering of the Spirit that move us from death to a resurrected body. The public witness of Pentecostals and Charismatics from the very inception of the revival at Azusa neglected, avoided and even worked hard to deny the experience of pain and grief. An accounting of the public witness of the Azusa revival readily reveals this propensity to bury pain.

The flames of the Pentecostal fire burned at Azusa and around the world. 'Azusa' refers to 312 Azusa St. in Los Angeles, California, where in April, 1906, a revival centered at a building at that address that came to be called, The Azusa Faith Gospel Mission. It was formerly a church,[13] but had fallen into disrepair and at the beginning of the revival was described as a 'barn'.[14] The Pentecostal revival that broke out is described by Wayne Warner as follows:

> A day at the Azusa Street Mission could begin at 9 a.m. and run conti-
> nuously until after midnight. Even then, some were reluctant to go
> home and would stand under a street light to talk about the Lord and
> what was happening…. Vigorous singing and hand clapping could ab-
> ruptly end after only 15 minutes; at other times it would shake the raf-
> ters and stir the neighborhood for two hours or more…. A.C. Valdez,
> an eyewitness, said the crowd at times seemed to forget how to sing in

presented in Church of God Theological Seminary Chapel, 2006); 'The Holy Spirit: Your Personal Guide', in *Endued With Power: The Holy Spirit in the Church* (ed. Robert White; Cleveland, TN: Pathway, 1995), pp. 15-31; 'Worldliness' (presented at Seminar of Practice of the Doctrine of Holiness in the Church of God, Lee College, 1970); *After Moral Failure: Forgiveness vs. Ministerial Fitness* (Cleveland, TN: Pathway, 1994); and Kimberly Ervin Alexander and R. Hollis Gause, *Women in Leadership: A Pentecostal Perspective* (Pentecostal Leadership Series; Cleveland, TN: Center for Pentecostal Leadership and Care, 2006).

[13] 'The Purchase of a Building', *The Apostolic Faith* 1.6 (Feb.-Mar., 1907) in *The Azusa Street Papers: A Reprint of The Apostolic Faith Mission Publications, Los Angeles, California (1906-1908) William J. Seymour, Editor* (Foley, AL: Harvest, 1997), p. 30. *The Apostolic Faith* became the chronicles of the Azusa Street Revival. The revival began in April, 1906, and by September, 1906, a regular newspaper averaging four pages per issue was begun. The paper was actually a journal or chronicle of the events at and emanating from the Azusa revival.

[14] Tom Hezmalhalch, 'Gracious Pentecostal Showers Continue to Fall', *The Apostolic Faith* 1.3 in *The Azusa Street Papers*, p. 18.

English. 'Out of their mouths would come new language and lovely harmony that no human being could have learned,' he reported.[15]

Other places where the Spirit was falling included Europe,[16] Canada, India, China, Africa, South America[17] and other locations in the United States and the Pacific.[18] Nevertheless, the public witness of contemporary Pentecost in the United States focused on Azusa.

The primary record and historically the public witness of the revival at Azusa were captured in a newspaper, *The Apostolic Faith*, published by the Apostolic Faith Gospel Mission on Azusa Street. The paper is credited by some to have been edited by William J. Seymour,[19] though his name does not appear as editor in the paper itself. The 'leading editors and promoters of the paper' were Florence Crawford and Clara Lum.[20] Later, the paper and the Azusa Revival would discontinue after 1909 when Crawford and Lum moved to Portland, Oregon,[21] pointing to the importance of the role of public witness in perpetuating the revival.

The paper was at first issued monthly, then bi-monthly and at times tri-monthly. The first 13 issues, reprinted in 1997 under the title *The Azusa Street Papers,* are especially helpful in chronicling first-hand perceptions of the events at and surrounding Azusa from within the revival itself.[22]

[15] Wayne E. Warner, 'The Miracle of Azusa', *The Azusa Street Papers,* p. 4.

[16] Paul Schmidgall, *From Oslo to Berlin!, European Pentecostalism* (Erzhausen, Germany: Leuchter-Edition, 2003), pp. 10-25. In this fine work, Schmidgall chronicles the many sources of Pentecostalism throughout Europe, providing ample reason and justification that there were many 'Azusas' or beginnings of Pentecost simultaneous with Azusa.

[17] Stanley M. Burgess and Gary B. McGee, 'The Pentecostal and Charismatic Movements', in *DPCM* (ed. Stanley M. Burgess and Gary B. McGee; Grand Rapids, MI: Zondervan, 1988), p. 3.

[18] 'Pentecost Both Sides The Ocean', *The Apostolic Faith* 1.6 (Feb.–Mar., 1907) in *The Azusa Street Papers,* p. 30. The sixth issue of the paper, on the occasion of the twelfth month of the revival, described various places around the globe that had been experiencing Pentecost, including, London, Stockholm, Sweden, Honolulu, Calcutta, India; and Norway.

[19] 'Pentecost Both Sides', p. 1.

[20] Vinson Synan, 'The Lasting Legacies of the Azusa Street Revival', *Enrichment, A Journal of Pentecostal Ministry* 11.2 (Spring, 2006), pp. 142-52 (p. 149).

[21] Synan, 'The Lasting Legacies', p. 150. Synan writes, 'In 1909, Crawford and Lum moved to Portland, Oregon, where they founded a congregation using the same name as the mother church in Los Angeles-Apostolic Faith Mission. When Lum moved, she took *The Apostolic Faith* mailing list with Seymour's initial blessing and continued publishing of the paper from Portland. This cut off Seymour from his followers and caused the eventual decline of the Azusa Street Mission.'

[22] *The Azusa Street Papers, A Reprint of The Apostolic Faith Mission Publications, Los Angeles, California (1906-1908) William J. Seymour, Editor* (Foley, AL: Harvest, 1997), p. 1.

Politics, Power and Pentecost in the Absence of Grief's Confession

A review of the sections and content of the first 13 issues of *The Apostolic* Faith lend insight into the nature of the revival and the emergence of politics and power issues as well as the fire of Pentecost. The paper was essentially made up of three parts. The first part was a section that provided fresh insight into what was actually happening at the scene of the Azusa Revival itself. The second part was a section, usually on page two, giving editorial notes and details about organization and structure of The Apostolic Faith Movement, the name cited as the publishing agent of the paper. The third part consumed the majority of the paper, giving testimonies of persons being blessed at and as a result of the Pentecostal revival at Azusa. Beginning with the sixth issue, testimonies also included stories of the Spirit's outpouring at other locations around the world.

The fresh insight portion of the paper was generally the lead article and other articles near the beginning of the paper. The lead article headlines of the 13 issues point toward a desire to report and interpret what was happening at Azusa.[23]

The focus was upon the Pentecostal revival in Azusa, as was the apparent mission of the paper. While this first part of the paper consistently functioned to report what took place, issues that were consistently held in the forefront were blessing, power, revival, prophetic fulfillment of Pentecost, signs, wonders and miracles. These testimonies would average nearly 80% of the paper's content. The following excerpt is representative of this emphasis:

> Canes, crutches, medicine bottles, and glasses are being thrown aside as God heals. That is the safe way. No need to keep an old crutch or medicine bottle of any kind around after God heals you. Some, in

---

[23] The lead headlines for the first 13 issues were as follows: (1) 'Pentecost Has Come, Los Angeles Being Visited by a Revival of Bible Salvation and Pentecost as Recorded in the Book of Acts'; (2) 'The Pentecostal Baptism Restored, The Promised Latter Rain Now Being Poured Out on God's Humble People'; (3) 'Bible Pentecost, Gracious Pentecostal Showers Continue to Fall'; (4) 'Pentecost with Signs Following, Seven Months of Pentecostal Showers. Jesus Our Projector and Great Shepherd'; (5) 'Beginning of World Wide Revival'; (6) 'Pentecost Both Sides The Ocean'; (7) 'Many Witnesses to the Power of the Blood and of the Holy Ghost'; (8) 'Los Angeles Campmeeting of the Apostolic Faith Missions'; (9) 'In the Last Days'; (10) 'Everywhere Preaching the Word'; (11) 'Good Tidings of Great Joy, Pentecost in Many Lands-News of Salvation-Jesus Soon Coming'; (12) 'The Lord is Speaking in the Earth Today'; (13) 'Fires are Being Kindled, By the Holy Ghost Throughout the World'.

keeping some such appliance as a souvenir, have been tempted to use them again and have lost their healing.[24]

The other 20% of the paper included occasional commentaries on societal issues such as money, politics and status as well as denominational organization. They gave attention to finances, preachers and, in one instance, to feeding the hungry.[25] They also addressed neutrality among churches.[26] Two articles cited the humbling impact of the Holy Ghost in contrast to the pride of 'well-dressed preachers'.[27] Comments about socio-economic concerns only served to highlight the work of the Spirit, primarily in demonstration of power, healing, signs and evangelism. They were not extensive political commentaries.

The second part of the paper contained editorial comments and information about the production of the paper itself and the organization of The Apostolic Faith Movement. There were strong, consistent indications that Azusa truly desired to be a 'movement' rather than an organization, as indicated by the very name. And yet, there were indications that there were also political and organizational struggles within Azusa and what was happening there. Politics and organization became part of Azusa. The publisher's official name in the first two issues was 'The Apostolic Faith Movement of Los Angeles'. It was changed in the third through fifth issues to 'The Pacific Apostolic Faith Movement'.

[24] *The Apostolic Faith* 1.2 (Sept. 1906) in *The Azusa Street Papers,* p. 11.

[25] 'What mean these salaried preachers over the land that will not preach unless they get so much salary?...The ministers of today have wandered from the old landmarks, therefore they are seeking salary over the land.... Do you want to be blest [sic.]? Do you want the approbation of God? Be a servant to humanity. The loaves and fishes did not multiply in the hands of our blessed Redeemer till He began to give out to the hungry.... He is sending out those who will go out without money and without price.' Quoted from the article, 'Back to Pentecost', *The Apostolic Faith* 1.2 (Oct. 1906) in *The Azusa Street Papers,* p. 16.

[26] 'A leading Methodist layman of Los Angeles says, "Scenes transpiring here are what Los Angeles churches have been praying for for years.... I bless God that it did not start in any church in this city-but in a barn, so that we might all come and take part in it."' Quoted from the article, 'Gracious Pentecostal Showers Continue to Fall', *The Apostolic Faith* 1.3 (Nov. 1906) in *The Azusa Street Papers,* p. 18.

[27] 'Proud, well-dressed preachers come in to "investigate." Soon their high looks are replaced with wonder, then conviction comes, and very often you will find them in a short time wallowing on the dirty floor, asking God to forgive them and make them as little children.' Quoted from, 'Pentecost Has Come, Los Angeles Being Visited by a Revival of Bible Salvation and Pentecost as Recorded in the Book of Acts', *The Apostolic Faith* 1.1 (Sept. 1906) in *The Azusa Street Papers,* p. 10. 'One who came for the first time said, "The thing that impressed me most was the humility of the people, and I went to my room and got down on my knees and asked God to give me humility".' Quoted from 'Beginning of World Wide Revival', *The Apostolic Faith* 1.5 (Jan. 1907) in *The Azusa Street Papers,* p. 26.

The sixth issue settled on the name that remained through the 13th issue, 'The Apostolic Faith Mission'. The preamble that appears under the publisher's name changed during the early issues, indicating changes in the articulating of mission and structure.[28]

What is surprising is a note in the editorial and organizational section in issue six indicating that the property had to be purchased and funds had to be raised. A board of trustees and secretary had been selected to hold the property. The purchase price was reported at $15,000 with a down payment of $4,000. After emphasizing in each of the previous issues that advertisements and solicitations were not permitted, funds were here actually solicited by the Azusa leadership.[29] The building was eventually demolished in 1931 due to termite infestation.[30]

Interestingly, two issues earlier, *The Apostolic Faith* publisher's section stated, 'We were not to tax the people or put ourselves in debt to the people and in bondage.... We have no advertisements.... No debts will be formed. The Lord can stop it [the Paper] at anytime.'[31] This statement appears to stand in contrast to the Azusa paper's appeal two issues later for enough funds to pay off the indebtedness incurred from the purchase of the Azusa Street building.

The politics of leadership appeared in articles in the first sections of the paper, fresh insights, as well as the second editorial/organizational sections, indicating at best a struggle, probably a theological wrestling and at worst, a political division.

In the first issue, in the first column, the second and third articles, there were apparently two leaders of the revival identified. W.J. Seymour testifies, 'The Lord sent the means, and I came to take charge of a mission on Santa Fe street....'[32] Then, a few lines down, the follow-

---

[28] *The Apostolic Faith* 1.5 (Jan. 1907) and 1.10 (Sept. 1907) in *The Azusa Street Papers*, pp. 27, 51.

[29] 'Any friends wishing to have a share in buying this Mission for the Lord may send offerings to Bro. Reuben Clark, who is secretary to the board of trustees....' The explanation for the purchase was as follows, 'It was necessary to buy this mission as a headquarters for the work, in order to hold it, as it would soon have been sold for other purposes. The situation is favorable, being centrally located and in surroundings where no one will be disturbed by prayers or shouts going up sometimes all night. Praise God! The Mission building was formerly a place of worship where souls had been saved years ago, and the spot thus made sacred; and during the past year, hundreds have been saved, sanctified, healed, and baptized with the Holy Ghost.' Quoted from *The Apostolic Faith* 1.6 (Feb.-Mar., 1907) in *The Azusa Street Papers*, p. 31.

[30] Robeck, 'Azusa Street: 100 Years Later', p. 42.

[31] 'Published Free by Faith' *The Apostolic Faith* 1.4 (Dec. 1907) in *The Azusa Street Papers*, p. 25.

[32] 'Bro. Seymour's Call', *The Apostolic Faith* 1.1 (Sept. 1906) in *The Azusa Street Papers*, p. 10.

ing is recorded, 'Bro. Charles Parham, who is God's leader in the Apostolic Faith Movement....'[33] That article anticipates Bro. Parham coming to Azusa as the leader. In the next column of that same issue, in an article entitled, 'The Old-Time Pentecost', it is further noted about Parham's leadership,

> This work began about five years ago last January, when a company of people under the leadership of Chas. Parham, who were studying God's word, tarried for Pentecost in Topeka, Kan.... The meetings in Los Angeles started in a cottage meeting.... The meeting was then transferred to Azusa Street, and since then multitudes have been coming.[34]

Three months later, in the fourth issue, seven months into the revival, in the lead article entitled, 'Pentecost with Signs Following, Seven Months of Pentecostal Showers. Jesus, Our Projector [sic] and Great Shepherd', Parham is declared not to be the leader as admittedly and previously stated by the paper, and Seymour is declared to be the leader.[35]

Leadership issues persisted during the revival for as late as the ninth issue of June-September, 1907, in an article spanning a column and a half, signed simply, 'W.J.S.', no doubt for William J. Seymour, entitled, 'The Holy Spirit Bishop of the Church', the Holy Spirit, and 'not men', is declared to be the leader.[36] Robeck, in one of the most thorough inventories of the leadership of Azusa, notes several forms of leadership during the revival, the example of Seymour, training, planning, staffing, volunteers, teaching of Scripture, preaching, teaching on doctrinal boundaries, and church discipline; but there is no reference to any leadership having to do with testimonies from or benevolence for the suffering.[37]

Our Heritage of Azusa's Public Witness and the Pentecostal /Charismatic Movement

It may be that the problems of one-sided focus only on miracles, inconsistencies in organization and mission, and a vulnerability to the

---

[33] 'Letter from Bro. Parham', *The Apostolic Faith* 1.1 (Sept. 1906) in *The Azusa Street Papers*, p. 10.

[34] 'The Old Time Pentecost', *The Apostolic Faith* 1.1 (Sept. 1906) in *The Azusa Street Papers*, p. 10.

[35] 'Pentecost with Signs Following, Seven Months of Pentecostal Showers. Jesus, Our Projector [sic] and Great Shepherd', *The Apostolic Faith* 1.4 (Dec. 1906) in *The Azusa Street Papers*, p. 22.

[36] 'The Holy Spirit Bishop of the Church', *The Apostolic Faith* 1.9 (June-Sept. 1907) in *The Azusa Street Papers*, p. 48.

[37] Cecil Robeck, *Azusa Street, Mission and Revival, The Birth of the Global Pentecostal Movement* (Nashville: Nelson, 2006), pp. 87-128.

politics of leadership can be attributed to the sheer absence of genuine observance of grief, pain and suffering. Unfortunately, we have inherited and perpetuated the public witness of Azusa – a parade of power[38] with little penance or pain. A painless Pentecost produces a political power struggle about who is in charge. It is the groaning of the Spirit that calls us to confess humbly that the Spirit leads us. A painless Pentecost brings puritanical doctrinal disputes[39] and a piety that strives to be correct more than it sides with the suffering.

In the witness of *The Apostolic Faith* and thereby of Azusa, we find little mention of pain, no effort to weep, no desire to embrace the powerless,[40] but rather only a quest to escape infirmity through healing, rapture and praise,[41] at best occasional, episodic references to the plight of the tragic[42] while apocalyptically looking for a revival, and an ab-

---

[38] An example where this can occur in modern Christendom is given by Juan Segundo, who describes the decisions where the church has sided with privilege and power, 'judgment concerning the greater good or the lesser evil. The church [in Argentina] fixed upon the preservation of Christian privileges as an adequate and self-sufficient criterion itself … is it not clearly an alliance when church authorities refuse to speak out against dictators who trample the most basic human rights under foot?' Juan Luis Segundo, *The Hidden Motives of Pastoral Action, Latin American Reflections* (Maryknoll, NY: Orbis, 1972), p. 41.

[39] By December 1906, in the fourth issue of *The Apostolic Faith*, doctrinal purity was a major concern, occurring and reoccurring through much of that issue. By the tenth issue, in September 1907, a year after the paper began, doctrinal expositions on healing, the ordinances, marriage, divorce, sanctification, were common in the paper. The witness and after effect can be observed in the work of John Belcher who found in research with Pentecostal married couples that 'many classical Pentecostal spouses are struggling with some of the orthodox rules which they are expected to follow.' John R. Belcher, 'Living as Deprived and in the Shadow of the Second Coming: Counseling Classical Pentecostal Couples', *Marriage and Family: A Christian Journal*, 5/2 (2002), pp. 193-203 (p. 200).

[40] Chan notes the discipline of Pentecostal ascetics to pray for '"unutterable groanings" drawing them ineluctably to identify themselves with the birth pangs of creation. They feel keenly the pain of a fallen creation and of the oppressed….' So Simon Chan, *Pentecostal Theology and the Christian Spiritual Tradition* (New York: Sheffield Academic Press, 2000), pp. 84-85.

[41] For many Pentecostals, spirituality is a quest to escape. As I note in an article summarizing Pentecostal/Charismatic spirituality and spiritual direction, 'The questions are about things unfamiliar. Questions include why there is a disease that is not healed, a loved one who remains unemployed, or a wayward son or daughter who continually rebels against God. Growth occurs but with unanswered questions. As a result, spiritual formation is frequently resisted.' The transformation he referred to was the transformation that comes through reflection and perseverance and not necessarily through deliverance. See my 'A Living Stream: Spiritual Direction within the Pentecostal/Charismatic Tradition', *JPsyT* 30.4 (Winter, 2002), p. 339.

[42] Volf carefully but clearly advocates 'embracing' the tragic, even the unjust, as part of the spirituality of the believer when he says, '…there is the *risk of embrace*. The risk follows both from nonsymmetricity and systematic underdetermination. I open my arms, make a movement of the self toward the other, the enemy, and do not know whether I

sence of sitting with the suffering while building an empire called a movement; that is the public witness of Azusa that we carry with us to this day. The pain of Pentecostals today is that we are so political. The politics of Pentecost today is the same as it was at Azusa, the virtual absence of pain.

Oh, pain was there, it was all around them. The people of California and Azusa were poor, they were hungry, they had even experienced that same year of 1906 in the north one of the greatest natural disasters ever known in the United States in the San Francisco earthquake of 1906. But, did Azusa weep, did it even moan? It blinked and testified to 'a spiritual earthquake – but with a much happier ending'. [43]

Was Azusa just about striving for a 'happy ending?' No, there were glimmerings of suffering that were skirted and touched upon, tucked away in the corner of the record of Azusa from time to time. In the first issue of *The Apostolic Faith*, on the last page, in a one-paragraph article entitled, 'Victory Follows Crucifixion', the paper noted that, 'Jesus suffered', and that there would be 'a crucial hour in every man's and every woman's life'. The article continued to talk of the manner in which the hour of suffering would come but the goal was to 'get on the resurrection side of the cross, the glory and victory will be unspeakable'. [44]

Even when Azusa talked about suffering, it was very infrequent and very far between. In the thirteenth issue, in May 1908, two years after Azusa began, the goal was still to get beyond the pain, not bear it together. [45] On the next to last page of that issue, in an article entitled, 'Pentecost at a Funeral', the story is told of a grieving father and mother at the funeral of their three-month old child. The parents were unsaved. The parents were in such grief that the mother could not attend the service. She was carried by 'three or four' to the viewing and was so weak that she 'fainted away and was unconscious for some time during the burial service'. Most of the article chronicles the effort to lead the mother to salvation. The capstone of the story occurred when the mother accepted Christ and realized that she would join her daughter in heaven. She then stopped grieving. Stopping her grief, rather than grieving with her was the goal. The removal of pain was

---

will be misunderstood, despised, even violated or whether my action will be appreciated, supported, and reciprocated. I can become a savior or a victim – possibly both.' See Miroslav Volf, *Exclusion and Embrace: A Theological Exploration of Identity, Otherness, and Reconciliation* (Nashville: Abingdon, 1996), p. 147.

[43] Volf, *Exclusion and Embrace*, p. 5

[44] 'Victory Follows Crucifixion', *The Apostolic Faith* 1.1 (Sept. 1906) in *The Azusa Street Papers,* p. 2.

[45] Galatians 6.2, 'Bear ye one another's burdens and so fulfill the law of Christ.'

the Pentecostal blessing. The legacy was the perception that the Spirit was *only* acting to make the pain stop. The end of the article notes, 'Several were present who had been very much opposed to the baptism with the Holy Ghost and the speaking in tongues, but they were convinced' when they saw 'the mother ... smiling and waving her hands ... and she was singing and speaking in a foreign language....'[46]

This is not a critique of Azusa. There are many things that occurred at Azusa that are not recorded in *The Apostolic Faith* paper/chronicles. However, this is a commentary and beginning of an analysis of the public witness conveyed by *The Apostolic Faith*. *The Apostolic Faith* was and is the most public witness of Azusa. It was what people then and now first and foremost know about the revival. Whatever happened there, whether the hungry were fed, the thirsty given drink, the strangers brought in, the 'naked' clothed, the sick or prisoners visited,[47] the chronicles do not emphasize these matters. On these topics, the public witness of that Pentecostal revival is at best virtually silent.

Why do we not hear about the painful experience of the 'groaning' and 'intercession' of the Spirit along with the resurrection power of the Spirit?[48] Why do we not hear about those who were never healed, who continued to wander, remained in prison,[49] were destitute and were never delivered in this world?[50] Why do we not hear about people 'bearing one another's burdens?'[51] These elements very well may have been there. However, according to the painless witness of the primary mode of telling the story of Azusa, *The Apostolic Faith*, we will at best not know.

If *The Apostolic Faith* represents our heritage of public witness, it contains politics as well as power. It contains struggles for leadership,

---

[46] 'Pentecost at a Funeral', *The Apostolic Faith* 2.13 (May 1908) in *The Azusa Street Papers*, p. 64.

[47] These are the areas uplifted by Jesus at the judgment as communicated in Mt. 25.31-46.

[48] Romans 8.11, 22, 26; This is portrayed by Pseudo-Maricus, 'You have no other way to become worthy of these amazing and blessed types, except that day and night you pour out tears according to him who says: "Each night I wash my bed and water my mattress with my tears" (Ps 6.6).... For this reason the Prophet boldly declares: "Do not silence my tears" (Ps 39.13).' Quoted from 'Homily 25' found in *The Fifty Spiritual Homilies and the Great Letter* (ed. George A. Maloney, S.J.; New York: Paulist Press, 1992), pp. 162-63.

[49] 'True, justice must be pursued, and the punishment of the criminals must be appropriate. But even at their worst, criminals remain human beings and, therefore, "neighbors" for whom we must care.' Miroslav Volf, 'Original Crime, Primal Care', in *God and the Victim: Theological Reflections of Evil, Victimization, Justice, and Forgiveness* (ed. Lisa Barnes Lampman and Michelle D. Shattuck; Grand Rapids, MI: Eerdmans, 1999), p. 34.

[50] These are the categories of the 'others' in Heb. 11.36-39.

[51] This is the admonition of Gal. 6.2 whereby one fulfills the law of Christ.

the hope of a better tomorrow and the way to a more prosperous world. These are the themes that those in pain, those left in the shadows of the pages of Pentecost's public witness, must observe – those for whom the ministry of healing turned into the ministry of condemnation when they were not healed.[52] We have been a movement of the outcasts, but we have tried hard to 'get in' through a witness of power. What of our witness of pain? Might bearing the pain of Pentecostals who are not healed, who do not get rich and who remain without power change our public witness?[53]

Continuing Public Witness and Grief Not Observed

The public witness of Pentecostals and Charismatics since Azusa indicates some expression of concern but not a central confession of suffering. A review of articles in the official publication of the Church of God, Cleveland, Tennessee, the *Evangel*, from 1960-2007 indicates an average of thee and one-half articles, commentaries or sermon outlines a year dealing with suffering.[54] The trend is not encouraging, because from 1960-1969 the average was five per year but from 2000-2007 the average was less than one per year. In the most widely read Charismatic publication, *Charisma and the Christian Life*, the average from 1980-2007 was less than two per year.

Observing Our Grief

Grief has not gone unnoticed by Pentecostals and Charismatics. Robeck in chronicling Azusa did note that the Pentecostal and Charismatic movement 'has functioned as an icon of hope for oppressed people'.[55] There was a theology of love at Azusa, as noted by Jacobsen,[56] that may have been the closest form of their observation of grief. Alexander has

---

[52] Charles Farah, Jr. *From the Pinnacle of the Temple, Faith or Presumption?* (Plainfield, NJ: Logos International, 1977), p. 33.

[53] As Adewuya points out, the community ministering to one another is 'the decisive edge' that the Spirit-filled community has in the world. J. Ayodeji Adewuya, *Holiness and Community in 2 Cor 6:14-7:1, Paul's View of Communal Holiness in the Corinthian Correspondence* (New York: Peter Lang, 2003), p. 168.

[54] Some of these articles of note include Duran M. Palmertree, 'The Christian and Suffering', *Evangel* 52.43 (Dec. 31, 1962), pp. 4-6; William H. Pratt, 'The Sick and the Dying', *Evangel* 52.1 (Mar. 5, 1962), pp. 6-7; James N. Layne, 'How to Deal with Suffering', *Evangel* 63.23 (Feb. 12, 1979); Margaret Gaines, 'Depression Blessings', *Evangel* 53.8 (Apr. 22, 1963), p. 19.

[55] Cecil Robeck, 'Azusa Street: 100 Years Later', *Enrichment, A Journal for Pentecostal Ministry* 11.2 (Spring, 2006), pp. 26-42 (p. 42).

[56] Douglas Jacobsen, 'The Gracious Theology of William J. Seymour and the Azusa Street Mission', *Enrichment, A Journal of Pentecostal Ministry* 11.2 (Spring 2006), pp. 56-62 (p. 62).

written extensively on the suffering of Pentecostal saints in their emphasis on healing.[57] Land has emphasized, 'Praying together, and not just for one another, bearing burdens and confessing to one another is essential for any Christian community....'[58] In her work, *Pentecostal Formation: A Pedagogy Among the Oppressed*, Cheryl Bridges Johns identifies the real roots of Pentecostals in being among the oppressed and being formed as a confessing, dialogical community.[59] Thomas probes the New Testament text concerning questions of sickness and suffering in *The Devil, Disease and Deliverance: Origins of Illness in New Testament Thought*.[60] Priscilla Patten Benham notes in her 1972 Masters thesis that Jesus exercised empathy for the sick, a model for therapists today.[61] I have written about care, counsel and discipleship for the oppressed, handicapped and ill.[62] Yong has approached issues of phenomenology, pneumatology and religions by addressing the work of the Spirit in the community of believers as they interact with issues of human relationship and need.[63]

The importance of observing one's grief and communicating with others about the grief experience has been underscored by caregivers and counselors in general. Kubler-Ross noted that 'we displace all our knowledge onto machines, since they are less close to us than the suf-

---

[57] Kimberly Ervin Alexander, *Pentecostal Healing: Models in Theology and Practice* (JPTS 29; Blandford Forum, UK: Deo Publishing, 2006); *idem*, 'Models of Pentecostal Healing and Practice in Light of Early Twentieth Century Pentecostalism' (Ph.D. diss., St. John's College, Nottingham, UK, 2002).

[58] Steven J. Land, *Pentecostal Spirituality: A Passion for the Kingdom* (JPTS 1; Sheffield: Sheffield Academic Press, 1993), p. 218.

[59] Cheryl Bridges Johns, *Pentecostal Formation: A Pedagogy among the Oppressed* (JPTS 2; Sheffield: Sheffield Academic Press, 1993).

[60] John Christopher Thomas, *The Devil Disease and Deliverance: Origins of Illness in New Testament Thought* (JPTS 13; Sheffield: Sheffield Academic Press, 1998).

[61] Priscilla Patten Benham, 'A Comparison of Selected Principles in the Counseling of Christ and Carl Rogers' (Master's Thesis, Wheaton College, 1972).

[62] Oliver McMahan, *The Caring Church* (Cleveland, TN: Pathway, 2002); *Scriptural Counseling: A God-Centered Method* (Cleveland, TN: Pathway, 1995); *Becoming a Shepherd: Contemporary Pastoral Ministry* (Cleveland, TN: Pathway, 1994); *Deepening Discipleship: Contemporary Applications of Biblical Commitments* (Cleveland, TN: Pathway, 2000); Oliver McMahan and Shea Hughes, *The Caring Christian, Intensive Care* (Cleveland, TN: Pathway, 2004).

[63] See Amos Yong, *Beyond the Impasse, Toward a Pneumatological Theology of Religions* (Grand Rapids, MI: Baker Academic, 2003); *Discerning the Spirit(s), A Pentecostal-Charismatic Contribution to Christian Theology of Religions* (JPTS 20; Sheffield: Sheffield Academic Press, 2000); *The Spirit Poured Out On All Flesh: Pentecostalism and the Possibility of Global Theology* (Grand Rapids, MI: Baker Academic, 2005); and *Spirit-Word Community: Theological Hermeneutics in Trinitarian Perspective* (Aldershot, UK: Ashgate, 2002); notwithstanding Yong does not address the need for confession of suffering or grief within the Spirit-community as a vital hermeneutic or aspect of global theology.

fering face of another human being which would remind us once more of our lack of omnipotence....'[64] Marvin Gilbert, a Pentecostal, commented, 'The counselor must resist the temptation to become the dispenser of God's power if exercising that role would rob the client of self-reliance and the personal discovery that God is the source of strength, power, and encouragement.'[65] Commenting on the grieving adult, Shapiro observed that '... the newly bereaved feel the first blow of grief almost as a death blow, a heartbreak they might in fact not survive.'[66] Koenig, McCullough and Larson have extensively documented the positive effect of religion upon health and coping with pain.[67]

The Crossroads of Confession for Pentecostals and Charismatics

Suffering has certainly placed Pentecostals and Charismatics at a crossroads, to tell or not to tell, to observe our grief or continue to proclaim the public witness of only the miracles at Azusa. Suffering has been called a 'gracious gift' by Hicks[68] who was commenting on Paul's words in Phil. 1.29 while the apostle was in chains, '... not only for you to believe on him, but also to suffer for his sake.' Yet for Pentecostals, Cox, in citing the reasons for the rise of Pentecostalism, noted that 'Pentecostalism confronted chaos, normlessness, and ennui by affirming and then transforming them.'[69] However, the public witness of Pentecostals and Charismatics may argue differently.

What is the challenge to Pentecostals and Charismatics in confronting their own griefs and surprises of suffering? The challenge may be one of reflection. Kierkegaard, in *The Present Age* described this challenge as 'a noose which drags one into eternity ... by leaping into the depths, one learns to help oneself, learns to love others as much as oneself'.[70] It is a theology of praxis that requires a corporate witness of

---

[64] Elizabeth Kubler-Ross, *On Death and Dying: What the Dying Have to Teach Doctors, Nurses, Clergy and Their Own Families* (New York: Macmillan, 1969), p. 9.

[65] Marvin G. Gilbert, 'Individual Psychology: The Theory and Psychotherapy of Alfred Adler' in *The Holy Spirit and Counseling, Theology and Theory* (ed. Marvin G. Gilbert and Raymond T. Brock; Peabody, MA: Hendrickson, 1985), p. 219.

[66] Ester R. Shapiro, *Grief As a Family Process: A Developmental Approach to Clinical Practice* (New York: Guilford Press, 1994), p. 21.

[67] Harold G. Koenig, Michael E. McCullough & David B. Larson, *Handbook of Religion and Health* (Oxford: Oxford University Press, 2001).

[68] Peter Hicks, *The Message of Evil and Suffering: Light Into Darkness* (Bible Themes Series; ed. Derek Tindbill; Downers Grove, IL: InterVarsity Press, 2006), p. 166.

[69] Harvey Cox, *Fire from Heaven: The Rise of Pentecostal Spirituality and the Reshaping of Religion in the Twenty-First Century* (Reading, MA: Addison-Wesley, 1995), p. 120.

[70] Soren Kierkegaard, *The Present Age* (New York: Harper and Row, 1962), p. 58.

dealing with a past while experiencing a future, a dilemma described by Hans Küng, 'The problems of the past should not have priority, but the broad and many-layered problems of men and women and human society today.... Believable theory and livable practice, dogmatics and ethics, personal piety and institutional reform are not to be separated....'[71] As the Pentecostal movement contemplates its own cross, it looks to the statement of the cross. As Brueggemann confesses, 'There is no more radical criticism than these statements [the passion announcements of Mark], for they announce that the power of God takes the form of death and that real well-being and victory only appear via death.'[72]

Pentecostals and Charismatics, in pondering the observance of their griefs, may be standing between the cross and Pentecost, just as the saints as described by Roger Stronstad, 'They had abandoned themselves to the person and ministry of Jesus, but in His death they had experienced a betrayal of their commitment, their hopes, and their aspirations. Shattered, disillusioned, and afraid of possible action against them ... they had drifted....'[73] Yet these are conditions of poverty, pain and privation that Pentecostals and Charismatics profess to have overcome, 'to rescue souls from a fallen world'.[74]

The problem of whether to observe what we profess to have left behind is, according to Schaull and Cesar, to 'relate the survival of the poor – their day-to-day struggle – with the infinite richness of the transcendental'.[75] And this involves not just the economically poor but also the pained, the dying and the discouraged. Schaull and Cesar's analogy applies to all of the pains we may have left behind, 'When churches that began with the poorest people are no longer poor, what effort is made to live in dialogue with the history out of which they have come?'[76] When we confess our healing, how do we relate to those who remain sick? When we profess our power, how do we relate to those who are still powerless? When we have analyzed our rights, how do we understand the righteousness of the cross?

It may be that the observance of our pains, our sorrows and our griefs may draw us nearer the cross. And once having made this obser-

---

[71] Hans Küng, *Theology for the Third Millennium, An Ecumenical View* (New York: Doubleday, 1988), p. 205.

[72] Walter Brueggemann, *The Prophetic Imagination* (Nashville: Fortress, 1978), p. 92.

[73] Roger Stronstad, *The Charismatic Theology of St. Luke* (Peabody, MA: Hendrickson, 1984), p. 59.

[74] Johns, *Pentecostal Formation*, p. 66.

[75] Richard Schaull and Waldo Cesar, *Pentecostalism and the Future of the Christian Churches: Promises, Limitations, Challenges* (Grand Rapids, MI: Eerdmans, 2000), p. 40.

[76] Schaull and Cesar, *Pentecostalism and the Future*, p. 136.

vance, we may experience the signpost of the suffering of the Spirit, pointing to the reality of the resurrected body. Telling this observance was the message of Vest and Land in *Reclaiming Your Testimony, Your Story and the Christian Story*, 'Christian people without a testimony – a story to tell – are a people without a future'.[77] Cartledge described the power and necessity of observance incumbent on Pentecostals and Charismatics,

> ... the individual aspects of knowing are integrated socially by the notion of testimony. It is the social mechanism of testimony that is of supreme importance to Pentecostal and charismatic understanding of our knowledge of God. We do not believe and know God in isolation; rather, we are part of a worshipping and witnessing community.[78]

We carry the observances of our sorrows to one another, so that we might see the Spirit and tell others about new life.

The decline of the revival at the building at Azusa Street may have been marked in 1909 with the cessation of its public witness in *The Apostolic Faith* newspaper. Or, it may have been destined by its leaders' refusal to observe the grief many of them continued to experience. Maybe in the future we will be known not as a movement, rallying the cause of the Spirit, but a church raising the sign of the cross, of One Who suffered and died for us, and bids us to come and follow Him, take up our cross all the way to the sacrifice and pain of Calvary; to enter the door of death, joining with the Spirit as we suffer together.

Then we may meet Him on the road to Jerusalem, much as the two joined on the Emmaus Road. Hollis and Val Gause wrote in a volume they co-authored called, *The Emmaus Road*, an account of the two on that road. As they shared their sorrows with each other and the Saviour, 'the flame of their burning hearts burned away the veils on their eyes....The flames of Pentecost had begun to burn already.'[79] Perhaps, as we share our griefs with one another as well as with our Lord, as we journey with the Spirit who suffers with us on even the road to death, the flames of Pentecost may truly burn as they transform us on the road to a new body, a new life and a new heaven and earth.

★★★★★★★★★★★★★★★★★★

[77] R. Lamar Vest and Steven J. Land, *Reclaiming Your Testimony: Your Story and the Christian Story* (Cleveland, TN: Pathway, 2002), p. 21.

[78] Mark J. Cartledge, *Practical Theology, Charismatic and Empirical Perspectives* (Carlisle, UK: Paternoster, 2003), p. 53.

[79] Val Gause and Hollis Gause, *The Emmaus Road* (Longwood, FL: Xulon Press, 2005), p. 79.

Abstract

In this paper the topic of the confession of grief and suffering of the Spirit is discussed, comparing the observance of grief and surprise by joy of C.S. Lewis with the testimony and witness of the Spirit by R. Hollis Gause during times of suffering and tragedy. The Pentecostal Charismatic heritage of public witness, it is argued, has shown a tendency to deny suffering and thereby mask the movement's vision of the work of the Spirit, especially in the transformation of the body. Finally, the future direction of the movement's witness is called into question relative to its willingness to confess its grief.

16

Complementarity and Mutuality in the Bonds of Marriage

Douglas W. Slocumb[*]

Created in Relationship with God

Women in the Body of Christ has long been the interest of R. Hollis Gause and his wife Beulah Gause, as reflected in their jointly authored book in 1984.[1] A more recent work, *Women in Leadership: A Pentecostal Perspective,* which Hollis Gause authored jointly with Kimberly Ervin Alexander,[2] showed the importance of the leadership role of women in the body of Christ.

Life for all humanity began in union with God. As God says in Gen. 1.26, 'Let us make [humanity]...' As Virginia Ramey Mollenkott points out, 'Adam and Eve were created on the sixth day, both of them in the image of God, and together they were given command over the rest of creation'.[3] According to Hollis Gause this passage gives us

> a record of a divine council in which God chose to create a creature who would be described as created 'in the image of God.' This account is unique in two ways. The first is that no other act of God in the events of creation is introduced in this way. All other events in the creation story are simply represented in decree with such statements as 'and God said ... , and there was ... ,' the second unique factor is that no other creature is described as bearing the image of God.[4]

[*] Douglas W. Slocumb (D.Min., Eastern Baptist Theological Seminary) is Associate Professor of Marriage and Family at the Pentecostal Theological Seminary, Cleveland, TN.
[1] R. Hollis Gause and Beulah Gause, *Women in the Body of Christ* (Cleveland, TN: Pathway, 1984).
[2] R. Hollis Gause and Kimberly Ervin Alexander, *Women in Leadership: A Pentecostal Perspective* (Cleveland, TN: Center for Pentecostal Leadership and Care, 2006).
[3] V.R. Mollenkott, *Women, Men, and the Bible* (rev. ed.; New York, NY: Crossroad, 1988), p. 43.
[4] Gause and Alexander, *Women in Leadership*, p. 30.

In creation God breathed into Adam's nostrils and he, Adam, became a living personal being (Gen. 2.7). Man and woman were the crowning act of God's creative work. They were created in the image and likeness of God. They were created male and female. They were persons. God is a person. A person can think, feel and will. A person is conscious of self and of other selves or persons. 'Man and woman, on the highest level, find their fulfillment in communication with God, the one who created them in his image.'[5] Commonness of relationship requires communication.

Created for Relationship with Others

Paul states in Gal. 3.28, 'there is neither male nor female; for you are one in Christ Jesus'. Man and woman are one in relationship with each other. They are also one in relationship to Christ.

'Adam' (humanity) was created in the image of God (Genesis 1). In Genesis 2, the single 'Adam' needed an equal with whom to communicate in order to be in relationship. God then created woman from the side of Adam (the individual) for them to be together as one. They were created suitable to one another both spiritually and in physical intimacy. This unity provided for physical fulfillment and for the procreation of the race. Each was also suitable to one another physically and psychologically. They belonged together and would find their fulfillment in each other.

Man and woman were created in physical union to become 'one flesh' (Hebrew בסר, Greek σάρξ). Maston states that this term points to more than just physical flesh; it also refers to the total person. The man and woman were one in more ways than just physically. They were also one in their capacity to communicate with one another as well as with their Creator.

Male–Female Duality/Sexuality

In being created in God's image, 'Adam' (humanity) was created male and female. The divine decree determined humanity's being made in the image of God and that they were given rulership over their environment, according to Gen. 1.26-27. Humans alone were given authority over their surroundings. They alone were given authority over God's creations.

This decree elevated humanity above all other creatures of God's creation. This likeness or image of God, according to Gause, included

---

[5] T.B. Maston and W.M. Tillman, Jr., *The Bible and Family Relations* (Nashville, TN: Broadman, 1983), p. 37.

intelligence, the spiritual nature of human existence, holiness, emotional capacity and humanity's deliberative and volitional nature. This gave humanity the special identity with God. This humanness consisted of male and female in creation. This duality gave humanity wholeness. God saw that it was not good for Adam to be alone (Gen. 2.15). Adam had been created for relationship. Therefore, the companion for 'Adam' (humanity) was created directly by God and in the image of God. The female immediately was equal with the male. Only an equal could provide the companionship that was needed by the other.

Even though the female was created out of the male, the pattern of creation produced equal but complementary creatures. They were equal in that they were of the same order of creation and they both bore God's image. As Gause puts it, 'In their humanity (i.e., being in the divine image), they are the same.'[6] In their humanness and dignity, they are one. In bearing the image of God, they are one. For in creation of humanity, God said 'Let us make man (humankind)' and this constitutes a divine council of God. He chose to create a creature (humanity) who would be created 'in the image of God.' No other creature of God's creation is made with this unique factor of bearing the image of God. 'The most fundamental fact of creation is that the man and the woman are complementary to each other because they are both created by God in His own image.'[7] As Gause observes, 'Neither is dependent on the other for the presence of that image and the high estate it gives.'[8] This makes each a steward of God and then a steward to each other.

This equality is integral to humanity's social, physical, and spiritual needs. As humans face each other, each mirrors the other in a way that helps both to see themselves and to make themselves accountable to each other. They share the obligation to obey God and the ability to function as personal creatures. They also equally share the consequences of failing in this obligation.

The divine decree to the man and the woman in Gen. 1.28 to multiply and fill the earth illustrates the mutual dependency of each on the other. Since the woman is out of man, it is possible to unite physically and spiritually in marriage. Their sexuality is holy and natural to the character of man and woman. Neither is the servant of the other but both are equals. They are one flesh. This oneness is designed to characterize the nature of marriage.

---

[6] Gause and Alexander, *Women in Leadership*, p. 25.
[7] Gause and Alexander, *Women in Leadership*, p. 31.
[8] Gause and Alexander, *Women in Leadership*, p. 31.

Biological distinctiveness is created through physical union. As the sperm fertilizes the ovum, the human's sexuality is determined. When the XX chromosomes are united, femaleness occurs and when the YY chromosomes are united, maleness results. This gender identity becomes the human's biological heritage.

'Adam' (humanity) possessed the potential for masculine/feminine identification. 'Male and female' refer to our gender identity (XX or YY), but 'masculine and feminine' refer to the ways in which a particular culture sociologically and publicly defines each gender role. The direction for gender roles is largely determined by the society and culture in which one lives. Divine decree in creation has prepared the way for our gender identity to be established. As Paul K. Jewett says, '... to be created in the image of God is to be male and female. Not only do men and women alike participate in the divine image, but their fellowship as male and female is what it means to be in the image of God.'[9] However, our gender role is not established this way. It is a learned behavior.

Nature of Human Relatedness

The word 'complement' points to that which fills up or completes by bringing together mutually completing parts. God created male and female to complete each other. They have been designed physically and emotionally to complement each other in establishing a new completeness in life. They complement each other in their mutual awareness of their sexuality. Male and female complement each other toward wholeness as persons.

Marriage brings the male and female into complementary personal partnership. As J.C. Howell brings out the sense of Gen. 2.18, 'Eve is Adam's ... help, corresponding to him.' Eve thus complements Adam, just as Adam complements Eve, with the result that it is the two together, man and woman, who form what the Genesis text denotes by the term 'Adam' (Gen. 5.12).[10]

Paul in 1 Cor. 7.3-5 states that in the Christian marriage the couple is equal in sexual responsibility. They complement each other in the sexual union. They are in partnership with each other. They have become one flesh (Gen. 2.24). They complement each other in emotional intimacy. Intimacy can only come as the authentic personhood of each partner's worth is made equal. Oneness in the concept of one flesh is the potential for intimacy. In this emotional intimacy the partners risk greater openness. This results in a greater degree of caring for

---

[9] P.K. Jewett, *Man as Male and Female* (Grand Rapids, MI: Eerdmans, 1975), p. 24.
[10] J.C. Howell, *Equality and Submission in Marriage* (Nashville, TN: Broadman, 1979), p. 38.

each other. Jesus spoke of this oneness in his relationship with the Father (Jn 17.11, 22-23). According to Mt. 19.5-6, man and woman in marriage were made one. They are unique. 'In one-flesh union of marriage, by analogy, the one[ness] which is possible is a dynamic unity of persons in which equality of personhood exists yet functional subordination to one another also exists for the fulfillment of tasks related to family life'.[11]

The unity that is exhorted in Scripture is based on Trinitarian unity. So, this unity in God is a paradigm for unity in redemptive and social situations. If we understand this, we can also understand: (1) the significance of unity; (2) the severity and unnaturalness of brokenness; and (3) the place that unity and brokenness has equals the spectrum of holiness and sin.

Humankind and Brokenness of Relationship: 'Alienation'

The harmony or complementariness of the male and female relationship was unique and explicit in original created state. Sin is not natural for those created in the image of God; it is a foreign and disruptive element in human nature. Humankind was created to be under the influence of the Spirit of God. However, in the sinful state, humanity lives in distortion to God's original intent. Scripture treats sinful humanity as dead.

Male and female both bear an equal responsibility for sin. Genesis (2.17) clearly states that if one eats of the forbidden tree that one will surely die. Romans (3.23) states that all have sinned because of the first Adam's sin in the garden. Paul in Ephesians (2.1, 2) describes this condition as being dead in trespasses and sins, and takes note of the indwelling of a foreign spirit in God's creation. The human race became sinful by lack of faith in God and by yielding to temptation.

This fallen state is a violated relationship and a break in the union with God; the nakedness of man and woman is brought to their awareness. They were ashamed. This was a reversal of their earlier state with each other. They were intimidated in their nakedness and fear filled their lives. Fear produced the will to subdue. The disruption and threat to equality and complementariness begins with the Fall of Adam and Eve.

Adam and Eve were afraid of the presence of God. The excuses that they gave God brought damning results. First, they became divided and belligerent toward each other. Second, they aborted any prospect of repentance toward God and forgiveness toward each other.

Their sin bought a curse upon all creatures. Paul states that the sin of disobedience by Adam and Eve brought sin on the whole human race

---

[11] Howell, *Equality and Submission*, p. 42.

(Romans 5). The Spirit of God and the spirit of man and woman were alienated. Henceforth, all humanity from Adam and Eve bore the sin of Adam and Eve. With the curse came the promise that Satan would be defeated; and in Genesis (12.1) the hope of restoration was given to humanity. This is the birth of hope for humankind.

Humanity exists outside of God in distress, sorrow and alienation. The woman would have sorrow in childbirth and would now be subject to her husband (Gen. 3.16). The man would have his livelihood cursed by the earth bringing forth thorns and thistles. He would produce his living by the sweat of his brow. They were both sentenced to the dust in death (Gen. 3.17-19).

This brokenness brought a break in the covenant that God had with Adam and Eve. Fear and distrust were brought into the marriage relationship. There was a break in the relationship between them and God. They were cast out of the Garden. No longer in relationship with God, they were cursed along with the earth and all creation.

The eating from the tree of the 'knowledge of good and evil' was not the reason for the 'Fall'; it was the breaking and the transgression of the commandment of God. It was the breaking of trust and covenant agreement God had made with His creation. The 'Fall' ushered in new and complex conditions and circumstances for the world.

Before the 'Fall', human beings were not ashamed of their nakedness. However, after the 'Fall' they felt the need of covering with fig leaves. As J. Murray states, 'This covering of themselves was apparently the instinctive reaction to the shame and fear which were the result of sin' (cf. Gen. 3.10).[12] There were emotions of shame and fear along with the sin and guilt. The whole nature of humanity was depraved. The Fall brings revolutionary changes into human life; 'yet, these ordinances [the procreation of offspring, the replenishing of the earth, subduing of the same, dominion over creatures, labor, the weekly Sabbath, and marriage] are still in effect and they indicate that the interests and occupations which lay closest to man's heart in original integrity must still lie close to his heart in his fallen state'.[13]

Humankind and Restoration of Hope

This alienated state leaves human beings in need of being restored to the earlier relationship with God. Whereas once they were in union with God, now they are alienated from God. There is need for redemption to restore harmony, harmony with oneself and with God. This restoration is necessary both spiritually and physically. Christ makes this restoration possible. As Murray comments,

---

[12] J. Murray, *Principles of Conduct* (Grand Rapids, MI: Eerdmans, 1957), p. 4.
[13] Murray, *Principles*, p. 44.

> Through the Incarnation, [God] joins both creation and redemption, and embraces the entire human race.... In His incarnation He stands for both men and women, not as an accommodation to women, but as an acknowledgement that He is Creator-Redeemer of the whole human race.... Whether in creation or redemption, God gathers all things and all people together under one Head, Jesus Christ who is the eternal Word/Decree of God.[14]

The purpose of Christ's death was for humankind to be restored again in union with God. In Christ's atoning suffering and death we see the restoration as applied in the New Testament (Mt. 8.17; 1 Pet. 2.24, 25).

Here the Holy Spirit works with unredeemed humanity to call humans back to union or back to their origin and purpose. As the Spirit was the agent in creation, He is also the agent of human re-creation (Jn 3.5-8 and Titus 3.5). The Spirit's work in unredeemed and imperfect humanity cultivates and perfects the human spirit in relation to God's Spirit.

This new creation in Christ does not do away with the personhood of the individual. As Manfred Brauch puts it, 'The salvation event does not create a new personality; it creates a new situation ... the justified "new creature" or person'.[15] Those who accept Jesus Christ, the last 'Adam', as the sacrifice for sin are justified again in righteousness with God. In Romans, Paul deals with the fact that humans were made righteous through Christ. In the Old Testament 'righteousness' was basically a relational concept. This was designated in the action of partners in keeping a covenant relationship. When Paul spoke of Abraham, who was before the law, Abraham was accounted righteous because of his faithfulness. David, who was under the Law, was accounted righteous because of his faithfulness, according to Gause.[16] Thus, righteousness is synonymous with faithfulness, according to Brauch.[17] Paul seems to use interchangeably steadfast love, faithfulness, and peace. Righteousness and faithfulness are words which God used with His relationship in creation. Therefore, it is a new situation that is given to those who believe. They are brought into a new relationship with God through His Son, Jesus Christ. Brauch states it this way: 'Christian existence is characterized by a change of lordship, not by a change within our inmost being.... The Christian has moved into the possibility of the new obedience.'[18] Paul is saying that Christians have become

---

[14] Murray, *Principles*, p. 27

[15] Manfred T. Baruch, *Set Free to Be* (Philadelphia, PA: The Eastern Baptist Theological Seminary, Jan. 1989), p. 11.

[16] Gause and Alexander, *Women in Leadership*, ch. 3.

[17] Manfred T. Brauch, 'Theology of Marriage and Family', Lecture, January 1989.

[18] Brauch, 'Theology of Marriage', pp. 26-27.

the righteousness of God. Thus, to become the righteousness of God means to become the incarnation of his restoring love in the midst of our world. The incarnation also shows the equality of woman with man. Aware of these new possibilities, one must recognize both the freedom and responsibility of that kind of existence. One becomes the mediator of God's reconciling, forgiving, and healing love in the midst of our broken and confused world.[19]

Brauch says this justification is 'that action of God's relation restoring love in Christ (God's righteousness), which calls humanity out of alienation/separation into a restored relationship with God.'[20] I am free to become what God intended me to be. Here in the operation of God's Spirit, my old 'Adamic' (fallen) nature is being put off and a new nature is being put on (Eph. 4.22-24). In this new nature I am to live in peace (Rom. 5.1), in reconciliation (Rom. 5.10-11; 2 Cor. 5.13), and as a new creation (2 Cor. 5.17) with God.

I live under the curse of the old 'Adam', with my hope in the new 'Adam', Jesus Christ. These two natures are overlapping in this life that I now live. Paul states there is a struggle within me (Eph. 6.10). This old nature's desire to rule and dictate my behavior keeps me in that broken relationship. The 'Adamic' nature alienated and separated me from the created order. This nature placed walls between brothers and sisters in the human community. The fallen nature brought emptiness, meaninglessness, anxiety, and despair. This nature boasts of a righteousness whose consequences become judgmental. This nature was bound with wrongdoing (Rom. 1; 1 Cor. 6-10; Col. 3.5-9).

I become free through God's unconditional love and grace. He sets the believer free through Jesus Christ. Through my faith in Christ, who shared Himself with humanity, I am free from the bondage of sin and death. The old 'Adamic' nature is dealt with in Christ.

Paul states, 'I am crucified with Christ; nevertheless I live, yet not I but Christ which lives within me.' I am a bondservant of Christ in love and submission to Him. I must now walk in the Spirit hoping and waiting for the new age to come that Christ has promised. 'By the Spirit all believers have been baptized into the eschatological events of Christ's death and resurrection and have been given the Spirit (1 Cor. 12.13), a sign that they belong to the new age.'[21]

This new life in Christ is one to be lived in love. Even the exercise of the charismatic gifts, such as glossolalia and prophecy, are to be governed by love so that the Christian community can be built up in

---

[19] Brauch, 'Theology of Marriage', p. 31.

[20] Brauch, 'Theology of Marriage'.

[21] French L. Arrington, *Paul's Aeon Theology in I Corinthians* (Washington, DC: University Press of America, 1977), pp. 143-44.

harmony, unity, and public worship that edifies all (1 Cor. 12; 13). Love, though imperfect, should be our aim in this Christian experience. 'It (love) exists in this age along with faith, hope, and pneumatic qualities. Based on the Christ-event as the turning point of the two ages, it is the mark and mode of Christian existence ... the believer's experiences of the transcendent in this age'.[22] Humanity lives in dialectical tension between the 'already-not yet' situation.

Psychology does not address relationship to God but rather the relationship of human being to each other. Psychology and theology are often two different languages being used to try to express the relationship of humanity to each other. God desires for us to be whole persons. Whole persons live in community with each other through Christ. In Christ I am protected, I am secure, I belong, and I am loved, meeting what psychology sees as my basic psychological needs.

In this renewed relationship with God through Jesus Christ, I find identity, I find intimacy or sharing of self, I find direction for my life; and there is integrity in my life. I live in a new covenant relationship with God.

Marriage is built on relationship to one's spouse. A good relationship between a husband and wife needs to begin with their individual relationship to God, if they are going to be able to build a good relationship with each other. When we understand our relationship with God, we can then understand and build a foundation of 'complementariness' or commonness for marriage. I realize that all marriages will not be Christian. Yet, I see this as a place for a husband and wife to begin a stronger marriage relationship with each other.

Nature of Christian Marriage

This background is where we begin to view the role of man and woman in the marriage relationship. Man and woman were created in the image of God, renewed from an alienated state to a new relationship in the last 'Adam', Jesus Christ. What is the relation of man to woman in the Christian marriage?

Man/Woman and the New Way in Christ

Man and woman were equally guilty in sin and invited to become Christian by faith in Christ. Thus, it must follow that man and woman achieve equal personhood in Jesus Christ.

Jesus permitted women to travel with Him (Lk. 8.2-3). This gave them a place that they had not received from society. 'These were women that Christ had raised from degradation and servitude to fellow-

---

[22] Arrington, *Paul's Aeon Theology,* p. 56

ship and service. It is true that Jewish culture would not let women learn
from the rabbi, but here He let them travel with Him. He was called
rabbi. Jesus was showing that all people (humanity) are equal under
God.'[23]

Jesus showed equality in ministry in relation to the needs of males
and females and even broke the cultural tradition defined to them in
public (Jn 4.4-32; 12.2-3). He treated women not as females but as
human beings.

Paul treats men and women equally and even comments on the
contributions of both in the church. He is always concerned for the
reputation of the church and gives counsel to women in the young
congregation. He noted that there was fundamental freedom of the
gospel, there was freedom to exercise responsibility (Gal. 5.13), and
women in worship and service must not flaunt or misuse their freedom. Here the public reputation of the young church was at stake
(1 Cor. 11.2-6; 14.34-36; and 1 Tim. 2.11-15).

The Christian Partnership of Complementarity

Howell summarizes the relationship of husband and wife this way: 'In
the one-flesh union of marriage, by analogy, the oneness which is
possible is a dynamic unity of persons in which equality of personhood
exists yet functional subordination to one another also exists for the
fulfillment of tasks related to family life'.[24] Gause asserts, 'Subordination
is not a term of inferiority. It is a term of order and it is an issue of
decorum'.[25] The marriage relationship is one of complementariness,
mutuality, belongingness, diversity, openness, identity, and unity. This
can only come about with the man and woman in a covenant relationship. Covenant is based on a promise binding two individuals together
to love one another unconditionally. Jesus demonstrated this when He
gave Himself on the cross to die for humanity and as an expression of
love (1 Cor. 13; 1 Jn 3.4).

Paul Jewett rejects the 'hierarchical model of the man/woman relationship in favor of a model of partnership ... man and woman are
properly related when they accept each other as equals whose differences
are mutually complementary in all spheres of life and human endeavor'.[26]

Maston states 'real freedom for the child of God comes through union with and enslavement to Christ.... Even in human relations, such

---

[23] Douglas W. Slocumb, 'Societal Relationships: Respecting the Role of Women' in
A Bold New Vision, Personal Enrichment Guide (ed. F.D. Carey and H.E. Stone; Cleveland,
TN: Pathway, 1988), p. 128.
[24] Howell, *Equality*, p. 42.
[25] Gause and Gause, *Women in the Body*, p. 72.
[26] Jewett, *Man as Male and Female*, p. 14.

as the home, the fullest freedom comes through mutual submission and unselfish devotion and service to and for one another'.[27]

Men and women were created equal and they are equal in submission in life. The Greek word used in the New Testament, *hupotasso,* may be translated as 'subjected or being subordinate to a person or persons in authority'.[28] It also may be translated 'submission in the sense of voluntary yielding in love'. Paul and Peter use this type of reference to designate the yieldedness given by one person to another on the basis of voluntary choice because of the relationship. Paul (Eph. 5.21) is dealing in this voluntary or mutual submission. Peter (1 Pet. 5.5) uses this type of reference with the younger submitting to the elder.

Jesus Christ Himself illustrated this type of submissive relationship to His earthly parents (Lk. 2.51). Also, He illustrates it with His death on the cross (Lk. 23.46). This same voluntary yieldedness is required of believers in salvation and if they are to become a participating member of a local church.

A relation of submission by both partners, which is a calling to 'voluntary yieldedness in love', is a vital exercise to the relationship. Voluntary yieldedness in love needs to include not only the husband/wife relationship but also the family and other social relationships of the Christian community. It is therefore submission in a mutually reciprocal relationship.

As Paul describes it (Eph. 5.19-21), a Spirit-filled life should be one of joy, thankfulness, and mutual submission. A life of submission is a distinguishing characteristic of a life in the Holy Spirit. Kenneth Wuest interprets *hupotasso* in Eph. 5.21 as 'subjecting one's self to another as the opposite of self-assertion, the opposite of an independent autocratic spirit. It is the desire to get along with one another, being satisfied with less than one's due, a sweet reasonableness of attitude'.[29]

If one compares these definitions of submission to Paul's description of love in 1 Cor. 13.4-7, the similarities are obvious. Submission in Eph. 5.21 can be very appropriately translated as 'voluntary yieldedness in love'.

Paul points out that submission and love are to be the same for the husband and wife as for Christ and the church, just as we recognize our need for God and humbly surrender ourselves to Him, our creator. Paul is saying that such yielded-ness is to be expressed by each family member toward the other – not just by the wife to her husband.

---

[27] Maston and Tillman, *The Bible*, p. 169.

[28] Howell, *Equality and Submission*, p. 55.

[29] Kenneth S. Wuest, *Wuest's Word Studies from the Greek New Testament for the English Reader,* vol. 1 (Grand Rapids, MI: Eerdmans, 1975), pp. 128-29.

Therefore, neither man nor woman is to lord over the other. But the relationship should be more of a surrendering of one's power to the control of another out of voluntary yieldedness in love and respect for one another.

Conclusion

The marriage relationship is one of mutual submission, not authority or dominance over one another. This kind of relationship is based on mutuality and respect, one for the other. Authority can be easily misused in the home. If one remembers to show the proper understanding and respect for each individual in the family unit, each can grow and find one's place in God's creation. Each is important and each has a vital contribution to the world in which we now live.

The same love that attracts and develops into friendship and marriage is the love that can continue if nurtured in the home. This love is one that is modeled by the parents to the children. This is a love that is unselfish and caring. The Greeks described love with three words, *eros,* sexual love; *philia,* friendship love; and *agape,* affection involving goodwill and benevolence. Sexuality is very important in marriage; so is friendship love. Yet, every marriage needs the unconditional affectionate love that Christ showed us. The affectionate, benevolent love is unconditional and open to every member of the family, respecting each person's own personal identity.

In the Holy Spirit may we each fully become what God wants us to be in the new life given to us through the Incarnation of Jesus Christ.

★★★★★★★★★★★★★★★★★★

Abstract
This study emphasizes the need for the Wesleyan Pentecostal Church to continue to look at the marriage relationship as being one of complementarity, mutuality, belongingness, diversity, openness, identity and unity. This can come about only when a man and a woman are living in a covenant relationship with God and with each other. In addressing this important theological issue in his works, R. Hollis Gause has directed the Wesleyan Pentecostal movement again and again to the Incarnation of Jesus, recognizing that God's gift of His Son to the world has made possible the theological grounding and shaping of our human relationships. He has lifted this up early in his ministry and perhaps before many in our movement were ready to accept complementarity and mutuality within the original creation of humankind.

17

The Triune God in Salvation History: Pentecostal Perspectives on Holistic Church Mission Today

Richard E. Waldrop[*]

All mission begins in and emanates from the Triune God. In this way the missionary character of God is revealed. Our God is a missionary God and so the life of the Church must be characterized as missionary existence.[1] Christian faith is intrinsically missionary,[2] or as the Swiss theologian, Emil Brunner, has said, 'the Church exists by mission, just as fire exists by burning'.[3] Having made those foundational statements, additional questions always arise concerning the particularities of Christian mission. The 'why' and the 'how' of mission, as an ecclesial and human enterprise, rest upon the missionary character of the Triune God. My own reflections on this theme are the result of more than thirty years of relationships and ministry among the peoples of Latin America and of involvement in the life and mission of the Pentecostal churches of the continent in contexts of violence, marginalization, poverty, and oppression. These reflections have been further enriched by my years of interaction and dialogue with my valuable colleagues at the Church of God Theological Seminary, who have helped to open up new vistas for me in constructive Pentecostal theology, especially as it has related to my work and concerns for holistic mission in and from Latin America. From the days of my childhood, growing up in a Pentecostal family and church, I have been conscious of a special missionary vocation to and with the people of Latin America, and during the years

[*] Richard E. Waldrop (D.Miss., Fuller Theological Seminary) is Adjunct Professor of World Mission and Evangelism at the Pentecostal Theological Seminary, Cleveland, TN, and Missionary Educator under appointment of Church of God World Missions, Cleveland, TN.
[1] David Bosch, *Transforming Mission: Paradigm Shifts in Theology of Mission* (Maryknoll, NY: Orbis, 1992), p 9.
[2] Bosch, *Transforming Mission,* p. 8.
[3] Emil Brunner, *The Word and the World* (London: SCM, 1931), p. 108.

of my missionary engagement there and here, I have made advances, I believe, in terms of my own comprehension of the deepness and wideness of the *missio dei*, or mission of God, in its cosmic, ecological, social, political, and of course, personal and spiritual dimensions. Thanks to many persons and realities which God has placed in my life through these years, I sense that I have been enriched and fulfilled as a person on mission for and with God, and hope that I have been able to contribute in some way to the missionary formation of God's people and to the advancement of missionary consciousness in the churches and educational institutions in which I have been privileged to participate.

The Missionary God in Creation

In creation, God is revealed as 'Missionary', if by missionary we understand the idea that God is 'Self-sent', 'Self-extended' and 'Self-revealed' outwardly through the divine creational activity. In Genesis, we find one of the great principles of missionary existence: the creative desire and ability to open oneself outwardly and take concrete steps to draw near to others with the intention of entering into relationships which seek others' welfare and salvation.

In fact, the original foundation of this principle rests upon the social and communal nature of 'trinitarian mutuality',[4] or the Economic Trinity. In the first words registered in Sacred Scripture, it is revealed to us that it was the Spirit (breath or wind) of God that moved upon the empty and void 'face of the deep' as the Creator Spirit (feminine voice) of Life. In the history of Christian thought, the Spirit of God has been recognized in her missionary role as the agent that generates and sustains life in all its dimensions.[5] Consequentially, to believe in the Triune God and to do mission in trinitarian fashion is an affirmation of full and abundant life, and must be, at the same time, a negation of anything which diminishes or destroys the life of the creation including, especially, human life in its spiritual, social and physical sense.

In regards to the various missionary ventures of the Church (missions or *missiones ecclesiae*),[6] it should also be recognized that the Spirit precedes and inspires all legitimate ecclesial and human initiatives, as an already active missionary presence in the world. In this way, we understand that from the beginning, we follow and participate in the missionary initiative of the Triune God and not our own. This must be reaffirmed with firmness and clarity, especially in a time in which Christian

---

[4] Jürgen Moltmann, *The Spirit of Life: A Universal Affirmation* (Minneapolis: Fortress, 1992), pp. 71-72, 248-66.

[5] Moltmann, *The Spirit of Life*, pp. 144-60.

[6] Bosch, *Transforming Mission,* p. 10.

mission has been twisted and confused, too often, with impure motives and equivocal actions related to neo-liberal economic imperialism, attitudes of cultural and spiritual superiority and the manipulation of resources by the cultures of consumerism and 'prosperity', and their corresponding *un*civil 'civil religion' in the Global North at the expense of the majority cultures and Pentecostal churches of the Global South.

Regarding the missionary nature of the social Trinity, the words registered in Gen. 1.26 are illustrative: '*let us* make humankind in *our* image, according to *our* likeness'. The *missio dei* is an enterprise that is realized in divine community. The mission of the Church, under the *missio dei,* must be carried out among all the sectors and groups that comprise the ecclesial community, and not simply by a group of 'professional missionaries' who too often form an elite class of 'super-spiritual' individuals.

The biblical idea of the image of God, or *imago dei*, in human beings, also has clear missiological implications. Human beings, because they carry the image of God and because they are the creation of God, must be treated with dignity and justice. Therefore, the whole missionary enterprise of the Church has as one of its principal objectives the recognition of the value of human life in all of its dimensions. Because God is the Spirit of Life, the Church must be clear in her prophetic proclamation of the dignity of life and in her prophetic denunciation of violence, slavery, racism, abortion, addiction, poverty and war, which are all instruments of sin, death and destruction.[7] This is a truly a completely 'pro-life' position. Holistic Christian mission signifies the full humanization and dignification of life in light of the image of God in each human being.

In addition to what is said above, in the creation story registered in Genesis, it is clear that the mission of God is delegated and shared, in the first instance, with human beings, that is to say, with the first human couple, Adam and Eve. In this way, the mission becomes a commission. This fact also points clearly to the social nature of the Trinity.

[7] On the issue of war and peace from a Pentecostal perspective, see the many pacifist statements issued by early Pentecostal leaders and denominations through the 20th century, compiled at the Thirdway Peace and Justice Fellowship-San Fransisco website (www.thirdway.cc), including many quotations from A.J. Tomlinson, e.g. 'War is butchery and contrary to the spirit of Christianity', *Church of God Evangel* 8.13 (Mar. 31, 1917), p. 1. See also, recent statements from Pentecostal theologians, including information on the website of the Pentecostal Charismatic Peace Fellowship (www.pentecostalpeace.org), and Steven J. Land's statements that 'many early Pentecostals were pacifists and quite critical of society' and that 'early Pentecostal pacifism, in a nuclear age of extensive poverty, is the best strategy for the church today', in *Pentecostal Spirituality: A Passion for the Kingdom* (JPTS 1; Sheffield, UK: Sheffield Academic Press, 1993), pp. 180, 207.

God's first discourse directed to human beings in Gen. 1.28-30 has been referred to as the *cultural mandate.*[8] Here are also references to human participation regarding the stewardship or care of the natural environment or God's creation. From this point we see emerging the idea of an ecological responsibility that should occupy an important space in the missiological agenda of the Church. In addition to the environmental responsibility given to human beings, the symbiotic human-ecological relationship is established with the result of providing wellbeing and sustainability to the inhabitants of the planet. This relationship between God, creation and human beings is established within the framework of social responsibility and submission to divine purpose.[9]

With the human disobedience and sin registered in Genesis 3, the panorama of human life, and as a result, creation, is altered dramatically, although not irreversibly. For this reason, the *missio dei* and the *missio ecclesiae* are directed toward the restoration of full life which would later reach its zenith in the redemption effectuated by the Son of God, Jesus of Nazareth, on the cross which is situated at center stage of salvific history. The good news of the incarnation of God in human history and of a new way of living (the Reign of God) would become the heart of evangelization and would occupy the center of the missionary task of the Church.

In this sense, the whole plan of God's mission revealed in the Old Testament should be seen in anticipation of its definitive fulfillment in the death and resurrection of Jesus Christ, finding its course in a commission or mandate given by him to his followers who would form the Church empowered for mission by the Holy Spirit. In this way, the Church participates in the *mission dei* as sign, agent and sacrament unto the consummation of the Reign of God at the *eschaton*.

The Missionary People of God

From the stark reality of human sin, the mission of God expands as it moves in new directions and takes on new dimensions. And because the mission of God is linked to God's relationship with human beings, God initiates and enters into a covenant alliance with a specific people, beginning with a relationship with the person of Abram (Gen. 12.1-9).

---

[8] Pablo Deiros, *Diccionario hispanoamericano de la misión* (Miami: COMIBAM Internacional, 1997), p. 267.

[9] See, for example, the recent excellent work done by Dr. Cheryl Bridges Johns, a member of an interdisciplinary and interdenominational task force which issued 'An Urgent Call to Action: Scientists and Evangelicals Unite to Protect Creation', National Press Club, Washington, DC, Jan. 17, 2007.

Upon reading the biblical text, it should be obvious that God's intention is to bless all the peoples of the earth through a particular chosen people. Israel, the people of God, is 'blessed to be a blessing',[10] in this way revealing the missionary purpose of God through the particular history of a specific people for all of humanity. Far from constituting a theological or biblical basis for some kind of rigid Zionism, in which the modern geo-political State of Israel has become an idol of North American fundamentalist churches (including, unfortunately, too many Pentecostal churches), God's Old Testament covenant with Israel should be understood as a salvific act of love and commitment on behalf of all humanity.

With the covenant established between God, Abraham and his descendents, there begins a long process of gestation and formation of a people who would reflect, at its best moments, God's missionary concern toward other nations. This period of formation passes through the stages of immigration of the people to Egypt, slavery under the yoke of a malignant and oppressive empire, the calling and preparation of a national liberator in the person of Moses, and in the great miracles wrought by God in favor of Israel in the Exodus.

Exodus and Liberation, then, figure as indispensable elements of any biblical and practical theology of holistic mission. Mission that does not liberate, in the broadest sense of the word, is not faithful to the *missio dei*.

Upon arriving at the wilderness, the missionary people of God continue the process of conscientization and learning in regards to the nature of their unique and special relationship with God and with their specific context. Sinai symbolizes the *law* (formation), *holiness* (ethics) and *shalom* (salvation, wellbeing, health, peace, community). In this case, shalom is revealed as God's design and desire, first of all, for Israel, and through them, for all of creation. To be faithful to its missionary vocation, Israel is to live as a model of holiness, which is wholeness, before the surrounding nations and in so doing, bear witness to the benefits of this way of life.

One of the adjectives used to describe the mission of God through Israel is the word 'centripetal'.[11] This word communicates the idea of movement from the periphery toward the center. The people or nations neighboring Israel would be attracted to the true God, Yahweh, by means of the light that would shine in and through the peculiarity of Israel's testimony and ethics, reflected in a legal and moral code given through Moses.

---

[10] W. Douglas Smith, *Bendicidos para bendecir* (El Paso, TX: Casa Bautista de Publicaciones, 1992), p. 9.
[11] Deiros, *Diccionario*, p. 287.

With regard to social ethics and mission, it is clear that God desires to bless all people, but there are special provisions for three classes of people: orphans, widows, and aliens in the land—the poor of the earth. This 'preferential option for the poor'[12] is to be practiced and is made visible in the legal and historical framework of the life relationships of the people of God as it regards these special people. The *Year of Jubilee* (Leviticus 25) is perhaps one of the best examples of a legal code that favors and protects, not only the poor of the earth, but also the *earth itself*. It signifies liberation and rest for human beings and the land, and shows the symbiotic relationship of interdependence between both.

Continuing on the way of salvation history, the pilgrim people of God arrive at last to the promised land and continue the process of formation and consolidation, which includes the development of a firm identity in terms of nationhood (Israelite), culture (Jewish), language (Hebrew) and religion (Monotheism), in contrast to the surrounding nations.[13] The social, political and cultic structures of the nation also continue to be developed through the judges, kings and the priestly class, with a liturgy characteristic of this period.

In the cultic life of Israel, liturgy served to keep the people's collective memory alive, so that the mighty acts of God in history would be rehearsed repeatedly through the telling of the stories of Creation, Covenant, Exodus, and Liberation. In the liturgy, there is also the constant reminder of the missionary design of God for the people of God with regard to their relation to the other nations, seen especially in the Psalms such as Psalm 67. At the same time, in the wisdom literature of Israel there is constant reference to the special love of God toward those who are poor and excluded, and to the moral and social responsibility of the nation, in the fulfillment of their mission of justice and peace in the world that surrounds them.

Later, with the vicissitudes of unethical behavior and the moral and spiritual decadence of the nation, which resulted in the lack of disposition of Israel towards God's purposes, the prophetic movement is raised up to announce judgment upon the people, denouncing their rebellion and calling them anew to the restoration of the covenant.[14] For example, on repeated occasions the prophet Isaiah (42.6; 49.6; 60.2-3) reminds Israel of the missionary purpose of God, in order that they would be 'light to the nations and to the ends of the earth'. The prophetic vocation always includes a component of social justice which is expected of the people of God regarding their behavior toward the

---

[12] Gustavo Gutiérrez, *A Theology of Liberation: History, Politics and Salvation* (Maryknoll, NY: Orbis, 1988), pp. xxv-xxvi.

[13] John Bright, *A History of Israel* (Philadelphia: Westminster, 1981), p. 120.

[14] Walter Brueggemann, *The Prophetic Imagination* (Philadelphia: Fortress, 1978), p. 20.

poor and oppressed (Amos), the hungry and naked (Isa. 58), and those who are broken and captive (Isa. 61), echoing again and again the ideal established by God in the 'favorable year of the Lord' (Lev. 25; Isa. 61.2; Lk. 4.19).

It is always the 'Spirit of the Lord', the ruach-agent of the *missio dei*, who is always moving, first over the empty and formless deep, and later over the lives of the patriarchs and matriarchs, judges, and kings throughout this salvation history, but especially upon the prophets.

This is evident, for example, in passages such as Isa. 61.1, where it is declared that 'the Spirit of the Lord is upon me, for he has anointed me to preach good news to the poor'. In short, the mission of the Tri-une God is revealed in the Old Testament through the covenant made with the people of Israel and in God's desire that they serve to bless others as a model of the shalom of God and light to the nations. Fur-thermore, it is the Spirit of God who anoints the prophets for the task of denunciation of injustice and for the proclamation of the good news of holistic liberation, especially for those who are poor and crushed.

Later, after a long 'intertestamental' period of dispersion and (appar-ent) silence, the prophetic, future and eschatological dimensions of the trinitarian mission would take on its most transcendental form in the most radical historical fact that the world had witnessed: *the salvific in-carnation of God in the history of humanity in the person of Jesus of Nazareth, his redemptive crucifixion and resurrection, and the re-formation of the mission-ary people of God, the Church.*

Incarnational Mission

In creation, the missionary God is self-revealed, and self-sent toward that which did not yet exist. This was a gesture of supreme creativity in a desire to extend divine relational capacity outwardly. Now in the specifically human context, the incarnation constitutes God's second great act of universal scope and cosmic redemption.

The attempt at explicating the fact that God 'bore' a Son and that this Father God 'sent' his Son into the world certainly transcends the capacity of human reason and must remain, to a great degree, a mys-tery of divine grace. But even as it is a mystery, the incarnation reveals to us much of the nature of the *missio dei*. The noble missionary ideal of opening oneself and of risking one's own existence for the good of someone or something else, has its origin in the salvific history of a humanized and crucified God.[15] The incarnation, then, establishes the pattern for all subsequent missionary activity in various ways. It is not

---

[15] Jürgen Moltmann, *The Crucified God: The Cross of Christ as the Foundation and Criti-cism of Christian Theology* (New York: Harper and Row, 1974), p. 4.

only opening oneself, but also is the fact of *being sent on mission* for the purpose of the salvation of others. Etymologically, the word 'mission' carries with it the indispensable element of the action of sending.[16] It also signifies becoming like the other or identifying oneself with the condition of the other persons to whom one is sent. This idea is well expressed in the words of a popular Latin American gospel chorus,

> I am sent by God
> and my hand is ready
> to build a fraternal world with Him,
> The angels have not been sent to change
> a world of pain into a world of peace,
> It has fallen to me to make this a reality,
> Help me, Lord, to do your will.[17]

From the earliest times of Christianity, then, mission has carried the trinitarian idea of divine sending:[18] the Father is self-sent *in* creation, and later sent *to* creation in the incarnation of the Son, Jesus Christ, and at the same time the Holy Spirit is sent *to and throughout* the world as the divine agent of the *missio dei*.

Jesus of Nazareth, sent from God, is the missionary *par excellance*, and is the perfect model of what holistic and liberating mission means.[19] In the inauguration of his ministry and announcement of his messianic platform in the synagogue of Nazareth, Jesus textually cites the prophetic passage of Isaiah 61, making it his own. He proclaims himself as the Sent One from God and Anointed of the Spirit to preach good news to the poor. Here is a clear missiological agenda, which covers all the spheres of human life, unless one attempts to twist the text with a dispensationalist and fundamentalist hermeneutic, leaving only a spiritualist shell, which is empty, and lacking the consistent flavor of holistic mission.

From the specific particularity of the geographical and social location of Galilee, and from the point of departure of Jesus' identification with repugnant lepers, abused women, forgotten children and marginalized Samaritans, Jesus demonstrates the way of mission. It is the road of solidarity with those who suffer persecution, the poor in spirit, those who are thirsty for righteousness, the humble peacemakers, those who

---

[16] Horst Rzepkowski, *Diccionario de misionologia: Historia, teologia, etnologia* (Navarra, Spain: Verbo Divino, 1997), pp. 357-58.

[17] Author unknown, but originating in Cuba according to Dr. Reinerio Arce, Rector of the Seminario Evangelico Unido de Mantanzas, Cuba.

[18] Bosch, *Transforming Mission*, pp. 1-2.

[19] Dario López Rodriguez, *La mision liberadora de Jesus: El mensaje del evangelio de Lucas* (Lima: Puma, 2004), p. 46.

are merciful and of a pure heart: because the Reign of God belongs to them (Mt. 5.3-12).

However, one cannot speak adequately of the incarnational mission of the Triune God without recognizing the medullar place of the *cross*. The cross is situated at center stage of salvific history and constitutes the hinge upon which the *kairós* of God turns. Everything before it anticipates it, and all that proceeds from it depends upon it as it is remembered. God's entire salvific work is sealed upon the cross and there 'it is completed' (Jn 19.30). With regard to mission, then, the cross is the example and the reminder of the suffering and martyrdom that is required of all faithful missionaries. On the road of mission there will be sacrifice, cross and death, for the sake of reaching others with salvation. But, after the cross of death comes the victory of the resurrection, and after the sacrifice and martyrdom of mission comes the full life of redemption in persons who are evangelized, societies transformed and in the creation renewed.

In this way, the evangelical message of the life, death and resurrection of Jesus Christ was and always shall be: 'The time has been fulfilled and the Reign of God has come near; repent and believe on the Gospel' (Mk 1.15). The Reign of God, then, becomes the vertebral cord of Christian mission and seeks the restoration of 'all things' in Christ Jesus (Rev. 21.5). The Church, as such, is not the final goal of the *missio dei*, but the penultimate goal.[20] The Church belongs to the Reign, but the Reign extends beyond the Church. The Reign is the realization of the final goal of the full manifestation of God's shalom in the world, when in the *parousía* of Jesus Christ, all that has been created will be completely renewed and the image of God will be totally recuperated in all of humanity at the eschaton.

In the interim, we continue to move forward in the missionary age of the missionary Church by the power of the missionary Spirit.[21] The Church has been chosen as an indispensable instrument in the 'hands' of God in the fulfillment of the divine mission. The Church may not be the only instrument available to divine agency but has been called out (*ecclesia*) to occupy a singular place of special prominence and privilege in the vanguard of God's mission. As John the Baptist prophetically made the way straight in preparation for the coming of the Son of God (Mt. 3.1-17), in the same way, the true Church prepares the way for the coming and final consummation of the Reign of God.

---

[20] Orlando Costas, 'Crecimiento integral y palabra de Dios' in *Iglesia y Misión*, no. 3 (1984). Also, see Costas, *The Integrity of Mission: The Inner Life and Outreach of the Church* (New York: Harper and Row, 1979), pp. 56-57.

[21] Jürgen Moltmann, *The Church in the Power of the Spirit: A Contribution to Messianic Ecclesiology* (Minneapolis: Fortress, 1993), pp. 7-11.

The faithful Church continually lives the experience of the 'coming and going' of mission. She is called to union with God in Jesus Christ, to the communion (fellowship) of the saints, and to reunion (meeting) for temporal worship. But she is also called to go out in the dispersion of mission, in evangelization and in the transformation of life in all its facets. In this sense, the mission of the Church has a *centrifugal*[22] character somewhat distinct from the *centripetal* character of that of the Old Testament people of God. Said differently, the Church moves from the center of her faith, worship, and commitment to Christ toward the periphery of mission in the world and, in this way, overcomes the multiple barriers of time and space, culture and race, and idiom and ideology.

The Holy Spirit is always the agent of mission, the force and power of the Church-in-mission, animating her so that, in the words of the Lausanne Covenant affirmed at the International Congress on World Evangelization in Lausanne, Switzerland in 1974, 'the whole Church will take the whole Gospel to the whole world'.[23] Under this rubric, the Jewish Festival of Pentecost (Acts 2) becomes not only a celebration of another annual cycle of Spring harvest, but the beginning of a new, end-times, worldwide cycle of ingathering by the Lord of the harvest (Mt. 9.38), with the sending out of workers so that the mission of God will be carried out in the world. Pentecost has the significance of both missionary event and movement. It is the humble and insignificant Galilean peasants who are converted into the protagonists and actors at the center stage of divine mission as they lend their voices to the xenolalia of the Spirit so that the festive representatives of the United Nations in Jerusalem are able to capture the salvific significance of the death, resurrection and ascension of Jesus and thereby answer the question which spontaneously arose from the multitude, 'What is the meaning of this?' (Acts 2.12).

Pentecost, then, represents a new wind of the Spirit with the same character of the breath of creation life imparted by the Spirit of God as she brooded over the face of the deep on the first day of creation, and gave life to the first human beings on the sixth day of creation (Gen. 1.1, 27-31). Pentecost also signifies the purifying, sanctifying fire of God, which cleanses and separates the people from the profane unto the sacred uses of missionary service, such as what happened to the people of God when the fire fell on Mount Sinai (Exod. 19). Pentecost is the prophetic and miraculous announcement of the good news of

[22] Deiros, *Diccionario,* p. 287.

[23] See Article No. 6 of the Lausanne Covenant in Gerald H. Anderson and Thomas F. Stransky, CSP, eds., *Mission Trends No. 2: Evangelization* (New York: Paulist, 1975), pp. 239-48.

the Reign of God in Christ Jesus in the languages of the world, represented that day by the various delegations of pilgrims gathered in Jerusalem.

As a result of Pentecost, the people of God, the Church, is revived by the Spirit for her mission in the world and through her existence begins to demonstrate the evangelical values of communion one with another, of the sharing of bread and other belongings (including properties), and of perseverance in the teachings of Jesus Christ and the apostles (Acts 2.42-47; Mt. 28.18-20).

Finally, in the new post-Pentecost era, eschatological hope comes to play a catalytic role which orients, motivates, and mobilizes the mission of the Church in its multiple expressions (word, sign, deed), dimensions (incarnational, liturgical, diaconal, numerical), and directions (vertical, horizontal).[24] Far from giving in to an escapist scheme of a rigid fundamentalist eschatology, or of falling prey to a neo-liberal economic, globalizing ideology, or to imperialistic neo-colonial politics, Christian mission recovers new energies in the promise of God to liberate the whole creation, so that on the final day of the eschaton, the Day of the Lord, the great multitude from all the nations, tribes, people and tongues, will cry in a loud voice saying, 'Salvation belongs to our God who is seated on the throne, and to the Lamb' (Rev. 7.9-10). Then, the *missio dei trinitaria*, will be completed, having finished its course from the Creation, to the Covenant, to the Incarnation and the Cross, and passing through Pentecost until the Consummation of all things in Christ Jesus to the glory of the Triune God, Father, Son and Holy Spirit! AMEN!

★★★★★★★★★★★★★★★★★

Abstract

Since all mission originates and proceeds from God, the divine missionary nature is revealed through God's great salvific acts in history. This is revealed biblically in creation, in the covenant and formation of Israel, the incarnation, Pentecost and in the consummation of all things in Christ Jesus in the eschaton. The Church fulfills her holistic mission as she is faithful to the missionary character of God.

[24] Jürgen Moltmann, *Theology of Hope* (New York: Harper and Row, 1967), pp. 353-76; Land, *Pentecostal Spirituality*, pp. 122-81; Juan Stam, *Profecía bíblica y misión de la iglesia*, Quito: Consejo Latinoamericano de Iglesias, n.d.), pp. 98-102.

Recommended Bibliography in English

Bosch, David J. *Transforming Mission: Paradigm Shifts in Theology of Mission*. (Maryknoll, NY: Orbis, 1991).

Orlando Costas, *The Integrity of Mission: The Inner Life and Outreach of the Church*, New York: Harper and Row, 1979.

R. Hollis Gause, *Living in the Spirit: The Way of Salvation*, Cleveland, TN: Pathway, 1980.

Gustavo Gutiérrez, *A Theology of Liberation: History, Politics and Salvation*, Maryknoll, NY: Orbis, 1988.

Catherine Mowry LaCunga, *God for Us: The Trinity and Christian Life*, San Francisco: Harper Collins, 1973.

Steven J. Land, *Pentecostal Spirituality: A Passion for the Kingdom*, JPTS 1; Sheffield: Sheffield Academic Press, 1993.

—— 'The Triune Center: Wesleyans and Pentecostals Together in Mission', *Pneuma* 21.2 (Fall, 1999), pp. 199-214.

Darío López R., 'The Liberating Mission of Jesus: The Message of the Gospel of Luke', trans. Richard E. Waldrop; unpublished manuscript; Cleveland, TN, 2006

Jürgen Moltmann, *The Spirit of Life: A Universal Affirmation*, Minneapolis: Fortress, 1992.

—— *History and the Triune God: Contributions to Trinitarian Theology*, New York: Crossroad, 1992.

—— *Theology of Hope*, New York: Harper and Row, 1967.

—— *The Church in the Power of the Spirit: A Contribution to Messianic Ecclesiology*, Minneapolis: Fortress, 1993.

—— *The Crucified God: The Cross of Christ as the Foundation and Criticism of Christian Theology*, New York: Harper & Row, 1974.

Donald Senior and Carroll Stuhlmueller, *The Biblical Foundations for Mission*, Maryknoll, NY: Orbis, 1983.

John R.W. Stott, *Christian Mission in the Modern World*, Downers Grove, IL: Intervarsity Press, 1975.

Index of Names[*]

---

[*] Index compiled by Robert S. Blackaby

Index of Biblical References

Journal of Pentecostal Theology
Supplement Series

Volumes 1-28 were originally published by Sheffield Academic Press/Continuum. Subsequent titles are published by Deo Publishing under ISSN 0966 7393:

Pentecostal Commentary series titles are now also published by *Deo Publishing*.
Also published by Deo Publishing:
John Christopher Thomas, *The Spirit of the New Testament*. ISBN 90 5854 029 4 / 978 905854 29 4.